THE
TRANSPORTATION
RESEARCH BOARD

EVERYONE INTERESTED IS INVITED

1920
2020

SARAH JO PETERSON

The National Academies of
SCIENCES · ENGINEERING · MEDICINE

TRANSPORTATION RESEARCH BOARD

THE NATIONAL ACADEMIES PRESS
Washington, DC
www.nap.edu

THE NATIONAL ACADEMIES PRESS
500 Fifth Street, NW
Washington, DC 20001

Transportation Research Board publications are available by ordering individual publications directly from the TRB Business Office, through the Internet at www.TRB.org or nationalacademies.org/trb, or by annual subscription through organizational or individual affiliation with TRB. Affiliates and library subscribers are eligible for substantial discounts. For further information, contact the Transportation Research Board Business Office, 500 Fifth Street, NW, Washington, DC 20001 (telephone 202-334-3213; fax 202-334-2519; or e-mail TRBsales@nas.edu).

Printed in the United States of America

International Standard Book Number-13: 978-0-309-49371-0
International Standard Book Number-10: 0-309-49371-4
Digital Object Identifier: https://doi.org/10.17226/25472
Library of Congress Control Number: 2019953088

Suggested citation: Peterson, S. J. 2020. *The Transportation Research Board, 1920–2020: Everyone Interested Is Invited*. Washington, DC: The National Academies Press.

The National Academies of
SCIENCES · ENGINEERING · MEDICINE

TRB Centennial Task Force

Sandra Larson (*Chair*), Transportation Innovation Strategies Leader, Stanley Consultants, Inc.*

Asha Weinstein Agrawal, Education Director, Mineta Transportation Institute, San Jose State University*

Coco Briseno, Former Deputy Director, Planning and Modal Programs, California Department of Transportation

James Crites, President, James M. Crites LLC*

Audrey Farley, Associate Administrator for Administration, Pipeline and Hazardous Materials Safety Administration

Chris Hendrickson (**NAE),** Hamerschlag University Professor Emeritus, Carnegie Mellon University

Jack Jernigan, Team Director, Research and Tech Program Development, Federal Highway Administration

Joung Lee, Policy Director, American Association of State Highway and Transportation Officials

Debra Miller, Former Secretary, Kansas Department of Transportation

Dale Peabody, Director, Research and Innovation Office, Maine Department of Transportation

Alan Pisarski, Principal, Alan Pisarski Consulting*

Robert Skinner, Former Executive Director, Transportation Research Board, National Academies of Sciences, Engineering, and Medicine* (*Subcommittee Chair*)

Michael Townes, Former Senior Vice President and National Transit Market Sector Leader, HNTB

Michael Trentacoste, Former Associate Administrator for Research, Development, and Technology, Federal Highway Administration

Katie Turnbull, Executive Associate Director, Texas A&M Transportation Institute*

Daniel Turner, Emeritus Professor of Civil Engineering, The University of Alabama

*TRB Centennial Task Force Publication Subcommittee.

Acknowledgments

THIS PROJECT COMMENCED in September 2017 and benefited from the ability to spend hours with the current executive director, Neil Pedersen, and two former executive directors, Thomas Deen and Robert Skinner, as well as Bettie Deen and Dianne Skinner. In addition, Lillian Borrone, Ann Brach, Damian Kulash, Lisa Marflak, Tom Menzies, Mark Norman, Katie Turnbull, and C. Michael Walton recounted decades of experiences. Gwen Chisholm-Smith, Christopher Hedges, Sia Schatz, and Lori Sundstrom shared what makes the cooperative research programs tick, and Scott Babcock, Bernardo B. Kleiner, Stephen F. Maher, and Thomas M. Palmerlee related the finer points of how the Technical Activities Division works. Finally, Pam Hutton, American Association of State Highway and Transportation Officials, and Amy Lucero and Carin Michel, Department of Transportation, offered their insights into Strategic Highway Research Program (SHRP) 2 Solutions.

Daniel Barbiero and Janice Goldblum at Archives and Records helped immensely in orienting me to the complexity of the National Academies of Sciences, Engineering, and Medicine and pointing me to just the right sources. William Mcleod likewise oriented me to the Transportation Research Board's (TRB's) publications and its TRID bibliographic database. Holly Sten assisted with photo identification and design. Beth Schlenoff designed the dust jacket and interior pages. Taylor Horner and Julie Phillips led copyediting and Rachel D'Agostino provided proofreading. Dorothy Lewis and Rachel Marcus of the National Academies Press shepherded the book through the production and printing process.

Alexandra Briseno, TRB's librarian, came to my assistance sometimes multiple times a day. She also led the research for photographs and other illustrations. Stephen Mautner, National Academies executive editor, was generous with encouragement and guidance. Russell Houston, TRB associate executive director, managed the project for TRB and was always willing to listen and quick to be helpful.

This publication was reviewed in draft form by individuals chosen for their diverse perspectives and involvement in TRB. The purpose of this independent review is to provide candid and critical comments that will assist TRB in ensuring the book's clarity and that it accurately portrays TRB's history. The review comments and draft manuscript remain confidential to protect the integrity of the process.

I am grateful to the following individuals for their review of the draft manuscript: Asha Weinstein Agrawal, education director, Mineta Transportation Institute, San Jose State University; Daniel Barbiero, manager, Archives and Records, National Academies; Ann Brach, director, Technical Activities, TRB, National Academies; Scott Brotemarkle, Marine Board program director and senior program officer, Marine Transportation and Intermodal Freight, TRB, National Academies;

James Crites, president, James M. Crites LLC; Thomas Deen, principal, T. Deen Consultant, and former executive director, TRB, National Academies; Susan Hanson (NAS), Distinguished University Professor Emerita, Graduate School of Geography, Clark University; Christopher Hedges, director, Cooperative Research Programs, TRB, National Academies; Sandra Larson, transportation innovation strategies leader, Stanley Consultants, Inc.; William Mcleod, manager, Transportation Research Information Services, TRB, National Academies; Thomas R. Menzies, Jr., director, Consensus and Advisory Studies, TRB, National Academies; Neil Pedersen, executive director, TRB, National Academies; Alan Pisarski, principal, Alan Pisarski Consulting; Robert Skinner, former executive director, TRB, National Academies; and Katie Turnbull, executive associate director, Texas A&M Transportation Institute.

Reviewing selected chapters were Neil Hawks, former director, SHRP 2; Christopher Jenks, former director, Cooperative Research Programs; Damian Kulash, consultant and former executive director, SHRP, National Research Council; William Millar, former president, American Public Transportation Association; Mark Norman, resident scholar, TRB, National Academies; Robert Reilly, former director, Cooperative Research Programs, TRB, National Academies; and Lori Sundstrom, deputy director, Cooperative Research Programs, and manager, National Cooperative Highway Research Program, TRB, National Academies.

Although the reviewers listed above provided many constructive comments and suggestions, they were not asked to endorse the content nor did they see the final draft. The review of this publication was overseen by Chris Hendrickson (NAE), Carnegie Mellon University; Karen Febey, senior report review officer, TRB; and Adrienne Archer, report review associate, TRB. They were responsible for making certain that an independent examination of this publication was carried out in accordance with standards of the National Academies and that all review comments were carefully considered. Responsibility for the final content rests entirely with the author.

Sarah Jo Peterson
January 12, 2020

Transportation Research Board Century Patrons

As of October 31, 2019

Diamond

Emerald

Sapphire

Sapphire

Topaz

Transportation Research Board Century Club

As of October 31, 2019

$5,000 to $10,000

Deb (Butler) Painter in Honor of TRB
  Volunteers
William C. Rogers and Judith K. Jones in Honor
  of TRB Staff

$2,500 to $4,999

Thomas and Bettie Deen
John and Deanna Horsley
Craig Philip and Marian Ott Honoring
  Joe Sussman
Greg and Frances Winfree for TRB and
  USDOT Staff
Claudia E. Zapata and Matthew W. Witczak

$1,000 to $2,499

Vicki Arroyo
Ann Brach in Memory of Philip L. Brach, Sr.,
  and Margaret R. Brach
In Memory of Don Capelle
Adrian (Ray) and Melanie Chamberlain
James M. Crites
Mortimer L. Downey III
The Econolite Family
Nicholas and Ada Garber
Jerry and Loretta Hall
Stephen Hargarten in Honor of Susan Baker
  and Steve Teret

David and Chris Harkey
Leszek Janusz for TRB's Influence on Society
Geraldine Knatz
Jane Lappin
Hani S. Mahmassani
Michael D. Meyer
William and Barbara Millar
Hyun-A Park
Neil and Barbara Pedersen
Joyce C. Pressley
Herbert Richardson
Sandi Rosenbloom
John Samuels
Kumares Sinha in Memory of Purdue/
  TRB Mentors
Dan and Sandy Sperling
James M. Tien for TRB's Global Contributions
Katie Turnbull
Linda C. and Daniel S. Turner
University of Nevada, Reno, Civil Engineering
C. Michael and Betty Walton

$500 to $999

Curt and Joan Beckemeyer
Allen Biehler
L. Borrone Honoring Executive Committee
  Chairs
Paul Carlson
Joni Casey on Behalf of All IANA Members

Patrick C. Casey

Gwen Chisholm-Smith in Honor of
   Sharon D. Banks and Rosalyn M. Simon

DJ Choupin and Stephan Alexander Parker

In Honor of George Cochran

Philip Benton Demosthenes

Ginger Evans

Mark and Adela Felag

King W. Gee

Ralph Haas

Amir and Margit Hanna

Christopher and Dalia Hedges in Memory of
   Michael Salamone

Cynthia Jones in Memory of Barnie P. Jones

Stephen Lane

Joel Leisch and in Memory of Jack Leisch

Steve Lockwood for Walt Hanson and
   All AMVers

Stephen F. Maher

Joan McDonald

Lance Neumann

Harold "Skip" Paul

Robert Peskin in Honor of Joseph Schofer

Bob and Marilyn Reilly

Robert J. Shea

Bob and Dianne Skinner

Shiraz Tayabji

Martin Wachs

Charlie Zelle

Katie Zimmerman

Johanna Zmud

$250 to $499

Pam Keidel-Adams and Gary Adams

Siegy Adler

Rose M. Agnew

Current and Former Employees of
   Argonne CTR

Frank Barich

Gregory Benz

France Bernard

Carlo Borghini for Isa and Giuseppe Borghini

Kanok Boriboonsomsin

Shelly Brown in Honor of James McDaniel

In Recognition of Don Capelle from Tad Widby

Linda Cherrington

Lowell Clary

In Honor of Past and Present Committee Chairs

Sally Hill Cooper

Malcolm Dougherty for TRB's Many Volunteers

William J. and Rita M. Dunlay

O. A. Elrahman (Sam)

Asif and Surraya Faiz

Barbara Fraser in Tribute to Steve Kale

Georgios A. Giannopoulos

Geoffrey Gosling

Campbell Graeub

Susan Hanson

Chris Hendrickson

Isaac L. Howard

Roger Huff

Christopher Jenks in Recognition of TRB's
   CRP Staff

Robert Johns

Ben Block Jones II in Honor of Margaret P. Ellis

Jay Kavi in Honor of My Parents and Siblings

In Memory of Ray Krammes from TTI Friends

Dan Lamers

Sandra Q. Larson

Joung H. Lee

Carol Abel Lewis in Recognition of Earl and
   Hazel Abel

Hope E. Luhman
Pat and Jim McLaughlin
Jean-Pierre Médevielle
Abbas Mohaddes
Michael Morris
Mary Lou Ralls Newman
David Orr in Honor of Lynne H. Irwin
Mark L. Reno
Peter Schauer
Susan Shaheen
Venkataraman N. Shankar
Robert Sheppard
Clayton and Brittany Stambaugh
Ling Suen in Honor of Jim Scott
Tsuchi and Margurita Teng
Marshall R. Thompson
Amy Van Doren
Steve Varnedoe
Montie Wade, Emeritus
Thomas F. Zimmie

$100 to $249
Asha Weinstein Agrawal
Ibrahim Aldubabe
Giorgio Ambrosino
Felix Ammah-Tagoe
Le An and Ting Ma
Jeffrey Ang-Olson
Jamshid Armaghani in Honor of TRB Volunteers
J. Peter Ault
Thank You to Aviation Committees
Linda and Scott Babcock
Chris Baglin Honoring TRB Staff
    and Volunteers
Geni Brafman Bahar

David Ballard
David Beal and Kathleen Almand
Robert Lawrence Bertini
Susan J. Binder
Jason J. Bittner
Cynthia Bland
Phillip B. Blankenship
Ronald E. Boénau, P.E.
Jeff and Jill Borowiec
LTG (Retired) Tom and Renee Bostick
Marcus Brewer
In Memory of G. Sadler Bridges
Mary R. Brooks
Jeffrey Busby
Mark S. Bush
Mara Campbell in Fond Memory of Tony Kane
Carlos Campo
Maria Carbone
Dean Carlson
Regis Carvalho
Javier Castaneda
Mary N. Cearley
Mecit Cetin
Susan Chrysler in Appreciation of Rick Pain
Lowell Clary
Cary Coglianese
Francis (Buddy) Coleman
Benjamin and Lizette Colucci
Edward N. Comstock
John and Janice Contestabile
Alison Conway
Sally Hill Cooper
Antonio Gomes Correia
C. Douglass Couto
Selby Coxon

For Mentors James M. Crites and C. Michael
  Walton
Graham V. Currie
Michael J Cynecki
Steven DeWitt
Shelly deZevallos
Mary Ann Dierckman
Arlene Dietz
Michael Dimaiuta
Davis Dure
Barry Einsig
William Eisele
Jon Epps
Ahmed Faheem
Karen Febey
Cecilia Feeley
Conrad Felice
John W. Fischer
Donald L. Fisher
Kay Fitzpatrick
Gerardo Flintsch
Frederic Dean Fravel
William Frawley
Dan Frazee in Honor of Michael Salamone
Chuck Fuhs
Daba Gedafa
Koonstantinos S. Giannakos
Brittney N. Gick
Tullio Giuffrè
Genevieve Giuliano
Richard Golaszewski in Memory of
  Aaron Gellman
Joseph M. Goldman
Aaron D. Golub
Deepak Gopalakrishna

Robert E. Gorman, Jr., and Mariann Gorman
Daniel Haake
James P. Hall
Abdul-Rahman Hamad
William H. Hansmire
Douglas W. Harwood in Memory of
  Raymond A. Krammes
Marwa Hassan
Patrick Hasson
Larry Head
Brendon Hemily
Jens Hennig - GAMA
Susan B Herbel
Ann Hershfang
Michael L. Holder
Andy Horosko
William Horrey
Beth and Russell Houston
Linda Howard
S. Jack Hu and Jun Du
Gloria J. Jeff
Average Joe
In Memory of Crystal Jones
John Kaliski
Prithvi (Ken) Kandhal
Bryan, Katie, Emily, and Ethan Katz
Jay Kavi in Memory of Antonio Estevez, P.E.
Thomas Kern
Timothy Klein
Harvey S. Knauer
Thomas P. Knight
Ratna Krishnan and Krishnan Viswanathan
David Kuehn
Beverly Kuhn
Jane Lappin

Thomas F. Larwin

Michael Lawrence

Andrew C. Lemer

Kevin and Natassja Linzau Family

Henry Liu

Kristine Liwag

Mohammad Longi

Rex Luk in Honor of M. B. Lee

Rajib Basu Mallick

Lisa Berardi Marflak

Shravya Markandeya

Susan Martinovich

Elmer Marx

John Mason

Deborah Matherly

Ross McKeown

Anne McKinnon in Honor of Kathleen Stein

Deb Miller

Elly Mixsell

Philip Mok

Patricia Mokhtarian

Jacklyn Rene Montgomery

Adrian Moore

Robert Murphy

Shashi Nambisan

B. Nanjundiah in Honor of
   C. S. Balasubrahmanya

Bob Newbery and Nancy Sugden

Wilfrid Nixon

James F. Nolan

Ghim Ping Ong

Valerio Oricchio

Juanita Owens

Gale Page

Maureen Palmer and Steven Cliff

Fanis Papadimitriou

Alagusundaramoorthy Paramasivan

Eun Sug Park

Terri H. Parker

Ellen L. Partridge

Cristina Pastore

Anthony Perl

David and Linda Plazak

Jackie Ploch

Steven Polunsky

Ingrid Potts in Memory of Raymond A.
   Krammes

Gonzalo Rada

Sharif Ramsis

John L. Renne

Jewelene Richardson

Shana-Lynn Rogers and Jack Klodzinski

Sougata Roy

Jonathan Rubin for a Civil Society

Eugene Russell

Paul Ryus

Stuart Samberg in Memory of
   Scott Rutherford

Ida van Schalkwyk

Doug Scheffler

Robert James Schneider

Suzanne Schneider

Joseph Schofer in Memory of Ralph Schofer

David Schrank

Matthias Schueller

Amy M. Schutzbach

Carol L. Schweiger

Gian-Claudia Sciara

In Memory of Jim Scott

Chi-Hsin Shao

Arunprakash Shirole

Steven E. Shladover

In Memory of Gordon Shunk

Frank Spielberg

In Honor of Robert Stein

Paul Steinberg

Ruth Steiner

Jack Stickel

Anne Strauss-Wieder

Hisham Sunna

Ramakrishna Reddy Tadi

Scott Taylor

Taylor and Francis Group

Honoring Susan Tighe, University of Waterloo

Knowles Tivendale

Jack Tone

Melissa Tooley

For TRB Staff

Michael Trentacoste

Shawn Turner

Hannah Twaddell

Sharada Vadali

Amiy Varma

Patricia Vieira

Juan Carlos Villa

Thomas Wakeman III

Joan Walker

Jason Wang

James Watson

Rick Weiland

Kevin White in Recognition of
    TRB Volunteers

Kristine Williams in Honor of Vergil Stover

Shawn D. Wilson, DOTD Secretary

Kum L. Wong

In Memory of Charley Wootan

Steve Yaffe

Duk-Geun Yun

Mariia Zimmerman

Samuel Zimmerman

Mia Zmud in Honor of My Sister
    Johanna Zmud

January 12, 2020

Dear Colleague,

The Transportation Research Board (TRB) of the National Academies of Sciences, Engineering, and Medicine marks its 100th anniversary this year, and we are proud to celebrate its many achievements. For a century, TRB's work has laid the foundation for safer, more efficient U.S. transportation that has connected millions of Americans and spurred unprecedented economic growth and prosperity. You can read about many of these accomplishments on the following pages.

This milestone anniversary also prompts us to look ahead at the many transportation issues that will shape our future. The U.S. and global transportation systems are facing myriad and complex challenges that are unlike those of previous generations. TRB's evidence-based guidance and advice will be more critical than ever to spark needed innovation and advancements.

Greenhouse gas emissions from transportation systems must be reduced, and we must prepare for extreme weather events resulting from climate change that can wreak havoc on transportation systems. At the same time, the roads, bridges, ports, waterways, airports, and public transit systems that underpin the modern world are in desperate need of repair and improvement. Governance and funding mechanisms are shifting rapidly, and changing demographics and workforce needs are introducing new stressors to aging systems. New technologies offer the potential to change radically how people and goods move and significantly enhance safety—but only if they are implemented wisely and for the benefit of all.

For 100 years, TRB has been an incubator for cutting-edge technologies and solutions that help solve some of the nation's most pressing transportation challenges. Our success is made possible because of our world-class and committed base of volunteer experts, talented staff, and the steady support of state and federal sponsors. We are grateful for their continued dedication, and confident that TRB will help lead society into a new era of progress in the years ahead.

Sincerely,

Marcia McNutt, President
National Academy of Sciences

John L. Anderson, President
National Academy of Engineering

Victor J. Dzau, President
National Academy of Medicine

Foreword

Thomas B. Deen and Robert E. Skinner, Jr.

THE TRANSPORTATION RESEARCH BOARD (TRB) celebrates its 100th anniversary in 2020. During those 100 years, the scale and scope of TRB's activities expanded steadily, no doubt well beyond anything the founders imagined in 1920. Starting with a handful of committees intended to foster technical exchange between highway researchers and practitioners, today it is a robust organization that serves virtually all modes of transportation, manages independent research programs, maintains information databases, and conducts studies of national transportation policy issues. Its first Annual Meeting hosted 30 attendees; today's attendance is closing in on 14,000. At the outset, 32 individuals served on TRB's three technical committees; today TRB's standing technical committee and task force volunteers number more than 5,000.

This growth in both scale and scope seems particularly remarkable given the challenges that professional organizations now face. For example, according to polling data and numerous articles, the credibility of institutions of all sorts—government, business, media, and nongovernmental organizations—has been in widespread decline for a long time. Credibility is the lifeblood of any organization, including TRB, whose mission involves generating, vetting, and disseminating information. Moreover, volunteer-based organizations have been hit especially hard in recent decades. In his best-selling book *Bowling Alone*, Robert Putnam reported on the drop in volunteerism throughout the United States, its impact on long-established institutions, and the resultant loss in what he termed "social capital." TRB is completely dependent on volunteers to populate its numerous committees, not just the standing technical committees but also the panels that oversee individual research projects and the committees that conduct consensus studies. Finally, TRB's "century" has been an extraordinary one for the United States and the world, which has seen a worldwide depression, World War II, and the Cold War with the constant threat of nuclear annihilation, revolutionary improvements in transportation and communication, energy crises, climate change, and security threats. These in turn have spawned a host of public concerns about the social, environmental, and economic impacts of transportation systems and individual projects that go well beyond the scope of TRB as envisioned in 1920. TRB had to adapt to all of these new challenges or lose its relevancy.

How is it that TRB continues to thrive in a climate that has proved so difficult for many organizations? How has it adapted to new challenges facing transportation? What have been the key success factors? As former executive directors, we had front row seats for a total of 35 years, more than one-third of TRB's life. When volunteer participation is counted, Deen has been involved for an almost unbelievable 64 years. So given these long-standing close connections, it should not be surprising that we have some thoughts about the answers to these questions.

Location within the National Research Council (NRC) of the National Academy of Sciences (NAS). This decision by TRB's founders proved providential for several reasons. Being part of NRC provided immediate recognition and credibility, as well as the institutional wherewithal to handle added assignments that came later. More importantly, TRB had a parent organization with a strong culture of quality, belief in the scientific method, and process-oriented safeguards to ensure high standards in publications and other products coming from the organization. NRC and NAS insulate TRB from political and financial pressures that otherwise would be difficult to resist. And because NRC was a relatively new organization itself in 1920, it had not yet developed a rigid sense of the activities in which it would and would not engage—a perfect place for a new board that needed some flexibility of its own to fully define its mission.

Mixing researchers and practitioners. TRB's founders, as noted in this book, had ties to academia and state highway agencies. They wished to "coordinate" research, not through top-down direction and not by just having researchers talk among themselves, but rather by having individual researchers and practitioners collaborate on the state of the practice, emerging needs, promising avenues for research, and research results in need of dissemination. Consequently, a constructive tension between the interests of researchers and the interests of practitioners was built into TRB from the outset, helping to keep research and TRB itself relevant to the needs of state and local highway agencies (and later transportation agencies).

No credentials or disciplinary requirements needed. TRB's founders—almost all civil engineers—were not trying to duplicate a professional engineering society. They had a specific mission in mind to promote innovation through better-coordinated research. And because they expected that the new organization would appeal primarily to practitioners and researchers already working in the field, they saw no need for participants to possess or demonstrate specific credentials or meet disciplinary requirements. This is important because, over time, as transportation became more complex and TRB expanded its scope to cover other modes, it could seamlessly adapt and become a multidisciplinary organization, welcoming students, researchers, and practitioners with a diverse array of professional backgrounds.

Empowering committees; providing bottom-up leadership. At the outset, the founders and first members of TRB's Executive Committee determined which topic areas merited having a committee of their own. These committees were the earliest of TRB's standing technical committees, which today number around 200 and are the foundation of TRB. Rather than the Executive Committee always in the role of commissioning new committees, momentum gradually shifted to the individual committees and their volunteer members. Often they were in the best position to identify emerging or evolving topics; and they sought to establish new subcommittees, task forces, and ultimately committees. Of course, the Executive Committee exerted oversight and established guidelines for commissioning new committees, but eventually the oversight responsibility itself was referred to the Technical Activities Council, comprising the leadership of the various groups of standing technical committees. The result has been that individual committees and volunteers have a direct role in shaping the direction of TRB. Thus, TRB does not depend on its Executive Committee to keep the portfolio of committees fresh and relevant, but rather allows the volunteers themselves to regenerate and refresh the portfolio, many times supporting multidisciplinary specialist communities that have no other institutional home.

Sponsors: the essential ingredient. Although TRB collects fees from meeting attendees and publication sales, the funds are not nearly sufficient to cover the full costs of running its core program—its standing technical committees, the annual meeting, publications, and related activities. From the outset, the founders envisioned an organization that would serve the interests of state and local highway agencies and that would be supported by the federal Bureau of Public Roads, acting on behalf of states and localities. Later in the 1940s, coincident with an expansion of the portfolio of committees and—perhaps more importantly—staff support for those committees, much of the burden was shifted directly to state departments of transportation (then highway departments). Today, state departments of transportation collectively are TRB's major sponsor, supplemented with major support from the Department of Transportation via the Federal Highway Administration and other modal administrations plus selected transportation associations and others. In a domain that most observers agree has difficulty dealing with long-term issues and faces perpetual financial challenges, such sponsor commitment is extraordinary. While we strongly believe that TRB's role in technology transfer and innovative practice is highly cost-effective, proving it in quantitative terms is not easy. The steadfast support of these sponsors for the Core Program has been essential to TRB's success, and their support over the years has extended to other missions conducted by TRB—managing cooperative research programs, overseeing special time-limited research programs, conducting policy studies, and maintaining bibliographic databases.

Serendipity. Regardless of how one describes the key factors that shaped TRB during its 100-year history, one must also acknowledge the role that serendipity played. It was established at the right time, surrounded by a supportive institutional environment, led by successive generations of far-sighted transportation professionals, and received the long-term support of dedicated volunteers and sponsors. None of this was guaranteed, and looking back we cannot help but be awed by the good fortune that TRB, its volunteers, and its sponsors have enjoyed during the past 100 years.

TRB's remarkable story is well documented in this wonderful, engaging book by Sarah Jo Peterson. Despite TRB's institutional complexity, its unique mission, the mind-numbing collection of acronyms it uses to facilitate internal communications, and the far-reaching changes that have taken place in its first 100 years, Dr. Peterson provided us with a view from 30,000 feet, which highlights the macro-level changes that have taken place in response to the social, political, and economic context in which transportation (and TRB) must function. At the same time she has attended to the details of key events, individuals, and the human motivations that have shaped TRB's evolution. Her skills as a historian, her experience in the transportation field, and her manifest ability to tell a good story have produced a book that all transportation professionals will find both engaging and informative and an essential reference text for their bookshelf.

Thomas B. Deen
Executive Director, 1980–1994

Robert E. Skinner, Jr.
Executive Director, 1994–2015

January 12, 2020

Contents

Key Events in the Transportation Research Board's History

1863   Congress charters the National Academy of Sciences (NAS).

1905   Logan Page becomes head of the federal Office of Public Roads.

1914   American Association of State Highway Officials (AASHO) is organized.

1916   NAS organizes the National Research Council (NRC) to serve the federal government during World War I.

1916   Federal-Aid Road Act establishes federal–state partnership for highway building.

1919   Thomas MacDonald becomes head of the federal Bureau of Public Roads (BPR).

1920   NRC's Division of Engineering and BPR convene the organizing meeting for the Advisory Board on Highway Research (the Board), a federation of member organizations, on November 11.

1921   William K. Hatt becomes the Board's first director.

1921   Federal-Aid Highway Act focuses federal–state partnership on primary and secondary highways.

1922   First Annual Meeting of the Board is held in January and the second in November.

1924   Charles M. Upham becomes the Board's second director.

1925   The Board changes its name to the Highway Research Board on January 1.

1928   Roy W. Crum becomes the Board's third director.

1931   The first *Highway Research Abstracts* is published as part of the Board's new research information service.

1934   Hayden-Cartwright Act authorizes states to spend federal aid on highway planning surveys.

1935   The Board organizes its technical committees into departments.

1936   Congress funds studies of highway safety, managed by the Board and BPR.

1944   Federal-Aid Highway Act authorizes a National System of Interstate Highways and states to spend federal aid on research.

1945   The Board launches the Research Correlation Service, funded by the states.

1948   AASHO adopts procedures for states to pool funds for research projects to be administered by the Board.

1951   Fred Burggraf becomes the Board's fourth director.

1952   NRC convenes the Maritime Cargo Transportation Conference.

1953   MacDonald retires as head of BPR.

1954   The Board expands its studies of urban transportation, with seed funding from the Automotive Safety Foundation.

1955   AASHO requests that the Board administer the AASHO Road Test.

1956   Federal-Aid Highway Act accelerates funding for the National System of Interstate and Defense Highways and expands the AASHO Road Test.

1956   The Board launches the Highway Laws Project with funding from the Automotive Safety Foundation and AASHO.

1961   NRC founds the Maritime Transportation Research Board on October 9.

1962   The National Cooperative Highway Research Program is established by agreement with AASHO, BPR, and NAS.

1962   Federal-Aid Highway Act establishes the 3C—continuing, comprehensive, and cooperative—planning process.

1962   The Board, through bylaw changes, becomes more closely aligned with NRC.

1963   *Highway Research Record* replaces the annual meeting *Proceedings*.

1964   D. Grant Mickle becomes the Board's fifth director.

1964   National Academy of Engineering is organized.

1966   William N. Carey, Jr., becomes the Board's sixth executive director.

1967   The Board rebrands the Research Correlation Service as Technical Activities.

1967   The new U.S. Department of Transportation (USDOT) consolidates many federal transportation agencies, and the Federal Highway Administration (FHWA) absorbs BPR.

1967   The Board pushes the start button on its first computerized Highway Research Information Service.

1969   NRC approves a new purpose and scope for the Board that includes urban transportation.

1970   The Board reorganizes its technical committees into groups defined by transportation system phases.

1971   The Urban Mass Transportation Administration becomes a Board sponsor.

1973   AASHO becomes the American Association of State Highway and Transportation Officials (AASHTO).

1974   The Highway Research Board dissolves and the Transportation Research Board (TRB), a unit of NRC's Commission on Sociotechnical Systems, is born on March 9.

1977   New TRB sponsors include the Maritime Administration, the Association of American Railroads, and the USDOT's Office of the Secretary, Federal Railroad Administration, Federal Aviation Administration (FAA), and National Highway Traffic Safety Administration (NHTSA).

1980   Thomas B. Deen becomes TRB's seventh executive director.

1982   TRB becomes a stand-alone unit of NRC and takes on the responsibility for policy (consensus) studies.

1982   NRC's Marine Board, which dates to 1965, absorbs the Maritime Transportation Research Board.

1987   Congress authorizes the Strategic Highway Research Program (SHRP).

1991   Congress authorizes the Transit Cooperative Research Program, to be sponsored by the Federal Transit Administration, in the Intermodal Surface Transportation Efficiency Act.

1993   The SHRP's IDEA—Innovations Deserving Exploratory Analysis—program joins TRB after the completion of SHRP.

1994   Robert E. Skinner, Jr., becomes TRB's eighth executive director.

1995   TRB launches its first home page on the Internet.

1999   The Marine Board joins TRB.

2003   Congress authorizes the Airport Cooperative Research Program, to be sponsored by FAA.

2003   TRB's standing technical committees reorganize into 11 groups representing modes and system functions.

2005   Congress authorizes the second SHRP.

2013   TRB co-sponsors the first annual European Union–United States Transportation Research Symposium.

2015   Neil J. Pedersen becomes TRB's ninth executive director.

2017   TRB assumes management of the Behavioral Traffic Safety Cooperative Research Program, together with NHTSA and the Governors Highway Safety Association.

2021   TRB celebrates its 100th Annual Meeting, January 24–28, 2021.

"We repeat, everyone interested is invited."

Roy W. Crum, Director
Highway Research Board
On the Eighth Annual Meeting
October 1928

Introduction

TRANSPORTATION RESEARCH has always been part of the National Academies of Sciences, Engineering, and Medicine (the National Academies). Three studies initiated in the founding institution's first year, 1863, examined problems of ship design and navigation. The original congressional charter for the National Academy of Sciences (NAS) created a select organization of America's scientific elite. Its mission was simply to advise the government of the United States upon request.

As the Transportation Research Board (TRB), a program unit of the National Academies, celebrates its Centennial in 2020, it hosts more than 200 standing technical committees, involving thousands of researchers and consumers of research. TRB boasts participation from students to senior scholars and from universities small and large, from all over the world. Researchers from government and industry are instrumental as well. TRB's Centennial also celebrates a century of partnership with state governments that has been the foundation, and then model, for large and continuing research programs. Yet, TRB still fulfills the original mission of advising the federal government upon request.

This book is the story of how people and institutions created today's TRB. It emphasizes origin stories, and some of what defines the modern TRB is very old. That those with expertise should volunteer their knowledge without payment is rooted in the federal charter of 1863. That the expertise required to advise government is found not in the individual, but in the group—organized as a committee—also dates to the National Academies' founding. Each of the unique aspects of TRB also has its own origin story, and some of them were years, if not decades, in the making. Implicit also in a centennial history is a celebration of continuity. Although the historian, like modern society, is often drawn to change and to what has become different, TRB's history confirms that continuity, too, can be a source of strength.

The book builds, for the most part, off of TRB's annual reports, Executive Committee meeting minutes, internal memos, newsletters, conference proceedings, selected interviews, and research reports. The action typically takes place within TRB or the National Academies. Given time constraints, little primary research was possible in the records of the federal agencies, Congress, TRB's partners and sponsors, or individual participants. Although the research made every effort to examine the most significant events and programs in TRB's history, much got left behind and some tantalizing hints went unexplored. This is not the definitive history of TRB.

As an organization of literally thousands of participants, when acknowledging everyone seems impossible, TRB has an understandable tendency to name no one. This history has chosen to name names, attempting to at least include committee chairs and their home institutions. These individuals are also symbols. For every person named in the 1920s and 1930s, tens more were doing faithful work in committees. For the middle decades, every individual recognized stands in for hundreds and, by the end, thousands.

How TRB Works

TRB has often been said to defy analogy. It is not a professional association or an industry organization, despite superficial similarities to both. Although it produces research reports, much of the nuts and bolts of the research itself is contracted to others external to the organization. This book argues that TRB can be best understood as an infrastructure, one that people purposely designed, carefully constructed, and devotedly maintained to facilitate communication and generate knowledge about transportation.

To say that the basic functional unit of TRB is the committee is true, but incomplete. TRB committees should not be confused with self-organizing affinity groups. Inscribed on the National Academies' DNA is that every committee is responsible for a set of tasks or objectives, and all individual volunteers are appointed through a selection process that prioritizes the success of the group. While membership in the National Academies is a select honor, it is not a prerequisite for appointment to the National Academies' committees. Anyone with the right mix of knowledge, experience, and willingness to work may be tapped for most committees. Someone is always designated—by TRB or the National Academies—as the chair, and the job of chair is recognized as a specialized skill. (Although this book uses "chair" instead of "chairman" throughout, the National Academies did not adopt the gender-neutral term "chair" until the 1990s.) Committees may take other names—council, task force, or panel, for example—but the essential group structure of chair, task, and appointed volunteers remains constant.

The overall structure of TRB's technical committees and other functions within the National Academies appears hierarchical, but it is equally a support structure—like for a bridge—as it is a command structure. TRB is a board, which today is essentially a collection of technical committees that have continuing responsibilities, an Executive Committee charged with giving strategic advice, and a staff with the capacity to manage studies, research programs, convenings, and publications, all overseen by a specialized committee that safeguards standards for quality and conduct. Historically, however, TRB's predecessors had quite a different organizational structure, and TRB's maturation required it to transform itself to meet new demands from its home organization.

Committees have meetings, and this is where TRB's founders innovated in a way that differed from NAS's usual procedure of inviting top specialists and leaders. In 1928, they invited everyone interested to attend their annual meeting. The invitation was sincere. They followed it up by writing to state governments and universities asking them to send anyone involved in highway research to the meeting in Washington, D.C. The invitation built on a culture that already valued a broad definition of who held expertise and the ability to contribute to research. This openness and desire for a broad reach has continued to find expression throughout the organization, including that the meetings of its standing technical committees are still open to everyone who is interested. This model—the open invitation, followed by the personal act of asking—pushed against without supplanting the older model of selected appointment. The two philosophies of knowledge, the open invitation and the selected appointment, exist side by side.

Key Developments in TRB's History

One year before the founding of NAS, Congress passed a landmark law that was equally critical to the development of TRB. The 1862 Morrill Act encouraged the states to found colleges that would specialize in the agricultural and mechanical arts, and the 1887 Hatch Act further encouraged these "land-grant universities" to engage in research. Land-grant universities would play an outsized role in TRB's formative years.[1]

In addition to NAS's founding precedents of appointed volunteers organized into committees, in the 1880s its members engaged in an internal struggle over the centralization of scientific research. Ultimately, the proponents of centralization lost, and NAS became an advocate for the decentralization of research. For highways, this preference for decentralization would make NAS's National Research Council (NRC) a congenial fit for the federal–state partnership pioneered in the landmark Federal-Aid Road Act of 1916.

NAS founded NRC in 1916 in preparation for World War I, and in May 1918 President Woodrow Wilson signed an executive order establishing NRC as a permanent organization and perpetuating its mission "to stimulate research." NRC acted as NAS's operating arm and gave it a continuing mission, in addition to responding to federal requests.

The organizers of the Advisory Board on Highway Research embraced NRC's mission when they founded the Board under NRC's umbrella on November 11, 1920. One of six advisory boards founded within NRC's Division of Engineering, it alone would thrive, eventually becoming large enough to warrant the status of stand-alone unit within the National Academies. The Board was originally founded as a federation of organizations, only two of which were the American Association of State Highway Officials (AASHO) and the federal Bureau of Public Roads (BPR). Among the other organizations were those representing the private sector, including the motor vehicle industries and highway materials providers.

Strictly speaking, highways are not a mode of transport; they are a type of infrastructure. To the Board's founders, a highway was a good road that was used for more than just a local means to access land. Over the century, the definition of "good" has constantly changed, growing in complexity, and has often been contested. It would not be until the 1960s, however, that the term "highway" began to be closely associated with high-speed travel.

Advisory Board on Highway Research
Division of Engineering, National Research Council

Member Organizations, First Annual Meeting, January 16, 1922

American Association of State Highway Officials	Association of American State Geologists
American Concrete Institute	Bureau of Public Roads (Department of Agriculture)
American Institute of Consulting Engineers	Engineering Foundation
American Society for Municipal Improvements	National Automobile Chamber of Commerce
American Society for Testing Materials	National Highway Traffic Association
American Society of Civil Engineers	Society of Automotive Engineers
American Society of Mechanical Engineers	U.S. Army Corps of Engineers
	Western Society of Engineers

Source: Minutes, January 16, 1922, TRB Executive Committee Meeting Minutes Record Group, NAS-NRC Archives.

The early highway builders—confronted with the reality that they had little control over vehicles, and their increasing numbers, types, uses, and capabilities, or the behavior of people driving and walking—sought out cooperative research as a way to achieve some sort of coordination. TRB's founders purposely created an organization where those responsible for policy could come together with researchers and practitioners to think: to mull over problems, develop a path for solutions, and, in later decades, promote innovation. With its first funded research project, the member organizations changed the name to Highway Research Board in 1925.

BPR was the Board's largest single financial sponsor for its first two decades, and its successor, the Federal Highway Administration, continues its long relationship with TRB. During the 1930s, the Board charged its technical committees with the identification of research needs, establishing the best practice that the identification of research priorities should also be a collective, cooperative task. Frustrated with the limits of an organization essentially run by volunteers, in 1944 the state highway departments and the Board developed a sponsorship arrangement for the Research Correlation Service, which supported professional staff for the technical committees and various communication functions. In 1948, AASHO and the Board negotiated a cooperative research funding mechanism that was deployed for the AASHO Road Test in the 1950s and laid the foundation for the National Cooperative Highway Research Program launched in 1962. At certain times throughout TRB's history, the private sector has also been a noteworthy source of research support and sponsorship.

The Highway Research Board's federation structure lasted until 1962, when the Board fully joined NRC, and the Board's Executive Committee became an NRC-appointed committee. The Board expanded its scope to include urban transportation in 1969 and, after nearly a decade of debate, became officially charged with "total transportation" on March 9, 1974. Although internally its leaders referred to the Highway Research Board as "the Board" (not "HRB") for short, the Transportation Research Board was immediately and universally nicknamed "TRB." The book follows these name traditions, using "HRB" only when necessary for reasons of clarity.

In 1964, the National Academy of Engineering (NAE) was formed within NAS. In 2015, the Institute of Medicine (IOM), established in

1970, was elevated to the National Academy of Medicine (NAM), and the organization took its present name. This book uses "National Academy" to refer to the organization as a whole up to 1964 and then "National Academies" thereafter. When the constituent parts are acting individually or interacting with each other, the book refers to them as NAS, NRC, NAE, IOM, and NAM.

The Urban Mass Transportation Administration became a sponsor in 1971 and by the end of the 1970s, the National Highway Traffic Safety Administration, the Federal Aviation Administration, the Federal Railroad Administration, the Maritime Administration, and the Association of American Railroads had also become sponsors. The American Public Transportation Association became a sponsor with the launch of the congressionally funded Transit Cooperative Research Program in 1992. NRC's Marine Board, which has its roots in the 1940s, joined TRB in 1999, and TRB developed even closer ties to aviation when Congress funded the Airport Cooperative Research Program in 2003.

Fulfilling NAS's founding mission, the Board answered its first congressional research request through managing investigations of highway safety during the late 1930s, and the Board incorporated directions from Congress into the AASHO Road Test. In 1982, TRB expanded its capacity to manage the National Academies' consensus studies that advise the federal government on questions of policy. Consensus studies also prepared the ground for both the first and second Strategic Highway Research Programs, authorized by Congress in 1987 and 2005, respectively.

TRB's Annual Meeting, its signature event, has been nearly constant for its first century. The first two annual meetings were held in January and November 1922, and then the Board continued to meet in November or December in Washington, D.C., until World War II. In 1941, the meeting left Washington, D.C., at the request of the federal government. The 1944 meeting went unassembled, although they produced a volume of proceedings. They next met in January 1946 and then the meeting returned to Washington, D.C., in December 1946. With a 13-month interval between the 1949 meeting and the 30th Annual Meeting held in January 1951, the Board adopted the annual meeting schedule used through today.

The Question of Impact

TRB has typically addressed the question of its impact by pointing to the usefulness of the thousands of applied research projects that it has managed or the decisions that flowed from the consensus studies that it has convened. This book can include only a sampling of these stories. Understanding TRB as infrastructure, however, lends itself well to stories of initiative, determination, and leadership, and the book includes the stories of people who exhibited all three to spectacular effect. On the other hand, while there is no doubt that any intellectual history of, for example, pavement design, traffic flow theory, or transit quality of service would include a role for TRB, TRB's infrastructure would only be one part of a larger story. The same is also true of most policy issues. Instead, this book asks: What has TRB been used for? How? What is it capable of being used for? What couldn't be done, if it wasn't there? All in order to better imagine: what will TRB be used for next?

CHAPTER 1

The National Academy of Sciences and Transportation, 1863–1919

WASHINGTON, D.C., during the Civil War attracted inventors and entrepreneurs, eager to aid the war effort. They brought their devices and proposals to Congress, the War Department, and the Navy. A parade of innovations in armaments, shipbuilding, and logistics—deploying the telegraph, railroad, and observation balloon for military purposes— demanded to be embraced or dismissed. In the midst of war, a small band of scientists found themselves in the advantageous position of being responsible for evaluating these schemes while also harboring an audacious proposal of their own.[1]

Two of the band were also engineers. Alexander Dallas Bache was the great-grandson of Benjamin Franklin. Educated at West Point, in 1843 he left a position at the University of Pennsylvania to become superintendent of the Coast Survey. Founded in 1807 by the Navy and made a civilian agency in 1832, the Coast Survey was responsible for hydrographic surveys and nautical charts and had thrived as a federal center for science. Charles Henry Davis, a naval officer, had been called to Washington, D.C., in 1862 to head up the Navy's Bureau of Navigation. Bache and Davis were part of a small group of friends led by Louis Agassiz, Harvard professor of zoology and geology, who saw in the mounting number of technical problems, proposals, and inventions an opportunity to pursue an idea they had been kicking around for years.[2]

They dreamed of an American version of Great Britain's Royal Society or France's Académie des Sciences, elite organizations that promoted science, but also advised their national governments. The United States already had scientific and technical societies. The American Association for the Advancement of Science dated to 1848 and the American Society of Civil Engineers was founded in 1852, but these organizations aimed to be broad professional organizations. Their proposed National Academy of Sciences (NAS) would be distinguished from other American organizations by its federal charter and limited, select membership. In their wartime review responsibilities, Bache and Davis now had a problem that their proposed NAS could help solve, or so they could argue to Congress.

Winning over one senator turned out to be enough. Agassiz persuaded Massachusetts Senator Henry Wilson, who saw merit in both serving the war effort and cultivating national prestige. As the final session of the 37th Congress wound down, Wilson, Agassiz, Bache, and Davis were among the small group that quickly drafted a bill for

The painter Albert Herter depicts President Abraham Lincoln signing the charter of the National Academy of Sciences on March 3, 1863. In this apocryphal scene, Senator Henry Wilson and the founders look on. Left to right: Benjamin Peirce, Alexander Dallas Bache, Joseph Henry, Louis Agassiz, President Lincoln, Senator Wilson, Admiral Charles Henry Davis, and Benjamin Apthorp Gould (NAS-NRC Archives).

Wilson to introduce on February 20, 1863. Amidst a flurry of resolutions on March 3, the Senate passed Wilson's bill on a voice vote and then adjourned. Hours later the House did the same. Before midnight, President Abraham Lincoln signed the charter into law. Not momentous debate, but a small and quiet legislative act gave birth to NAS.

Science in Service to Government

As originally enacted, the federal charter limited "ordinary members" to 50 and gave NAS the freedom to set up its organization as it saw fit. The act set forth three requirements: to hold an annual meeting, to make reports to Congress, and "whenever called upon by any department of the government, investigate, examine, experiment, and report upon any subject of science or art." The act authorized no funds to operate this new academy. Indeed, just the opposite. NAS "shall receive no compensation whatever for any services to the Government of the United States." Its members would be volunteers in service to their government.

The act listed the inaugural 50 incorporators, men of science handpicked by Agassiz and company. The founders made no attempt to turn NAS into a mirror reflecting the best of American science. Although natural history dominated science in the United States, NAS emphasized the physical sciences and technology. Many members held military posts.

Bache became the first NAS president. To provide financial stability, Bache also amended his will to name NAS as trustee of his sizeable estate. As the first requests for assistance arrived in 1863, Bache devised what would become the basic functional unit of NAS: the committee of experts who make a report. For simple problems, Bache believed written correspondence among committee members would suffice, but he envisioned in-person meetings for committees charged with major

The U.S.S. Monitor, 1862: two studies in NAS's first year investigated ironclad ships (Library of Congress, LC-DIG-cwpb-01058).

investigations. Already in 1863, he also anticipated that a committee should not act unsupervised, but that its work might "be perfected" by another unit or the academy as a whole.

The First Transportation Studies

Transportation was well represented in NAS's first studies, not surprising given the founders' ties to ships and navigation. During NAS's first 2 years, the Navy made five transportation-related requests, half of the total number of studies.[3] NAS's wartime transportation studies outlined the organization's promise and pitfalls for peacetime. Although NAS could convene the best minds on a topic, government's desire for an answer could be fleeting and would not necessarily translate into adequate research funding. However, NAS could be useful in reviewing the work of others and, in the process of review, set standards for scientific conduct. Finally, NAS could be the source of a neutral opinion in controversies.

Ironclad ships powered by steam first saw battle in the U.S. Civil War, and from their earliest encounters proved their might over wooden ships. Iron as a construction material, however, reacted poorly to saltwater. The Committee on Protecting the Bottoms of Iron Vessels, NAS's second committee, reported that unfortunately no effective coatings yet existed to protect a ship's iron cladding. The committee offered to conduct its own tests and even arranged to use the Smithsonian Institution laboratories, but neither the Navy nor Congress was forthcoming with additional funds. Iron also interfered with the magnetic compasses used for navigation. Here, NAS had more impact. "The Compass Committee," as it was nicknamed, recommended that magnets be carefully mounted to counteract the deviation. The committee eventually supervised the installation of magnets on 27 vessels.[4]

NAS's final naval assignment in 1863 allowed it to take a strong stand for sober science. Davis asked NAS to assess two of the Navy's publications, *Wind and Current Charts* and *Sailing Directions*. They had been prepared starting in 1847 by Matthew Fontaine Maury, who during his long Navy career came to be internationally renowned as the "Pathfinder of the Seas." Maury's innovation was data collection.

He distributed logbooks to ship captains for daily records of winds, storms, currents, temperatures, and other marine phenomena. Maury used the data to map routes that took days, even weeks, off of sailing times. Over the years, however, Maury added hundreds of pages to these official government publications promoting his personal—unscientific and even fanciful—theories of the marine environment. Providentially, Maury hailed from Virginia and joined the Confederacy. Calling the publications "a most wanton waste of valuable paper," the NAS committee advised that only the data-driven charts should continue to be published. The Navy discontinued the publications altogether.[5]

Controversies sparked the two transportation-related committees formed in 1864. The Navy tasked a committee with resolving a feud among naval engineers over using compressed steam to reduce the cost of fuel. Although the committee, jointly appointed by NAS, the Navy, and the Franklin Institute, embarked on an ambitious program, the study languished for years without conclusion for a lack of funds.[6]

A tragedy brought NAS into a different type of dispute. The Navy steamer *Chenango* exploded soon after being put into service, killing 28 sailors. The local inquest produced a majority and a minority opinion, the former finding fault with the boiler and its design, a Navy responsibility. The Navy then turned to NAS, and committee members traveled to Brooklyn Navy Yard to inspect what remained of the ship. Less than 4 months after the explosion, the committee submitted a detailed report offering a third conclusion, which placed most of the blame on the private contractors charged with the ship's construction.[7]

The transition to peace seemed to bode well for the new academy. Six requests for advice arrived in 1866, including the first from the State Department. An American company had invested in the harbor at Greytown on Nicaragua's Atlantic Coast. Once capable of hosting deep, large ships, the harbor had filled with silt, and shifting sandbars threatened to close its entrance entirely. On behalf of the Nicaraguan government, the Secretary of State requested NAS's advice on saving the harbor. The committee, assembled in Washington, D.C., and consulting maps

Landslide!

THE CUCARACHA SLIDE had first bedeviled the builders of the Panama Canal in 1907. It appeared along the Gaillard (Culebra) Cut that carried the canal through the mountains and over the Continental Divide. A huge break in January 1913 pushed back the canal's opening to August 1914. Slides continued and dredging struggled to keep pace. A fast-growing island appeared in the canal, eventually forcing its closure on September 18, 1915. With two new active slides near the quiet, but still threatening, Cucaracha Slide, skeptics began openly predicting that the engineers' plans to out-dredge the slides would be futile.

At President Woodrow Wilson's request, the National Academy of Sciences appointed a team of nine experts led by Charles R. Van Hise, a geologist and president of the University of Wisconsin, to investigate, and by December 19, 1915, they were in Panama. The committee recommended extensive drainage of the hillsides, but were otherwise optimistic. Their preliminary report issued in 1916 advised the president that "the Committee looks to the future of the Canal with confidence."[a]

The Panama Canal did indeed "serve the great purpose for which it was constructed," as the committee predicted, but 26 slides between 1914 and 1986 led to temporary closures. Much work still needed to be done to understand—and prevent—landslides.[b]

The Highway Research Board's Committee on Landslide Investigations formed in 1951.

Chaired by Edwin B. Eckel of the U.S. Geological Survey (USGS), it brought together geologists and highway engineers "to attempt to cover the entire field of landslides, from causes to cures." At the time, no comprehensive synthesis on landslides existed in English, let alone one that integrated experiences in North America. The committee sent a detailed questionnaire to highway departments, state geologists, and universities across the United States. With the assistance of Rockwell Smith, a committee member from the Association of American Railroads, they also surveyed American and Canadian railroads.[c]

The final report, *Landslides and Engineering Practice*, appeared as Special Report 29 in 1958. Divided into two parts—Definition of the Problem and Solution of the Problem—the report covered geology and engineering, but also economic and legal aspects. Although committee members took the lead responsibility for different chapters, teamwork created a cohesive whole that proved immediately useful. Within just a few years, the report sold out.

Despite being out of print, interest in the report continued, and in 1972 the Highway Research Board appointed a task force, chaired by Robert L. Schuster, USGS, that took on an update. American and Canadian geologists and engineers with experience in highways and railroads took the lead on individual chapters. TRB published *Landslides: Analysis and Control* (Special Report 176) in 1978. In 1990, a study committee led by A. Keith Turner, Colorado

School of Mines, began the process of producing a third update. *Landslides: Investigations and Mitigation* (Special Report 247, 1996) repeated the winning formula, with sponsorship from the National Science Foundation. A 2016 Transportation Research Board (TRB) survey of practitioners showed 61 percent still used the publication.[d]

Individual careers grew alongside their participation in the reports. Ta Liang, a pioneer in using aerial photography to detect landslides and a professor of civil and environmental engineering at Cornell University, and David J. Varnes, a geologist with USGS, worked on both the 1958 and 1978 editions. Varnes even contributed his 50 years of experience to the 1996 update.[e]

The National Academies of Sciences, Engineering, and Medicine, in their more than a century of advising on mitigating landslides to keep transportation moving, have contributed to the massive expansion in knowledge and refinement of guidance. In 1958, geologists had only identified three types of landslides: falls, slides, and flows. By 1978 they had added two more: topples and spreads. A comprehensive survey in 1958 required only 232 pages. By 1996, the project ranged more than 650 pages. In 2005, a task force of volunteer reviewers and authors, again led by Turner, started work on just rockfalls. Published by TRB in 2012, *Rockfall: Characterization and Control* weighs in at 658 pages, plus a DVD with videos.[f]

Workers dredge the Cucaracha Slide on the Panama Canal, 1910–1914 (Library of Congress, Detroit Publishing Company Collection, LC-DIG-det-4a24729).

and other materials, did not hold out much hope. The committee outlined one potential solution, which in its details communicated that they thought success unlikely.[8] After 1866, NAS received only one additional assignment directly related to transportation until into its sixth decade. The Navy adopted many of the changes to its Nautical Almanac that a committee convened in 1877 recommended.[9]

After the war, NAS struggled to be seen as relevant to the federal government and also to fend off threats from competing organizations. To address both challenges, in 1870, NAS designated Washington, D.C., as its permanent home and location of its annual meeting and lifted the cap on membership, electing a maximum of 10 new members each year. Between 1878 and 1908, however, NAS issued only 20 reports.[10]

Notably absent was any NAS involvement in the greatest transportation transformation of the 19th century: railroads. Although the War Department's Military Railroads took over southern railroads during the Civil War, operating by war's end 2,000 miles of service including 642 newly built or rebuilt miles of track and 26 miles of bridges, it made no requests for NAS assistance.[11] Throughout the second half of the 19th century, railroad officials and professionals founded numerous technical and professional organizations that confronted common problems and achieved desired coordination. Today's Association of American Railroads has its roots in the conventions first held in the 1870s to coordinate local time and railway time. Technical associations targeting track maintenance, bridges and building, railway engineering, and signals and communications were also founded during the 1880s and 1890s, and today are organized under the banner of AREMA, the American Railway Engineering and Maintenance-of-Way Association.[12]

The coming of the railroad did trigger, at least indirectly, what came to be celebrated as NAS's first big success. The Central Pacific Railroad started construction in Sacramento of the western section of the first transcontinental railroad in 1863; the Union Pacific followed suit out of Council Bluffs, Iowa, in 1865. Though the Golden Spike would not join the two in Promontory Summit, Utah, until May 10, 1869, the federal government used the new rail lines to launch survey expeditions as early as 1867. By the mid-1870s, six expeditions under the jurisdiction of three different federal departments were traipsing over the Great

Plains and the Rocky Mountains. Although each survey had different combinations of methods and purposes—geology, geography, topography, and parcel surveys for homesteading—accusations of duplication and waste aggravated a conflict between the Engineering Corps of the Army and the Department of the Interior and its allies in the universities. They argued over whether Army officers or scientific experts should be in charge of the expeditions. Congress stepped in to investigate after two rival survey teams—military and civilian—crossed paths to ill effect in Colorado in 1873.[13]

In 1878, the House Committee on Appropriations had had enough. It refused to continue to fund surveys and looked to NAS to propose "a plan for surveying and mapping the territories of the United States on such general system as will, in their judgment, secure the best results at the least possible cost." To protect the study's integrity, NAS excluded from the committee any member of a government survey team, leading to vigorous protest from the Army's Chief of Engineers. NAS's committee sided with the Department of the Interior and scientific expertise, recommending geological surveys be consolidated in a new agency, the U.S. Geological Survey (USGS). Military surveys should be done for military purposes only. The House incorporated the committee's final report directly into its bill. The Senate dropped some of the report's recommendations, but USGS took its place in the Department of the Interior on March 3, 1879. NAS had had a direct impact on how the federal government organized and conducted one of its most significant scientific functions.[14]

This study also set two precedents that would continue into the era of highways and beyond. Government valued advice on the sometimes politically difficult task of deciding how best to organize and administer its own scientific activities and technical research. Not conducting research, as NAS's founders had imagined, but advising government on how government should conduct research would be an ongoing role for NAS. Additionally, frustrations with—or fears of—duplication and

Geological survey pack train along the Yellowstone River, [1871] (Library of Congress, LC-USZ62-20198).

its attendant waste could motivate federal calls for assistance, implying a potentially significant role for NAS in the coordination of research activities.

Decentralized Science

In 1886, Congress rejected NAS's boldest proposal since its founding: a federal Department of Science. President Grover Cleveland did not think much of the idea either, but more importantly, neither did one of NAS's own powerful members, Alexander Agassiz, son of Louis Agassiz. The proposed Department of Science came in response to growing concerns in the 1880s about how best to manage the multiplying number of scientific activities—including the Coast Survey, the Geological Survey, and the Weather Bureau—taking place across the federal agencies. In 1884, a joint commission of the House and the Senate on the organization of science in government requested a report from NAS. After making minor recommendations, the committee then took the initiative and critiqued the government's scientific agencies for being "absolutely independent" and recommended that one central authority, managed by a commission that would include the president of NAS, coordinate all of the government's scientific work.[15]

Agassiz testified against the Department of Science and resigned, temporarily as it turned out, his NAS membership. A successful mining engineer who had made his fortune in copper and then followed in his father's footsteps into zoology, Agassiz opposed the centralization of science in Washington, D.C., and government endeavors that competed with universities and other scientific enterprises. He sided with those who believed that NAS's role was to counsel government, not promote science in government. Finding allies, he returned to the NAS fold and eventually rose to president, serving from 1901 to 1907. Yet, even he wrestled with how to encourage government to request NAS's advice more often.[16]

At 50 years, NAS had survived and proven itself useful to government, but major questions remained. Should NAS go beyond answering government's occasional call? Should it draw government's attention to research that NAS deemed of public importance? If so, how? In addition, over the years NAS had distanced itself from its roots in practical problems and the government experts who were responsible for them. At its founding, military and naval engineers had made up one-fifth of the original members. By 1912, only one remained. Nor had NAS responded to the rise of industrial engineering, leading one observer to call its Physics and Engineering Section "something of a misnomer." NAS's ability to counsel government in the applied sciences was faltering.[17]

World War I and the National Research Council

For George Ellery Hale, the 50th anniversary of NAS in 1913 presented an opportunity for renewal. An astronomer, Hale had been only 33 years old when elected to NAS in 1902. Like many before him, he felt frustrated that NAS remained an honorary society, without even an address of its own, that occasionally organized the delivery of advice to the federal government. The 50th anniversary, Hale wrote, should be "the beginning of a new epoch." In three essays published in the journal *Science,* he argued that NAS should aim to be a national center of science, housed in a state-of-the-art building in Washington, D.C. It should strengthen its ties to the federal government not by competing with the government's own capable scientists, but by leading in new areas of science, including engineering and the social sciences.[18]

War would provide Hale the needed catalyst to propose major changes to how NAS interacted with the federal government. Soon after the May 1915 sinking of the *Lusitania*, he began reaching out to fellow members in his capacity as NAS's foreign secretary. One year later, the NAS Council, its governing body, agreed to Hale's proposal to bring the engineering societies and NAS together to offer their services to the government in the event of American entry into war. With President Woodrow Wilson's quiet approval, Hale formed the Committee on the Organization of the Scientific Resources of the Country for National Service. NAS approved the committee's proposed National Research Council (NRC) in June 1916, and President Wilson appointed federal officials from the military and scientific bureaus to NRC in August.[19]

Although a unit of NAS, NRC from the outset had two key operational differences: it invited participation by *representatives*

NRC aviation research during World War I included overseeing the development of George W. Stewart's system to detect and locate aircraft using 18-foot listening horns at Ellington Field, Texas, 1918 (NAS-NRC Archives).

of other organizations in government, industry, and academia, and it set up committees in advance of requests from government. Indeed, the Engineering Foundation, the philanthropic arm of the United Engineering Societies, devoted its entire income in 1916 and 1917 to funding the new NRC and provided staff support and space in the Societies' offices in New York. By the end of 1916, NRC had formed 28 committees, and in 1917 the American Society of Civil Engineers joined the societies for mechanical, electrical, and mining engineers that made up the United Engineering Societies.[20]

For Hale, NRC was not a temporary structure for war, but a template for peace. Hale had also planned that the wartime NRC would be a mechanism to support basic research, hopes that were quickly dashed as the reality of war intruded. Practical applications targeting the problems of the military and battlefield dominated. NRC's wartime contributions to transportation mostly addressed aviation, including advances in instrumented weather balloons, aerial photography, optical glass, and the psychology of pilots. Roadbuilding was not completely left out. NRC's Geology Committee led an investigation on rapid road construction and fortification in coastal areas that influenced practices in concrete construction.[21]

The wartime NRC project that received the bulk of government funding, however, did not require scientific research at all. Through its Research Information Service, NRC showed how cooperation and technology could be used to rapidly communicate technological advances and research needs. In spring 1917, British scientists reached out to the American military, suggesting a liaison with their American counterparts. NRC took charge of the effort, which grew into four scientific offices in Washington, D.C., London, Paris, and Rome staffed by NRC and military intelligence officers. The science attachés made daily or weekly reports by cable or uncensored mail, and NRC staff in Washington, D.C., met weekly to review the reports and distribute their findings to appropriate parties. On airplanes, NRC staff received and circulated 330 foreign reports during the war. Robert Millikan, who along with Hale had helped found NRC, believed the Research Information Service to be "the first demonstration in history of the possibilities of international cooperation in research on a huge scale." The Research Information Service had devised mechanisms to move innovations from one location to the next to be "applied there as soon as possible" and "to stimulate carefully selected groups of competent technical men" to make additional advances. Although the government stopped funding the Research Information Service at war's end, developing a peacetime version would be a priority for NRC during its first decade.[22]

NRC's Transition to Peace

Even as NRC fulfilled its first wartime requests for advice, Hale began making preparations for a permanent organization. The wartime NRC encouraged collaboration with industry, scientific and technical societies, and government experts. NAS members made up less than half of NRC's staff, although they held a majority of leadership positions. For Hale, these collaborations were not just a wartime expediency. He proposed that the National Academy continue to appoint nonmembers from industry, government, academia, and other societies to the operational structures of a peacetime NRC.[23]

Despite its size and broad scope, administratively NRC was still just built on a request in a letter from President Wilson. Hale sought a stronger footing, proposing to the president that he issue an executive order addressing NRC's future. After reassuring the government's scientific bureaus that NRC was not a means for the National Academy to supervise the government's work, Hale got his executive order on May 11, 1918. President Wilson requested that NAS "perpetuate" NRC and outlined six continuing "duties." The National Academy finally had a national service role that went beyond giving advice upon request.

NRC's first duty was "to stimulate research" in the sciences and "in the application of these sciences ... with the object of increasing knowledge, of strengthening the national defense, and of contributing in other ways to the public welfare." The second duty included "to formulate comprehensive projects of research." The third and fourth duties addressed promoting cooperation "at home and abroad," including with the military and civilian departments of government, in such a way that "give[s] encouragement to individual initiative." The fifth spoke directly to the problems associated with war, and the sixth gave NRC the responsibility to be a clearinghouse for information, including making sure new information got into the hands of "duly accredited persons." Finally, the executive order called on the departments of government to cooperate with NRC's efforts.[24]

Within a year, two significant additional pieces of Hale's plan had fallen into place. The Carnegie Corporation awarded the National Academy a $5 million gift for a permanent endowment to support NRC's mission and a building in Washington, D.C. They selected a site within view of the Lincoln Memorial on today's Constitution Avenue. Located within the McMillan Plan, the building's architecture furthered the plan's vision for a mall surrounded by monumental buildings. The National Academy's "Temple of Science," as President Calvin Coolidge called it during the dedication ceremony on April 28, 1924, provided grand rooms for meetings and offices for NAS and NRC staff.[25]

Between 1913 and 1919, NAS had gone from an honorary society with almost no engineering presence to a home for robust partnerships with American engineering societies. The wartime NRC had renewed

the National Academy's commitment to applied science and solving practical problems. NRC also provided a structure, formally endorsed by the federal government, designed to promote an ambitious, continuing mission that required the participation of experts from government, industry, and academia beyond those elected to NAS membership. Finally, the National Academy could promise those who saw in NRC an opportunity to cultivate advances in their own technical areas that there would be resources for a permanent presence in Washington, D.C., even as it continued its traditional encouragement of decentralized research.

As World War I drew to a close, Hale and his National Academy colleagues began transforming NRC. Building on NRC's wartime

The National Academy of Sciences' long-awaited building was dedicated in 1924 (NAS-NRC Archives).

momentum, Hale arranged to stand up NRC's new organizational structure all at once. In February 1919, the NAS Council approved a plan that structured NRC around seven divisions of science and technology. Each division would arrange for technical committees grouped under advisory boards. By the end of 1919, the revamped NRC had launched some 80 committees involving more than 1,000 participants. In addition, they had approved a proposal for six committees grouped under an Advisory Board for Highway Research.[26]

CHAPTER 2

From Rural Roads to Highway Research, 1890–1920

AS THE NATIONAL ACADEMY OF SCIENCES largely ignored the applied sciences and practical problems at the turn of the century, a new center of technical research was growing larger and stronger within the federal government. What would become the technologically triumphant Bureau of Public Roads (BPR) began as the tiny Office of Road Inquiry (ORI). Housed in the Department of Agriculture, federal officials offered technical assistance and outreach designed to increase the roadbuilding capacity of local and state governments. During World War I, state highway officials confronted the engineer's nightmare. Their best roads failed, crumbling seemingly overnight, and they did not know how to prevent it. To the highway builders, the need for research would not seem just pressing, but imperative. Thus, despite the National Academy's orientation toward national service and the federal government, the National Research Council's Advisory Board on Highway Research would see itself as equally responsible for meeting the needs of state governments. In addition, the new Board would define expertise broadly, tapping into experts at prestigious universities and in the highway departments of the smallest states.

But it all started with the bicycle.

Bicycles, Mail Delivery, and Good Roads

Two innovations—a chain drive to the rear wheel and pneumatic tires—revolutionized bicycling in the 1890s and attracted multitudes of American men and women to the bicycle for recreation, but also transportation. The League of American Wheelmen (LAW), founded in 1880, proselytized for good roads at all levels of government. Bicyclists wanted to ride in the countryside, but farmers feared the higher taxes for road improvements. To counter charges that urban bicyclists were trying to get rural property owners to pay for their recreation, LAW developed a political campaign that promised to improve rural life. At a time when twice as many Americans lived in rural areas as in cities, LAW's arguments for good roads—better access to markets and to manufactured goods, education, and civic institutions—attracted the attention of a wide range of lawmakers.[1]

LAW's campaign also revealed that governments lacked even basic knowledge about the quantity and quality of their roads. Local governments built the roads. New Jersey, a rare LAW success, was the first state to approve state aid for roadbuilding in 1892. Massachusetts founded the first state highway department in 1893, tying state aid to minimum construction standards. At the turn of the century, only six states had highway commissions. Nor were universities filling the gap. Harvard University, first to launch a program in highway engineering, started offering courses only in the 1890s.[2]

Although Congress rejected LAW's federal agenda, it did agree that better information was needed and in 1893 earmarked a small amount for road investigations in the Department of Agriculture's budget. ORI distributed technical information for practical use, modeling itself after the other respected bureaus in the Department of Agriculture. With more than 40 publications in just its first 2 years, ORI quickly built a reputation as the place to go for road construction methods and solutions. By 1895, ORI was preparing county road maps and had embarked on its first formal technical investigations. From the beginning, federal involvement in roads centered around collecting and sharing information.[3]

After America's first bicycle craze collapsed at the end of the century, Rural Free Delivery (RFD), launched in 1896, accelerated demand for dependable roads. The U.S. Postal Service promised to bring mail directly to farmsteads, as long as there was a reliable road. Local interest in quality rural roads exploded; the U.S. Postal Service reached 5 million people along its RFD routes by 1903. The addition of package delivery in 1913 brought the era's boom in mail-order purchasing to the far corners of rural America.[4]

Railroads stepped in to promote good roads, confidently predicting that quality local roads would funnel traffic to intercity railroads. Illinois Central Railroad ran the first Good Roads Train from Chicago to New Orleans in 1901. Good Roads Trains soon traversed the country, attracting crowds to the roadbuilding demonstrations. The Office of Public Road Inquiry, as renamed in 1899, received thousands of requests for technical information from local roadbuilders.[5]

Numerous photographs illustrated poor roads in Massachusetts as part of the Report of the Commission to Improve the Highways of the Commonwealth, 1893 (State Library of Massachusetts).

A Federal Center for Road Science

Logan Page concurred with the railroad's vision for transportation, even as the first horseless carriages ventured onto American streets. Page came to Washington, D.C., in 1900 to run the Office of Public Road Inquiry's new materials testing laboratory. One of the first graduates of Harvard's engineering program, Page had toured France's renowned national engineering corps, bringing to Washington, D.C., cutting-edge knowledge of road construction and materials testing. He invited the railroads, local roadbuilders, government officials, and even the general public to submit materials to be judged, free of charge, for their suitability for road construction. Advanced laboratory methods tested the strength of rock and cement and analyzed the chemistry of oil and asphalt. Page's laboratory soon tested hundreds of samples a year.[6]

Page became director of the renamed Office of Public Roads (OPR) in 1905, after scandals prompted Congress to require that the office be headed by a scientist or engineer. Page greatly expanded the construction of demonstration roads, a program started in 1896 for which federal

A horse team pulls a drag used to maintain dirt roads (used with permission from Iowa Department of Transportation).

engineers supervised the building of short lengths of quality local roads. Page also initiated a demonstration program for road maintenance and offered federal experts for local training in construction and financial management. In 1906, OPR developed a partnership with the U.S. Post Office: construction of OPR's recommended improvements would make a community eligible for RFD. Hundreds of RFD petitioners requested OPR's advice.

In addition to public outreach, Page pushed the profession forward. New federal laboratories provided more capacity for materials testing. OPR engineers also devised new testing methods, including the use of field tests, culminating in the opening of an experimental field station in Arlington, Virginia, in 1912. OPR hosted a 1-year postgraduate program on highway engineering and established standards for materials testing, road construction, and bridge specifications. For new economic investigations, it gathered and analyzed data on the nation's roads, including their costs and benefits. Page also installed OPR staff, starting with himself, in influential positions on the new Road Materials Committee of the American Society for Testing Materials (ASTM), the leading body for sanctioning standards across both private industry and governments. Between 1904 and 1914, an additional 100,000 miles of improved road increased the nation's inventory by more than 60 percent.[7]

OPR's technical expertise and service orientation gave Page a platform from which to openly advocate for legislative reforms at the state and federal levels. OPR's demonstration programs meant the agency knew firsthand the difficulties in bringing construction expertise to the thousands of counties, parishes, and townships that made up rural governments. Increases in road funding also risked attracting fraud and corruption. Page concluded that state governments needed to be more heavily involved, and OPR began circulating model state legislation that authorized state governments to grant their counties funds for road-building, conditioned on supervision by professional engineers.[8]

Page also continued to espouse the farm-to-market foundation of OPR, despite growing interest in national highways. By the 1910s, Washington, D.C., was crowded with advocates touting proposals for federal spending on roads. Motor vehicle registrations in the United States grew from 79,000 in 1905 to more than 450,000 in 1910 and then skyrocketed to 2.5 million in 1915. Road bills circulating in Congress numbered in the dozens. One school of thought, espoused by the American Automobile Association (AAA) and promoters of the Lincoln Highway, wanted federal investment in hard-surfaced roads that would crisscross the county. An ambitious proposal even floated a 51,000-mile national network of federal highways. Page, however, endorsed federal aid for local roads and advocated for a limited, advisory role for the federal government. Congress followed his lead in 1912, funding a modest $500,000 experiment in federal aid to post roads as part of the 1912 Post Office Department Appropriation Bill.[9]

For Page, the post road experiment only confirmed that building better roads required empowering state governments. States and counties, both eligible to receive federal aid, struggled to implement even this small program. Despite ambitions to funnel funds to all 48 states, federal aid from the 1912 appropriation supported only 17 projects in 13 states. A majority of states did not even have the legal authority to spend federal aid.[10]

The Founding of AASHO

The Fourth American Road Congress, held in Atlanta in November 1914, attracted more than 3,000 registered attendees, and advocates for better rural roads and proponents of national highways continued their pointed debate. In a letter read to the Congress,

A mail truck drives through snow to deliver packages as part of Rural Free Delivery service, 1915 (Wisconsin Historical Society, WHS-71650).

President Woodrow Wilson took the side of better "community roads" to rail stations, and OPR's Page continued his push for federal funding for rural roads. AAA's representative clarified that the association did not oppose state and local investment in better rural roads, but federal funding should be dedicated only to "important roads" making up a "dedicated system of highways."[11]

Also in Atlanta, a new organization prepared to enter the political debate. The state highway engineers from Maryland, North Carolina, and Virginia formed the organizing committee for what they called the American Association of State Highway Officials (AASHO) and issued a call for representatives of state highway commissions to gather in Washington, D.C., 1 month later to draft their own version of a federal road bill. On December 12, 1914, state highway officials or their proxies representing 27 states elected Henry G. Shirley, chief engineer of the Maryland State Roads Commission, to be the new organization's first president. Page attended AASHO's meeting with President Wilson at

Children help illustrate the crown for a dirt road (used with permission from Iowa Department of Transportation).

the White House, but OPR officials did not join in as AASHO's leaders hammered out the first version of their preferred federal bill.[12]

The relatively good roads and robust highway programs in Maryland, North Carolina, and Virginia aligned their state highway officials, and by extension AASHO, with AAA's vision for federal investment in important highways only. Midwestern states protested: a national coalition of states required a broader approach. Into the breach stepped Thomas MacDonald, chief engineer of the Iowa Highway Commission since 1904. Instead of a limited network of federal highways, MacDonald persuaded AASHO to endorse federal aid for state road construction. In the long run, he argued, using federal aid to increase the size and improve the competence of state programs would leverage federal dollars and result in an even larger highway network than federal funds alone could produce.[13]

AASHO's first foray into federal legislation proved successful. The Federal-Aid Road Act of 1916 appropriated $75 million to be spent over

5 years for rural post roads and outlined the terms of the federal–state highway partnership for decades to come. Even in 1916, $75 million was small, less than 2 percent of all annual spending on road construction. Federal aid would be granted only to state governments. Congress distributed the funds among the states according to an apportionment formula, first defined by AASHO, based on population, land area, and road mileage. To be eligible, states had to meet the renamed BPR's criteria for strong state highway departments. Moreover, federal aid was tied to specific projects, which a state had to show met BPR's management and construction specifications, including provisions for long-term maintenance. BPR provided an equal match for expenses up to $10,000 per mile, a limit designed to prevent the construction of grand boulevards.[14]

At the outset, only California's state highway department met minimum standards. By the end of 1917, every state had a conforming highway agency. BPR worked cooperatively with AASHO to establish standards and inspection procedures for materials, construction, and management. Construction began slowly, and the American entry into World War I in April 1917 eventually halted construction entirely. Mobilization for war tested American transportation in ways not yet imagined, and both rails and roads would be found wanting.[15]

Railroads, Highways, and World War I

War mobilization quickly overwhelmed the railroads. At first, the federal government rationed space on railcars, but in December 1917 the government resorted to nationalization, instituting centralized planning for shipments and movements. Reacting to the congestion—up to 100-mile backups of railcars out of port cities such as New York—and government control, enterprising shippers started looking to the improved roads for freight movement. Motor trucks, which had been designed to carry freight to and from rail stations, were pressed into service for longer hauls between cities. Roy D. Chapin, president of Hudson Motors and member of the federal government's Highway Transport Committee, arranged for trucks manufactured in the Midwest and bound for France to be driven to the ports. Surmounting winter weather, 30,000 trucks reached Philadelphia and Baltimore in early 1918.

The trucks may have exceeded expectations, but the roads they drove on succumbed to their numbers and weight. Hundreds of miles of highway surfaces crumbled. A government engineer reported, "These failures were not only sudden but also complete, and almost overnight an excellent surface might become impassable." The *Engineering News-Record* declared that the success of long-haul trucking meant "A New Era in Highway Transportation," and this new era raised new questions that went beyond how to build hardier, all-weather road surfaces. Intercity freight trucking was mainly a commercial function in a complex relationship with the costs borne by governments—and taxpayers— for good roads. Federal aid to roads was no longer simply about improving rural life. Congress, however, wanted more good roads and appropriated an additional $200 million in 1919, on top of the 1916 Act's $75 million, for road improvements.[16]

With railroads weakened and trucking ascendant, advocates for a federally constructed national highway system had new momentum. Page defended the policy of federal aid to state highway departments for rural roads, but his position was faltering. Page went to AASHO's Annual Meeting in December 1918 hoping for an endorsement of his plan for limited reforms, but he died of a heart attack during the meeting. Iowa's MacDonald, again playing the mediator, stepped in to propose a compromise that would have concentrated federal aid on primary highways, but highway interests split over continued federal aid versus a federal highway commission.[17]

AASHO recommended that MacDonald replace Page as chief of BPR. But before taking the job, MacDonald wanted assurances of support for his plans to improve state relations and speed construction. MacDonald knew only too well that state highway engineers had chafed at what they had perceived to be Page's rigid enforcement of the new standards. MacDonald's BPR would be founded on a more cooperative footing. From 1919 until his last day in office in 1953, MacDonald held fast to his belief in a federal–state relationship built on checks and balances "so that the states and the federal government both have to agree before they can accomplish a positive program." MacDonald's colleagues and counterparts in state government would come to treat

Mobilization for World War I proved the feasibility of moving freight long distances by truck (Library of Congress, LC-USZC4-10126).

him as first among equals, and MacDonald's approach to federalism would strongly shape everything he touched.[18]

The National Research Council and Highways

As NRC set out to rebuild for peace, its Division of Engineering maintained the strong wartime ties to the Engineering Foundation and its parent, the United Engineering Societies, including sharing staff and office space in New York. Government service during World War I connected the Division's chair, Comfort A. Adams, professor of electrical engineering at Harvard University, and Anson Marston, dean of engineering at Iowa State College and one of three representing the American Society of Civil Engineers on the NRC division. Adams had led groundbreaking work in welding and procurement during the war, while Marston had joined the Engineering Corps of the Army in 1917 and by war's end was a lieutenant colonel. The Western Society of Engineers designated Arthur N. Talbot, professor of engineering at the University of Illinois and one of the founders of the Illinois engineering experiment station in 1903, to be its representative to the Division of Engineering.[19]

Unlike NAS's relatively simple committee formation process—government made a request and NAS formed a committee to respond—NRC built a more formal structure. The process that eventually produced the Advisory Board on Highway Research on November 11, 1920, started with a small meeting convened by the Division of Engineering in Chicago on October 8, 1919. Marston and Talbot met with representatives from BPR and state highway officials, including MacDonald and Albert T. Goldbeck, then BPR's engineer of tests, and Clifford Older, Illinois State Highway Department, represented the Mississippi Valley Conference of State Highway Departments.[20]

They came to discuss using NRC to advise on a national program of highway research, responding in part to a call to arms published in August 1919 in BPR's new magazine, *Public Roads*. In the article, Thomas R. Agg, chair of AASHO's Committee on Tests and Investigations and, like Marston, a professor at Iowa State College, called on BPR to launch a large-scale, long-term research program on materials and construction methods. Agg insisted that BPR was the only organization capable of leading the needed research. Aware of NRC's interest in highways, Agg thought NRC should be advisory to BPR and a mechanism to reach out to academia in a way similar to how AASHO connected BPR to the states. AASHO's president, A. R. Hirst of Wisconsin, endorsed Agg's proposal.[21]

Marston and Talbot submitted a formal proposal to NRC that touted the research capabilities—and potential—of BPR, state highway departments, and the engineering colleges. The need, moreover, for a national program of highway research was dire. Citing the billions of dollars to be spent on building highways in the next 15 to 20 years, they argued that research was desperately needed "to establish the fundamental data." Without "coordination," the research results would be "more or less desultory," suffer from "unnecessary duplication," and "omit important researches." NRC's Division of Engineering soon approved the report's recommendations: to form a committee (later Board) for highway research and to petition the President of the United States to appoint the chief of the BPR to membership in the Division of Engineering. MacDonald formally joined the Division in December 1919.[22]

Marston also presented the plan to AASHO at its December 1919 meeting, where MacDonald played the skeptic. In an exchange between former professor and student that was later printed in *Public Roads*, MacDonald voiced the concerns of "a number of the executive officers of

Rotary cement mixer on the grounds of Cornell University in 1909 (Bureau of Public Roads).

TRB's Iowa Roots

Anson Marston, Thomas R. Agg, Thomas MacDonald, Walter H. Root, and Roy W. Crum

FIVE MEN FROM IOWA shaped the Transportation Research Board's earliest decades with their expertise and commitment to research. They succeeded in part because Iowa exemplified in the extreme the close relationships between universities and state highway departments during their earliest years.[a]

In the early 20th century, Iowa was a large state with a dispersed population heavily dependent on agriculture. Iowa's 2.4 million people in 1920 ranked it 16th in population among the 48 states. With 125,000 residents, Des Moines was the only city with more than 75,000 people. Ames, home of Iowa State College, housed fewer than 6,500 people.[b]

As agriculture mechanized, the heavy, steam-powered equipment that moved from field to field tore up Iowa's roads, crashed through bridges, and crushed culverts. Good roads became imperative, and Iowa State College led the state's good roads transformation. The state's highways then positioned it to take advantage of the new freight trucking industry. During World War I, Iowa was a recognized leader in designating and managing highways for year-round truck use.[c]

Of the five, Anson Marston was the senior scholar, teacher, and mentor. He had come to Iowa State College to teach civil engineering in 1894. Ten years later, at age 40, Marston used a competitive offer from the University of Wisconsin to pressure the college to fund an engineering experiment station and the state legislature to create a state highway commission. Marston built Iowa State College into a powerhouse of highway research, helped by a state law that required the experiment station to spend annual sums—in 1920, at least $10,000—on highway research.[d]

Marston encouraged his students, including Thomas MacDonald, to conduct research and to make policy recommendations based on their findings. In 1904, MacDonald co-authored a senior thesis revealing that the amount of power required for a team of horses to pull a wagon over dirt roads could be seven times higher than over macadam roads. The thesis concluded that the best way to systematically improve Iowa's roads was through a state highway commission.

That same year, MacDonald became the new commission's chief engineer, by virtue of being its only full-time employee. At first, the commission was just advisory and technically a unit of Iowa State College. Marston and MacDonald pushed for it to have independence and authority, a goal they achieved in 1913. When MacDonald left Iowa in 1919 to become the chief engineer for the federal Bureau of Public Roads, the commission had 156 employees and oversaw the state's primary road system.

Even after becoming an independent state agency, the highway commission stayed in

Engineering Hall (right), which housed the State Highway Commission until 1924, and engineering shops at Iowa State College pictured in 1911 (Iowa State University Library Special Collections and University Archives).

Ames and operated in tandem with the college's engineering experiment station. In 1913, Thomas R. Agg—a former student of Marston—returned to Iowa State College from a job at the Illinois State Highway Commission managing experimental roads. After publishing what would become a standard text, *Construction of Roads and Pavements*, in 1916, he became chair of the American Association of State Highway Officials' (AASHO's) newly founded standing committee on tests and investigations. Agg used the position to advocate that universities with federally supported agriculture experiment stations follow Iowa's lead in creating engineering experiment stations.[e]

The state highway commission depended on the college's experiment station for tests of materials until 1919, when it appointed Roy W. Crum to head its new department of materials and tests. Crum had begun working at the experiment station while still a student and rose to associate professor before moving to the highway commission. His work simplifying the tests needed for aggregate used in concrete was considered seminal at the time.

The youngest of the five, Walter H. Root graduated from Iowa State College in 1911 and joined the highway commission 1 year later. In 1919, the commission tapped him to found its maintenance division. In 1922, he would do the same for the Advisory Board on Highway Research, eventually serving as chair of the Board's Department of Maintenance from 1935 to 1949.[f]

All five men dedicated decades of their lives to the Highway Research Board. Marston, Agg, and MacDonald helped found the Board, and both Crum and Root died with their boots on: Crum as executive director in 1951 and Root during his term as chair of the Executive Committee in 1954. Their legacies, however, will last well into the Board's second 100 years.

highway departments," who "found it difficult to enthuse very much" over NRC's plan. They worried, MacDonald shared, "that the results would be delayed until after the roads are built." He advised Marston that NRC's committee should not be "a reviewing body, or the investigative body, but simply the correlating body" and to make sure results were available to all "immediately." In response, Marston emphasized that coordination was to be accomplished only by tracking research and publicizing results. To concerns about delays, Marston colorfully replied, "The results are to be taken right off the griddle, as it were, as the meal proceeds."[23]

During 1920, Marston led the formation of three of the six technical committees recommended in the original proposal. Agg chaired the Committee on Economic Theory of Highway Improvement; BPR's Goldbeck chaired the Committee on Structural Design of Roads; and Horatio S. Mattimore, engineer of tests, Pennsylvania Highway Department, chaired what started as the Committee on Tests and Properties of Road Materials. After ASTM protested that testing was its province, Mattimore's committee became the Committee on the Character and Use of Road Materials. The other three technical committees, for road construction, maintenance, and bridges and culverts, temporarily took a back seat.[24]

ASTM's intervention is indicative of the crowded field that NRC was attempting to enter. Although highway research still felt new, numerous organizations had a piece of the puzzle and turf to protect. In addition to the federal government and state governments, the long-standing engineering societies had been joined by new organizations catalyzed by the motor vehicle. The National Automobile Chamber of Commerce represented manufacturers, and the Society of Automotive Engineers, which dated to 1905, had grown to 5,000 members by 1920. Many of the organizations that formed to advocate for good roads or national highways also had technical committees, as did the various industry organizations for roadbuilding materials.[25]

By 1920, education and research on highways had also spread to American colleges and universities, often in close cooperation with state highway departments. Although only 15 engineering colleges offered specializations in highway engineering, 111 institutions of higher learning provided at least one course. Universities also partnered with state highway departments to hold short courses or extension courses on highway topics, usually in the winter. West Virginia University and the University of Tennessee held annual short courses that closed with multiday conferences for all state highway officials. The University of Georgia's "good roads department" traveled the state, taking instruction to local roadbuilders. At least 10 state highway departments depended on university engineering laboratories and experiment stations for materials testing, including Georgia Polytechnic Institute, Iowa State College, Kansas State Agricultural College, The Ohio State University, University of Idaho, University of Kentucky, University of Maine, University of Michigan, University of Minnesota, University of Missouri, and University of Nevada.[26]

Many who would attend the Board's organizing conference in November 1920 participated earlier that spring in a series of meetings as part of the Conference on Education for Highway Engineering and Highway Transport, sponsored by the federal government's Bureau of Education. Concerned in part with educating the workforce needed for the sudden expansion of both highways and trucking, the meetings purposely brought together highway interests, motor vehicle interests, and university educators. MacDonald chaired the Committee on Highway Engineering, and motor vehicle interests dominated the Committee on Business Education. Both committees saw a pressing need for research and discussed a role for NRC. The civil engineers in attendance bemoaned the lack of knowledge about "the methods to be used in the fundamental problems" of good pavement. Further troubling to the highway engineers was that in commercial trucking, unlike for the railroads, those who designed, owned, operated, and maintained the "rolling stock" and the infrastructure were completely separate industries. Engineering and economics, however, were not so easily separated, and the engineers welcomed NRC in a coordinating role.[27]

The motor vehicle interests, not surprisingly, prioritized "the economics of the situation" including research into "how traffic over the highways can be made to go at the least possible cost per mile, be it per ton-mile or per passenger (traffic) mile." However, they were more interested in universities as training grounds for future industry researchers than that the automotive industries should themselves become part of a coordinated research effort. The Society of Automotive Engineers used the conference to announce a new research effort into "the science of truck operation."[28]

The Organizing Conference

In designing the organizing conference for the Advisory Board on Highway Research, NRC's Division of Engineering attempted to transcend the

Charles D. Curtiss, Pyke Johnson, and Albert T. Goldbeck (pictured from left) attended the organizing meeting of the Advisory Board on Highway Research in 1920 and celebrated the Highway Research Board's 40th Annual Meeting in 1961 (George Kalec).

divide opening between highway engineering and highway economics. Invitations went to national organizations representing governments, engineering professionals, and industry organizations, and one-third of the 36 attendees represented the automotive industries. The Advisory Board on Highway Research would be made up of the designated representatives of member organizations and a few at-large individuals, mostly from academia, appointed by the Division. New organizations joined the Board upon vote by existing members. A small Executive Committee, supported by a director employed full-time by NRC, handled administrative matters including forming technical committees.[29]

Although the organizing conference for the Advisory Board on Highway Research took place at the Engineering Societies Building in New York, both NRC's Division of Engineering and BPR shared the duties of host. Marston was quickly elected chair, and Charles D. Curtiss, BPR, secretary. The academics in attendance, though few, were significantly older than many of those representing the highway and automotive industries. Chapin, the leading automotive industry voice during the proceedings, had just turned 40. For BPR, MacDonald was not yet 40, and Curtiss and Goldbeck were in their early 30s, as was Pyke Johnson, representing the National Automobile Chamber of Commerce. Goldbeck, Johnson, and Curtiss, like MacDonald, were at the beginning of a lifelong association with the Board, each rising to serve as chair of the Executive Committee in 1934–1935, 1960, and 1963, respectively.[30]

Both Adams and MacDonald welcomed attendees with words meant to capture the purpose and urgency of the gathering. MacDonald warned, "We can no longer think of highways merely as good roads." Eight million vehicles had "descended upon the highways like an avalanche," meaning that "the expenditures for highways are already very large and will constantly grow larger, and we have not adequately developed the science of highway building and maintenance." Adams expressed hope that highways would be a model for "cooperative attack" because "we are not faced with the same degree of commercially competitive interests as some of the fields."[31]

To Marston fell the task of laying out the specific functions and organization of this new NRC Advisory Board. But first he outlined the overwhelming need for research using dramatic examples that communicated both the sheer magnitude and the complexity of the problems. Soon the country would spend "twice the cost of the Panama Canal ... in highway construction annually," he observed, in ways "which affect the daily life of every person in the country." Iowans now had 400,000 registered vehicles, meaning that "we could all escape from the state on a few hours notice, provided it did not happen to rain just then." Most disturbing to Marston, highway administrators lacked the theories and knowledge to make sound decisions. Should they flatten a 108-foot hill or relocate the road? Should they build concrete, brick, or bituminous roads? Which would hold up best under the weight of trucks? How should they designate primary versus secondary roads? What were the best ways to deal with contractors and share risks? Ultimately, what was the "proper relation" of highways, railways, and water transportation? Concluding that "it is impossible for us to organize it on too large a scale," Marston threw down the challenge: "The greater the number of research committees we can organization and properly finance, the better."[32]

Marston also placed his faith in science, the scientific method, and hard work. The Board's committees should be chaired by "scientific research men" who "actively engage in the research personally." He worried that "the practical side of highway engineering" had become overly dominant, admonishing "we must not be afraid of mathematics in highway engineering, must not be afraid of the word 'theory.'" Committee membership, however, should include a balance of scientists, practitioners, and commercial interests. Marston touted the ASTM in which committees were "quite equally divided between consumers and producers." Everyone on a committee, however, should come to work. "We have no room for inert material," he warned.[33]

Finally, Marston addressed the need for financial support. As general policy, he advised seeking authority for the federal government and state highway commissions to dedicate a fraction of highway spending—"one percent would be ample"—to research. Confident that the research would save costs, he argued that "such a plan would furnish all the funds we want without increasing total expenditures at all." For the Board's own projects, he envisioned asking "public spirited men" or commercial organizations for funding or in-kind donations of materials and equipment, including to publish and widely distribute results. Marston also flagged a problem that would take the Board decades to overcome. State highway departments "would be glad to cooperate" he surmised, "if they had the authority to do so."[34]

By the end of the day, the Board's bylaws were in place. Its primary purposes included "outlining a comprehensive national program of highway research and coordinating activities thereunder," organizing committees, and "act[ing] in a general advisory capacity."[35] Over the next 6 months, with support from the Engineering Foundation's Alfred D. Flinn, who acted as interim director, the Division of Engineering officially invited organizations to join as members of the Board, put in place its first Executive Committee, and raised funds to pay an executive director. Marston continued as chair, with Flinn as vice chair. MacDonald, George S. Webster, president of the American Society of Civil Engineers and director of the Department of Wharves, Docks, and Ferries in Philadelphia, and Charles F. Kettering, past president of the Society of Automotive Engineers and president of Dayton Engineering Laboratories, rounded out the Executive Committee. In the end, they raised $14,500 for fiscal year 1922, with $12,000 from BPR slated for the director's salary and expenses. The Engineering Foundation and the Connecticut State Highway Department each gave $1,000 and NRC contributed $500.[36]

During the 14 months between the Board's organizing conference and its first annual meeting in January 1922, the last legislative showdown took place between those desiring a federal highway commission and national highways and those wanting to continue the federal-aid-to-states approach formalized in 1916. MacDonald won genuine consensus for his plan to concentrate federal aid on 7 percent of each state's roads, split between a primary and secondary highway network. States were also responsible for maintaining federal-aid highways. The requirements for system classification and maintenance promised to produce a national network of highways, while still furthering the partnership with states. The Federal-Aid Highway Act of 1921 became law in November.[37]

CHAPTER 3

The First Three Directors: Hatt, Upham, and Crum, 1921–1939

THE ADVISORY BOARD on Highway Research was built on the "strong frame work," as its first director would call it, provided by "the triangular relation between" the federal government, the states, and the National Research Council (NRC).[1] In different ways, the first three directors, William K. Hatt, Charles M. Upham, and Roy W. Crum, all strengthened the new Board. Hatt was the respected academic, who facilitated cooperative research projects and believed that everyone, including practitioners and students, could contribute to advancing knowledge. Upham, coming from state government, was a builder. He would not be content with advising at a distance and, instead, positioned the Board to conduct research itself. Crum was the organizer. Welcoming to all, he nurtured leadership and experimentation in the committees in ways that enabled them to grow and flourish. He would also stretch himself to co-direct the Board's first congressionally mandated studies on a subject far beyond his own technical expertise: highway safety.

Although the federal government's Bureau of Public Roads (BPR) and its chief, Thomas MacDonald, paid their salaries, none of the first three directors felt limited by the federal-aid highway legislation that restricted BPR to a partnership with state governments to construct

The first three directors: William K. Hatt, Charles M. Upham, and Roy W. Crum (TRB).

primary and secondary highways in rural areas. By pressing for the study of highway economics, local roads and streets, and traffic safety, all three encouraged the Board and its committees to go beyond the federal government's purview.

Hatt and Cooperative Research

The Executive Committee of the Board convinced William K. Hatt, head of engineering at Purdue University since 1906, to take a 2-year leave of absence to become the Board's first full-time director. Hatt's hiring built on his previous relationships with both the Department of Agriculture and MacDonald. He had established the first timber testing laboratory on behalf of the Department of Agriculture at Purdue in 1902.[2] Hatt had also served on the same committee as MacDonald during the Conference on Education for Highway Engineering and Highway Transport the previous year. During the conference's deliberations, Hatt had counseled, "I think the spirit of research could be stimulated if the National Research Council … would draw up a comprehensive program and let the student understand that he is making the researches as a part of a big national program." Hatt's philosophy—that they could meet the pressing need for highway research by inspiring the voluntary coordination and cooperation among researchers, including students—would have much in common with BPR's ideas for the Board.[3]

Hatt served as director from July 1921 through the end of 1923 and managed three annual meetings, the organization of additional technical committees, and experiments with different ways of engaging in research. In his first months in office, the Executive Committee finalized the Board's structure and operating procedures. NRC remained the financial agent for the Board, but the Executive Committee operated the Board, including approving the director's activities and all appointments to technical committees.[4] Although NRC's Division of Engineering remained headquartered in New York, the Board moved to Washington, D.C., where BPR provided Hatt with an office.[5]

William K. Hatt's outline of a highway research program was circulated in advance of the First Annual Meeting (*Engineering News-Record*, September 15, 1921, 451).

September 15, 1921   ENGINEERING NEWS-RECORD   451

TENTATIVE OUTLINE OF THE FIELD OF HIGHWAY RESEARCH

ECONOMICS

TRAFFIC STUDIES (REGIONAL)

Distribution in Region (Traffic Blank)
Character
  Vehicle
  Weight and Distribution
  Speed
  Tire (condition)
  Commodity
  Length Haul
Method of Expressing Unit of Traffic
Predicted Changes
Other Traffic on Steam and Electric Roads
Central Sources of Traffic

COMMUNITY NEEDS

Systems of Roads in Classes for Industries, etc.
Intangibles

COST OF TRANSPORT

Capital Cost
  Road
  Vehicle
Fixed Charges
Overhead
Operation
  Maintenance
  Routine
  Replacement on Road
  Replacement on Vehicle
Equivalent Units X-Auto-Y-Ton Truck, etc.
Economic Life

ECONOMICS OF LOCATION

Cost of Distance
Rise and Fall
Curvature
Ruling Grade
Ruling Curve

FINANCING

Bonds
Taxes
Fees, etc.

HIGHWAY VALUATION

Increment of Land Values

OPERATION

CONTROL OF TRAFFIC

Routing
Terminals
Franchises
Police Regulations

ACCIDENT INSURANCE

PLANNING SYSTEMS OF TRANSPORT

Financing
Environment
Relation to Other Transport Organization

FINANCING

Bonds, Taxes, Fees

DISTRIBUTION OF COSTS

Traffic
Property
Political Units

MAINTENANCE SYSTEMS

MAINTENANCE MACHINERY

MAINTENANCE METHODS

Routine
Replacement
Snow Removal, etc.

TRAIL MARKING

COST ACCOUNTING

SAFETY

DESIGN (ROAD)

SUBSOIL STUDIES

Properties
  Physical
  Mechanical
  Chemical
Drainage
Supporting Power
Improvement by Treatment
Effect of Road Deformations
Effect of Climate
Distribution of Pressure

BASE COURSE

Character, Type
  Thickness
  Materials
  Cross Section

SURFACE

Character
  Thickness
  Materials
  Cross Section
Wear by Traffic
Wear by Elements
Impact of Traffic
Tractive Resistance
Wear of Tire
Wear of Vehicle
Dusting
Influence of Locality

CROSS SECTION

Width
Crown
Shoulders
Ditches

LOADS

Static
Impact
Surface Integral as Effected by Design of Vehicle

DESIGN OF INTEGRAL SLAB

Strength and Stiffness of
  Solid
  Precast
  Cellular

VOLUME CHANGES

Joints
Shoving

REINFORCING

Theory of
Amount
Kind
Distribution
Direction

DESIGN (VEHICLE)

DESIGN OF VEHICLE

Power Gear Ratio
Braking
Etc.
Etc.

EFFECT ON LOADS

Sprung
Unsprung
Distribution

ECONOMY OF OPERATION AND MAINTENANCE

(See Automotive Industry)
Economic limit of size of truck in various situations
Cost of truck transport (Schedule of elements)
Economic limit of haul
Cost accounting

SURFACE

Tractive Effort
Wear on Tires
Loads

MAINTENANCE OF VEHICLE

ALIGNMENT

Curves (Speed)
Grades

CROSS SECTION

Width
Crown

SAFETY

CONSTRUCTION

MATERIALS

Bituminous
Non-Bituminous
Fundamental Mechanical Properties
Methods of Test
Standard Tests
Specification
Preparation and Treatment
(See Special List)
Proportioning

MIXING

Efficiency of Mixer
Central Mixing Plants

PLACING

METHODS OF TESTING ROADS

Instrument
Cores

DESIGN OF EXPERIMENTAL ROADS

DRAINAGE (And Drainage Structures)

IMPACT ON BRIDGES (See Design)

REINFORCING (Handling and Placing)

INSPECTION

PLANT DESIGN AND CONTROL

COST ACCOUNTING

CONSTRUCTION CONTRACTS

Meeting of Advisory Board on Highway Research of Natl. Research Council, Washington D.C. Nov 28, 1926.

Forty men stand outside NRC for a photograph memorializing the Second Annual Meeting, November 1922 (TRB).

Less than a month into his term as director, Hatt presented the Board's first outline of a highway research program at a conference at the University of Maryland, and the proposed program was published soon after in both *Automotive Industries* and *Engineering News-Record*. Embracing comprehensiveness, Hatt's scheme put transport economics as a research category on par with highway design, operations, and construction. In addition, Hatt's research categories all targeted both roads and vehicles, as did his concerns about safety. He admitted that "the answers to these questions cannot be made without data that are at present unavailable," yet announced that NRC "will not engage in research directly." The Board's role would be the "coordination of such research."[6]

Hatt expanded on the Board's coordination role in a meeting with the American Association of State Highway Officials (AASHO) in December 1921, in preparation for the Board's first annual meeting. Although he pushed for studies of highway economics, he acknowledged that "community welfare, safety, and social values" could justify road expenditures with no need for the complicated economic studies that commercial trucking and intercity bus service seemed to demand. Hatt announced that the Board would begin with a research census and hoped to initiate a research information service "by which data may be marshalled, boiled down, and put in useful terms" for states, counties, and cities. Hatt also celebrated the research work that states were already doing and pushed them to do more because "the best field of effort … is often a local problem." AASHO adopted a resolution pledging its support to the Board.[7]

Both BPR and NRC rebuffed a proposal, floated at the First Annual Meeting, that the Board should strive to be a direct recipient of large amounts of federal funding for highway research. Preferring decentralized, even individual, initiative was consistent with National Academy of Sciences norms that dated back to the controversy in the 1880s won by Alexander Agassiz against a proposed federal Department of Science. In 1919, NRC's leaders had persuaded The Rockefeller Foundation to drop a proposal for a centralized research institute, substituting instead postdoctoral university fellowships administered by NRC. Hatt, too, pondered in several of his speeches exactly how to encourage individual initiative, yet still avoid duplication and concentrate resources on the most pressing and promising research projects.[8]

By the Second Annual Meeting in November 1922, the Board had formed two additional committees, a Committee on Highway Traffic Analysis, chaired by George E. Hamlin of the Connecticut State Highway Department, and a Committee on Maintenance, chaired by Walter H. Root of the Iowa State Highway Department. They also adopted the annual meeting format that would last throughout the decade. The 1-day meeting started with the report of the director on the state of the organization, followed by reports of the chairs of each of the technical committees. The technical committee reports gave overviews of major developments in their subject areas and updates on the projects that followed, which the proceedings recorded verbatim, and the chair was not shy about calling on people to provide their perspective on a question or a point of dispute.[9]

Hatt experimented with several models for research: consulting, surveying, and advising large, cooperative projects. The Board's first involvement in a research project was in partnership with BPR and the Connecticut State Highway Department, which had contributed $1,000 to the Board's initial round of funding. Both Charles J. Bennett, the state's highway commissioner, and Charles J. Tilden, professor of engineering mechanics at Yale University, had attended the Board's organizing conference and participated in discussions of how typical traffic studies—which only counted vehicles—were inadequate for economic studies of highways. With BPR's approval, Hatt, Tilden, and J. Gordon McKay, an economist from the University of Wisconsin, traveled to Hartford in August 1921 to set up the state's first comprehensive traffic survey. In Enfield, on the highway between Hartford and Springfield, they counted not only the number of vehicles, but also the number of passengers and the types, value, and weight of freight, and inquired about origins and destinations. When repeated in October in Greenwich, fines from overweight trucks recovered in just 14 days the cost of purchasing the 25-ton scales. In total, they tabulated 75,000 vehicles and uncovered that one in three trucks violated Connecticut's weight limit. *Engineering News-Record* published the resulting studies in 1922.[10]

A census of research, however, was Hatt's top priority. Conceived as a tool for coordination and as the first step for an eventual research information service, Hatt and staff on loan from BPR contacted those in universities, industries, and federal, state, and local governments likely to be doing research on highways or geology. They uncovered 479 projects from governments or universities in 43 states and the District of Columbia. The census, limited to unpublished research or research in progress, did not include results to spare researchers "the embarrassment of premature announcements of conclusions." The Board published the census as an NRC Bulletin in October 1922, in time for discussion at the second annual meeting that November.[11]

The research project that generated the most excitement during Hatt's tenure, however, was on the tractive resistance of trucks. In part through the Board's dual roles as coordinator and advisor, what started as a doctoral dissertation proposal became a large—estimates upward of $40,000—research project involving two branches of the federal government (Quartermaster Corps of the Army and BPR), two state highway departments (Massachusetts and Connecticut), and researchers at two universities (Massachusetts Institute of Technology and Yale University), with major assists from four other universities (Harvard University, Iowa State College, Kansas State Agricultural College, and University of Michigan). Thomas R. Agg, as chair of the Committee on Economic Theory of Highway Improvement, made connections to the researcher community while Comfort A. Adams, as chair of the Division of Engineering, and Hatt worked to raise funds and attract partners to the project. They coordinated with the Society of Automotive Engineers and raised funds or in-kind contributions from truck, asphalt, concrete, and tire companies.[12]

For Hatt and Agg, the tractive resistance project epitomized the spirit of cooperation that was the Board's very reason for being. The project also epitomized the unified approach to highway economics—the road and the vehicle together—that they both espoused. They aimed to take tests of vehicles and their rolling resistance on different surfaces, air resistance, and performance traveling on hills and connect the results to the capital and operating costs of both highways and vehicles. In other words, they approached highways as if they were managing railroads. The Society of Automotive Engineers resisted. Studying vehicles was its turf. In response, the Board convened its first specialty conference on July 14–15, 1922. In addition to defining key terms and concepts, the Conference on the Tractive Resistance of Motor Vehicles produced an agreement that automotive engineers, not the Board or government, would take the lead on studies of vehicle performance. The Society continued on the Board, but studies on "relations of road and vehicle" were moved to the Committee on the Structural Design of Roads, chaired by BPR's Albert T. Goldbeck. Whether this was a friendly division of responsibility or more a competitive delineation of territory, Hatt did not hide what he thought. In his next director's report, he emphatically stated, "*It is increasingly evident that the highway engineer and the automotive engineer must join forces in coordinated highway research* [emphasis in original]."[13]

Upham and the Highway Research Board

Hatt returned to Purdue University at the end of 1923, and after MacDonald received approval from the Department of Agriculture, the Board's Executive Committee hired Charles M. Upham as director in March 1924. Unlike Hatt, Upham was firmly in the world of state highway building. Then in his late 30s, Upham had quickly risen to highway management roles in Massachusetts and Delaware before becoming chief engineer for North Carolina's State Highway Commission. His time in Delaware would prove important to the Board. Upham had left Massachusetts in 1912 to work on the DuPont highway, privately funded by the business giant T. Coleman du Pont. Upham became du Pont's chief engineer, and after du Pont donated the 100 miles of paved highway to the state, he was appointed the chief engineer of the Delaware State Highway Department. During the 1920s, du Pont continued his philanthropy and also became a politician, serving in the U.S. Senate from 1921 to 1922 and 1925 to 1928. At the time of his hiring, Upham also held leadership positions in AASHO, ASTM, and the American Road Builders Association (ARBA), and his former boss, North Carolina's State Highway Commissioner Frank Page, would become AASHO's president in 1925–1926.[14]

Symbolizing the Board's independence from BPR, Upham moved into the National Academy's new building soon after its April 1924 dedication. ARBA donated funds for the Board's office furniture.[15]

Program

AND

Summaries of Papers and Committee Reports

OF THE

Ninth Annual Meeting

HIGHWAY RESEARCH BOARD

DIVISION OF
ENGINEERING AND INDUSTRIAL
RESEARCH

NATIONAL RESEARCH COUNCIL

View of the Entrance to the
National Academy of Sciences and
National Research Council

December 12 and 13, 1929

AT THE BUILDING OF THE NATIONAL ACADEMY
OF SCIENCES AND THE NATIONAL RESEARCH COUNCIL,
B AND 21ST STREETS, WASHINGTON, D. C.

The Ninth Annual Meeting program, the oldest in TRB's collection, includes presentations on soil investigations in Russia and road conditions in Latin America.

Upham's close ties to state governments and the highway building industry was consistent with a larger organizational shift occurring within NRC. Frank B. Jewett had replaced Adams as chair of the Division of Engineering in 1923. Jewett headed what would soon become Bell Telephone Laboratories and was also a vice president at AT&T. At NRC, Jewett managed the reorganization of the Division of Engineering into a Division of Engineering and Industrial Research and used his position as chair of the new division to mount a significant outreach effort to promote research in industrial corporations.[16]

Further strengthening the Board's tie to state governments and the highway industries, in 1923 Arthur N. Johnson, dean of engineering at the University of Maryland, replaced Anson Marston as chair of the Board's Executive Committee. Johnson had served stints as chief engineer for Massachusetts, Maryland, Illinois, and the Office of Public Roads, arriving at the university in 1920 after 4 years as consulting engineer with the Portland Cement Association. His deanship, moreover, coincided with the founding of the Maryland engineering experiment station, following an agreement between BPR and the State Roads Commission. Johnson chaired the Executive Committee through 1926.[17]

Johnson and Upham, not surprisingly, worked to make the Board more responsive to the states. One of their first initiatives asked state highway departments to appoint "contact men" to the Board. Although AASHO remained the official member organization, through contact men the Board extended ties to individual states and cultivated their research leaders. Contact men received copies of Board publications without charge. More importantly, the Board aimed to use the contact men to create a network of researchers in the state highway departments, with the Board acting akin to a central switchboard, quickly connecting those with problems to solutions and research programs. States responded enthusiastically with the names of their appointees.[18]

The advent of contact men began a subtle shift in the Board's orientation from organizations to people. The Board soon extended the privilege, and free publications, to university contact men, which numbered more than 120 by the end of 1925, including from the University of Mexico.[19]

Goldbeck's attempt to resign as chair of the Committee on Structural Design of Highways augmented this shift to people. Goldbeck had left BPR for a position with the National Crushed Stone Association and offered his resignation because he now worked for "an industry serving the highway field." Signaling that expertise and integrity resided in the individual, the Executive Committee refused his resignation.[20]

Not content to be just a facilitator of research, Upham led the Board into funded research projects. With funding from BPR off the table, private industry or individuals were the most likely sources of funds. The National Steel Fabric Company, a subsidiary of Pittsburgh Steel Company, provided $10,000 for the Board's first privately funded study, a "fact finding survey" about "the economic value of reinforcement in concrete pavement systems." The sudden appearance of a well-funded, defined research project drove the Board to quickly adopt guiding policies. Led by MacDonald and Agg, the Executive Committee outlined its ideal research process. First, the Executive Committee should decide which topics merited the Board's investigation. For approved topics, the director should first seek funding for "a general survey made to disclose the present status." Once such a survey was completed, the Board "will formulate a research project or series of projects to supply the additional information, facts, or data that may be necessary to complete the conclusions and recommendations of policies." In addition, appointed project committees should guide any Board-hired investigators. The Executive Committee also decided that no research conducted under the auspices of the Board should be released to the public, including for discussion at an annual meeting, without prior review by the Executive Committee.[21]

Once the Board officially committed to doing research, Upham made another lasting contribution to the history of transportation research. He proposed changing the Board's name. As he explained to the Executive Committee, "At a convention, ten or twelve engineers said in commenting about this Board, 'Who is going to do the advising? They never built a mile of road in their lives?' I cannot see any advantage in having the word

TRB and AASHTO

A Partnership from the Beginning

Be it resolved that the American Association of State Highway Officials welcomes the establishment by the National Research Council of the Advisory Board on Highway Research, and that the Association pledges its support to the Advisory Board in this much-needed effort to stimulate and coordinate highway research. —December 8, 1921[a]

ONE MONTH BEFORE the National Research Council's (NRC's) new Advisory Board on Highway Research was to hold its first annual meeting, the Board's director, William K. Hatt, traveled to Omaha, Nebraska, to address the Seventh Annual Meeting of the American Association of State Highway Officials (AASHO). His presentation on the coordination of highway research would be just one of many, many conversations between the association and the Transportation Research Board (TRB) over the decades to come. Both worked to leverage the Board's dedication to advancing innovation through research to help AASHO (after 1973, the American Association of State Highway and Transportation Officials [AASHTO]) meet its responsibilities for setting standards and promoting best practices.

Fruits of this partnership include the founding of the Research Correlation Service in 1945, the predecessor to state transportation departments' sponsorship of TRB's core technical activities. Together, they developed a procedure for pooling research funds in 1948 that led to major research projects including the $27 million AASHO Road Test that ran from 1954 to 1962. AASHO's leadership was instrumental to founding the National Cooperative Highway Research Program in 1962, which became a model for similar cooperative research programs for transit and airports. More recently, working through AASHTO, the states committed $60 million to the $172 million fund to implement the findings of the second Strategic Highway Research Program.

Today, TRB staff serve in a nonvoting capacity as secretary to AASHTO's Research Advisory Committee and Special Committee on Research and Innovation, and AASHTO's executive director is an ex officio member of TRB's Executive Committee. In addition, numerous current and former state transportation officials continue to offer TRB their time and talent in leadership roles.[b]

The founders of AASHO as they gathered with federal officials in December 1914 (AASHTO).

'Advisory' as it is misinterpreted." Indeed, the word "advisory" meant something completely different among senior academics and high-level federal officials than it did in federal–state relations. The Executive Committee quickly approved dropping the troublesome word. The Board rechristened itself the Highway Research Board on January 1, 1925.[22]

Attracting research funding, however, proved difficult and filled with unexpected pitfalls. Few companies or associations just turned over large checks, as had happened with the reinforced concrete study. Instead, sponsored research followed the cooperative pattern of the earlier study on tractive resistance of trucks. The Board had learned at least one lesson from the truck study: maintain control of the publication process. The Board had had little leverage when the Army—the owner of the study's results—did not prioritize putting them into publishable form.

The Board launched its most ambitious study during Upham's tenure on what was planned in 1925 to be a 2-year, comprehensive survey of earth roads and low-cost roadbuilding across the United States. Upham's close ties to T. Coleman du Pont, who contributed $17,000, and to ARBA, which contributed at least $4,000, helped bankroll most of the study. Despite hopes of making definitive recommendations, the project exhausted its funds on "descriptions of practically all of the low-cost road types in use in the United States" and the Executive Committee concluded it had to settle for an "informational" report. Yet, printing the report, including plans for an edition in Spanish, was delayed until the end of 1928 as the Board scrambled for additional funds. The Board eventually published the final report as Part II of the Proceedings of the Seventh Annual Meeting. A research project on culverts faced similar budget and fundraising hurdles, even though this project had stronger support—at least in-kind—from BPR.[23]

Crum and Institution Building

When Upham resigned in December 1927, the Board was struggling financially, forced to go hat in hand to its member associations to cover operating costs for 1928. Hiring Roy W. Crum as the next director solved two problems. Although an accomplished and respected researcher with significant experience with state highway departments, Crum did not have the stature of either Hatt or Upham. He came a bit cheaper. In addition, Crum had taken charge of the culvert investigation in 1925.

The Board hired him with the understanding that he would restart the defunct culvert study as part of his responsibilities as director, saving both the investigation and additional operating expenses. Crum served as director until his death in 1951. Upham took a position as engineer-director for ARBA and maintained close ties to the Board, including years of service on its Executive Committee.[24]

Crum would provide the Board—in his person and in his accomplishments—the stable foundation to both weather the difficult years ahead and enter a period of spectacular growth. Crum's special talent was outreach. His friendly, personal tone soon filled the Board's relaunched newsletter, sent to members of technical committees and contacts in member organizations, states, and universities. Nor was he afraid to be frank about problems, or funny. In one of his first newsletters, he noted about the 1927 Annual Meeting: "It was regretted by many that there was very little time available for discussion of the various papers and reports."[25] Those who worked with him described him as full of ideas, a "quiet, deep thinker" and a "wise, perceptive visionary" who was often "in a gentle way, very effectively persuasive."[26]

With Crum's hiring, the Board began a multiyear effort to broaden participation and reframe the role of committees. They started with the annual meeting. Consistent with National Academy traditions, the Board's annual meeting had been an invitation-only affair. In 1928, the Board decided instead to hold an open meeting. Crum used the October 1928 newsletter to explain the new policy and preview the meeting's coming attractions, closing with "We repeat, everyone interested is invited."[27]

In addition, the Board approved writing to the presidents of universities and heads of state highway departments to urge them to send their researchers to the meeting every year. The Board also welcomed municipal contact men, who represented 53 cities by 1931. Although annual meeting attendance stayed right around 300 as the Great Depression took hold, it started to increase in 1935, reaching more than 500 at the 19th Annual Meeting in December 1939. Researchers from Canada and Mexico also regularly attended during the 1930s.[28]

Next, they broadened their approach to member organizations. Although originally limited to technical organizations that emphasized research, they invited associations that were primarily educational or merely "interested in technical development within an industry" to apply. Acceptance, however, still required a majority vote of the Board's member associations. Although BPR increased its annual contract to $15,000 in 1930 and to $20,000 in 1936, the Board resorted to instituting dues for both organizations and individual affiliates in 1937. State and local governments, universities, and individual affiliates paid a low flat fee; associations were charged on a sliding scale based on mission and income.[29]

Bringing even more new blood and energy to the Board was the work done to revitalize the committees. At its low point in 1929, the Board had only five technical committees and two small-project committees for research funded by industry. They started by expanding the Executive Committee to 11 members. In 1930, Frank H. Eno of The Ohio State University, Agg, and Tilden represented academia; Horatio S. Mattimore, Pennsylvania Highway Department, and Hamlin represented state highway departments. There were committee slots for two BPR officials, including MacDonald, and one for NRC's engineering division. Three represented private industry: Upham from ARBA; Alfred J. Brosseau, president of Mack Trucks and the designated representative of the National Automobile Chamber of Commerce; and Hobart C. Dickinson. Although Dickinson worked at the Bureau of Standards, he was heavily involved in the Society of Automotive Engineers and would serve as its president in 1933 before becoming the Board's chair in 1936.[30]

Next, they began preparing for the 10th Annual Meeting, to be held in December 1930, by tasking the existing committees with not just reporting research results, but also outlining research needs. Dedicating the Ninth Annual Meeting to reviewing the compilation of research needs, they concluded that the Board's current organizational structure was not up to the task. Over the next 5 years, they put in place several different committee structures and objectives and, just as importantly, studied how well they performed. During the Board's first decade, the interests of the committee chair had heavily influenced a technical committee's activities. In the 1930s, the Board aligned its committees according to its survey of research needs, bringing in both new topics and new people. Dickinson, for example, led the Committee on the Highway and the Vehicle, outlining research needs for headlights, the mechanics of steering, and brakes. Burton W. Marsh, in 1930 the traffic engineer for the city of Philadelphia and a founder of the Institute of Traffic Engineers (ITE), became active in the Board's new traffic and safety committees. He would become the second president of ITE in 1932 and become the Board's chair in 1938. Marsh would serve on the Board's Executive Committee through 1967 and in 1970 was still on its safety committees.[31]

In 1935, the Board adopted the department and project committee system that would sustain and grow with the organization through the 1960s. Experience had taught that committees organized around *general* topics often fell short of the expectation that they would keep up with progress in their fields and plan and promote needed research. To be effective at promoting research required that a committee target a *specific* problem and outline a plan of action. The Board created six departments to replace general committees: Finance and Administration; Highway Transportation Economics; Design; Materials and Construction; Maintenance; and Traffic Control and Safety. A seventh department—Soils Investigations—was soon added. All technical committees within a department would be project committees, responsible for specific research activities around a defined topic. The Board charged departments and their members with arranging for research papers to be presented at annual meetings; suggesting and organizing project committees; and reviewing project committee reports. The Board outlined three types of project committees: those overseeing funded research, those conducting surveys of information on a specific topic, and those with continuing responsibilities to "correlate" all information on specific topics.[32]

One virtue of the project committee concept was its ready adaptability to cooperative research projects. Each cooperative partner could have representatives on the project committee, while the Board's department structure provided connections to additional expertise and the stamp of approval offered by its final review. In 1932, AASHO and the Board created a joint Committee on Roadside Development

HIGHWAY RESEARCH BOARD ANNUAL MEETING

1936

DATES November 18–20, 1936
LOCATION National Academy of Sciences on Constitution Avenue
CHAIR Hobart C. Dickinson, Bureau of Standards

ATTENDANCE 400
NUMBER OF PAPERS 31
ORGANIZATION OF TECHNICAL ACTIVITIES
Seven departments hosting 37 project committees

TOPICS
- Highway finance
- Gasoline consumption and tire wear
- Relation of curvature to speed
- Durability of concrete
- Estimating traffic volume

BIGGEST HIT Time designated for informal departmental meetings expands from 1 to 2 days
CHANGING TIMES The last year that papers were presented without prearranged time limits

WHAT ELSE IS HAPPENING AT HRB IN 1936?
HRB's highway safety studies, the first congressionally funded studies, begin

charged with making a comprehensive set of recommendations on "the art of highway beautification" in rural areas. The Roadside Development Committee continued to publish regular reports until 1962. ARBA and Iowa State College also conducted joint projects with the Board during the 1930s, and several industry-funded research projects also proceeded on the older cooperative model, where the Board hired a special investigator. Topics included the curing of concrete pavements and using calcium chloride as a dust palliative. Project committees were also a tool to formalize the Board's role as adviser to cooperative research projects that were led by BPR or state highway departments.[33]

Starting in 1930, the Board could also finally claim to have at least the beginnings of the long-desired highway research information service. With initial support from BPR, they started publishing *Highway Research Abstracts* in 1931; the monthly publication continued through 1975. The abstracts cast a wide net, summarizing studies published in academic journals as well as research results from experiment stations and student projects. In 1935, AASHO and the Board began conducting joint censuses of ongoing research. AASHO collected information from the states, and the Board surveyed colleges and other research organizations. The Board stored all of the census files in its offices for use by researchers.[34]

Highway Safety: Fulfilling NRC's Promise

The particular promise of NRC lay in its ability to draw on research expertise from across the scientific disciplines. Despite the Board's home in NRC's Division of Engineering and Industrial Research, engineering was not the source of the Board's most fruitful collaborations during its first decades. The Division stayed in New York tied to the Engineering Foundation, whereas the Board and the rest of NRC resided in Washington, D.C. The Division's efforts promoting research in industry had been a success. Private research laboratories had grown five-fold in number by the early 1930s. As the Great Depression deepened, however, the Division became a shadow of its former self. By 1936, it had only two other committees, in addition to the Highway Research Board.[35]

Highways, however, depend on more than engineering, and the Board's home in Washington, D.C., supported cross-fertilization with

An automobile crash on
U.S. 40 in Maryland, 1936
(Library of Congress,
LC-DIG-fsa-8b28380).

other NRC divisions. The Division of Geology and Geography had obvious
overlapping interests with the Board, but the Board also connected early
on with NRC's Division of Psychology and Anthropology. For example,
all three divisions came together to promote advances in archeology.
At a joint conference in April 1931, leaders of the three divisions invited
highway engineers and others managing excavation projects to work with
NRC on a plan to anticipate, report, and manage the discovery of ancient
remains and other human artifacts.[36]

In addition, the Board's interest in the overlap between safety
and psychology dated nearly to its founding. The National Safety
Council, a nonprofit formed in 1913 to promote industrial safety,
joined the Board in 1922. At the Second Annual Meeting in November
1922, Raymond Dodge, chair of NRC's psychology division, made a
special presentation on "The Human Factor in Highway Safety and
Regulation." Psychological research, Dodge argued, could improve
understanding of perception, inattention, and confusion in both
drivers and pedestrians, as well as offer insights for safety education
campaigns. In addition, Dodge believed that the field of psychology
should influence the standardized tests needed for licensing different
types of drivers.[37]

The Board's cooperative relationship with the psychology division's
Committee on the Psychology of the Highway would be its most significant

The Bureau of Standards tests paint used for safety zones and streets, 1937 (Library of Congress, Harris & Ewing, LC-DIG-hec-22548).

cross-NRC activity during its first decades and would eventually lead to the Board's first federally funded research project, directed by an act of Congress in 1936. The Committee on the Psychology of the Highway had its origins in highway safety activities promoted by the National Safety Council and organized by the Department of Commerce under Herbert Hoover. The future president espoused what historians call "associationism." Instead of top-down, expert-driven regulation, Hoover proposed using cooperation to solve the problems created by motor vehicles. To practitioners of associationism, it was proper for government to give those directly tied to a problem the opportunity to take responsibility and voluntarily devise and support its solution.[38]

In conjunction with the Department of Commerce, Alvin B. Barber, head of transportation for the Chamber of Commerce of the United States, directed a series of four National Conferences on Street and Highway Safety in 1924, 1926, 1930, and 1934. Alarm over the mounting rate of deaths and injuries had prompted the original conference, but the forum quickly expanded to cover a comprehensive set of problems related to the regulation of traffic, drivers, and vehicles. The conferences brought together businesses, social organizations, and delegates chosen by state and local governments and charged them with coming to consensus on model laws and practices for states and municipalities to adopt. Although representatives of the streetcar and bus transit industries participated in the conferences, businesses associated with the manufacture and operation of vehicles and delegates from state automobile clubs outnumbered delegates from other transportation industries.[39]

The substantive work of the safety conferences began in their committees, which circulated draft recommendations in advance of the conferences. The conference gatherings themselves were more like political conventions, where the delegates adopted a platform—model laws and practices—that they then pledged to promote in their home states and cities. The unquestioned goal was uniformity across municipalities and states. Although the Highway Research Board was not formally represented

Secretary of Commerce Daniel C. Roper (right), Representative Edith Nourse Rogers of Massachusetts, and Representative Emmot O'Neal of Kentucky at a meeting on accident prevention, [1936 or 1937]: Their interest in traffic safety led to the Highway Research Board's first congressionally funded studies (Library of Congress, Harris & Ewing, LC-DIG-hec-33608).

until the 1934 conference, half of the 24 members on the 1924 conference's Committee on Construction and Engineering had some tie to the Board. Upham, then the Board's director, but representing AASHO, served on the key Committee on Public Relations, while Johnson, then the Board's chair, served on both the construction committee and the statistics committee. Both also participated in the 1926 conference.[40]

As the first safety conference closed, plans were already under way for the second conference, which would attract more than 1,000 delegates, including those appointed by 43 state governors. In preparation, NRC formed the Committee on the Psychology of the Highway in 1925 and became a cooperating organization responsible for supporting the second conference's Committee on the Causes of Accidents. This committee's report shocked Hoover, and he lamented during his opening address that uniform laws properly enforced would mean little if the fundamental causes of accidents remained "elusive and mysterious." Hoover endorsed the report's "plea for exhaustive and extensive research work."[41]

The Board founded its own Committee on the Causes and Prevention of Highway Accidents and tried to build momentum for research projects during the late 1920s. But by 1931, the Board had all but ceded advising and conducting highway safety research to NRC's psychology division, although the Board's traffic committee still outlined and promoted needed safety research. The Board also publicized the research that NRC's Committee on the Psychology of the Highway facilitated at universities on topics such as the visibility of highway signs and signals, the design of license plates, and the development of tests for drivers.[42]

A project done in cooperation with the psychology committee, Chrysler Corporation, and the United Motor Coach Company of Chicago in 1934 and 1935 really got people's attention. At the Board's annual meeting in 1930, Sidney J. Williams, director of public safety for the National Safety Council, had outlined the need for research on "the accident-prone driver" in commercial fleets. Running with Williams's suggestion, Alvhh Ray Lauer, a young professor of psychology at Iowa State College, led the cooperative study. The researchers aimed to correlate tests of drivers' skills with the companies' accident records. Although their tests were not yet predictive, the analysis confirmed Williams's hypothesis: more than half of vehicle crashes in commercial fleets involved a small number of repeat culprits. Here was a research finding with clear economic and policy implications for business and government. In December 1935, Barber—in his dual role as director of the safety conference and staff of the Chamber of Commerce—petitioned the Highway Research Board to take on an even larger "investigation of accident repeaters."[43]

Federal Funding for Safety Research

The Board was primed for another attempt to build up its safety research. For the first time, BPR had become a cooperating organization of the National Conference on Street and Highway Safety in advance of its 1934 meeting. Moreover, AASHO and the safety conference had formed a joint committee in 1932, chaired by BPR's Edwin W. James, to bring together their respective rural and urban manuals of signs, markers, and signals. After endorsement at the 1934 conference, their effort gave birth to the first *Manual of Uniform Traffic Control Devices for Streets and Highways* in 1935.[44]

A decade after the first safety conference, the stubborn toll of 30,000 dead and 800,000 injured per year heightened the sense of urgency. In the conference's opening address, Secretary of Commerce

Daniel C. Roper minced few words: "Death on wheels has become one of the most shocking and terrifying evils in the life of our nation." The delegates endorsed updates to the model laws and a new publication, "Guides to Traffic Safety." Written by the conference's Executive Committee and published by BPR, this remarkable document briefed government officials and safety activists in plain language on everything from highway engineering to accident investigation, from traffic courts to preschool safety education. Moreover, specific research needs were woven throughout, culminating in an outline for a comprehensive research program. In its 1934 resolutions, the conference thanked BPR for its leadership and also urged "Chief MacDonald" to continue activities in support of "the further study of accident hazards and remedies." Dickinson and Marsh, both in attendance and soon to serve back-to-back terms as the Board's chair, gave testimonials in support of additional studies, as did representatives of the National Automobile Chamber of Commerce and the American Automobile Association.[45]

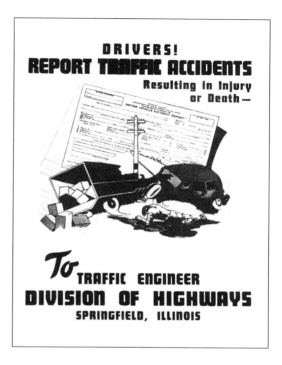

An exhibit from *Inadequacy of State Motor-Vehicle Accident Reporting*, Motor-Vehicle Traffic Conditions in the United States Part 3 (Government Printing Office, 1938, 8).

Studies at the scale that the conference envisioned would take significant resources. When the safety conference's Barber came to the Board in late 1935, the Board agreed that it would be "a desirable project" if funding could be found. Representative Edith Nourse Rogers, Republican of Massachusetts, had twice introduced resolutions in 1935 to authorize funding for the studies, and congressional funding finally came through in June 1936, in an act authorizing $75,000 and directing BPR to study traffic safety conditions and make recommendations for their improvement. In September the Board authorized a Special Project on Highway Safety and a cooperative agreement with BPR. At the Board's 16th Annual Meeting, the National Safety Council's Williams celebrated the success, calling it "tremendously encouraging," that "the patient pioneer work of psychologists like Lauer" was finally "receiving the support it deserves."[46]

Dickinson, then the Board's chair, headed the Highway Safety Committee that advised BPR. The committee contained both experts from academia—including Tilden and Lauer—and representatives from nine associations related to automobiles or motor vehicle safety. Marsh represented the American Automobile Association, and AASHO was represented by Arthur W. Brandt of New York and a past president of the organization. BPR submitted the six-part report to Congress in early 1938, a truly astonishing time line given the depth of the research. To continue the momentum, BPR sponsored an additional special investigation by the Board during 1938–1940 that examined speed regulations on rural highways.[47]

Crum and BPR's James co-directed the studies, produced by different combinations of BPR staff and Board-hired investigators. BPR handled the study of "Nonuniformity of State Motor Vehicle Traffic Laws," which concluded that "chaotic nonuniformity prevails," including for "provisions that are essentially fundamental" to safety. The report "Skilled Investigation at the Scene of the Accident Needed to Develop Causes," contained its recommendation in its title and was conducted in conjunction with the Michigan State Police and the International Association of Chiefs of Police. For the report "Inadequacy of State Motor-Vehicle Accident Reporting," Peter J. Stupka, a founder of ITE, traveled to 38 states. Most states kept some data on accidents, and the author commended the 24 states that kept accident spot maps and the 4 states—Connecticut, Massachusetts, New Jersey, and Oklahoma—that went even further and conducted accident location studies. The fourth study, "Official Inspection of Vehicles," did a deep dive into the 15 states with vehicle inspection laws, finding failures rates between 34 and 85 percent of vehicles.[48]

Parts five and six of the report to Congress showcased the power of research using large data sets. Yale University's Tilden led "Case Histories of Fatal Highway Accidents." The researchers collected local investigative reports and other information on 1,715 recent fatal collisions from around the country. They then created detailed case histories, from conditions before the collision to final legal penalties for drivers who survived, which they constructed as narratives. They concluded that few fatalities had a single cause and that the courts were an inadequate means to prevent future deaths. The decision to include 103 complete case histories—all compellingly written and invariably tragic—in the main body of the report to Congress went beyond analysis and made a profound political statement.[49]

Connecticut's advanced accident record keeping made "The Accident-Prone Driver" possible. The Board hired Mary J. Cairns, a longtime employee of the Connecticut Department of Motor Vehicles and the supervisor of records, to take charge of compiling the necessary data from official files. They randomly selected 30,000 licensed drivers and cross-referenced them with the state's accident records. Harry M. Johnson of Tulane University, who had built a national reputation as the first aviation psychologist during World War I, took charge of interpreting the analysis. The study confirmed that "accident repeaters" were indeed a measurable phenomenon. In addition, they were surprised to discover that drivers under age 25 were especially accident prone, causing fatal accidents at a rate far higher than older drivers. The researchers found this result especially perplexing because these young drivers often excelled at the tests the psychologists had devised to assess driving skill.[50]

BPR and AASHO took their safety messages to the public. As the studies got under way, MacDonald and AASHO President Gibb Gilchrist of Texas and other state highway officials participated in an NBC radio broadcast provocatively titled, "Can Road Design Make Highways Completely Safe?" As the highway officials listed all the dangers of roads that needed to be fixed, the announcer bluntly asked: "Now why did you … allow them to be built into the roads to begin with?" Gilchrist replied, "[The] road builders have not been able to keep pace with the vehicle builders. The roads last longer than the vehicles." Gilchrist also

Speed limits varied by vehicle type were one solution to vehicle capabilities outpacing highway design and construction (Waco, Texas, 1939; Library of Congress, LC-DIG-fsa-8a27563).

Events such as a football game between the University of North Carolina and Duke University showed that traffic was not just an urban issue (near Duke University Stadium, 1939; Library of Congress, LC-USF34-052649-D).

promoted building sidewalks, especially for schoolchildren. MacDonald, however, emphasized that he did not fault vehicles for being capable of greater speeds, but the drivers who "speed *at the wrong place* that's to be condemned" [emphasis in original].[51]

BPR promoted the safety studies to the public through radio addresses and a summary bulletin of findings and recommendations. Although BPR's official recommendations were limited to highlighting the importance of uniform laws and best practices and calling for more research, BPR did emphasize the problem of young drivers. In addition, on the bulletin's first page, BPR commended the Highway Research Board. BPR credited the Board with convening the "leading authorities" and experienced researchers, "who have devoted their best efforts to the studies and the resulting reports."[52]

The safety studies were the result of forces that pressured the federal government to broaden its approach to transportation. Highway traffic did not stop just because a rural area had become urban, and the consequences of the motor vehicles were larger than the impacts of trucks on rural highways. Through its traffic department and the leadership of men such as Dickinson and Marsh, the Highway Research Board too had expanded into transportation topics far beyond the building of rural highways. In 1939, BPR officially shed its rural past and left the Department of Agriculture for the Federal Works Agency.

CHAPTER 4

Mission Building: Research Correlation Service, 1940–1950

EIGHT WEEKS BEFORE the Highway Research Board gathered to celebrate its 20th Annual Meeting in early December 1940, cars and trucks began speeding across Pennsylvania on a landmark in highway development, the Pennsylvania Turnpike. Unlike the popular parkways of the 1930s, Pennsylvania built the turnpike for speed, intercity travel, and trucks. Crews working around the clock constructed 160 miles of access-controlled expressway in just 2 years. Dynamite and power shovels helped flatten mountains, fill valleys, and straighten natural curves. Before its official opening, General Motors and the military sent fleets of vehicles to test their handling and durability at speeds in excess of 75 miles per hour and in the rain. Radiators boiled over and trucks broke down under the strain. Highway builders had finally gotten out ahead of the capabilities of motor vehicles.[1]

Pennsylvania and the federal government financed, constructed, and managed the turnpike outside of the Bureau of Public Roads (BPR)/ state highway department nexus. In response to requests in 1938 from the newly created and independent Pennsylvania Turnpike Commission, the federal Reconstruction Finance Corporation purchased $41 million in bonds and the Public Works Administration ponied up $25 million in grants for labor.[2]

President Franklin D. Roosevelt, excited about the prospect of transcontinental "superhighways" funded by tolls, requested a feasibility study from BPR. In 1939, shortly before BPR left the Department of Agriculture for the Federal Works Agency, Thomas MacDonald delivered *Toll Roads and Free Roads*. The report argued against transcontinental superhighways, laying out a detailed forecast that concluded that toll collections would not cover costs. Instead, the country should focus on upgrading the federal-aid highway network where it was most needed: in and around America's metropolises.[3]

At the Highway Research Board's 20th Annual Meeting, only one paper, "Curve Design and Tests on the Pennsylvania Turnpike," addressed the new superhighway. MacDonald, chair of the Board's Department of Finance, dedicated his report to promoting off-street parking.[4]

Superhighways soon took a backseat to preparing for defense and then war. In May 1940, President Roosevelt stunned the country and the military with calls for an aircraft industry capable of producing 50,000 planes per year, more planes than had been built since Kitty Hawk. Constructing the massive manufacturing plants for airframes and engines and expanding the shipyards soon taxed supplies of steel and aluminum. Airports and landing fields took precedence over highways. In the second half of 1941, President Roosevelt vetoed the federal-aid highway bill for failing to target defense needs, and federal officials ordered the curtailment of automobile production, which came to a halt altogether in January 1942. Americans left their farms and small towns for the manufacturing metropolises to work in the war industries. In response to rubber shortages for tires, the government rationed gasoline, required manufacturers to encourage carpooling, and dictated a top speed limit of 35 miles per hour nationwide. Ridership surged on mass transit. Highways built for speed had little place in wartime America.[5]

The National Academy of Sciences and World War II

In the run up to war, the National Academy of Sciences (NAS) and its National Research Council (NRC) reoriented themselves to their founding missions. Frank B. Jewett, who had

The Pennsylvania Turnpike in 1942 (Library of Congress, LC-DIG-fsa-8d06851).

chaired NRC's Division of Engineering and Industrial Research in the 1920s, became NAS president in 1939, serving until 1947. Vannevar Bush helped direct the federal government's investment in research. As chair of NRC's engineering division, Bush had transitioned it from serving industry to government and moved it from New York to Washington, D.C., in 1941. He also chaired the government's National Defense Research Committee and headed the federal agency that superseded the committee, the Office of Scientific Research and Development.[6]

Rubber shortages and thinning tires led to reduced speed limits during World War II (Library of Congress, LC-USE6-D-010878).

To aid Bush's work, the National Academy conducted censuses of expertise and research facilities, which Bush then used when placing federal research contracts in universities and research agencies. NRC itself accepted 34 wartime research contracts totaling just more than $5 million. Many of the contracts called for NRC to advise on research projects contracted to others. Experts continued to serve on National Academy committees without compensation, but the federal government set an important precedent by agreeing to cover overhead expenses. Although few of NRC's wartime projects related to transportation, one of its largest contracts guided the selection and training of airplane pilots.[7]

The Highway Research Board, however, spent the war years anticipating the return to peace. Its federal funding stayed flat at $20,000 per year for the duration of the war. In response to Washington, D.C.'s congestion, annual meetings were convened in Baltimore (December 1941), St. Louis (December 1942), and Chicago (November 1943). The Annual Meeting for 1944 went unassembled, although they produced a *Proceedings*. The Annual Meeting for 1945 was delayed until January 1946 and held in Oklahoma City.[8]

Starting in 1942, the Board began publishing *Wartime Road Problems*, short bulletins on practical topics such as the curing of concrete pavement, maintenance of concrete slabs, and the removal of snow and ice. The pamphlet-sized publications "present[ed] the best available information in understandable language" for practicing engineers. Pleased with the bulletins' usefulness, the Executive Committee looked to expand this approach, so "that the men on the firing line" would not have to "wait 3 or 4 years until the research men have the best answer." With their focus on research implementation, the bulletins were precedents for everything from the *Highway Capacity Manual* to the synthesis reports of the cooperative research programs. Through 1963, the Board arranged via its technical committees to periodically update some of the original 13 under the postwar title *Current Road Problems*.[9]

A New Source of Funding

The Board's most significant innovations of the 1940s were institutional. The Board worked closely with federal officials and the American Association of State Highway Officials (AASHO) to forge two landmark agreements that dramatically expanded the Board's ability to be both a convener of researchers and a manager of research. The chairs of the Executive Committee during this transformation hailed from road construction and state highway departments. Warren W. Mack, chair for 1940–1941, was chief engineer of the Delaware State Highway Department, where earlier in his career he had worked under Charles M. Upham, the Board's second director, who was still on the Executive Committee representing the American Road Builders Association (ARBA). The chair for 1942–1943, Fred C. Lang, had served on the Board's original Committee on the Character and Use of Road Materials since the early 1920s. When he became chair, Lang was employed in the dual role as professor of highway engineering at the University of Minnesota and engineer of tests and inspections for the state highway department. Stanton Walker, chair for 1944–1945, represented the National Sand and Gravel Association. Fred V. Reagel, engineer of material for the Missouri State Highway Department, was chair for 1948–1949.[10]

The first landmark agreement funded a Research Correlation Service. Ongoing concerns about duplication in research, compounded by a sense that a lot of good investigations being produced in state highway departments were never reaching a wider audience, spurred leaders into action. Although these concerns were not new—they dated to the

Board's founding—as more state highway departments had embarked on research, the scale of potential duplication and loss had only grown. During Lang's tenure as chair, he led an effort to propose "a program for stimulation of research" that fully articulated a new solution to the perennial problem. The Board should hire expert "field agents" on a permanent basis, and these engineers should also support the work of the technical committees. The expansion of professional staff should go hand in hand with improving the Board's research information service, including library services and *Highway Research Abstracts*.[11]

Moreover, the Executive Committee was willing to put a request for significant funding on the table, distinguishing Lang's proposal from the Board's reforms of the 1930s. The desire for field agents who would "go from state to state and carry firsthand information" institutionalized a practice from the Board's special investigations, including the research censuses. Nearly all of these investigations had required that the engineers hired (or loaned) for the studies travel widely to gather information on-site and in person. Funds raised for specific projects, however, had supported these investigators and their travel. Although the Board had new sources of revenue from membership and affiliation dues and publication sales, these sources did not come close to providing a foundation for the expansion of professional staff. Only two possible sources of funding held promise for what they proposed: the federal government or the states, acting in concert through AASHO. Moreover, in the ideal, the source of funds would be a self-renewing funding stream.

The solution to the funding conundrum lay hidden in the Hayden-Cartwright Act of 1934. Primarily a road funding bill, a new provision had allowed states to use 1½ percent of their federally apportioned funds "for surveys, plans, and engineering investigations of projects for future construction." The Federal-Aid Highway Act of 1936 had added economic investigations to the list.[12]

With this funding carrot, BPR had launched a push for statewide highway surveys that built on new techniques such as Bruce D. Greenshields' pioneering methods to study

View from U.S. 40 in Colorado, 1942 (Library of Congress, LC-DIG-fsac-1a34858).

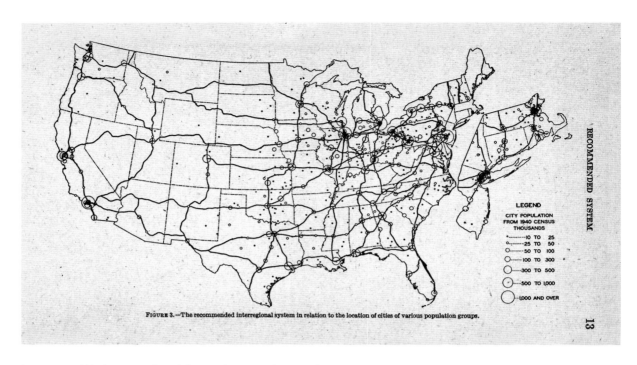

LEGEND
CITY POPULATION
FROM 1940 CENSUS
THOUSANDS

•----10 TO 25
○----25 TO 50
○----50 TO 100
○----100 TO 300
○----300 TO 500
⊙----500 TO 1,000
◯----1,000 AND OVER

FIGURE 3.—The recommended interregional system in relation to the location of cities of various population groups.

13

Interregional Highways analyzed data and proposed routes that set the stage for the National System of Interstate Highways (BPR, 1944).

traffic behavior using 16-millimeter cameras and the Board's 1932 special investigation on traffic survey methods, funded by the Metropolitan Life Insurance Company. For states, the surveys and plans were voluntary, their content a product of a cooperative agreement with BPR. Missouri's statewide highway planning survey, for example, included inventorying and mapping all roads, conducting widespread traffic counts to make traffic flow maps, and collecting financial data on all government expenditures for roads and streets.[13]

The statewide surveys of the 1930s created the foundation that made both *Toll Roads and Free Roads* and its follow-up, *Interregional Highways*, possible. Whereas the first report made the case against transcontinental toll roads, *Interregional Highways* presented the analytical rationale for what the country should build instead: 39,000 miles of "interregional" highways—or express routes—with limited access, including an estimated 5,000 miles of routes distributing traffic within urban areas. President Roosevelt had appointed the National Interregional Highway Committee in 1941 to produce a report outlining a plan for postwar construction, and the Defense Highway Act of 1941 had funneled $10 million to the states for additional surveys and studies. MacDonald chaired the president's committee; vice chair went to G. Donald Kennedy, Michigan's state highway commissioner, AASHO's president for 1942, and future Board chair for 1954–1955. MacDonald credited Herbert S. Fairbank, a career employee promoted to head of research in 1943, for leading the research and writing of the final report. When they submitted the report to the president and Congress in January 1944, Fairbank also chaired AASHO's Highway Transportation Committee and the Board's Department of Economics, Finance, and Administration. On Fairbank's team of engineers was Olav K. Normann, who next would lead the production of the first *Highway Capacity Manual*.[14]

Interregional Highways set the stage for authorization of a National System of Interstate Highways in the Federal-Aid Highway Act of 1944. The report was also the fullest realization to date at the national level of the powerful use of data for transportation policy and planning. The analyses incorporated studies of traffic volumes and origin–destination surveys and examined the performance of alternative networks against criteria including construction costs, population, location of cities, employment, manufacturing products, and agricultural products. For urban areas, although the report assigned the choice and location of routes to local study, its recommended urban transportation planning principles and designs take up nearly one-third of its 130 pages.[15]

Just as significant for the future of transportation research, *Interregional Highways* epitomized the blurred line between research and planning. Decades earlier, the spread of highway research had been reinforced by the overlap between the types of activities required to routinely test the properties of highway materials and to investigate the performance of innovative highway designs. Similarly, the federal government endorsed an approach to highway planning that not only built on previous research studies, but also required the collection of data, the application of theories, and analyses leading to conclusions and

Freight movement by truck continued to frame highway research needs and the importance of interstate highways during the 1940s (Library of Congress, LC-DIG-fsa-8d27813).

recommendations as part of the production of new plans, such as *Interregional Highways.*

The Board's records do not indicate who first suggested funding its postwar ambitions by tapping into federal aid for state planning surveys. In 1943, AASHO formed a special committee, which paralleled the Board's committee led by Lang, to develop a cooperative plan for research services and in December adopted a resolution "recognizing the need for an increased program of correlation and utilization of research." At its meeting in February 1944, the Board's Executive Committee discussed raising funds through the set-aside for state planning surveys, although it noted that "physical research" of pavement designs or construction techniques was not listed as an authorized use. The committee empowered MacDonald and J. S. Williamson, chief highway commissioner for South Carolina, to reach out to AASHO on its behalf.[16]

At the same time, AASHO was circulating proposed legislation for what was to become the Federal-Aid Highway Act of 1944 and working the halls of Congress as it always did for highway bills. When the legislative wrangling ended in late 1944, the Interstate System was authorized, but not funded. However, the section authorizing 1½ percent of apportioned funds for planning surveys had two important amendments. The previous law's "may" had been replaced with "shall." These funds could only be used for the listed planning, engineering, and economic studies, and—new to the list—"for highway research necessary in connection therewith." MacDonald quickly issued guidance that the Board's and AASHO's plans for a Research Correlation Service qualified for this funding.[17]

The Work of Research Correlation

The Research Correlation Service (RCS) was launched July 1, 1945, and by the end of the fiscal year, 42 states, the District of Columbia, and the territories of Hawaii and Puerto Rico had paid for "subscriptions." The executive secretary of AASHO became an ex officio member of the Board's Executive Committee. The Board's operating budget increased more than three-fold, from $40,000 in 1945 to $130,000 in 1947, the first full year of operation, while federal funding stayed flat at $20,000. The Board and AASHO worked out budgets, typically on 3-year cycles, that were then divvied up among the states according to federal-aid apportionment rules. However, the Board signed separate contracts with each state or territory.[18]

In the RCS's first year, the Board hired research engineers for materials and construction, soils and foundations, design, and equipment and maintenance. The Board also hired a full-time librarian. The next year an engineer of traffic and operations joined the staff. Fred Burggraf, as associate director and second in command to Roy W. Crum, the long-time director, supervised the RCS.

BPR's move to the Federal Works Agency in 1939 broadened its purview for research to include urban highways; left turn lane on University Avenue, Berkeley, California (BPR, 1944).

Burggraf first held a Board appointment in 1929, when the Illinois State Highway Department had loaned him to work on a special investigation of concrete curing. He stayed until 1932, picking up an investigation into the use of calcium chloride as a dust palliative, a special project supported by the state highway departments of Kansas, Missouri, Nebraska, and South Carolina, and the Calcium Chloride Association. After 8 years with the Calcium Chloride Association, he returned to the Board in 1940. The launch of the RCS also brought a young William N. Carey, Jr., to the Board, hired as executive assistant to the director in 1946.[19]

The Board's new engineers were directed "to do everything possible to be helpful to the highway researchists [sic] throughout the nation and to aid highway administrators and engineers in the solution to problems," Crum explained in his first annual report to AASHO. The work of the departments, and their technical committees, would no longer depend solely on volunteers. Each research engineer served a specific department and was a liaison to the volunteers on the department's technical committees. Often left unsaid, the Board also provided its research engineers with secretarial assistants. In addition, the contact men in each "subscribing" state became part of the RCS's advisory committee. In the RCS's first year, the field engineers visited every state and 69 engineering colleges and held more than 1,000 "personal conferences" with state highway engineers, federal researchers, and other researchers in academia and industry. The field engineers conducted their visits every year and recorded the questions, problems, concerns, developments, experiments, and innovations that they heard and saw in a series of reports. The visits also became recruiting opportunities for new participants to annual meetings or on the Board's committees.[20]

But what exactly was a "correlation service"? Even Crum struggled to explain it without using the word in the definition. "Correlate" and its variants appear frequently in NRC and transportation professional circles in the first half of the 20th century, but in few other contexts. The Board's RCS was more than a research information service, although like NRC's World War I Research Information Service, it aimed to move knowledge and innovation quickly across a dispersed geography. Emphatically, "correlation" did *not* describe the centralized or government-directed coordination of research. The Board's staff would continue to encourage the voluntary coordination of research, in ways that respected individual initiative.[21]

"Correlate" could also mean a mode of research, much larger in concept than the term's use today in statistics. The closest contemporary word is "integrate." When a researcher set out to correlate, his or her topic may have been narrow, but the sweep of information and knowledge considered relevant was broad. Valuing both structured, published research and innovations developed in the field of practice, the researcher integrated the theoretical and the empirical and set laboratory findings against real-world results. In pursuit of solutions to specific problems, correlation went beyond cataloguing research findings to include assessing research needs. In addition, the term encompassed providing for and studying research implementation, a word that they did not use, instead resorting to descriptions of how they aimed to put "the worthwhile results of technical studies … into practice as soon as possible." By extending into the field and into "development" as well as research, Crum proclaimed, "practically all responsible highway workers" were welcome under the big tent of the Highway Research Board.[22]

The work of correlation also encompassed the Board's technical committees. The RCS published the technical committees' products, from identifying research needs to reporting investigation results, and distilling best practices. In his 1948 chairman's address, Reagel examined how the committees played a vital role in getting research into practice. "Accumulation of data" was "essential," he argued, "but much of the ultimate benefit of research must await the evaluation and sponsorship of groups such as are available in our committees ... [that] perform this very useful and necessary function which translates research into terms of practice." Lang, too, in pushing for the RCS, had emphasized "the necessity for teamwork in highway research."[23]

Cooperative Projects Through Pooled Funds

The second landmark agreement of the 1940s enabled states to pool funds for research. For researchers such as Reagel and Lang, World War II had taught the benefits of teamwork in science in spades. Huge projects, some employing thousands of scientists, engineers, and technical personnel, made advances in chemicals, rockets, radar, radiation, and, of course, the atomic bomb. Advances in the techniques and skills required to manage large, complex research and development projects would have a profound impact on technological development in the postwar world.[24]

Before the lessons of teamwork could be applied to large research projects for highways, Lang, Reagel, and the Board needed to overcome

From left, Charles H. Scholer, Kansas State University; Fred V. Reagel, Missouri State Highway Department; G. Donald Kennedy, then with the Portland Cement Association; and Thomas MacDonald at the 1948 Annual Meeting (BPR).

Highway Capacity Manual

TRB's Instant Best Seller

A S THE COMMITTEE on Highway Capacity wrapped up its first big report in 1949, the Highway Research Board knew something special had happened. Olav K. Normann, the committee's chair, had pioneered studies of highway capacity in the late 1930s. His paper for the 23rd Annual Meeting had, for the first time, connected the combined effect of highway design factors—curvature, sight distance, and gradient—to how much traffic a highway, street, or road could carry.[a]

In 1945, Normann had gathered a crew of fellow federal highway engineers and researchers from state highway departments and city transport agencies to integrate the growing number of studies on capacity. Unsatisfied with the data, especially from urban areas, the committee guided additional field studies, and even arranged for new instruments that counted vehicles and also recorded their speeds, positions, and spacing.[b]

As the report neared completion, a private publisher approached the Board. The new manual had best seller written all over it. Tempted, the Board's Executive Committee soon came to consensus. Most of the research had been funded by governments. In addition, the Board wanted "maximum distribution." When *Highway Capacity Manual: Practical Applications from Research* came out in 1950, the Govern-ment Printing Office sold it for 65 cents, or less than the price of 3 gallons of gasoline. It would go on to sell more than 26,000 copies and be translated into nine languages. Its foundational role in highway planning, design, and operations continues through to today.[c]

The Committee on Highway Capacity launched anew in 1953, with Normann still chair, and started working seriously on a second edition in 1957. Like the first edition, the new edition was to contain the committee's best judgments on everything from rural two-lane roads to downtown urban streets, but the researchers were especially excited about incorporating recent studies on freeways, including ramps and weaving.[d]

The second edition also introduced the concept of "level of service" (LOS), with five levels of free-flow conditions graded A through E and a catchall category, F, for gridlock. Determining the capacity of streets and highways is not as simple as figuring out how much water can flow through a pipe. How much traffic a given roadway can carry depends on human behavior. People, moreover, have preferences and desires. Even in the 1940s, the researchers conceived of capacity to include dimensions such as the driver's desire to go fast, dislike of waiting, and comfort with an open road. As Carlton C. Robinson, chair of the committee for the

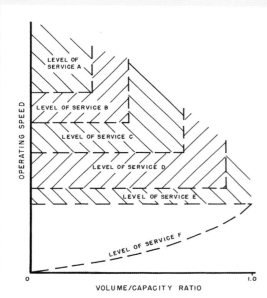

Figure 4.1. General concept of relationship of levels of service to operating speed and volume/capacity ratio. (Not to scale.)

Highway Capacity Manual 1965 introduced the concept of level of service, with levels assigned A–F (HRB Special Report 87, 1966, 81).

third edition, said "highway capacity involves human beings who are sensitive to the quality of the service they are receiving and capable of reacting to it."[e]

LOS was controversial from its inception, and so divisive were the competing philosophies that Normann felt he was failing as chair. Recognizing that its chair's job risked becoming thankless, the committee took the unusual step of honoring him with the gift of a watch inscribed, "To Mr. Capacity." Normann's unexpected death in 1964, however, meant he would not see the completion of *Highway Capacity Manual 1965*. With financial assistance for publication from the Eno Foundation for Highway Traffic Control, the manual came out

as Special Report 87 in 1966. It was another instant best seller.[f]

The committee became the Highway Capacity and Quality of Service Committee during the Board's 1970 reorganization. The manual's third edition, in 1985, took full advantage of the National Cooperative Highway Research Program (NCHRP) both to build on a coordinated series conducted by the Federal Highway Administration (FHWA) and NCHRP and to tap into NCHRP's panel process and paid consultants. To solve the conundrum that new research always outpaced manual updates, the Transportation Research Board (TRB) adopted the three-ring binder format still used today. Major updates in the 1990s came out in chapters that could be substituted for or added to chapters in 1985's Special Report 209.[g]

Highway Capacity Manual 2000 (HCM2000) divided the manual into three volumes: one on concepts for policy makers and one each for uninterrupted and interrupted flow facilities. HCM2000 also introduced online support materials and tutorials. Like the third edition, HCM2000 and HCM2010 continued to build off a coordinated set of FHWA and NCHRP research projects and involved hundreds of panelists and reviewers.[h]

In addition to integrating new research findings, the updated editions adapted to changing expectations. The evolving treatment of pedestrians illustrates this arc. The 1950 manual uses pedestrian counts to define different types of urban environments, but otherwise pedestrians are mentioned as sources of "conflict" or "interference." The 1985 manual includes a chapter on service quality from the perspective of people walking, but struggles to get beyond ideas of crowding and flow.

HCM2010 integrates service quality "scores" for people walking, biking, or taking transit into each section covering different types of streets and intersections.

LOS, however, continued to spark controversy, with intense debates recurring during every major revision. As understanding deepened of how people perceive and react to service quality, a limited number of seemingly simplistic "grades" became even more unsatisfactory to some, while at the same time the "grades" had become embedded in policy discussions and even standards. After HCM2010, three veterans of the LOS battles, Roger P. Roess, Mark A. Vandehey, and Wayne Kittelson, went public in the *Transportation Research Record* with their worries that LOS had been consuming time and talent out of proportion to its usefulness.[i]

In HCM's sixth edition, published in 2016, the committee revamped its content in response to federal legislation emphasizing the use of performance measures and to research coming out of the Strategic Highway Research Program 2 on travel time reliability. To signal the change, the committee added a subtitle for the first time since 1950. The manual is now also "A Guide for Multimodal Mobility Analysis" and covers quantity of travel, quality of travel, accessibility, and capacity. LOS levels A–F for motorists is still included in the most recent edition. However, the committee, chaired by Lily Elefteriadou, University of Florida, reminds HCM users that "there is no one right way to measure and interpret performance."[j]

Chinese edition of *Highway Capacity Manual 2000* (China Communications Press).

Over the decades, TRB's *Highway Capacity Manual* has been required for professional engineering exams and even inspired a spin-off. The Transit Cooperative Research Program's *Transit Capacity and Quality of Service Manual* had reached its third edition by 2013. The HCM committee began sponsoring an International Symposium in 1991, which has been convened in Australia, Denmark, Germany, Japan, and Sweden. And, finally, a fun fact: TRB's *Highway Capacity Manual* has its own Wikipedia page. Wikipedians created HCM's page in 2007 and updated the entry for the 2010 and 2016 editions.

another decades-old problem. A state joined cooperative projects by welcoming researchers and research projects into the state. Individual state highway commissions or departments were reluctant to engage in the messy politics of one state paying for another state's research.

The mandated spending on planning and research in the 1944 Highway Act provided AASHO a mechanism to do an end run around the politics stymieing truly cooperative projects. Because the 1½ percent funds, as they called them, had to be spent on planning or research, states became more willing to consider pooling funds. In September 1948, AASHO's Executive Committee adopted a formal procedure enabling AASHO's committees to originate research projects that would seek pooled funds from two or more states. The procedure designated the Board as the preferred project administrator, assigning it what amounted to the right of first refusal on all such projects. Once the project was accepted, the Board would enter funding agreements with individual states and any other interested partners including BPR. The Board would also appoint a project committee to plan, direct, and monitor the project; provide for any needed staff; and publish the final reports.[25]

World-Wide Distribution of Associates of the Board by Countries

By the Highway Research Board's 30th Anniversary, individual associates subscribing to its publications resided all over the world (HRB, Annual Report, 1951).

The Highway Research Board at 30

The Board that celebrated its 30th Annual Meeting in January 1951 differed significantly from the Board 10 years earlier. Its operating budget reached almost $190,000, nearly five times larger than the $40,000 in fiscal year 1941. Its permanent technical staff numbered 10, including 5 RCS engineers and a librarian. Total pages published annually had more than doubled to more than 2,500, and a typical initial print run called for 3,900 copies, 95 percent of which were distributed immediately to subscribers. Although still technically a federation of a limited number of member associations, individual and corporate associates totaled more than 1,100 and hailed from all over the world. Eight hundred and sixty attended the Annual Meeting, 50 percent more than typical a decade earlier.[26]

Just as significant to the Board's influence was the number of slots on its technical committees. They numbered more than 2,000. The basic structure—project committees organized into six departments—remained the same. That year the Department of Economics, Finance, and Administration had the fewest slots, 113 over 9 committees, and the Department of Materials and Construction the most with 229 over 20 committees. The project committees were supposed to study a specific problem, outlined in a project statement that covered its scope and objectives. Upon project completion, the committee was supposed to disband, unless another problem was already teed up to take its place. Individual appointments lasted only 1 year, but could be renewed indefinitely.[27]

The Board had also started to think through how best to publish the burgeoning number of reports and studies. To its two main publications, *Proceedings* and *Abstracts*, it added a third, the *Highway Research Board Bulletin*, and was about to launch a fourth, *Special Report*. In which of the four series a report or study would appear was not dictated by merit, but by how it would be used. Department chairs recruited research reports and papers for the annual meeting, and they also decided where to publish them. The annual volume of the *Proceedings* was reserved, in general, for papers of "permanent reference value." Because *Proceedings* appeared only once per year, anything of "immediate value" went out in the more frequent *Abstracts*. Reports that could be packaged around a theme or were just too long for *Proceedings* found a home in the *Bulletin* or the short-lived *Highway Research Report*. The *Special Report* series would finally solve the problem of what to do with the Board's own research, including reports produced by its technical committees. The *Special Report* series would also include the proceedings of Board-sponsored conferences and workshops held outside the annual meeting.[28]

Despite all the changes, the Executive Committee at the Board's 30th Anniversary was a remarkable site of continuity. MacDonald still represented BPR, which had been transferred to the Department of Commerce in 1949. Crum was still ably in charge as director. Pyke Johnson, who had attended the Board's organizing conference and was now president of the Automotive Safety Foundation, retained a seat, as did Burton W. Marsh, who had led the Board in the late 1930s during the safety studies requested by Congress. The Board's second director, Upham, although retired from ARBA, still served. Walter H. Root and Reagel had also both gotten started with the Board in the early 1920s. The Board's chair, Ralph A. Moyer, then a research engineer at the University of California's Institute of Transportation and Traffic Engineering, had come up through Iowa State College, working for its highway experiment station from 1921 to 1948.[29]

These men, plus many more, had brought the Board through its infancy and well into its adolescence. When they started, the highway professions were young, as were they, which gave the field of highway research room to define itself outside of the usual hierarchies of academia or government. But the inevitable generational change was at hand. Four months after the 30th Anniversary, Crum collapsed and died shortly after returning from presiding over a committee meeting in Columbus, Ohio. Burggraf assumed the role of director, an appointment then made permanent. MacDonald officially retired in 1951, when he reached the government's mandatory retirement age of 70, but he stayed as interim director until early in the Eisenhower administration, finally leaving federal service in April 1953. After moving to College Station, Texas, he helped build what would become the Texas Transportation Institute. The Secretary of Commerce appointed Francis V. du Pont, son of T. Coleman du Pont of Delaware highway fame, to take MacDonald's place as Commissioner of Public Roads. Charles D. Curtiss, who in 1920 had been appointed secretary to the Board's organizational meeting, served as BPR commissioner from 1955 to 1957, maintaining BPR's strong ties to the Board well into the late 1950s.[30]

ROY W. CRUM'S SEVEN PRINCIPLES

(Director, Highway Research Board, 1928–1951)

The secrets of TRB's success, as related by William N. Carey, Jr., on receiving the Roy W. Crum Distinguished Service Award for 1979.

1 Don't become elitist—the old-guard experts become outdated—make the young turks feel really at home.

2 Don't try to tell volunteer workers what to do—they know the problems and potential solutions better than you do.

3 The implementation of research results is the responsibility of the administrators. Researchers should try to ensure that their work is understood and then step aside.

4 Don't try to stamp out competition—if another organization is doing a job within your scope and doing it well, encourage them. There is more than enough for you to do.

5 In writing about technical matters, never use three syllables when two would do, or three words when two would do.

6 Get useful information out to the firing line.

7 Hire and keep staff who truly understand the place of TRB and the scheme of things and who are truly dedicated to the advancement of knowledge.

Source: "Roy W. Crum Award Given to William N. Carey, Jr.," *Transportation Research News*, March–April 1980, 11–12.

Crum's influence extended decades beyond his death. Both Burggraf and Carey, directors from 1951–1963 and 1966–1980, respectively, consciously modeled their tenures after Crum's example. Nearly 10 years after Crum's death and 4 years after MacDonald's, the Board dedicated its 40th Annual Meeting to their memory. As Burggraf stated simply during his address to the opening session, Crum was still "our beloved Director."[31] When Carey, close to retirement, received the Roy W. Crum Award for Distinguished Service at the 59th Annual Meeting, he used the occasion to share what Crum had meant to him and to the Board. Observing "this may be the last time for you to learn from one who worked for him," he continued, "If ever the nature, structure, and ideals of an organization are reflections of a single person, such is the case here." Carey then listed "Roy's basic principles," which had guided him and so many others as they had shepherded the Board through the tremendous opportunities and challenges of mid-20th-century transportation. These principles are reprinted above.[32]

CHAPTER 5

Cooperative Research and the AASHO Road Test, 1950–1962

THE DESIRE FOR larger and more elaborate field tests of pavement designs had motivated, in part, the development of the American Association of State Highway Officials' (AASHO's) 1948 procedure to pool funds for cooperative research. "Road tests" were not new, but had been limited to cooperative agreements between the federal government and the state in which the test roads or loops were constructed. The Bureau of Public Roads (BPR) had been conducting tests at Arlington Farms (now Turner-Fairbank Highway Research Center) in Virginia since 1919. For the Bates Road Test (1920–1923), the Illinois Division of Highways and BPR had built 2½ miles of test road consisting of six major types of pavement, let them weather for 2 years, and then drove heavy trucks over them until destroyed, proving that truck weight and solid rubber tires were destructive to roads. The Pittsburg Road Test (1921–1922) in California had been an early investigation of reinforced concrete pavement. Although the Advisory Board on Highway Research had tracked these tests closely, any advisory services rendered were informal.[1]

The road tests of the 1950s, culminating in the $27 million AASHO Road Test, brought the Highway Research Board back to highways' founding conundrum: the economics of trucks and freight movement. In ways strikingly similar to 1919, the Federal-Aid Highway Act of 1944 meant that the highway industry entered peacetime anticipating a highway building boom. The Board founded the Committee on Economics of Motor Vehicle Size and Weight in 1946, coming full circle to reembrace the contention of founding member Thomas R. Agg and first director William K. Hatt that the road and the vehicle needed to be considered together. Highway engineers, however, could not yet determine with any precision how the weight and frequency of truck traffic damaged pavements of different designs. Absent a better understanding, ascertaining the optimum economic case for freight movement by truck was impossible. The road tests, and their implications for the taxation of trucking, would eventually bring the Board to the attention of Congress as it debated the Federal-Aid Highway Act of 1956, the landmark law that increased gasoline taxes and created the Highway Trust Fund to accelerate construction of the rechristened National System of Interstate and Defense Highways.

The road tests of the 1950s were seeking the optimum point of balance between highway and trucking costs (HRB Special Report 73, 1962, 417).

Road Test One—Maryland and the WASHO Road Test

With the return to peace, truck traffic shot upward, doubling between 1945 and 1955, and the vehicles increased in size and weight. In 1946, AASHO recommended that state regulators maintain weight restrictions

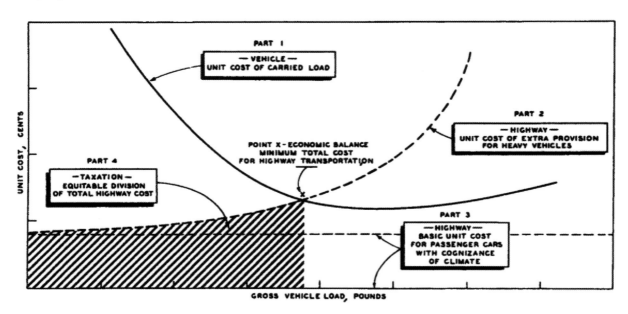

of 18,000 pounds per axle and 32,000 pounds per tandem axle. Before the war, only 13 axles per 1,000 trucks had been over this limit. By 1949 vehicle weight studies revealed excess weight on 86 axles per 1,000 vehicles. Indeed, Thomas MacDonald, concerned that the truck industry was increasingly carrying heavy freight formerly transported by rail, requested in 1948 that the Board reach out to the railroad industries about studies "from the standpoint of the welfare of transportation as a whole." No joint studies resulted from the requested outreach at the time.[2]

From the policy perspective, the objective in the ideal was the widespread adoption of uniform regulations of maximum truck size and weight that would be reflected in corresponding highway design standards, all paid for by "equitable taxation" on trucking. The Board's new motor vehicle economics committee studied how the operating costs of trucks varied with highway characteristics (chiefly hills and curves), while AASHO set out to conduct a new round of road tests on pavement design and damage from weight. State governors got involved too. The responsibility to regulate the use of vehicles typically fell outside the purview of highway departments, and vehicle regulations had economic development ramifications beyond the cost of building and maintaining highways.[3]

Regional coalitions of states organized the first two road tests. Because they were seeking the optimum regulation and taxation of vehicles, they limited the tests to common pavement designs. Eleven midwestern and eastern states and the District of Columbia collaborated on what came to be called Road Test One—MD. Using the AASHO procedure to pool funds, the Board launched the study in 1950. Fred Burggraf, who had worked on the Bates Road Test earlier in his career, served as chair of the test's advisory and executive committees, and BPR assigned its personnel as field researchers. The trucks came from seven different truck manufacturers, and 15 companies donated gasoline, oil, and grease. They tested four vehicle-load/axle combinations on a two-lane concrete highway, U.S. 301, constructed in 1941. The findings confirmed that modest increases in weight could cause dramatic increases in damage. Upon publication of the results in 1952, the Board celebrated Road Test One—

Highway leaders in the 1940s grew concerned that trucks were taking heavy loads formerly carried by trains (Chicago, 1943; Library of Congress, LC-DIG-fsac-1a34699).

The Hybla Valley Nonrigid Pavement Study, a cooperative project of the Bureau of Public Roads, the Asphalt Institute, and the Highway Research Board, under construction in 1949 (Bureau of Public Roads).

MD as "the greatest cooperative project ever undertaken in the field of highway research in this country."[4]

Even before Road Test One's results were in, AASHO encouraged other regions to organize road tests. The 12 states in the Western Association of State Highway Officials (WASHO) began planning the WASHO Road Test of flexible (asphalt) pavements in 1951. By constructing new roads for testing, the WASHO Road Test could also investigate a range of

Loops for the WASHO Road Test: The Highway Research Board conducted this test from 1952–1954 in Malad, Idaho (AASHTO).

pavement designs. Twelve states funded construction of two test loops in southern Idaho. Again, BPR contributed personnel, and motor truck and petroleum companies donated vehicles and fuel. Earle V. Miller, Idaho Department of Highways, chaired the advisory committee and William N. Carey, Jr., trained by Burggraf during the Maryland study, took over as study supervisor for the Board. The WASHO Road Test's published results came out in 1954 and 1955.[5]

Organizing the AASHO Road Test

The AASHO Road Test, which would end up costing two orders of magnitude more than the Maryland road test, started as the regional project of the Mississippi Valley Conference of State Highway Departments. As with the WASHO Road Test, planning began in 1951, but already AASHO members had an appetite to do something bigger. They aspired to build new test loops that would accommodate a wider range of both rigid and flexible pavement types and of axle loads. Crucially, some of the tested pavement designs would be purposely underdesigned, that is, designed to fail. The AASHO Committee on Bridges and Structures and the Board's motor vehicle economics committee also wanted in. Instead of planning the project regionally, AASHO's Committee on Highway Transport formed a national Working Committee that in addition to a cross-section of state highway engineers, included Carey for the Board and experts from BPR, Portland Cement Association, Asphalt Institute, American Trucking Associations, Automobile Manufacturers Association, National Highway Users Conference, and two branches of the Army. Subcommittees of the Working Committee were constituted just as broadly, including one subcommittee made up solely of representatives from motor vehicle manufacturers. Edwin A. Finney, director of the Michigan State Highway Department's research laboratory, chaired the Working Committee.[6]

At the request of AASHO, the Board created a short-lived Task Committee in late 1951 to write a research proposal, but AASHO's Working Committee led the detailed planning that took place from 1952 to 1955. The Working Committee chose the site, a stretch of land planned for Interstate 80 west of Ottawa, Illinois, in 1952. The Working Committee also drafted an increasingly detailed series of project programs that included cost estimates and a plan for sharing the costs among the states

Meeting of the AASHO Road Test National Advisory Committee, April 30, 1957: 200 volunteers served on the test's committees and panels and reviewed reports (AASHTO).

and private industries. In February 1955, with the states committed, AASHO formally requested that the Board administer and direct the AASHO Road Test. The National Academy of Sciences approved the request and also subsequently exercised approval authority over all appointments to Board committees, panels, and staffing. The Board opened a field office in Ottawa in July 1955 and the Illinois Division of Highways soon joined them to conduct preliminary planning and construction work.[7]

During 1955 and 1956, what had started as an $11 million research project grew to $27 million, in part because the AASHO Road Test became a mechanism to break a long-standing political stalemate in Congress over increased funding for the Interstate System. Although authorized in the Federal-Aid Highway Act of 1944, construction backlogs after World War II and then the Korean War had diverted the Truman administration's attention. Although the Eisenhower administration revived talks of accelerating construction of the Interstate System, congressional negotiations foundered over funding, in part because the American Trucking Associations had long opposed both tolls (which BPR also opposed) and differential—and higher—taxation on truck operations. To break what was shaping up to be another deadlock in 1956, the bill's leaders tempered proposals for new taxes on trucking and instead offered as a compromise a study on how to fairly allocate highway costs. The Federal-Aid Highway Act of 1956 called on BPR to conduct this cost allocation study in coordination with the Board and the AASHO Road Test. The law also singled out truck weight and width limitations for special treatment and instructed BPR to report to Congress the AASHO Road Test findings on "maximum desirable dimensions and weights for vehicles."[8]

To fulfill its congressional mandates, BPR requested two additional test loops for the AASHO Road Test, raising the total number to six. The 48 states, the District of Columbia, and the territories of Hawaii and Puerto Rico made individual payments totaling $11.82 million. BPR contributed $7.3 million, including roughly $1 million in services. Illinois fronted another $4 million for construction of lanes that the state planned to repurpose as I-80. The Automobile Manufacturers Association contributed $1.3 million and the American Petroleum Institute contributed $875,000. The Department of Defense loaned military personnel to drive the trucks, a service estimated to be worth nearly $1.5 million. Costs were roughly evenly split between construction of the test facility and building, operating, and conducting the research program.[9] But a true cost accounting could not be done, because it would require adding the value of the thousands of hours spent by upward of 200 volunteers serving on committees and panels and reviewing reports.[10]

In March 1956, the National Academy appointed Kenneth B. Woods, professor of highway engineering at Purdue University and chair of the Board's Executive Committee, to chair the AASHO Road Test's National Advisory Committee. In addition to being head of Purdue University's School of Civil Engineering, Woods directed the Joint Highway Research Project, a partnership between Indiana's Highway Commission and the university, which Hatt had founded in 1937 and recruited Woods to join in 1939. The Board had already awarded Woods its Distinguished Service Award in 1949, but a more telling precedent for his road test work was his award for best paper for the 1946 Annual Meeting. Authored with Harold S. Sweet and Tilton E. Shelburne, "Pavement Blowups Correlated with Source of Coarse Aggregate" used modern analysis of statistical correlations to rule out cement, fine aggregate, traffic, or subgrade soils as a cause of sudden pavement degradation, while determining that the correlation between blowups and coarse aggregate was "outstanding." Woods would guide the AASHO Road Test through to its completion in 1962.[11]

Expert panels began forming even before the formal appointment of the National Advisory Committee. At the request of the National Academy, the Board organized a panel of statisticians in 1955 and hired Paul E. Irick, then an associate professor in the Department of Statistics at Purdue University, to ensure that the project was designed and executed in ways supporting modern statistical analysis. In addition to expert panels on the highway and bridge elements, the Board also organized panels on data analysis and "public information." Another panel advised BPR on its cost allocation study. The National Advisory Committee had 34 slots for representatives from the states, BPR, the Army, and from the pavement, motor vehicle, trucking, and tire industries, plus a few academics. An 11-person steering committee, also chaired by Woods, allowed more frequent communication between the Board and the study's sponsors. To accommodate the AASHO constituency, they formed four regional advisory committees that each elected three representatives to serve on the National Advisory Committee.[13]

The National Advisory Committee took the problem definition and project purposes defined by AASHO's Working Committee and translated them into objectives that directed the research. AASHO defined the problem in terms of economics. It wanted to determine the "unit cost" of increased loads and stronger highways and the "basic unit highway cost" for highways carrying only passenger vehicles, so as to determine taxation or "the highway cost responsibility" of different types of highway users. Out of the AASHO Road Test, it wanted "facts" and "criteria" for the design, construction, and maintenance of pavements and bridges and "an engineering basis" for weight limitations and highway taxation. Reflecting a long-standing tradition between AASHO and the Board that AASHO recommended policy and set standards, the Board's research objectives discussed specifications such as "the number of repetitions of specified axle loads" and their "significant effects" on the "performance" of pavements and bridges.[14]

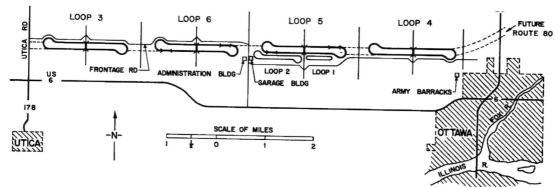

Figure 1. AASHO Road Test.

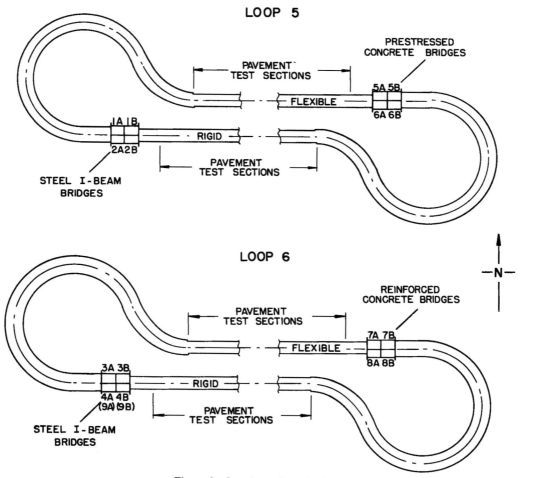

Figure 2. Locations of test bridges.

Map and design of loops and location of bridges for the AASHO Road Test in Ottawa, Illinois (HRB Special Report 73, 1962, 19–20).

In addition to Irick, the Board assembled a project staff carefully chosen to enhance the project's credibility. Walter McKendrick, Jr., had been chief engineer for the Delaware State Highway Department before taking on the position of project director. Carey, having completed the WASHO Road Test, became chief engineer for research, responsible for all the studies that eventually became Special Reports. Alvin C. Benkelman, engineer for flexible pavement, had been on BPR's team for its road tests, Road Test One, and the WASHO test. He was an old-school "man of the pavement," who valued close observation and walking a pavement to get its "feel." Like Irick and Carey, Frank Scrivner, the engineer for rigid pavements, was considered one of the mathematicians, well versed in the theories of stress and strain in concrete. James F. Shook, materials engineer and formerly with the National Sand and Gravel Association Laboratories, and his team were on the front lines making sure that materials met Irick's exacting uniformity standards.[15] In addition, the Road Test had access to consulting resident-observers from the Asphalt Institute, the Portland Cement Association, the American Trucking Associations, the Army, and from Canada and Germany.

Survey party working on an AASHO Road Test loop (AASHTO).

Construction of the loops began in August 1956 and test driving commenced in October 1958. At the project's peak, 170 researchers, technicians, mechanics, maintenance personnel, and clerical workers were employed in the field and 400 military personnel lived in the on-site barracks. To reach the goal of at least 1 million axle loads, drivers circled the test loops at 35 miles per hour for nearly 19 hours per day, 6 days per week—rising to 7 days per week in 1960—until hitting 1,114,000 axle loads on November 30, 1960. Ten different vehicle/load combinations, 16 bridges, and 836 randomly placed test sections meant that the traffic tests threw off an immense amount of data. Researchers designed instruments to electronically record as much of the data as possible, which was then processed for statistical analyses via a Bendix G 15-D computer on-site and the Datatron computer at Purdue University. Special studies continued on-site into 1961, while the researchers analyzed the test data. The field office closed in January 1962.[16]

AASHO Road Test Results

AASHO and the Board understood from the beginning that the Road Test was a public information minefield. Its unprecedented size and cost raised expectations, made even higher by Congress' inclusion of the Road Test in its mandated study on allocating highway costs. Beyond the policy implications, the Road Test had ventured into what the highway engineering community had long purposely avoided: the inclusion of roads and bridges designed to fail. Testing both flexible and rigid pavements, side by side, literally on the same loops only upped the public relations challenge. Rex M. Whitton, chief engineer for the Missouri State Highway Department, chaired the advisory panel on public information until he became Federal Highway Administrator in March 1961. The other members of this small panel were public relations specialists from the auto industry.

At AASHO's request, the Board adopted a public information strategy that broke with long-standing tradition and would end up fracturing long-standing relationships. No preliminary results were to be released or discussed publicly. In what was likely a coordinated effort, on January 13, 1961, BPR submitted its highway cost allocation study to Congress *without* the required AASHO Road Test results. The same day the Board's Executive Committee issued a statement "clarifying" that when the Board finally released the research reports, they would be providing only "engineering data" and "valid findings and conclusions" from "major experiments." The responsibility for answering the larger engineering and economic questions belonged to the study's sponsors. BPR did not submit the final piece of its cost allocation study to Congress until 1965, long after attention to the Road Test had waned.[17] Tensions with the Asphalt Institute and the Portland Cement Association over how to release the research results, however, grew to the breaking point. Desperate to get out in front of the findings, in March 1961 both organizations resigned from the Road Test and the Board's Executive Committee and withdrew their membership in the Board itself.[18]

The Board officially released the AASHO Road Test's results at a special conference held May 16–18, 1962, in St. Louis. Ralph R. Bartelsmeyer, chair of the Board's Executive Committee and, fittingly, chief engineer for the Illinois Division of Highways, presided. Reverend Ned Cole, dean of the city's Episcopal Cathedral, solemnized the occasion with an invocation for the 850 engineers, administrators, academics, and industry representatives in attendance. Despite the conference's size, Woods opened by emphasizing the importance of discussing all points of view in this forum and not later, in what he feared would be "a barrage of conflicting positions appearing in proprietary journals." After pleading with attendees to stay focused on the results, Woods explained that each day would end with an open period for discussion with no set time limit. The Board recorded all discussions and included transcripts in the conference proceedings, providing a remarkable record of how attendees received the results.[19]

Any hopes of leaving politics outside, however, were gone by the conference's second day. An editorial appearing that afternoon in the *St. Louis Post-Dispatch* not-so-helpfully outlined all the policy questions—from truck taxation to the choice of cement versus asphalt pavements—that the Road Test findings could guide. Making matters worse, the editorial took a direct swipe at the asphalt industry for lobbying that all highway pavement contracts be open to competitive bidding from both pavement types.[20]

By a quirk of the pavement experiments, although both the concrete and asphalt sections included a range of under- and overdesigned sections, the asphalt sections had had more failures. All of the concrete failures, moreover, had been preceded by "pumping," a phenomenon when the weight of moving vehicles causes the base underneath the concrete to erode. New techniques, which enjoyed wider adoption after the Road Test had been built, targeted such erosion. The asphalt industry was not pleased, and its representatives in the research community publicly announced that they thought the equations the Board's team had developed needed to be reworked. The concrete industry also protested, calling the implicit comparisons between plain and reinforced concrete unfair.[21]

The buzz of the conference, however, were the equations that described how pavement design inputs and traffic loads related to pavement deterioration. Even those who disagreed with their finer points conceded that the Road Test team had done something extraordinary in their creation. Edward H. Holmes, then assistant commissioner for research at BPR, spoke to his fellow men of the pavement who were uncertain about the paradigm shift that they were witnessing:

> We look with dismay on the bright young mathematicians who seemed to be way ahead of a lot of the older highway engineers. We question, perhaps, the way they handle the mathematics involved in strains, and stresses, and deflections, and other terms of that sort. Yet, the great importance of what they have done certainly should not be lost on any of us.

Moreover, the project had defined concepts such as load equivalency, pavement performance, and pavement serviceability in ways that allowed statistical analysis, recognized breakthroughs that were adopted the world over.[22]

The embrace of statistical rigor and exacting standards also led the researchers to adopt the caution of scientists in ways that clashed with the pragmatism of engineers. To the frustration of some attendees, the researchers insisted that the equations only reflected the specific materials, environments, and variables tested in Illinois, and they strongly cautioned against simply applying them to different circumstances. To critics such as California's respected asphalt engineer Francis N. Hveem, even worse was that the Road Test's most celebrated equations were correlations devoid of theory. The pavement serviceability index, for example, correlated the

When the AASHO Road Test's profilometer, which measured roughness, proved to be unnecessarily complex for routine use, William N. Carey, Jr., H. C. Huckins, and Rex C. Leathers, and other engineers invented the CHLOE profilometer, a simpler and more rugged device (Special Report 73, 1962, 126; Van pulling CHLOE profilometer, State Archives of Florida, Florida Memory, https://www.floridamemory.com/items/show/105566).

Marine Board

Ships, Ports, Offshore Energy, Safety, and Protecting the Environment

ALTHOUGH JOINING THE Transportation Research Board (TRB) in only 1999, today's Marine Board has its roots in the late 1940s, and it builds on a legacy of maritime research that dates back to 1863 and the founding of the National Academy of Sciences.

The modern era of maritime research began in the 1940s by providing advice on designing better ships. Committees formed within the National Research Council's (NRC's) Division of Engineering and Industrial Research on ship steel (1948) and ship structural design (1952) to advise an interagency committee of the Coast Guard, Navy, Maritime Administration, and American Bureau of Shipping.[a]

The National Academy then moved into logistics. Under a contract with the Office of Naval Research, NRC organized representatives of government and the shipping industries into the Maritime Cargo Transportation Conference (MCTC) during 1953 and in the late 1950s launched the Maritime Research Advisory Committee in response to the Maritime Administration's request for guidance. NRC consolidated all these activities in a new Maritime Transportation Research Board on October 9, 1961, under the directorship of Rear Admiral Edwin G. Fullinwider, retired from the Navy.

Even before the first commercial container ship, the *Ideal-X*, set out from Port Newark on

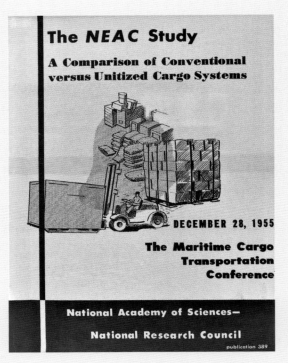

The NEAC Study, named after the Air Force's NorthEast Air Command, was part of a series of reports on the unitization of cargo produced by the Maritime Cargo Transportation Conference, a predecessor to today's Marine Board.

April 26, 1956, MCTC had begun issuing reports on the "unitization" of cargo, including using large metal boxes it initially called "transporters." MCTC produced a dozen reports on reducing the costs of cargo handling during 1954–1964. The largest project was a 5-year study of the San Francisco ports, and the study committee included representatives from the labor union and the Department of Labor as well as shippers and the military. Upon release of the San Francisco ports report in 1964, the Organization of American States sponsored its translation and distribution across Latin America.[b]

The National Academy of Engineering (NAE), founded in 1964, also looked to the oceans. What eventually became NAE's Marine Board started in 1965 as a Committee on Ocean Engineering. Its scope was broader than transportation, as it sought to "further the engineering application of oceanographic knowledge for the public welfare and defense." The Maritime Transportation Research Board and the Marine Board eventually merged in 1982.[c]

By the late 1980s, environmental issues had joined shipping economics as major areas of research for the Marine Board. Federal requests after the *Exxon Valdez* collided with a reef in March 1989, spilling 11 million gallons of oil into Prince William Sound, Alaska, prompted a series of studies on oil tanker design and safe navigation in the 1990s and beyond. In 2004, Congress directed the Coast Guard to adopt recommendations from *Environmental Performance of Tanker Design in Collision and Grounding* (TRB Special Report 259, 1991).

Numerous studies in recent years on offshore oil, gas, and wind energy production reflect the Marine Board's continued expertise in ocean engineering. After the April 20, 2010, blowout of the Macondo Well killed 11 workers on the *Deepwater Horizon* drilling rig and gushed oil into the Gulf of Mexico for months, the Department of the Interior sponsored a study, published in 2012, of its causes and means of prevention. Following up on its recommendations, the Marine Board and the National Acad-

emies of Sciences, Engineering, and Medicine's Board on Human-Systems Integration produced *Strengthening the Safety Culture of the Offshore Oil and Gas Industry* (TRB Special Report 321) in 2016.

Today's 20-member Marine Board continues to provide expertise in maritime transportation and marine engineering and technology. Geraldine Knatz, chair of the Marine Board 2005–2006, personifies TRB's intersection of research, practice, and public interest. After earning a Ph.D. in biological sciences, she rose through the ranks managing ports and was executive director of the Port of Los Angeles when awarded TRB's Thomas B. Deen Distinguished Lectureship in 2009. In the lecture, Knatz argued that "health impacts from ship and port operations cannot be discounted or justified by economic gains." She shared how ports can—and should—use their position as intermodal freight nodes to reduce air pollution and greenhouse gas emissions in the larger marine and surface transportation industries, while still expanding capacity for international trade.[d]

Federal agencies—Coast Guard, Army Corps of Engineers, Office of Naval Research, National Oceanic and Atmospheric Administration's National Ocean Service, Department of Transportation's Maritime Administration, the Department of the Interior's Bureau of Safety and Environmental Enforcement, and Navy's Supervisor of Salvage and Diving—sponsor the operations of the Marine Board. In addition, the Marine Group, part of TRB's technical activities, and its committees on ports and channels, inland water transportation, marine environment, and marine safety and human factors provide synergies and access to expertise in specific technical areas within the Marine Board's purview.

The AASHO Road Test also included tests of bridges (AASHTO).

design and load factors with subjective judgments of how pavements looked on their surface, without giving insight into the mechanisms causing failure.[23]

Despite the critiques, many others expressed excitement for what they recognized as the dawn of a new era of pavement research, if not transportation research. Research now meant that "staff at all levels found that it would be essential to become familiar with a new language, the language of the statistician," enthusiasts remembered. For F. H. Gardner, the engineer observer for the Army Transportation Corps, the Road Test was "the pinnacle of my 42 years in highway engineering." Echoing the engineers who founded the Board, Gardner continued, "we felt the burden of our responsibility, that we did not know what we were doing.... This is the first time I have felt that we were on the right road, finding out how to do our job."[24]

The bridge experiments did not attract the same controversy, perhaps because all of the bridges had been designed to fail and, after the traffic tests ended, were all stressed to failure. The Board's bridge committee, including Eric L. Erickson, chief of BPR's bridge division, had championed adding bridges in the Road Test back in 1951. More than 10 years later, Erickson opened the conference's bridge discussion by observing that "certainly it was demonstrated that overloading structures sufficiently is going to wreck them." Ivan M. Viest from the University of Illinois had led the bridge research on-site. Like the pavements, the 16 short-span bridges—8 steel beam, 4 concrete beam, and 4 reinforced-concrete beam—represented common designs and construction. Viest reported that the bridges performed as bridge theory predicted they would, a satisfying if anticlimactic result. Still, the bridge tests pointed the way to several modifications in design practices for AASHO to consider and, of course, fruitful directions for additional research.[25]

After an evening of congratulations alternating with frank, and sometimes brutal, assessments of the Road Test's methods and results, the Board teed up the final morning with reports from a select group that had already started to use the Road Test's findings and equations. Representatives from the New York State Thruway, the Illinois Division of Highways, the Texas Highway Department, and others described how to adapt the results to different situations, and the conference report includes lengthy appendixes of graphs, charts, and summary sheets ready for use, including for cost allocation studies. Both the AASHO Committee on Design and the AASHO Committee on Highway Transport also shared how they planned to incorporate the findings into their design procedures and vehicle size and weight recommendations.[26] In fact, AASHO's Committee on Design had already produced interim guides for flexible pavements and rigid pavements in October 1961 and in April 1962. They remained in use, and in interim form, until the 1980s.[27]

A Changed Highway Research Board

The AASHO Road Test's immersive experience affected a generation of researchers. Cohorts of young BPR engineers spent 6 months in Ottawa as part of their training. After the Road Test's completion, the research team dispersed to universities and research organizations. Burggraf called being unable to keep the Road Test researchers together a "great personal regret." Holmes, however, foresaw already in 1962 that the dispersal of its researchers would lead to a blossoming of research across the country, as people continued to evaluate "the great volume of data" that were "just crying for further exploration" and extended the original Road Test experiments. Carey returned to Washington, D.C., to be the Board's second in command. Irick also stayed on and soon headed up the Board's new special projects division dedicated to in-house research.[29]

Highway Research Board Director Fred Burggraf, known for his active interest in encouraging students and young engineers, chats with students at a BPR training program, 1954 (*Ideas & Actions*, 140).

The AASHO Road Test, however, was the end of an era defined by a cooperative ethos—embedded in the Board at its founding—that government and private industry should literally pool resources to solve the major problems of the day. This ethos depended on a shared belief that research, properly done, could transcend economic realities. The Board's structure—as a federation of member organizations—was increasingly out of sync with the rest of the National Research Council (NRC). In 1960, the Executive Committee got word that NRC's Governing Board had revived talk of spinning off the Highway Research Board as an independent organization. Woods, in a passionate defense of staying, argued, "Well I have said many times that if the Highway Research Board ceases to be a member of the Academy—Research Council I think it's done. I think the National Research Council is the reason that it has survived." The Board agreed to integrate itself into NRC, and bylaws adopted in October 1962 fundamentally changed the Board's structure. No longer would member organizations control the Executive Committee, which would instead be appointed by NRC and essentially advisory to the executive director and the National Academy.[30]

For Carey, the AASHO Road Test was formative to his sense of the proper role of both research and the Board. When he led the Board through the troubled waters ahead to its eventual transformation to the Transportation Research Board (TRB), he had a particularly acute sense of which transportation questions were amenable to research and which ones were matters of policy that research may inform, but will not resolve. Twenty years would pass before TRB proposed another blockbuster research program rivaling the AASHO Road Test. TRB would continue—even expand—cooperative approaches to research, but in less naïve forms. It would develop cooperative processes balanced by procedures filled with "checks and balances" that protected the research process from bias. Indeed, Holmes excitedly announced at the AASHO Road Test conference that the National Cooperative Highway Research Program was on its way.[31]

CHAPTER 6

Urban and Legal Research and the Origins of NCHRP, 1950–1974

FOR REX M. WHITTON, federal highway administrator, the St. Louis location of the American Association of State Highway Officials (AASHO) Road Test conference in May 1962 made his appearance there a celebratory homecoming. Whitton had joined the Missouri Highway Department just days after graduating from the University of Missouri in 1920. In 1951, he rose to chief engineer. His work preparing for the AASHO Road Test brought him into national leadership roles, first as AASHO's president in 1956 and then as chair of the Highway Research Board's Executive Committee in 1957. Whitton used the release of the results of the largest highway research project ever completed to urge investment in even more research.

Research funding, Whitton warned that day, was "ridiculously small in comparison with the billions being invested in highway construction." A fixed percentage of highway funding should be dedicated to research, he exhorted to the highway leaders in his audience. Moreover, this research should not limit itself to physical research, but should encompass studies of human behavior, land use, employment, and new technologies such as electronic controls. Governments needed to tackle what he termed "clearly a supreme challenge to research": moving people and goods in cities. One month later, the National Academy of Sciences (NAS), AASHO, and the Bureau of Public Roads (BPR) signed the three-party agreement creating the National Cooperative Highway Research Program (NCHRP).[1]

Highway officials in the 1940s had not anticipated the population and economic boom of the 1950s. Indeed, 1944's *Interregional Highways*, outlining the Interstate System, got its start as a plan for a postwar jobs program in anticipation of the return of Depression economics. As the baby boom hit its stride, the American population continued to urbanize. From 1950 to 1955, the 168 metropolitan areas with core cities of more than 50,000 captured 98 percent of the country's population growth. Within metropolitan areas, however, suburbanization ruled. Not just housing, but shopping and employment decentralized, often finding attractive locations along new suburban expressways such as Boston's Route 128, a circumferential highway that opened in 1951. Retail sales in downtowns stagnated. Car ownership shot up, while transit use plummeted, falling 25 percent between 1950 and 1955 in even the largest cities. Thomas MacDonald's "avalanche" of motor vehicles had returned. Unlike in 1920, this time the pattern of travel was decidedly urban.[2]

These trends were in full flower before the Federal Aid Highway Act of 1956 accelerated construction of the Interstates and designated more than half of its funding for routes in the burgeoning metropolises. Congress also gave state highway officials a budget and a deadline, originally just 13 years. State highway officials responded with a mix of solemn determination and panic, and AASHO released *A Policy on Arterial Highways in Urban Areas* (the "Red Book") in 1957, its first policy on urban highways. As Alfred E. Johnson, AASHO's executive director, explained to a group of state highway and municipal officials in 1958, the acceleration of Interstate construction "came about with such suddenness that some were not prepared for it. Both state highway officials and local authorities must nonetheless do the best they can to produce sensible, forward-looking plans to coordinate highway and general urban development."[3]

Throughout the 1950s and early 1960s, AASHO and BPR would use the Board to study urbanization, coordinate planning for urban transportation, and improve highway laws. The Board's expansion into urban and legal research in the 1950s would also be important precedents for

NCHRP. With the Board's staff focused on the road tests, much of this new activity would happen through the efforts of volunteers and contracted researchers, supported by the Automotive Safety Foundation (ASF) and spurred on by the highest levels of NAS.

The Problems of the Metropolis

The Board had long made room for studies touching on urban transportation, despite the limitations linked to funneling federal aid to states through, until 1939, the Department of Agriculture. Traffic surveys and highway finance studies made little sense without including urban traffic. Pedestrian safety and even the benefits of one-way streets made

From left, Kenneth B. Woods, leader on the AASHO Road Test; Edward H. Holmes, BPR's assistant commissioner for research; and Rex M. Whitton, Executive Committee chair and future federal highway administrator, at the 1958 Annual Meeting (TRB).

appearances at the annual meeting as early as 1923. The dangers to people walking influenced the Board's expansion into safety studies in the late 1930s, a time when the Board also had project committees studying pedestrian walk signals, yellow signals in stop lights, one-way streets, and near-side versus far-side bus stops. Parking became an increasing focus in the 1940s, including the potential for "fringe parking" to feed mass transit service into downtowns. To be sure, in the full spectrum of the Board's activities, urban transportation had only a minor place. In 1939, the soils department alone supported 29 project committees and subcommittees.[4]

What distinguished the Board's forays into urban transportation in the 1950s was that pressure started to build for the Board to organize at least a part of itself around not just traffic control, but the transportation needs of cities. Some of the push to embrace cities came from NAS's president, Detlev Bronk. A physiologist who had pioneered advances in biophysics, Bronk had trained as an airplane pilot during World War I and was a leader in aviation medicine during World War II. He became the National Research Council (NRC) chair in 1946 and the NAS president in 1950, serving until 1962. Bronk worked to integrate NRC more closely

NAS President Detlev Bronk speaking at the 1954 Annual Meeting (George Kalec).

into NAS and put science into service to society. He took special delight in challenging NRC's highway engineers to think broadly about the future of highways and the welfare of people.[5]

Bronk's addresses at the Board's annual meetings sparked reflection and action among the Board's leaders. At the 33rd Annual Meeting in January 1954, Bronk differentiated NAS from other scientific societies, which he thought were dangerously trending toward specialization, because "we are an organization for the synthesis of science," that is, moreover, "dedicated to the translation of science into the social welfare." Directly addressing "the problems of the metropolis," Bronk laid down the challenge: "If we are to make our cities more satisfying places in which to work and live, we shall require your assistance; for I need not remind you of the desperately difficult transportation problems which confront every modern center of population."[6]

Meeting just a few days later, both Pyke Johnson, representing ASF, and Herbert S. Fairbank, deputy commissioner at BPR, pushed the Board to form an Urbanization Research Committee.[7] Bronk was not alone in his crusade, but part of major national-level policy conversations about the future of cities that played out most significantly in introducing urban redevelopment and planning into the Housing Act of 1949 and urban renewal into the Housing Act of 1954. NRC quickly organized a meeting of all its divisions on the problems of urbanization. Although the divisions representing psychology and anthropology, biology and agriculture, geology and geography, engineering, and medical sciences agreed to assist, the consensus was that the Board should take the lead. The Board organized a 2-day conference on urbanization that April, bringing together 22 urban highway and traffic experts and representatives from the American Transit Association, the federal Housing and Home Finance Agency, Brookings Institution, and the Urban Land Institute, the research arm of the real estate industry.[8]

Upon receiving the urbanization conference's report, members of the Board's Executive Committee reacted in ways ranging from concern to bafflement. The conference had agreed that NRC should take on urban transportation research, but had concluded that it should be organized *outside* of the Board. Urban transportation, the conference had advised, was not just a list of problems to be solved. Instead, transportation was "only one phase" of the many "urban complexes" that needed to be integrated. Moreover, even for urban transportation, there was a desperate need for "a comprehensive approach … through organized research among all the disciplines involved." Even something as seemingly straightforward as ascertaining the relationships between the use of land and the movement of people and freight was actually caught up in the much larger processes of "urban redevelopment, dispersion, decentralization, or the development of new cities."[9]

The Board's Executive Committee did not agree, in an early appearance of what would be a long-running, sometimes heated, debate within NRC and at times the highest levels of government over how to organize research about cities and the appropriate place of highways in such research efforts. The Board's Executive Committee believed that either the Board should take charge of urban transportation or NRC should form a separate urbanization research effort, with which the Board would coordinate. D. Grant Mickle took on the task of forming a Special Committee on Urbanization Research for the Board with seed funding promised by ASF.[10]

ASF, funded by motor vehicle manufacturers and related industries, supported the early stages of many Board initiatives in the 1950s. Johnson, in his constant presence for more than 40 years including as chair of the Executive Committee in 1960, linked the Board to ASF's original parent organization, the National Automobile Chamber of Commerce, one of the Board's founding organizations. Mickle too would be a continuing bridge between the Board and ASF. He had built a career in traffic engineering, rising to director of traffic engineering for the city of Detroit, before joining ASF in 1943 to organize its traffic engineering division. He would become deputy federal highway administrator in 1961 and lead the Board as executive director in 1964, before returning to ASF in 1966 and chairing the Board's Executive Committee in 1970.[11]

ASF directed its contributions to the Board to studies on economics, planning, and safety. In the early 1950s, ASF provided $75,000 for a major series of studies on parking and retail sales in both downtown and suburban locations. Published in five parts from 1953 to 1956, the studies surveyed shoppers' attitudes, spending habits, and choice of travel mode and parking facility, and also examined corporate decisions about store locations. The researchers even conducted small before-and-after studies on the impact of expanding parking. The conclusions were ambivalent. Parking appeared to be only one factor, and an inconsistent one at that, among the many factors affecting downtown shopping districts.[12]

For the Board, however, the parking studies had marked an important expansion in topics and constituencies and a shift in research activities. Instead of a project spurred and managed by one of the Board's technical committees, ASF was clearly the client. Mickle chaired a large advisory group made up of representatives from all the industries involved, including transportation, municipal government, real estate, and consumer goods. AASHO and BPR participated, but as two organizations among many. An assigned project engineer managed the studies, but the Board contracted the research to the business schools of five universities.[13]

Urbanization Research and Urban Transportation

Seed funding from ASF allowed the Board to form a Special Committee on Urbanization Research in 1955. Although the committee shortened its name to simply Urban Research, urbanization of what it called the "urban-rural fringe" still captured a great deal of attention. At 30 members, plus 4 liaisons with other NRC divisions, the unusually large committee included only 3 with ties to state highway departments, one of whom was Whitton. E. Willard Dennis, the committee's chair, worked at Sibley, Lindsay, and Curr Company, a New York department store chain. More than half of the committee's members were connected to city planning, regional planning, city management, or the development of housing or stores. The academics too included experts, such as the sociologist Amos Hawley, the geographer Harold M. Mayer, and the demographer Donald J. Bogue, who were authorities on metropolitan growth and change. These three and others, moreover, constituted a critical mass hailing from northeastern Illinois, including J. Douglas Carroll who had recently moved from Detroit to direct what would become the landmark Chicago Area Transportation Study.[14]

The Board's Committee on Urban Research soon connected with the National Committee on Urban Transportation (NCUT). Formed in 1954 with representatives from BPR and eight American and

Canadian organizations related to managing local governments, NCUT had embarked on an ambitious project to prepare studies and plans to meet the "total transportation needs" of urban areas, as a representative explained to the Board's Executive Committee in June 1955. With the Federal-Aid Highway Act of 1956 suddenly adding even more urgency and ASF providing support, NCUT, ASHO, BPR, and the Board produced three major reports on urban transportation in 1958 and 1959: a how-to guide for urban transportation planning, a policy statement on state-local relations, and a brief on research needs.[15]

Better Transportation for Your City: A Guide to the Factual Development of Urban Transportation Plans (1958), produced by NCUT with the Board, AASHO, ASF, and the American Transit Association among its consulting organizations, advocated for a comprehensive approach to urban transportation planning. Remarkably thorough considering that it is less than 100 pages, the *Guide* stepped decision makers through the phases of the rational planning process: initial organization, fact-finding across modes, using service standards and land use plans to identify deficiencies and forecast future travel, preparing the plan, gaining plan approval, and finally "putting the plan to work." Mass transit and walking were not left out either, with studies and recommended standards

During the 1950s, the Board led and participated in studies of the urban–rural fringe and mass suburbanization. The Southdale Shopping Center, Edina, Minnesota, in 1956, the year it opened, and in 1966 (background), with buildings of a newly built medical center in the foreground (Minnesota Historical Society).

addressing their needs. The *Guide*'s technical committees also read like a Who's Who of the Board's volunteers, including a half-dozen past and future chairs of the Executive Committee and Alan M. Voorhees, who would be chair in 1972, then with ASF and the lead consultant on the project.[16]

The Board's Committee on Urban Research had a more direct role in the Sagamore (National) Conference on Highways and Urban Development, held in October 1958. The 5-day conference was a joint production of the Board's committee, the American Municipal Association's and AASHO's joint committee on highways, and Syracuse University, with funding from ASF. They brought together 55 officials from state highway departments, municipal governments, and civic leaders to hammer out a mutual understanding of roles and responsibilities for highway building in urban areas. The state highway leaders espoused a cooperative approach. They encouraged communities to take the lead in community and regional planning and hoped that local communities would respect that Congress had charged the states with taking the lead on Interstate Highway development.[17]

Whereas the *Guide* was a confident set of instructions for comprehensive planning for urban transportation, and the Sagamore Conference was at least hopeful about cooperative planning between state and local governments, the Board's own special report was much more sobering. Unusually, the Committee on Urban Research had commissioned an assessment from an outside expert, Coleman Woodbury, noted authority on housing and urban development from the University of Wisconsin. *A Framework for Urban Studies: An Analysis of Urban-Metropolitan Development and Research Needs* (Special Report 52, 1959) concluded that "shockingly little" research was being done in response to America's "exploding metropolises." Woodbury warned that both general theories of urban development and sound practices for urban planning were lacking. No solid foundation existed on which to build more specific studies of urban transportation.[18]

Woodbury's list of "policy questions re urban circulation" anticipated many of the challenges, including racial segregation, that would confront urban transportation in the coming decades. The location of expressways, he called, "a difficult and troublesome task" that was "a prime example of a problem that never can be solved by studies," although research was still needed "to enlighten and guide judgment." On mass transit, he lamented that research and policy had fallen into the trap of "constantly viewing the motor car and mass transit as natural enemies locked in a death struggle," instead of researching how they "might most effectively share the job of moving people (and goods)." He highlighted the need for studies of land use patterns and pegged new travel patterns, such as reverse commuting and intersuburban trips, as needing research. Finally, he worried about displacement. Urban expressways, along with urban redevelopment, were displacing homes, businesses, and communities on a scale unprecedented for American cities. Ad hoc responses would be inadequate, he warned, especially for African Americans, Puerto Ricans, and other low-income residents and businesses who would have difficulty relocating "because of racial and ethnic segregation practices."[19]

The Board's Committee on Urban Research also successfully introduced sessions on urban research at the annual meeting in 1958, at which President Bronk once again challenged the attendees to consider "what is to be the pattern of urban living," given "the great highways which you are building." But within a year, the Committee on Urban Research had exhausted its funding and the question of how to organize—and get sponsorship for—urban research within NRC was still unsettled.[20] The committee released *Framework for Urban Studies* with the hopes that it would inspire graduate students, researchers, and institutions to respond to "the severity of the need for urban research" to help guide "the judicious decisions so urgently wanted and needed in all aspects of urban life."[21]

AASHO and BPR could not wait, however, for NRC to move forward on urban research. A worried Whitton pointed out during the Board's June 1960 Executive Committee meeting that the state highway departments were spending millions to locate expressways in cities *now*. Harmer E. Davis, chair of the Executive Committee in 1959, too urged that the Board "should lose no time pursuing vigorously the transportation aspects of urban development." Indeed, AASHO had just that week established its own Operating Committee on Urban Transportation Planning. In June 1961, the Board followed suit, transforming its Committee on Urban Research that served all of NRC to a Special Committee on Urban Transportation Research.

Schuylkill Expressway (I-676) connects Center City and Philadelphia's northern and western suburbs, 1973 (U.S. National Archives, 412-DA-10227).

NCHRP's First Report

The Search for Inert and Innocuous Aggregate That Launched a Career

From extensive laboratory research and careful observation of field performance has come a realization that the aggregate phase of portland cement concrete is neither dependably inert nor inherently innocuous, as was once commonly supposed.[a]

THE FIRST SENTENCE of the first report to be published with funding from the National Cooperative Highway Research Program (NCHRP) will not be found in an NCHRP report. Thomas D. Larson, only a year after completing his Ph.D., led a group of young engineers at The Pennsylvania State University, including Philip Cady, M. Franzen, and Joseph Reed, in producing what was only supposed to be an interim report for NCHRP. Instead, their work was honored with publication as the Highway Research Board's 80th Special Report.

Tilton E. Shelburne, the first and longtime head of research at the Virginia Department of Highways, chaired the advisory committee for NCHRP 4-3: Development of Methods to Identify Aggregate Particles Which Undergo Destructive Volume Changes When Frozen in Concrete, and E. A. Whitehurst, University of Tennessee, chaired its Panel on Beneficiation of Aggregates. They were so impressed with the interim report from Larson's team, they did not want to wait until the final report for publication.[b]

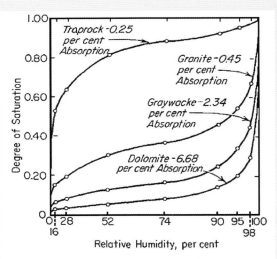

Fig. 1.—The Degree of Saturation Attained by Aggregates at Various Humidities Differs Widely and Reflects Their Different Pore Size Distributions.

For discrimination the scale for relative humidity has been plotted as proportional to (% RH)^2.

A graph illustrating how aggregates respond to humidity from G. Verbeck and R. Landgren, "Influence of Physical Characteristics of Aggregates on Frost Resistance of Concrete," *ASTM Proceedings* 60 (1960, 1063–1079), an article included in Special Report 80's annotated bibliography (reprinted with permission from ASTM International).

NCHRP was not ready to publish yet, so the Board's Special Report series stepped in. In addition to a 41-page annotated bibliography, Special Report 80 covers the history and current theory of freezing-and-thawing effects, summarizes methods to identify frost-susceptible aggregates, and recommends areas for research.

Larson was at the beginning of a relationship with TRB that would last more than four decades. After founding the Pennsylvania Transportation Institute at Penn State, he was tapped by Pennsylvania Governor Richard Thornburgh to be secretary of transportation, a position he filled from 1979 to 1987. He served as TRB chair in 1981 and chaired the steering committee for *America's Highways: Accelerating the Search for Innovation* (Special Report 202, 1984), the report that laid the groundwork for the first Strategic Highway Research Program.[c]

Larson went on to serve as the American Association of State Highway and Transportation Officials president (1986) and as federal highway administrator (1989–1993) in the Department of Transportation, where he played a significant role in shaping and then implementing the Intermodal Surface Transportation Efficiency Act (1991).[d]

Larson stayed connected to TRB well into his retirement. Forty years after HRB published Special Report 80, Larson shared his favorite model for successful leadership and management in an essay in *TR News*. His final sentence: "Has there ever been a time when these were needed more?"[e]

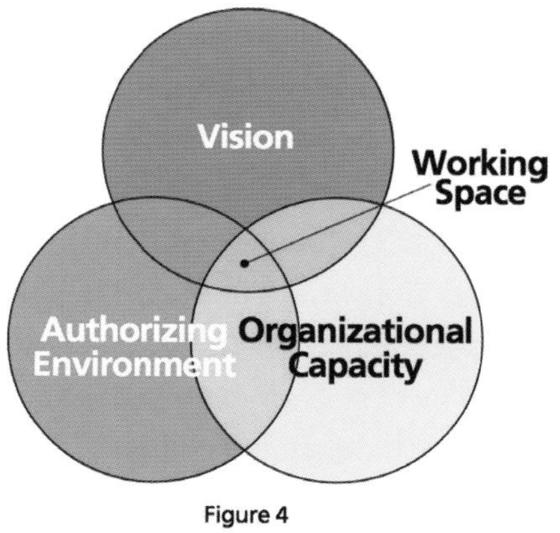

Figure 4

Diagram illustrating Larson's recommended model for leadership and management (*TR News*, November–December 2004, 16).

AASHO's focus on urban transportation continued too, and it emphasized urban transportation problems in the new NCHRP's second slate of research problems. In June 1963, the Executive Committee elevated urban transportation planning to a full department. By 1966, the new department had six committees and 148 slots for volunteers.[22]

The urban transportation activities cultivated by ASF, NCUT, BPR, AASHO, and the Board in the 1950s set the stage for the landmark "3 C" transportation planning process mandated in the Federal Aid Highway Act of 1962. The 3 Cs—continuing, comprehensive, and cooperative planning—carry through to today, structuring the policy foundation that organizes federal support for metropolitan planning and defines federal–state–local relationships for urban transportation.

In confronting the problem of the exploding metropolis, both Whitton and D. Grant Mickle had benefited from and used the Board's institutional structures and resources. Whitton had been one of the few from state highway departments on the Board's Committee on Urban Research, and he also attended the Sagamore Conference. He brought Mickle with him as his deputy when he became federal highway administrator in 1961. Whitton, moreover, would organize an Office of Planning and an Office of Highway Safety and bring into the agency civil rights specialists and behavioral scientists.[23]

Highway Law and Legal Resources

ASF was also instrumental in institutionalizing legal studies within the Board. Louis R. Moroney spearheaded the effort. An attorney, he headed Michigan's Motor Vehicle Department and helped organize the American Association of Motor Vehicle Administrators before moving to ASF after World War II to direct its law division. The Board's law project, at first, followed a tried and true path. In 1951, AASHO requested that the Board conduct a study of state laws relevant to highways. The Board hesitated: this would be a huge and unfamiliar undertaking. North Dakota, however, soon provided a model for success. Like most states, North Dakota's body of highway law had evolved as a mishmash of incremental changes. They were not even sure, for example, that they had the legal authority to stop farmers from planting crops in the right-of-way. The state formed a legislative research committee and over a year and a half developed a comprehensive modernization of relevant laws, which its state legislature readily adopted.[24]

The Board's new Committee on Highway Laws, chaired by Moroney, set out in 1954 to help other states repeat North Dakota's success. The committee produced its first report, on the relocation of public utilities, in 1955. The pace possible with volunteers, however, was clearly too slow, especially once the Federal Aid Highway Act of 1956 was posed to accelerate Interstate construction. With funding from ASF and BPR, the Board founded the Highway Laws Project and hired five attorneys to conduct the studies. AASHO advised which topics to prioritize and funded years 2 and 3 of the project. The states each contributed a set of their relevant laws and designated "legal liaisons" in addition to their regular contact men. When completed in 1960, the project had produced reports or memoranda covering 28 topics on everything from expressway law to billboards and eminent domain to system classification.[25]

Upon completion of the Highway Laws Project, its committee kept the momentum going by becoming a special committee of the Board in 1961 and organizing what would become an annual workshop, first held in July 1962. AASHO arranged to fund the Board's expansion into law with a 10 percent increase in the states' annual contributions to the Research Correlation Service. In June 1963, the Board promoted "legal studies" to department status, making a commitment to full-time professional staff.[26]

Morony continued to push the Board to expand its legal activities, organizing a new Committee on Motor Vehicle and Traffic Law in 1965. He took advantage of the Board's home within NRC to bring together researchers in public health, psychology, and behavioral sciences, as well as engineers, administrators, and even judges. Morony, nearing retirement, also recruited the next generation of attorneys to the Board, including a member of his staff, Victor J. Perini, Jr. When interviewed by *TR News* 20 years later, Perini still remembered how impressed and inspired he was at that first meeting to be mixing with a cross section of professionals and scholars all focused on motor vehicle safety.[27]

HIGHWAY RESEARCH BOARD ANNUAL MEETING

1956

DATES January 17–20, 1956
LOCATION Sheraton-Park Hotel
PRESIDING CHAIR G. Donald Kennedy, Portland Cement Association

ATTENDANCE 1,520
NUMBER OF PAPERS 196
ORGANIZATION OF TECHNICAL ACTIVITIES
Six departments hosting 66 technical committees

TOPICS
• Urban transportation
• Bridge tolls
• Future traffic predictors
• Moisture movement through soils
• Structural adequacy of highway bridges

ON THE MOVE Hotel required, as the meeting had outgrown the NAS building
ROAD TESTS Opening General Session shows a film of the WASHO Road Test

WHAT ELSE IS HAPPENING AT HRB IN 1956?
• Construction begins on the AASHO Road Test
• The five staff engineers make 172 visits to state highway departments and universities

Setting the Stage for NCHRP

Ideas & Actions, the history that the Board produced for its 50th Anniversary, contains a simple origin story for the Board's NCHRP. Edward H. Holmes, BPR's assistant commissioner for research, and Alfred E. Johnson, AASHO's executive director, were chatting one day in the late 1950s about Johnson's recent discovery that 32 state highway departments were researching the same problem! Duplication, a frustration dating back to the Board's founding, was once again undermining research progress. Out of their conversation, NCHRP was born. Without a doubt, many conversations of this type were likely to have occurred in the late 1950s, just as they had arisen many times before. But they alone do not provide an explanation for how this time an oft-repeated conversation led to the founding of a multi-million-dollar annual research program that would thrive for more than 50 years.[28]

When the Board began another of its periodic examinations of highway research needs in 1958, the activities catalyzed by AASHO and ASF during the 1950s had already expanded the universe of what the Board's leaders thought possible. The cooperative agreement of 1948 had resolved long-standing barriers to pooling state funds and led to the road tests. Studies such as the ASF-funded parking project had given the Board additional experience managing client-initiated research projects conducted by third parties. The Highway Laws Project had developed mechanisms for AASHO to choose research topics on a rolling basis. ASF funding had also shown the utility of quickly mobilizing research funds.

In addition, in 1956 the Board had reorganized the Executive Committee. They expanded it to 19 members and reduced the chair's term to 1 year. Former chairs served ex officio for 2 years after their term. By creating slots for a first and second vice chair and providing an order of succession, the Executive Committee would always have at least three members in leadership roles. The Executive Committee also created committees to improve its operations. In addition to the long-standing Ways and Means Committee, it formed committees on research interpretation and dissemination, research needs and project initiation, and publication policies. The Executive Committee continued to add members, rising to 21 in 1957 and 25 in 1961. With the October 1962 reorganization of the Board from a federation of organizations to a committee fully of NRC, there was no longer an inherent limit on the size of the Executive Committee. In 1969, it reached 28 members.[29]

With more hands on deck, the Executive Committee entered into a period of strategically driven change. Out of its efforts, for example, came a complete revamping of publications. Since the start of the Research Correlation Service (RCS), published pages had grown from 1,000 to 10,000 pages a year. In response to their own contribution to the mid-century information explosion, the Board capped total published pages and instituted more rigorous review standards. In 1963, it eliminated the annual meeting *Proceedings*, transformed *Highway Research Board Bulletin* into *Highway Research Record*, and introduced *Highway Research News*. In addition, the Board hired the long-sought-after public information officer, who turned *Highway Research News* into a true news magazine and introduced the Board's first logo in 1965. Although "HRB" was now an acceptable moniker, few of the Board's old-timers used the acronym.[30]

The Federal Aid Highway Act of 1956 had also pushed the panic button for those involved in traditional areas of highway research, just like it had for those responsible for urban and legal problems. When Johnson, as chair of the research needs and project initiation committee, made his report to the Executive Committee in June 1958, he framed its recommendations in response to "the largest road building program in the history of the world." His committee, as had been traditional practice, had collected research needs lists from the Board's six departments and from BPR. The items on the seven lists varied in specificity from simply calling for studies of "safety" to research into "overhead sign supports" and "cost of turnover in state highway department engineering and technician positions." Other than very rough cost estimates—$19.5 million to $36 million in total—no other detail was provided or prioritization indicated.[31]

What distinguished the effort, however, was Johnson's and the committee's recommended next steps. Instead of settling for an ad hoc publicity effort, the committee recommended that the Board advocate for the research needs list to be turned into a true research program that identified priorities and proposed a funding mechanism. Specifically, the committee recommended that the Board should work to persuade the state highway departments to not only make their own survey of highway research needs, but also "to pledge a substantial part of their 1½ percent funds annually to this work." The committee also recommended that a strategically small project committee—five "top research men" only—be responsible for shaping the research program proposal.[32]

The Holmes Report

The Executive Committee enthusiastically accepted the research needs committee's recommendations and appointed BPR's Edward H. Holmes to chair the committee that would produce what would come to be known as the "Holmes Report" (officially, *Highway Research in the United States: Needs, Expenditures and Applications*, Special Report 55). This landmark report broke new ground in three important ways. It led to the standardization of research needs statements. It proved it feasible for state highway administrators to collectively prioritize research projects. Finally, it conducted a census of research implementation.

On the five-member committee, Harmer E. Davis, founding director of the Institute of Transportation and Traffic Engineering at the University of California since 1948, was the lone university researcher. An expert in concrete and asphalt pavements and concrete structures, he was also a member of the Board's Committee on Urban Research, played a leadership role in the Sagamore Conference on urban planning, and would chair the Executive Committee in 1959. Holmes too had participated in the Board's urban research initiatives. Researchers affiliated with state highway departments held the other three slots. William A. Bugge, director of highways in Washington State and chair of the Executive Committee in 1961 and Fred V. Reagel, engineer of materials and tests in Missouri and who had been instrumental to the cooperative agreement to pool state funds for research projects, stayed with the project to its completion.[33]

The Holmes committee, with the cooperation of the states and many university engineering departments, conducted a thorough survey of research spending. The fiscal analysis was aimed at calculating one number: the percentage of total highway expenditures going into research annually, which they astonishingly concluded was less than 0.2 percent. They also gathered 101 more detailed—and newly standardized—research problem statements from the Board's departments. In what Johnson would call, in his dramatic retelling of the Holmes Report in his 1961 chair's address—"a cold appraisal of the field for broadened research"—the committee decided at its first meeting to assign research

Charley V. Wootan (center), Texas Transportation Institute, works with Texas Highway Department engineers on a study of the land use impacts of freeways and rural highways in the early 1960s. Wootan would chair TRB's Executive Committee in 1980 (Texas A&M Transportation Institute).

priorities solely from the perspective of the state highway administrators. The committee would only recommend research that, as its members phrased it, "will pay dividends." (This was not without controversy; all 101 problem statements ended up in an appendix to the Holmes Report.) The committee circulated a list of 17 research problem areas, with rough budgets, to state highway engineers and administrators for feedback, augmentation, and ranking, and eventually included 19 "adjudged to rate A-1 in importance and urgency" in the Holmes Report.[34]

The Holmes committee coordinated its work with a Board-led project documenting "applications of highway research findings." RCS engineers collected 348 examples from 47 states. They found, disappointingly, that state highway departments did not regularly track or assess the benefits of research in quantitative form (e.g., cost savings or time savings). They were able to conclude, however, that many states had institutionalized the review and adoption of research findings. More than half of the Holmes Report contains the list of the 348 research applications, complete with problem descriptions, research impact, and references to the actual research report or project.[35]

These activities, and the enormous amount of work involved, were all part of building the persuasive case, and the Executive Committee was going to leave little to chance. Upon receiving the Holmes Report in June

1959, the Executive Committee resolved that its aim was nothing less than "to achieve maximum results in advancing and expediting needed researches … and enabling the Highway Research Board to make its maximum contribution to highway research."[36]

The report, not published until 1960, outlined a 4- to 5-year research program with estimated costs of $34 million. Among the 19 problem areas, physical research on aggregates, soils, and "translating" the AASHO Road Test results took up over one-third of the estimated budget. Five problem areas targeted freeways, including design, maintenance, lighting, removal of snow and ice, and, finally, control of land development around interchanges. Another five areas examined the larger social and economic questions involved in freight movement; patterns of urban living; appraisal of the "tangible and intangible" benefits and consequences of highways for road users, nonusers, and communities; and forecasting traffic and revenue. The report recommended tapping the power of computers, including to create driving and traffic flow simulations, analyze how vehicles interact with roads, and experiment with the electronic control of vehicles. Finally, fully broadening the program, the report recommended research into setting standards for secondary and local roads, deploying teams of scientists to investigate accidents, and improving the efficiency of motor vehicle administration.

Ultimately, however, it was not the proposed research program, but the process that had the most impact. The Holmes committee proved it feasible for state highway officials, acting through AASHO and with assistance from the Board, to cooperatively design a broad-based research program. The shift from funding a multiyear program, as the Board proposed, to AASHO sponsorship of a continuing program may have indeed originated outside the Board. In November 1960, AASHO leaders officially endorsed a pooled, revolving fund for highway research and sent the proposal to a referendum among the states. With advocacy from Augustus Kinzel, chair of the NRC's Division of Engineering and Industrial Research in 1960, the Board convinced a skeptical NRC Governing Board to agree to accept ongoing operation of an applied research program. Using the 1948 pooled funds research agreement as the template, AASHO's committees developed the first program in 1961, and the Board began setting up its administrative structure for what was then called the "Continuing AASHO Research Program" in early 1962.[37]

Launching NCHRP

AASHO, BPR, and NAS signed the three-party agreement officially creating the National Cooperative Highway Research Program (NCHRP) on June 19, 1962. The states funded NCHRP through dedicating 4.5 percent of their federal aid designated by law for planning and research—also known as the 1½ percent funds and the same source that funded the Research Correlation Service. This funding mechanism is still used today. State contributions are voluntary, and very few states have ever opted out of their annual share.[38]

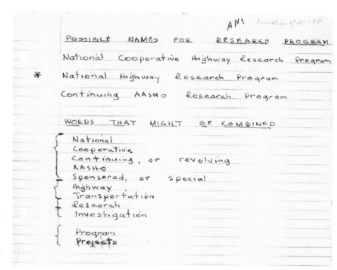

Handwritten notes exploring a name for the new highway research program (*TR News*, November–December 2012, 6).

From the beginning, only research problem statements receiving votes from two-thirds of the states have been eligible for final consideration, guaranteeing that research results have a wide audience. Although only state highway departments, AASHO committees, or the Federal Highway Administration (FHWA) may formally propose a research problem statement for a vote, the Board expected that AASHO's committees would consider the research needs statements regularly prepared by its technical committees when they crafted research problem statements for NCHRP.[39]

As in the Holmes Report, NCHRP's original administrative structure anticipated a comprehensive research program, covering a wide range of problem areas. The program anticipated research projects in 19 areas. Four problem areas covered the design of pavements and bridges, and another four areas dealt with materials and construction. Maintenance and traffic had three problem areas each. Administrative problem areas included economics, law, and finance, while transportation planning encompassed both traffic planning and urban transportation. Area 20 was reserved for special projects.[40]

Launching NCHRP was not easy. The responsibility fell to William N. Carey, Jr., deputy executive director, and M. Earl Campbell, the program's first director. Looking back from year 3 of the program, they recalled "the struggles to establish procedures, to establish advisory panels, to organize staff, and then to redo all of these things" as they developed experience.

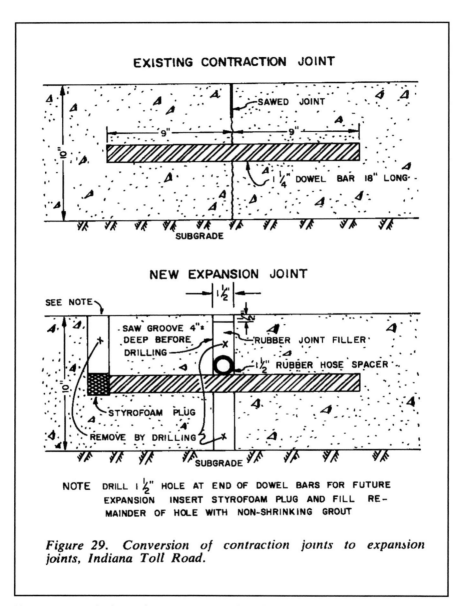

Figure 29. Conversion of contraction joints to expansion joints, Indiana Toll Road.

Numerous state highway departments contributed to *Evaluation of Methods of Replacement of Deteriorated Concrete in Structures*, NCHRP Report 1 (1964), including this figure from the Indiana Toll Road Commission.

Paramount was a concern for what they called "checks and balances": ensuring that each research project targeted the problem the states had identified, fit within BPR's aims for coordinated research, and met NRC's standards for appropriate research. A critical path analysis produced 125 "necessary major activities." Still, in 3 years, NCHRP's advisory panel process had turned the states' problem statements into 75 research contracts awarded to 44 research agencies including universities, nonprofit organizations, and consulting firms. NCHRP published 12 formal reports in 1964 on a wide range of topics from replacing deteriorated concrete to traffic signals, from snow and ice control to communicating with disabled vehicles. NCHRP's mailing list of interested researchers had grown to 2,000 and each "project statement" received, on average, 12 formal proposals from potential contractors. Carey and Campbell felt justifiably proud that NCHRP "cannot help but strengthen the highway research potential throughout the country."[41]

Research Implementation

Sponsoring and managing a continuing research program confronted AASHO and the Board with the problem of research implementation, a word not in general use until after 1970. Instead, NCHRP's early managers spoke of getting the program's findings "into the mainstream of highway thinking." Their first implementation strategy was built around reports and people. NCHRP distributed 10 copies of each report to state highway departments and FHWA. Universities also received reports. The Board charged its Research Correlation Service staff with being familiar with each report's results, and AASHO committees committed to reviewing all relevant reports.[42]

By 1967, Carey took to the pages to *Highway Research News* to share his concerns about "the transfer of information." The practicing engineer was "likely to be frustrated by the conflict between his desire to make a competent decision and his lack of time to study thoroughly even the abstracts provided." Carey noted the growing recognition of the need for updated handbooks, reports covering state-of-the-art practices, and other "super documents" that distilled key decision information into "bite size" pieces.[43] AASHO too began examining ways to bridge what it called the "utilization gap," or as NCHRP's third director Krieger W. Henderson described it: "that researchers and operating personnel seem to live in two entirely different metaphoric worlds." In response, NCHRP initiated the *Synthesis of Highway Practice* report series in 1968, and Henderson began advocating for "research-practice staff" in the field whose job was literally to translate research into practice.

Board publications also began periodically carrying advice on implementation. John L. Beaton, California Division of Highways, asked "Is Your Highway Research Being Implemented?" Beaton argued researchers should think of themselves as "a salesman with a real product and seek active support and cooperation with the ultimate users" and also advised researchers not to write reports, but "implementation tools."[44] This early body of work on implementation culminated in NCHRP Synthesis of Highway Practice 23, *Getting Research into Practice*, published in 1974. Among the report's conclusions, the authors advised that research projects should include funding to create the "guides, policies, standards, and specifications" that translate research into practice, and that research programs should consider funding "workshops, seminars, demonstrations projects, and training sessions" as part of research implementation programs.[45]

The "C" in NCHRP—cooperative—was the culmination of decades of relationship building among the states, BPR, and the Highway Research Board. As examined more in Chapter 13, with additional examples in Chapters 9–12, "cooperative" was not NCHRP's only strength, nor does it alone explain NCHRP's longevity. Because it was cooperative and applied, the program would evolve a broad definition of research, from planning to implementation. Because it was comprehensive at its founding, the program would build a diverse constituency for its research. The flexibility inherent in a continuing fund for annual research programs would make NCHRP agile: states would learn how to quickly deploy and re-deploy its resources in response to changing objectives. At the same time, NCHRP's constancy would encourage states to commit to conducting complicated, multipart, long-term research projects, including in coordination with others. Finally, NCHRP would inspire imitation: research advocates would look to the Transportation Research Board to host several short-term cooperative research programs and two long-term programs for transit and airports.

CHAPTER 7

A New Highway Research Board, 1960–1970

THE HIGHWAY RESEARCH BOARD had answered the challenge issued by the National Academy of Sciences' (NAS's) President Detlev Bronk in 1954 to take on the problems of the metropolis, including their total transportation needs. By early 1960, however, the National Research Council's (NRC's) broadly conceived Committee on Urban Research, managed by the Board but serving the National Academy as a whole, was running out of steam. Attempting to scale down, the Board proposed refocusing its work solely on total transportation. NRC agreed, as long as the Board clarified that it was only pursuing "total transportation in metropolitan areas." NRC's leaders were not willing to cede to the Board the responsibility for total transportation for the country or, in a semantic turn just emerging, the total transportation system.[1]

As the Board pursued "total transportation" in the 1960s, both definitions—needs versus system—vied for attention in ways that were not always clearly distinguished. The concept of total transportation needs, as developed in the 1950s, originally meant all the transportation needs of the metropolis. The concept of the total transportation system, on the other hand, applied systems thinking to transportation and would come to emphasize the interrelationships among transportation modes.

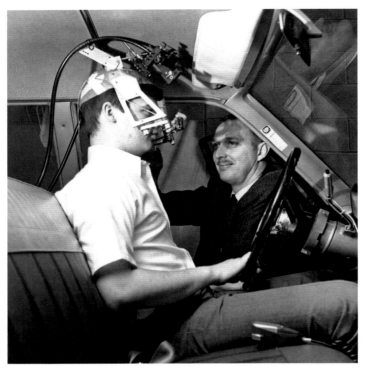

Research in the 1960s: Driver fitted with a television eye-marker system at The Ohio State University (The Ohio State University, College of Engineering).

However, throughout, there was a consensus within the Board, the National Academy, and the federal government that these concepts should shape how society organizes itself around transportation, including transportation research.

A Systems Approach to Transportation

Coincident to limiting the Board's total transportation work to metropolitan areas, the National Academy was in the midst of planning a major study on this new systems approach to transportation. NRC gathered 150 top researchers, federal transportation and military officials, and leaders from the country's transportation industries—the rail, air, maritime, pipeline, and motor vehicle manufacturing and fleet industries—at its center in Woods Hole, Massachusetts, for the month of August 1960. Sponsorship came from The Rockefeller Foundation, the National Science Foundation, and the Office of Civil and Defense Mobilization, which was then in the Executive Office of the President. The Board was involved: Harmer E. Davis, director of the Institute of Transportation and Traffic Engineering, University of California, Berkeley, and the Board's Executive Committee chair in 1959 also chaired the Woods Hole study. Fred Burggraf, the Board's executive director, attended, as did William N. Carey, Jr., then director of the American Association of State Highway Officials (AASHO) Road Test. Highways and urban transportation, however, would be last among equals. Edward H. Holmes was the lone attendee from the Bureau of Public Roads (BPR), and neither state nor local governments had any representatives. Absent, too, were experts in the roadbuilding industries.[2]

Institutionally, the Woods Hole Conference was a bit of a bust for the National Academy. No funding stream for additional studies flowed from it. However, the conference put on the table a new definition of "total transportation." The conference promoted the analytical concept of "system" for transportation because this concept focused researchers and policy makers on "how transport functions ... undistracted by the relative posture of the available modes at any one point in time." The conference defined "the total transportation system of the nation" to be all the infrastructure, services, activities, policies, and institutional arrangements that go into moving people and goods. They aimed to use systems analysis and the new power of computers to take a god's eye view and identify "modifications or adjustments in the system that will aid the economic, social, and strategic objectives of the commonwealth." Under this conceptualization, however, urban transportation was subordinate to the larger system of total transportation, as they admitted in their reminder that "studies of urban transportation should be pursued in close association" with studies of the system.[3]

The total transportation system concept gained momentum, eventually reaching federal policy. On January 12, 1966, President Lyndon Johnson announced in his State of the Union address his intent to create a new Department of Transportation (USDOT). Instigation for promoting transportation to a Cabinet-level department had come not out of BPR, the behemoth sitting in the Department of Commerce, but from the outgoing head of the Federal Aviation Agency. The fate of supersonic transport in particular had opened his eyes for, what he called, the need for "reasonable coordination and balance among the various transportation programs of the government."[4]

President Johnson endorsed the system concept when he introduced the legislation to Congress in March 1966: "America today lacks a coordinated transportation system that permits travelers and goods to move conveniently and efficiently from one means of transportation to another, using the best characteristics of each." Authorized by law in October 1966 and opened for business on April 1, 1967, USDOT consolidated 31 federal entities and programs, including the Federal Aviation Administration, the Federal Railroad Administration, and the Federal Highway Administration, which absorbed the functions of BPR. Although the Maritime Administration remained in the Department of Commerce, the Urban Mass Transportation Administration moved from the Department of Housing and Urban Development to the new department in January 1968.[5]

National Academy of Engineering

During the 1960s, the National Academy became more aggressive in pursuit of its mission. Near the end of Bronk's second and final term, he recommended that the National Academy formally merge the NAS president and the NRC chair with one full-time, salaried appointment. Frederick Seitz, professor of physics at the University of Illinois, assumed both offices in 1962 and transitioned to full time in 1965. Under Seitz, an NAS Committee on Government Relations founded in 1962 evolved into the Committee on Science and Public Policy. No longer content to wait for government to ask for advice, the committee was charged with long-range planning and coordinating with federal agencies and Congress to anticipate their needs and promote the National Academy's services.[6]

At the same time, leaders of the engineering professions were feeling frustrated with the gap between the importance of technology in modern life and the ability of the engineering professions to contribute to national policy discussions. Indeed, within the National Academy, the burgeoning diversity of scientific disciplines meant that engineering's influence had been waning. Moreover, the National Academy leaned heavily on published research as the measure of merit for membership, whereas the expertise of engineers was "often hidden in blueprints, design products, computer programs, and finished structures." In the early 1960s, the Engineers Joint Council, made up of representatives of the various engineering professional societies, sought "to make engineers more visible and vocal on the national scene" and to increase engineering's "contributions to the public welfare." Rapid suburban growth and the decline of inner cities, the spread of television and technology's influence on mass and personal communications, and the increasing number of practical applications for computers were just some of the topics they cited as in need of the engineering professions' guidance.[7]

The Engineers Joint Council looked to model its new organization after NAS-NRC, but as a separate entity with its own federal charter. Bronk and then Seitz worked to give the engineering professions the platform they desired, while keeping them within the National Academy fold. The original 1863 charter allowed it to found separate, autonomous organizations, Seitz offered, which would save the engineers the time and effort of seeking a federal charter. Negotiations succeeded. On December 5, 1964, the NAS Council approved, under the umbrella of NAS, the founding of the National Academy of Engineering (NAE). Within a year, NAE members numbered 95.[8]

Seitz hailed NAE as "a major landmark in the history of the relationships between science and engineering in our country," but NAE members soon chafed at their younger sibling status. At issue was control and conduct of NRC. In the original plan, NRC would be the operating arm of NAE, just as it was for NAS. NRC designated eight divisions by academic discipline, one of which was the Division of Engineering and Industrial Research, which housed both the Highway Research Board and the Maritime Transportation Research Board. NAE's Council was to exercise its separate authority through recommending individuals to be appointed chair of this division, which in 1966 changed its name to simply the Division of Engineering.[9]

In reality, however, the National Academy's committee formation process was not so straightforward. When NAE formed, 12 committees and boards stood outside NRC's division structure, including the Committee on SST-Sonic Boom, which advised the federal government on the commercial use of supersonic aircraft.[10] Moreover, members of NAE expected to play a large role in NRC's engineering-related activities, which they estimated amounted to 40 percent of NRC's programs in 1964. They had founded NAE as a "working organization" that aimed to get "as many members as possible" to participate. For example, under contract with the Department of Housing and Urban Development, NAE and NRC, working through the Highway Research Board, jointly conducted a study in 1967–1968 on the development of design criteria for "nonrail transit vehicles." Frustrated with "joint management" of NRC activities, however, NAE soon began forming its own committees for assignments conducted outside of NRC's formal structure.[11]

In 1967, NAE formed a parallel body to NAS's Committee on Science and Public Policy, and NAE explicitly oriented its Committee on Public Engineering Policy to "broad questions of national policy." NAE's independent work on transportation culminated in August 1970 in a contract with USDOT to form a Committee on Transportation. NAE's Committee on Transportation was envisioned as an ongoing activity that would provide "critical engineering review" of transportation plans and programs and other "broad counsel" as requested by federal agencies. The Committee on Transportation's first project, on urban transportation, recommended incorporating more input from social science research and conducting demonstrations to show "how changes in transportation can help fulfill broader social and urban objectives." NAE's Committee on Transportation had no intention of confining itself to giving advice on engineering.[12]

Research in the 1960s: Technician watches monitors of the Gulf Freeway Surveillance and Control Project in Houston (Texas Department of Transportation).

The Highway Research Board and Long-Range Planning

At its January 1965 meeting, 5 weeks after the founding of NAE, the Board's Executive Committee learned that little should change in the Board's relationship to NRC. The Board would just serve both academies, as requested. However, in preparation for the new academy, the engineering division's Long-Range Planning Committee had conducted a survey of "national problems" that anticipated "trends that will certainly affect social, economic, and political structures." NRC recommended that the Board form its own a long-range planning committee, and Alfred E. Johnson, executive secretary of AASHO and an ex officio member of the Executive Committee, formally proposed and won unanimous approval for an ad hoc committee that would develop the scope for such a committee. At its summer 1965 meeting, the Executive Committee charged its new Special Committee on Long-Range Planning with reviewing the Board's functions, structure, and finances and assessing existing transportation research programs in the context of future needs.[13]

Six months later, when the new Special Committee on Long-Range Planning updated the Executive Committee on its progress, the federal context for transportation had shifted dramatically. Nine days earlier,

DEPARTMENTS OF THE HIGHWAY RESEARCH BOARD, 1966

TOTAL NUMBER OF COMMITTEE ASSIGNMENTS: 2,437

DEPARTMENT OF ECONOMICS, FINANCE, AND ADMINISTRATION (16)

Administrative and Management Studies

Finance, Taxation, and Cost Studies

Economic Studies

DEPARTMENT OF DESIGN (18)

General Design Division

Pavement Division

Bridge Division

DEPARTMENT OF MATERIALS AND CONSTRUCTION (24)

Bituminous Division

Concrete Division

Construction Division

General Materials Division

DEPARTMENT OF MAINTENANCE (13)

DEPARTMENT OF TRAFFIC AND OPERATIONS (14)

DEPARTMENT OF SOILS, GEOLOGY, AND FOUNDATIONS (14)

DEPARTMENT OF URBAN TRANSPORTATION PLANNING (6)

DEPARTMENT OF LEGAL STUDIES (4)

SPECIAL COMMITTEES (7)

Numbers in parentheses refer to the number of committees.

Source: Highway Research Board, Annual Report, 1966.

President Johnson had announced his intention to form a department of transportation. The possibility of a new Cabinet-level department, especially one focused on coordinating the modes, added to the significance of the Special Committee's work. Chaired by Edward G. Wetzel of the Port of New York Authority, the committee notified the Executive Committee that it had split its charge in two—a study of future research areas and a study to be conducted later on sources of funding. This decision raised some comment, given that 80 percent of the Board's "present support" came from BPR and the state highway agencies. Johnson, AASHO's representative, first raised the two alternatives that would become fodder for future discussions and disagreements: they could move slowly and expand "to consider other forms of transportation as they affect highways" or they could go all in on a "transportation research board" and look for other sources of "support."[14]

"Support" was an elegant, but misleading way of describing how the Board actually funded its activities: it sold a limited number of services. Two of the three services, moreover, had been crafted and honed to meet the needs of one type of client, state highway departments, and one type of

TRID
Leadership on Information Technologies

IN A CENTURY when we google instead of perform manual searches, researchers can take instant information for granted. In the early 1960s, the Highway Research Board led the charge in developing "automated information systems" to replace searching by hand through card catalogs and publications such as *Highway Research Abstracts*. With more than $800,000 in funding from the National Cooperative Highway Research Program (NCHRP) and the federal Bureau of Public Roads and access to the National Academy of Sciences' computer, Board staff wrote the computer programs for storage and retrieval and then entered, one by one, descriptions of each highway research project and report.[a]

Work began in 1964. In summer 1967, when Paul E. Irick, the Board's assistant director for special projects, excitedly announced that they had "push[ed] the start button," computer tapes stored 14,000 references with summaries or abstracts. Computer searching was expensive, and turnaround on a search still took 1 week. The Board limited state highway departments to 625 requests per year and charged other Board affiliates $35 per search request.[b]

The Board's experience developing the Highway Research Information Service (HRIS) database made it a leader in computerized research information services. The Board soon earned contracts from the Maritime Administra-

Ashish Sen, director, Bureau of Transportation Statistics; Mortimer L. Downey, deputy secretary, USDOT; Rodney E. Slater, secretary, USDOT; and Robert E. Skinner, Jr., executive director, TRB, celebrate accessing TRIS on the Web at the ribbon cutting ceremony at the 2000 Annual Meeting (Risdon Photography).

tion for a Maritime Research Information Service (MRIS), the National Highway Safety Bureau for a Highway Safety Information Service (HSIS), and the Federal Railroad Administration for a Railroad Research Information Service (RRIS).

The Department of Transportation's (USDOT's) Office of the Secretary then tapped the Board in 1969 to write the software that would allow information databases to be compatible with each other, an effort first dubbed "TRIS." The work facilitated mutual exchange agreements with the International Road Federation and others.[c]

In 1973, the Board announced that TRIS was now "on line" and could be accessed remotely through the telephone. Searches now took just minutes.[d]

The new Transportation Research Board (TRB) continued its leadership in information technologies, serving as the administrative home for TRISNET, USDOT's network of transportation information databases from all over the country covering air, water, mass transit, pipeline, rail, and highway transport. TRB also

Retrieval specialist Rukmini Seevaratnam (seated center) shows attendees at the 1974 Annual Meeting how to search TRIS (USDOT, Jay Carroll).

took TRIS and HRIS (still two databases) on the road, setting up terminals at conferences and at the annual meetings in the 1970s and 1980s.

New transportation concerns sent HRIS managers on the hunt. When requests started coming in for information on energy conservation in 1973 and 1974, they sought out articles and reports from new sources and quickly added abstracts on topics such as fuel consumption, carpooling, and priority lanes for buses.[e]

As the cost of storage dropped over the decades, eventually the separate databases merged into just TRIS. By 1984, TRIS contained 185,000 abstracts from 2,500 journals from 72 countries. On January 1, 1985, TRIS could be dialed up worldwide. Ten years later, TRIS contained 360,000 records and became available in a boxed set of CD-ROMs.

At the annual meeting in January 2000, Secretary of Transportation Rodney E. Slater cut the ribbon to unveil TRIS free on the Web through the National Transportation Library.[f]

In 2011, TRIS became TRID—a merger of TRB's TRIS database and the Organisation for Economic Co-operation and Development's Joint Transport Research Centre's International Transport Research Documentation database. At 1.2 million records in 2018, TRID is the world's largest and most comprehensive bibliographic source on transportation.

funding source, federal-aid highway dollars designated for planning and research. The young National Cooperative Highway Research Program (NCHRP) amounted to managing a large, ongoing research program for a third party. The Research Correlation Service, still faithful to its original concept decades later, sold to clients a heterogeneous set of services built around a specialized transportation professional who liaised with technical committees, made regular visits to clients and constituents, prepared technical bibliographies, delivered talks, and helped organize the annual meeting. Although crafting research needs statements was a long-standing activity, the Board did not, for the most part, sell research. Only a small part of its activities were commissioned research projects leading to special reports. A fourth service, a computerized version of its research information service, was still only in the early development stage.[15]

As an organization, the Board was large and well funded. It was not at all clear, however, whether the industries and governmental agencies affiliated with other aspects of transportation would be interested in Board-style services and how much they would be willing to pay.

Research in the 1960s: The universal testing machine applies 300,000 pounds of pressure (Oklahoma Department of Transportation).

"Regardless of Mode"

The Special Committee on Long-Range Planning presented its report on how to respond to the "broad emerging concepts and needs of total transportation" to the Executive Committee in July 1966. The committee's rationale was both profound and practical. The Board's current scope—"to provide for the best in highways, bridges and appurtenances"—was inadequate to address the problems of "urban area growth in population and business activity." The current scope also did not match the Board's current activities. The new Departments of Urban Transportation Planning and Legal Studies, in addition to the expanding work of the Departments of Economics, Finance, and Administration and Traffic and Operations, all went far beyond physical research. In addition, the proposed federal department and New Jersey's creation of the first state department of transportation showed the path that those who claim leadership in transportation must take, the report argued. Moreover, if the Board stayed a "highway-oriented agency," it should expect that "some agency" dedicated to "transportation requirements as a whole" would "preempt" even the Board's highway work.[16]

The Executive Committee minutes carefully recorded at length the reactions of AASHO's Johnson and Rex M. Whitton, federal highway administrator, to the Special Committee's recommendations. Johnson signaled AASHO's support while noting that AASHO's Executive Committee was also discussing the need to broaden beyond highways. More importantly, he opined that the state highway departments "will not insist" that the Board use their funding for "strictly highway work." For example, studies of airport facilities would probably be deemed appropriate, Johnson thought, but "a new metal for supersonic air transport" would not. Whitton reinforced his agreement by arguing that "agencies with highway orientation ... should take the leadership in all considerations of total transportation."[17]

The Executive Committee agreed that "there is an urgent need" for action and issued a set of directives intended to transform itself into a "transportation research board." The Long-Range Planning Committee was to create a new statement of purpose and scope that "encompasses study and research in transportation, regardless of mode" in time for announcement at the 46th Annual Meeting in January 1967. In parallel, the executive director was to study restructuring the Board, especially its technical committees. Finally, the Long-Range Planning Committee was to outline how to tackle financial support. They decided to wait, however, on petitioning NRC to change their name until after the new scope was in place.[18]

Soon after, the Executive Committee accepted D. Grant Mickle's resignation as the Board's executive director and appointed Carey to take his place effective October 1, 1966. Carey was then deputy executive director, and his career with the Board spanned back to 1946. He had a reputation as "a person with a great imagination and willingness to listen" and the ability to foster "a spirit of cooperation." His new job would test these skills. Carey's deep, personal connection to the Board and its work would shine through in his regular columns in *Highway Research News*, from which he often spoke directly to the Board's expanding constituencies.[19]

At first, everything seemed to be going well with the Board's transformation. The Executive Committee adopted a new purpose and scope in January 1967:

> Purpose: The purpose of the Board is to advance knowledge concerning the nature and performance of transportation systems, through the stimulation of research and dissemination of information derived therefrom.

> Scope: The Board may give attention to all factors pertinent to the understanding, devising and functioning of systems for the safe and efficient movement of persons and goods, including: the planning, design, construction, operation and maintenance of transportation facilities and their components; the economics financing and administration of arrangements for providing transportation; and the interaction of transportation systems with the physical, economic, and social environment they are designed to serve.

J. Burch McMorran, superintendent of the New York State Department of Public Works, announced at the annual meeting's Chairman's Luncheon that "The Highway Research Board, if it is to continue to be in the research forefront, must modify its objectives and scope and must expand its involvement into the general transportation field."[20]

Carey followed up in the winter issue of *Highway Research News*. Cognizant of his audience, Carey assured everyone that the Board was not being rash and that it would continue to be good stewards of their funds. The Board was "not really embarking into completely unfamiliar waters" because many of its departments and committees "are already deeply involved" in the "interface between modes" and "have been considering the impact of other forms of transportation upon highways and vice versa." Moreover, the Board's materials, soils, and design research "is just as applicable" to railroads and airports. Repeating Johnson's example, Carey assured readers that the Board would not be venturing into "new metals for supersonic aircraft." For good measure, Carey included an extended quote from an editorial in the *Engineering News Record*, dated January 26, 1967, which argued that "since urban highways must be fitted into complex, coordinated systems … HRB's scope must be broadened further, and additional financial support must come from non-highway sources."

Executive Committee and Highway Research Board staff, 1967: Donald S. Berry (top row, second from right); D. Grant Mickle (middle row, center); and (front row, from left) J. Burch McMorran, Pyke Johnson, unidentified, Edward G. Wetzel, David H. Stevens, and William N. Carey, Jr. (BPR, Charles Ritter).

In closing, however, Carey revealed how daunting the road ahead actually was: "We at the Board are optimistic that such support will be forthcoming. It will have to be if we are to turn the concept into reality." [21]

By the time Carey penned the optimistic cover letter for the 1967 annual report, he already knew that the Board's ambitions had hit a snag. With Wetzel now chair, Davis had taken charge of the Long-Range Planning Committee. After chairing the Woods Hole Conference on Transportation, Davis had served on the Executive Committee for NRC's engineering division from 1962 to 1964 and was elected to NAE in 1967. Davis's experience with the Board's parent institutions gave him the credibility to deliver the bad news. When they had adopted the new scope in January 1967, the action "amounts to a decision on *our* part that we should proceed" [emphasis in original]. Only NRC's Governing Board had the authority to change the Board's scope. [22]

More concerning, informal discussions with staff in the engineering division and members of the Governing Board had turned up "divergent" reactions. Although Davis went into few details, "divergent" may have been a significant understatement. Davis advised against formally petitioning the Governing Board anytime soon. Without NRC's agreement, Davis acknowledged, their efforts to transform the Board were stalled. Pursuing funding could not proceed "until we can show that we have something to sell." But they could talk, and they should talk. "The effort must have the sincere concurrence of those associated with all aspects of the Board's activities," Davis reasoned. "Thus, we need to talk about it in many places and on many occasions."[23]

A New Highway Research Board

Despite the setback, the Board went ahead with the reorganization of its internal structure, and staff studied the technical committees. Carey divided the staff into four divisions: NCHRP, Administration, a new "Regular Technical Activities" division that replaced—in effect, rebranded—the Research Correlation Service, and a new "Special Technical Activities" division for funded projects. Then the real work began: reorganizing the Regular Technical Activities' 8 departments, 116 committees, and 2,437 committee members to be responsive to the broadened scope. In 1967, staff recommended against organizing by professional discipline, which they deemed infeasible, or by mode, which they feared would "be more divisive than helpful."[25]

The Executive Committee settled on an organizational structure for the Regular Technical Activities Division based on "functions, or phases of system development." They expressed enthusiasm for this approach's "flexibility" and the "merit of permitting gradual evolutionary development as conditions justify it." In January 1968, the Planning Committee proposed a process for reorganizing the Technical Activities committees: The Executive Committee should circulate an outline of a proposed structure in advance of a conference planned for spring 1968. The Planning Committee also developed several criteria for this new structure: new topics should be able find a natural home and the number of committees should grow and contract without pulling the overall structure "out of balance." In addition to addressing "modal interfaces," the new organizational structure should encourage projects that "cut across boundaries" and improve the Board's capacity to

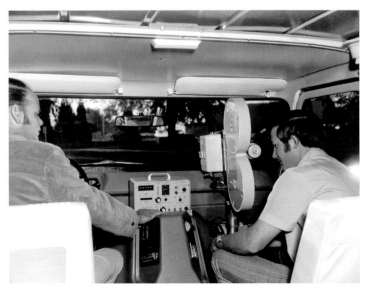

Research in the 1960s: Automobile with photo-log equipment (Idaho State Archives, Idaho Department of Transportation).

respond to "requests by government for advisory services on problems which involve various combinations of subject matter."[26]

With Executive Committee endorsement in hand, the Board's leaders took the proposal on the road. *Highway Research News* published Carey's address to the American Society of Civil Engineers' Transportation Conference, held in San Diego that February. In laying out the fullest case yet for transforming the Board, Carey positioned himself as an objective observer reporting on a revolution that was already nearing completion. This revolution was not content with just building better roads and bridges, but was asking "what system of facilities will maximize the social and economic well-being of the region." Moreover, highway administrators had been leading the charge, as evidenced by both the Board's annual meeting programs and federal highway legislation that required "a continuing planning function in the major cities." Research was critical, however, because "highway administrators know that they need to know more" about how transportation modes affect each other. Carey also shared a "side benefit" of total transportation. The Board's past expansion into urban planning and legal fields had resulted in the "mutual recognition of competence among those who in the past have been viewing transportation from independent and sometimes intolerant points of view and a reduction of the suspicion and distrust that goes with parochialism." Carey expected the reorganized technical committees to accelerate this comity.[27]

In May, Davis chaired the Board's Conference on Reorganization and Reorientation, a 3-day affair that hammered out the details for reorganizing the technical committees. Held at Airlie House, a retreat center in rural Virginia, the conference's recommendations soon became a touchstone referred to simply as the Airlie House Conference. The Board had been careful to create a coalition of the willing. From their volunteers, they selected participants "who recognize the directions the Board must take to be responsive to the needs of today and the future" and invited others who espoused "a broad approach to transportation and interest in counciling with highway specialists." In addition to

Research in the 1960s: Crushing a test cylinder of admixture concrete in the Materials and Tests Division, Texas Highway Department (Texas Department of Transportation).

transforming the technical committees, the conference touched on a long list of topics related to the conduct of the Regular Technical Activities Division, from the timetable for the transition to procedures for reviewing annual meeting papers and even how to fire unproductive committee members.[28]

Publicly, the Board's transformation appeared to be moving forward. Both *Highway Research News* and the *Annual Report* for 1968 covered the Airlie House Conference and shared the resulting reorganization plan. Inside the National Academies, however, the Board's future was still mired in uncertainty. Becoming a transportation research board was fundamental to the Executive Committee's overall long-term strategy, but 18 months after it had forwarded its proposed purpose and scope to the Division of Engineering, the division was still refusing the necessary step of putting it on the agenda for NRC's Governing Board. The Executive Committee was aware that what had seemed fairly straightforward, even inevitable, in 1965 was becoming more complicated by the day. The new federal transportation department, by consolidating the agencies responsible for the modes, made the department itself a huge prize, too big for either NAE or NRC to cede to a single board.[29]

By mid-1968, Carey's game was up. He had stayed the course when NRC's Division of Engineering had admonished him in April 1967 and again in May 1968 to stop acting as if the Board's broadened scope and reorganization were a done deal. When the division repeated its message in July 1968, he had no more pieces to move forward for a new transportation research board without explicit NRC approval.[30]

The internal struggle played out over who got to use the word "transportation." The Division of Engineering objected not only to "transportation" being in the name of a transformed board, but in the names of the proposed Technical Activities groups as well. As the division notified the Board's Executive Committee, NRC did not want "HRB to take on the appearance of, or become in fact, a Transportation Research Board" because this "would infringe on the missions of the other transportation-related committees" within the National Academies. In a tense exchange at the Executive Committee's summer meeting, the division's representative informed them that because the Board was "not equipped at this time to completely serve all of transportation," no approval of a broad

Research in 1960s: Automatic triaxial test apparatus in the Soil Mechanics and Bituminous Materials Laboratory, Institute of Transportation and Traffic Engineering, University of California, Berkeley (Institute of Transportation Studies, Berkeley).

new scope would be forthcoming. Davis protested. Without a broad scope and name, the Board had little hope of encouraging "support from other modal interests."[31]

The clashes within the National Academies over the word "transportation" were also a manifestation of a much larger intellectual and political puzzle. Some sincerely questioned whether an organization still largely dominated by highway engineers was appropriate for total transportation. Frank W. Lehan, USDOT's first assistant secretary for research and technology, had reached out to the presidents of NAS and NAE in March 1968 requesting a proposal for the National Academies to advise him on USDOT's research and development programs. New to transportation, Lehan reflected this larger skepticism when he explained why he had not supported a transportation research board in 1968: "The general attitude has been 'Well, gosh, you guys are a bunch of highway guys, and the problem is we got too many highways and the last thing we want you to do is to take over the entire transportation system.'" Lehan's wariness of highways also reflected the positions of his boss, Alan Boyd, the first USDOT secretary, and Paul Sitton, Boyd's deputy under secretary.[32]

Highway politics had indeed turned severe. Revolts against urban expressways had spread to city after city throughout the mid-1960s. In the Board's own backyard, Washington, D.C., and its suburbs were engulfed in a mammoth, multisided struggle among those arguing for and against completion of the planned urban freeways and those advocating for construction of a subway system. Protesters filled heated public meetings, and their leaders began circulating their own studies that methodically questioned the quality of the quantitative analysis offered by the highway engineers.[33]

Richard Nixon's election brought John A. Volpe to the position of USDOT secretary. Commissioner of public works and then governor of Massachusetts, Volpe had also served, on an interim basis, as the first federal highway administrator in 1956. Although widely presumed to be a highway builder, Volpe shocked highway advocates and opponents alike when in one of his first decisions he rescinded approval for construction of a riverfront expressway in New Orleans. In 1964, BPR had added the expressway, which affected the French Quarter, to the official plan for the Interstate Highway System, triggering years of protests by anti-freeway activists and historic preservationists. In July 1969, Volpe went even further and took the unprecedented step of canceling federal support for the New Orleans expressway altogether. In December, he attended the ceremonial ground-breaking for Washington, D.C.'s Metrorail subway system. In the passing of USDOT from Democratic to Republican administration, the questioning of urban expressways had only grown stronger.[34]

With the chips stacked against them, the Board's Executive Committee gave in. The chair, David H. Stevens, Maine State Highway Commission, negotiated the final agreement with NRC that provided a measure of face-saving for the Board despite the Executive Committee's thwarted ambitions. The Highway Research Board remained the Highway Research Board. The Board's new purpose continued to refer simply to "transportation systems," but its scope was officially broadened—or limited, depending on the point of reference—to only "highway and urban transportation systems and their interrelationships with other aspects of total transportation." NRC, however, accepted the Board's new organizational structure including the use of the word "transportation" in the names of the Technical Activities groups. NRC's Governing Board finally accepted the Highway Research Board's new purpose and scope on April 27, 1969.[35]

The reorganized Regular Technical Activities Division went live on February 1, 1970. Four groups replaced the eight departments. True to its aim to be organized "regardless of mode," no group or section name identified a specific transportation mode. Instead, following the Airlie House Conference recommendations, transportation as a system was broken down into three phases: planning and administration, design and construction, and operations and maintenance. Only 16 of the 115 technical committees included a mode in their names. The organization by system

Research in the 1960s: Extracting asphalt from asphaltic concrete in the Iowa Highway Commission Laboratories (used with permission from Iowa Department of Transportation).

phases meant, however, that the Department of Urban Transportation Planning would not be replicated in the new structure. Although urban transportation was now part of the Board's official scope, no group or section was dedicated to urban transportation. "Urban" found its way into the name of only one standing committee, the Legal Resources Group's Committee on Urban-Metropolitan Transportation Law.[36]

Already in January 1969, at least one skeptic had begun to rethink the stance that the Highway Research Board was not suited for total transportation. USDOT's Lehan reflected during an interview: "we castigate them for being nothing but a bunch of highway guys, so we've got them kind of in a box. And I'm not sure looking back ... that I wouldn't have been much wiser to encourage them to become the Transportation Research Board."[37] Implementing an Airlie House Conference recommendation, the new-except-in-name Board worked to build the "closer ties with architects, planners, social scientists and others" whose expertise the Board would need for its new scope. The Board also decided that "to maintain its position as the key research group in the transportation field" it needed to be "more aggressive" in reaching out to the highest levels of USDOT.[38]

Looking Forward at 50

The Highway Research Board also moved forward with plans to celebrate its 50th Anniversary. They looked backward with *Ideas & Actions: A History of the Highway Research Board, 1920–1970* and forward with a remarkable film. *Research: The Common Denominator* begins with spaceflight, but not rockets. The film opens with astronauts strapped into quaking seats as Rod Serling of *The Twilight Zone* television fame intones "Man reaches into space." Their mission is not complete, however, until they record what they have found so that others may learn from it. This is how "man completes another cycle in his search for knowledge." The film touts research that exploits computer technologies: driving simulations, electronic guidance systems, holographic signs, and in-vehicle navigation instructions. Yet, the researcher is in the frame too. A researcher—who is sometimes even a woman wearing a white lab coat—monitors the "space age" equipment, operates a tiny camera, reads a printout, and, in one rather shocking scene, runs with a caged rabbit through a tunnel of polluted air.[39]

Crash test conducted by the California Division of Highways (© 1970 California Department of Transportation, all rights reserved).

The highway—"the keystone of the transportation system"— dominates the film, and the images constantly reinforce that "highway" now means a singular type of infrastructure: the high-speed expressway. Speed carries into the highlighted safety research. In scene after scene, vehicles smash into guardrails and signposts and spin out on curves. Crash test dummies absorb the horrific forces of collisions. The Board struggled, however, with how to portray that urban transportation was now officially part of its scope or even what research in urban transportation meant for the rapidly suburbanizing metropolis. Instead of parking downtown, the film suggests, perhaps drivers will go to park-and-ride lots and take rapid transit into the city. A demonstration project in Ohio proposes that perhaps computers will route vans that offer door-to-door service. (They called this exciting new service Dial-a-Ride.) The film's only reference to the study of people walking, however, was set in between the buildings of an open-air, suburban-style campus.

The Los Angeles neighborhood of Watts is the film's case study of the incredible tensions between the national commitment to expressways and the social consequences of constructing them in urban areas. The vignette opens with people taking to the streets, not in protest, but to march in the Watts Summer Festival Parade. The narrator acknowledges the 1965 riot and the African-American community's distrust of outsiders with development ideas, and the camera lingers on a statue of a raised, clenched fist. The story that follows drew from presentations by Stuart L. Hill, supervising right-of-way agent for the California Division of Highways, who had been invited to present at two Board-sponsored conferences in 1968 and 1969. He was then working with the Watts Labor Community Action Committee, a local group founded after the riot, to relocate some of the 2,600 individuals in the path of the freeway—and the houses that they owned—to other sites within the Watts community.[40]

The film argues that, although highway departments were not required to consider the larger community, the Watts project "could prove to be a model" for highway planners and engineers. The National Environmental Policy Act, signed into law in 1970, and its mandated environmental impact analysis did require community consideration, argued the Center for Law in the Public Interest in a lawsuit filed in February 1972 to stop the expressway's construction. When the Century Freeway finally opened in 1993, it had become the most famous example of transportation planning by consent decree.[41]

CHAPTER 8

From Highways to Total Transportation, 1970–1974

DESPITE THE HIGHWAY RESEARCH BOARD'S thwarted ambitions to be a transportation research board by its 50th Anniversary, the pause allowed its leaders to take stock. The concept of total transportation would continue to animate transportation reform, and reformers still justified "total transportation" in terms of the total transportation needs of the metropolis. However, the term "total transportation" increasingly came to refer to the solution on which they put their faith: research and development of the total transportation system.

For the National Academies, the early 1970s was a time of significant reform, both procedural and organizational. Members of the Board would watch in somber recognition as the rest of the institution experienced the divisiveness and other dangers of venturing into politically controversial topics, a lesson that William N. Carey, Jr., the Board's director, and Paul E. Irick, head of special projects, had learned the hard way on the American Association of State Highway Officials (AASHO) Road Test. Despite those questioning the place of highways within the National Academies, out of the tumult, the Highway Research Board would finally become the Transportation Research Board (TRB).

Urban Mass Transportation

The Board's disappointingly limited new scope—highways and urban transportation—did have one advantage: it focused the Board's expansion efforts. In late 1969, Carey and Oscar T. Marzke, chair of the Executive Committee and vice president of Fundamental Research for the U.S. Steel Corporation, met with James M. Beggs, Department of Transportation under secretary, who signaled his willingness to consider a proposal for sponsorship from the Urban Mass Transportation Administration (UMTA). William L. Garrison, then with the University of Pittsburgh's School of Engineering and serving on the Board's Long-Range Planning Committee, was tapped to lead the effort. A geographer, Garrison had reinvigorated his field in the 1950s through applying sophisticated statistical methods to spatial analysis and in the 1960s had dedicated his research to transportation. The Board would come to depend heavily on his expertise and energy in the years to come.[1]

William L. Garrison helped lead the transition from highways to total transportation, and from the Highway Research Board to the Transportation Research Board (TRB).

Garrison had gained experience in mass transit in 1967 on a joint National Academy of Engineering (NAE)/National Research Council (NRC) Committee on Nonrail Transit Vehicles, funded by the Department of Housing and Urban Development (HUD) for UMTA. Conducted as a special project, the Board often cited the $150,000 study as it pursued additional funding for urban transportation. The study developed a comprehensive set of design and performance criteria. It had also explored, as they described it, "the possible utility of multi-phase systems involving small-vehicle door-to-door pickup, feeding larger trunk-line vehicles, and the control and communications systems essential to their efficient operation," a model of mass transit service that is still much debated 50 years later.[2]

To pursue new sponsorship, Garrison led the production of a 3-year action plan and a lengthy document titled "The Highway Research Board and Urban Mass Transportation: Questions and Answers," intended to guide communications with both the Board's traditional constituencies as well as potential new funders. The guide laid out the persuasive case.

The Board was not just made up of "civil engineers and economists," but in recent years had attracted "men and women" representing "mechanical engineers, physicists, mathematicians, statisticians, sociologists, psychologists, attorneys, planners, architects, computer specialists and many others." Using the mode-neutral reorganization of the Board's technical activities to its advantage, the document touted 17 technical committees applicable to mass transit, including the committees on Taxation, Finance and Pricing; Transportation Forecasting; Theory of Traffic Flow; and Social, Economic and Environmental Factors of Transportation. In addition, the document listed 49 papers related to mass transit published in *Highway Research Record* from the 1967, 1968, and 1969 Annual Meetings.[3]

For $250,000 in annual funding, Garrison's action plan envisioned a full range of activities, including technical committees and research correlation, which the plan defined as "developing contacts with staffs of mass transportation organizations, identifying ongoing research and research needs, reviewing the literature in the field, transmitting information, and disseminating the results of research." The Executive Committee endorsed all of Garrison's plan except point one: change the name of the Board to better reflect its actual scope of activities. Attempting another name change went down in a rare split vote, 18-1. Garrison, however, would become only more convinced that "Highway Research Board" weighed like an albatross around the Board's neck.[4]

One year later, sponsorship for mass transit remained elusive. Francis (Frank) C. Turner, federal highway administrator, urged the Board to try again with UMTA. New federal legislation improved the odds of success. The Urban Mass Transportation Assistance Act of 1970 was slated to invest $10 billion over the next 12 years to improve mass transit systems, an unprecedented commitment of federal resources to urban transportation.[5]

UMTA joined the Federal Highway Administration (FHWA) as a federal sponsor of technical activities on May 1, 1971. Carlos C. Villarreal, UMTA's administrator, became an ex officio member of the Executive Committee and addressed the Chairman's Luncheon at the annual meeting in 1972. Despite the heavy rail systems under construction in San Francisco and Washington, D.C., Villarreal argued that "the best prospect for relieving urban transportation congestion, at least in the near term, is a broader and wiser use of the city bus," making it a priority to "preserve urban bus systems before the species becomes extinct." UMTA's $100,000 annual contribution in support of regular technical activities, while smaller than the $376,000 then coming from FHWA, allowed the Board to begin developing a section of committees on public transportation and hire its first transit specialist. In late 1971, the Board also held a small conference, with sponsorship from the American Transit Association, on public transportation research needs that tackled transit operations, equipment, and marketing.[6]

With UMTA funding in hand, Garrison made another attempt to change the Board's name. Although no one was particularly happy with his "cumbersome" offering, they all recognized the urgency of getting the Executive Committee on record supporting a name that matched the Board's scope. Events inside and outside the National Academies were making the misconception that the Board solely a highway research organization even more untenable. After "no better name was suggested," the Executive Committee voted unanimously at its June 1971 meeting that the Board should take appropriate steps to change its name to "Highway and Urban Transportation Research Board."[7]

Scandals and Reform

When Philip Handler replaced Frederick Seitz as the National Academy of Sciences' (NAS's) president on July 1, 1969, he came into office knowing that the National Academies would benefit from significant reforms. Elected to NAS in 1964 and serving on NAS's top governing council when appointed president, Handler had been chair of the biochemistry department in Duke University's Medical School. His long record of public service included chair of the Board overseeing the National Science Foundation, and membership on the President's Science Advisory Committee. Handler served two 6-year terms as president and died just weeks before TRB awarded him its Distinguished Service Award in January 1982. The award citation recognized Handler's role in shepherding the Board from highways to total transportation, and also noted, without elaboration, that Handler had acted "unfailingly in proclaiming that the Board, as an integral unit of the National Research Council, was uniquely qualified to serve the national interest." Handler had not just helped transform the Board, but maneuvered to save its very existence.[8]

In 1968, as the Board's leaders were backing away from their ambitions for total transportation, the future of air travel was teaching the National Academies a wrenching lesson in the political pitfalls of new demands for transportation research. From 1947—when Air Force pilot Chuck Yeager broke the sound barrier—through the Eisenhower administration, the federal government supported supersonic transport (SST) for only military use. As the British and the French pushed SST toward commercial flight, American SST proponents persuaded President John F. Kennedy in 1963 to declare its commercial use to be a national objective. NAS became directly involved in May 1964. The Federal Aviation Agency (FAA) was conducting test flights over Oklahoma City to assess the effect of repeated sonic booms on buildings and people. When a state court judge issued a restraining order halting the flights, FAA immediately contacted NAS. President Seitz arranged for a Committee on SST-Sonic Boom, newly founded outside the NRC division structure, to be on the ground in Oklahoma City within 2 weeks. Despite numerous claims for property damage, a passage in the committee's second report, released in February 1968, appeared to minimize concerns that sonic booms would harm structures. SST proponents touted this finding, while SST opponents protested. With the help of an NAS member, opponents blasted the SST committee report in a letter sent to every member of NAS. Eventually 189 NAS members signed the request for a retraction. The National Academies finally released a formal clarification, attributing the error to poor editing, in an internal newsletter in February 1969.[9]

Handler took over as president in the aftermath of the first SST controversy, and he wasted little time launching efforts to reform and revitalize NRC. At the NAS autumn meeting in 1969, he outlined why NRC's organization by scientific disciplines no longer served its mission. Specifically identifying transportation, Handler argued that contemporary problems required "multidisciplinary attack." Six months later, in his first address to the NAS annual meeting as president, Handler confronted the controversies that he saw plaguing science inside and outside the National Academies. He admitted that those "questioning" science and its practices had brought many "grave and far-reaching problems" to the National Academies' attention. More concerning, "science was under attack by an appreciable sector of the public and Congress." NAS must play a role in restoring the public's faith in science "by demonstration that the benefits science can afford are essential to society."[10]

Philip Handler, NAS president, 1969–1981 (Smithsonian Institution Archives, Image #SIA2008-3326).

Human Factors Workshop

Bringing New People to TRB, Including Patricia F. Waller

THE HUMAN FACTORS WORKSHOP has a prominent place among the workshops that crowd the day before the Transportation Research Board (TRB) Annual Meeting. The oldest workshop, it dates to 1967. Not only did the workshop introduce new ideas to TRB, it became a pathway for leadership. Among these new leaders was a psychologist who had switched careers to dive headfirst into highway safety research. Her name was Patricia F. Waller.

Harold L. Michael, who had pioneered using computers for traffic engineering at Purdue University in the 1960s, was chair of the Highway Research Board's Department of Traffic and Operations in 1967, when its Committee on Road User Characteristics responded to what he termed "increasing national concern directed toward highway safety." In addition to founding a subcommittee dedicated to driver education research, the committee planned a new workshop on human factors in the design and operations of the highway system.[a]

They were ambitious. When the workshop got off the ground in 1968, the committee called it the "First Annual Workshop on Human Factors in Highway Transportation." True to the workshop form, no papers were presented. Attendees sat around tables "in their shirtsleeves" discussing the problems of drivers and passengers and people walking, bicycling, and

Patricia F. Waller receiving the Roy W. Crum Distinguished Service Award from Joseph M. Sussman, Executive Committee chair, at the 74th Annual Meeting in 1995 (Robert P. Turtil).

taking mass transit. By 1974, the workshop had grown into six full-day concurrent sessions.[b]

Waller had also embraced highway safety research in 1967. She had earned her Ph.D. in clinical psychology in 1959, but by the mid-1960s she had what in academia is called the "two-body problem." Her husband's appointment in experimental psychology at the University of North Carolina disqualified her from working in the university's psychology department. B. J. Campbell, founding director of the Highway Safety Research Center at the University of North Carolina in 1966, asked and asked again for her to join the new center. She finally said yes.[c]

Waller is pictured among the men attending the Human Factors Workshops in 1974 and 1975. Participants pondered questions such as "How do we distinguish a good sign from a poor one?" and "How do we designate a design-driver, or average driver, when people differ so much physically, physiologically, mentally, and emotionally?" After bemoaning "the gap" between what traffic engineers expect people to do and what people actually do, some participants suggested that instead "we should measure the intuitive behaviors of drivers and pedestrians" and then "design traffic control devices to reflect that behavior."[d]

Waller chaired a TRB Task Force on Driver Regulation, which produced *Future Role of Driver Licensing in Highway Safety* (TRB Special Report 151) in 1974. In 1976, she led a session at the Human Factors Workshop on driver skills and knowledge. By 1980, she was chair of Group 3, Operations and Maintenance of Transportation Facilities, yet she still stayed committed to the Human Factors Workshop.

She is pictured in the 1981 group photograph along with one other woman, Gerry Simone, the workshop's chair. In 1982, perhaps celebrating the workshop's record-breaking attendance, Waller stands smiling with Emily Larson, incoming chair for the 1983 workshop.[e]

Despite her TRB leadership roles, Waller was still at the beginning of her career. Taking to heart her research findings that people learn to drive by driving, Waller pioneered graduated driver's licenses, developed criteria for commercial driver's licenses, and served on the National Highway Traffic Safety Administration's Research Advisory Committee. She also led research on older drivers, pedestrians, truck safety, and driving under the influence of alcohol. TRB recognized Waller with the Roy W. Crum Distinguished Service Award in 1994.

In a remarkable memorial tribute to her in the journal *Injury Prevention*, Waller's colleagues wrote that although a psychologist by training, "she quickly recognized, however, that the relationships between the driver, the vehicle, and the road were largely interdependent and responsive to the larger societal context of laws and cultural norms." To honor her contribution, TRB established a new award for outstanding paper on safety and system users in her name in 2004.[f]

Over the next few years, Handler would put in place new requirements that brought all research-related activities of NAS, NAE, and NRC under a common set of procedures designed to protect the integrity of their products and the reputation of the organization. He also attempted to reorganize the National Academies to bring society's problems and science's new advances into supportive alignment. While transportation research had been emblematic of the problem, Handler also used transportation as a model—and guinea pig—for his vision, not only for a revitalized organization, but for how science should contribute to society. Through speeches at the Board's annual meetings in 1970, 1971, and 1973 that were reprinted, at least in part, in *Highway Research News*, Handler outlined straightforward critiques as well as gave praise, issued challenges, and concluded with calls to arms.

At the 49th Annual Meeting's Chairman's Luncheon, Handler subsumed highways in transportation, asking highway leaders to put their experience in the service of larger transportation problems. He opened by reminding those "serving the nation" in transportation that "the nation has become acutely sensitive to the impact that transportation has on our daily lives, on land use, on economic growth, on the quality of the environment, and just the simple daily comforts of each individual as well as society's well-being." Transportation was failing the "four-fifths of our population [who] very soon will live in urban centers." And he counted himself among those suffering: "It used to be amusing to be told that you could fly from here to New York in 45 minutes and then spend the next 2 hours getting to Wall Street. This story has lost its humor—it happened to me 2 days ago."[11]

Handler also unveiled his plan for transportation. He commended the Board for "beginning to act where others perhaps have not yet begun to meet their responsibilities." However, he also repeatedly emphasized that neither better data nor technological advances would solve the nation's transportation problems, unless applied "in the total social and economic framework in which our transportation systems must operate." He admitted that the Board's home, NRC, was "not at present an adequate instrument" and announced his plans to restructure NRC "to deal in a more systematic and orderly fashion with the totality of the nation's transportation problems." He called on the Board "to lend its talents, its experience, its

An engineer at the controls of an Amtrak train in 1974: Amtrak began passenger service on May 1, 1971 (U.S. National Archives, 412-DA-13630).

leadership, its devotion—so ably proven already—to aid all of us in this endeavor."[12]

During the coming months Handler worked to put his vision for transportation into action. In June 1970, he received NAS Council approval for a proposal to create a "Division of Transportation," on par with the Division of Engineering. As he wrote privately to the incoming chair of the Division of Engineering, he aimed for this new division to be "a most important event in the life of this institution" because he expected it to allow the National Academies to address "the more global and systematic aspects of transportation in the large" while being a "prototype for the remodeling of the NRC with the passage of time."[13] At the NAS autumn meeting, Handler drew attention to the increasing number and complexity of federal study requests by highlighting four examples, two of which involved transportation: extending the runways at John F. Kennedy International Airport and meeting Clean Air Act targets for automobile emissions by 1975.[14]

The Board's Executive Committee reacted to the proposal that it transfer to (not become) a new Division of Transportation with cautious optimism. The Executive Committee also, of course, formed a subcommittee, with

Sign for bus and carpool lanes on I-95 in Fairfax, Virginia, 1974 (courtesy of Virginia Department of Transportation).

Carpool office in Portland, Oregon, 1974 (U.S. National Archives, 412-DA-13064).

Garrison as chair and liaison to NRC. One fact hung over all future negotiations: the Board's sponsors and revenues contributed 85 percent of the National Academies' transportation-related funding and more than one-quarter of the National Academies' total sponsored activity. In its formal response, the Executive Committee offered its support, tempered with reservations. Protecting the integrity of sponsor relationships included avoiding controversial "policy studies" that advised the federal government. Despite Carey's somewhat strained insistence that neither the Board nor the Maritime Transportation Research Board "provide advice to their sponsors on matters of policy" and that it was "essential to maintain this separation of information activities from policy advice," he understood that an NRC unit for total transportation must have the capacity to advise government. In addition, the proposed new Division of Transportation had had much to do with the Executive Committee's sense of urgency about adopting the name "Highway and Urban Transportation Research Board."[15]

The Crises of 1971

At the end of 1970, controversy over the National Academies' supersonic transport research spilled out into the open in a dramatic fashion, pulling the Board into the line of fire as well. Stewart L. Udall, secretary of the Department of the Interior during the Kennedy and Johnson administrations, shocked those attending the annual meeting of the American Association for the Advancement of Science when he delivered a broadside against the scientific establishment and the National Academies. His speech, covered by the press including extended excerpts in *The New York Times*, castigated scientists for their lack of moral leadership on technology, society, and the environment. Calling the National Academies "virtual puppets of the government" and "political eunuchs," he proclaimed that he would "rather see scientists err on the side of activism and occasional hyperbole." Udall critiqued science in general, but his examples went after transportation. After describing NAS's work supporting "an airborne Edsel and an environmental disaster," Udall asked, "Is it any wonder science is on the defensive when it dutifully provides a convenient rationale for the SST lobby, highway contractors or the Defense Department?"[16]

Udall did more than criticize. He called for a "dispassionate and intensive study" of the National Academies and even named who should lead the effort: Ralph Nader and the Center for the Study of Responsive Law. Nader's 1965 surprise best-selling book, *Unsafe at Any Speed: The Designed-In Dangers of the American Automobile*, had prompted the Johnson administration to found the National Highway Safety Bureau (the forerunner to the National Highway Traffic Safety Administration) in 1966. Nader then founded the Center for the Study of Responsive Law, which marshalled young activists to conduct investigations of government agencies and social issues. By 1970, his force—nicknamed "Nader's Raiders" by *The Washington Post*—was 200 strong.[17]

Nader's center launched the investigation within months of Udall's speech, and Handler announced at the NAS annual meeting in April 1971 that he had instructed staff to cooperate, within limits. From that point on, Handler was in a race to get his reforms firmly in place before Nader's team published their study. In many ways, however, Udall, Handler, and leaders within the Board all agreed on the problem: the interaction between technology and its social and environmental contexts. They also advocated similar approaches, at least conceptually, to a solution. Udall echoed Handler's speeches when he proclaimed that day in Chicago, "Whether they deserve status as ecologists or not, we desperately need men and women of all disciplines who are not afraid of integrating their ideas into a larger context that embraces man, nature and technology." In other words, something very similar to what highway leaders sought with total transportation, both needs and systems.[18]

Just days before the Board's 50th Annual Meeting, another bombshell dropped, this one closer to home. *National Journal*, a political magazine based in Washington, D.C., published an article on the National Academies' need for reform, including comments from an interview with Harvey Brooks, dean of the Division of Engineering at Harvard University. Brooks, a member of both NAS and NAE and a recognized expert in technology and public policy, named the Board first among four NRC boards that "may be constituted too completely with those who have an economic or institutional interest in the outcome of their work."[19]

In his remarks at the Board's 50th Anniversary, President Handler began by offering, not words of congratulations, but of sympathy and even commiseration:

> Fifty years of service in designing highways has brought us up against an impatient American public, concerned about all aspects of travel. Those who are relatively thoughtless in these regards find it very simple to be critical, and to offer unconstructive, but occasionally devastating, comments with respect not only to our highway system but to our airports, aircraft, trains, buses, maritime system, and so on. But please do not be distressed or dismayed. It would appear that in this year 1971, every aspect of American life is up for reconsideration.

Yet, Handler acknowledged the critiques of highways and their negative impacts on cities and the natural environment. He believed he knew the solution—"an integrated, total transportation system ... where each portion of the system will bear its appropriate share of the total transportation burden"—but lamented that transportation research had yet to produce a path to success.[20]

In March 1971, President Richard Nixon added to the uncertainty around federal support for transportation research when he delivered to Congress a sweeping plan to reorganize and consolidate the federal departments. Instead of departments organized around functions, the Nixon administration proposed grouping governmental agencies and activities around societal objectives. The cabinet-level Department of Transportation (USDOT) would disappear, its functions split for the most part between a new Department of Community Development built around HUD and a new Department of Economic Affairs, to be focused on interstate and international commerce. UMTA was to return to a new Community Transportation Administration. For FHWA, the Nixon administration proposed, with the support of George Romney at HUD and John A. Volpe at USDOT, that highways should also become part of this new Community Transportation Administration. Once the Interstate System's construction was completed, Volpe argued, "highway programs from then on will be primarily community oriented." AASHO members were aghast; its president vigorously protested that "highways are national in scope and must be kept national in scope and never confined to what we have termed a community." Handler's proposed NRC Division of Transportation would have to wait until the Nixon administration's proposal finally died on the vine after his reelection.[21]

For the National Academies, the crisis of 1971 landed next on the health effects of airborne lead. During a congressional hearing, a House Committee staff member charged members of an NRC committee with conflicts of interest and dereliction of duty in their study of motor vehicle emissions for the Environmental Protection Agency (EPA). The report of the Committee on the Biologic Effects of Atmospheric Pollution had actually been produced under new report review procedures. NRC reports, which at the time could be anything from a letter to an agency to a hardcover book for sale to the public, now had to meet standards set by the independent Report Review Committee. For reports addressing significant public policy issues, NRC arranged for a separate set of experts to review a report's analysis, presentation of data, clarity of prose, and recommendations, including their relationship to the initial charge. Handler's report review process put the National Academies on the forefront of adopting exacting procedures for peer review to add credibility to scientific research in light of public criticism. Still, Handler warned that "because of the nature of these studies and their substantial political and emotional content, the Academy and its NRC committees must anticipate criticism and attack."[22]

Handler also introduced a requirement, adopted after much debate, that all members of committees advising government must submit a statement of personal bias. The statement went beyond financial conflicts of interest to include other sources of bias, such as having made strong public statements about government policy. The intent was not necessarily to exclude those with biases, but at least to acknowledge and balance them. Finally, Handler reformed the committee appointment process, requiring the regular rotation of members for all committees, except short-term project committees such as National Cooperative Highway Research Program (NCHRP) panels.[23]

Energy conservation affected highway lighting on I-5, 1973 (U.S. National Archives, 412-DA-12969).

Speaking with One Voice

Reorganizing NRC was crucial to Handler's vision for applying multi-disciplinary creativity to society's problems, and also to implementing the desperately needed procedural reforms. Study committees formed under the jurisdiction of NAS, NAE, or NRC, and after 1970, the new Institute of Medicine, created confusion for sponsors and complicated efforts to enforce new standards. Handler and the NAS Council wanted all studies brought under the jurisdiction of NRC. Leaders of NAE understood what was at stake, but they had also designed their academy to work. Over the years, NAE had developed its own portfolio of studies and relationships with federal agencies, which its leaders were not willing to simply hand over to an NRC controlled by the scientists.[24]

Transportation was right in the middle of the dispute. NAE's Committee on Transportation had formalized its role as advisor to USDOT's Secretary's Office. Moreover, NAE did not confine itself to engineering problems. The committee's 1972 study, *Urban Transportation Research and Development*, denounced the current systems of urban transportation as "more detrimental than beneficial to city life" and proclaimed that instead urban transportation "should help to make cities more livable—more pleasant and non-polluted, with jobs, recreation, and education facilities within easy reach of all city residents." The study called for federal investment in demonstration projects and design competitions to test a long list of potential solutions including dedicating streets to mass transit and "peak hour auto-use taxes" for congested downtowns.[25]

In October 1972, NAE dedicated its autumn meeting to urban transportation. James M. Beggs, under secretary of transportation, gave the keynote address on the need for innovative solutions. Sessions covered innovations such as vertical takeoff and landing aircraft, deep draft ports, and breakthroughs in telecommunications, but also addressed urban development more generally. Speakers from HUD and the Rouse Company, a real estate development firm, joined urban planners from Chicago, Dallas, San Francisco, and Washington, D.C., to discuss urban design, development, and renewal.[26]

The Board also continued to produce special reports on a growing range of transportation topics, and the staff of its Special Projects division provided support to committees convened to oversee research connected to government policy. Recent efforts had included an advisory

Rhode Island Avenue Station, 1977: Serving the Washington, D.C., region, the Metro opened in 1976 (WMATA).

committee sponsored by FHWA and EPA on highways and air quality and studies by the National Highway Safety Bureau evaluating driver education programs and developing design criteria for ambulances. More controversially, the Board had also accepted funds from Keep America Beautiful to manage a study of highway litter. The funders, a coalition of bottle and can manufacturers, had then used the study to argue against proposed state laws requiring deposits on beverage containers.[27]

With two growing loci for studies in just transportation alone, leaders of NAS and NAE struggled for more than 3 years to come to an agreement over managing technology-related studies within NRC. They framed the debate as whether science and technology could bridge their differences and advise the federal government, and nation, with one voice. Some of the scientists, however, blamed too-close ties with industry for the National

Academies' scandals, implicitly challenging NAE's broader concept of expertise. Although the scientists were genuinely concerned about "damage to the national interest and to the technical community" if the two academies went their separate ways, by spring 1973 negotiations had become so strained that NAE's membership endorsed preparing plans to become a separate not-for-profit organization, and NAS began moving forward on the NRC reorganization on its own.[28]

A demonstration project for radio-dispatched, door-to-door bus service in Haddonfield, New Jersey, ran from 1972–1975 (U.S. National Archives, 412-DA-14296).

Propriety of the Highway Research Board

Continued concerns also prompted the NAS Council to order a thorough investigation of three NRC boards, including the Highway Research Board. Handler appointed NAS members to small visiting committees charged with reviewing these boards' operations from top to bottom. Handler's instructions to the Visiting Committee for Highways, formed in September 1971, went beyond asking for recommendations for reforms. Ultimately, the Visiting Committee was to advise the Council on its "value to American society" and "the propriety and merit" of it staying within NRC.[29]

Carey worked closely with the Visiting Committee during its months of investigations, and Saunders Mac Lane, the chair and a mathematician from The University of Chicago, met with the Board's Executive Committee at its meeting in June 1972. Mac Lane reported that the Visiting Committee commended the Board's general operations, and they discussed the challenges of broadening the base of funding, especially for modes other than highways. Mac Lane also previewed the conclusion that they seemed to operate like a "professional engineering society," functions the Visiting Committee questioned. The Executive Committee mounted a defense, explaining how the funding and function of the Technical Activities Division was both broader in personnel and more focused on research than typical for engineering societies.[30]

Despite the preview, Carey was taken aback when he reviewed a draft of the Visiting Committee's report. One recommendation in particular sent him into a panic: that the Board should submit a separation plan within

2 years covering all of its activities that resemble a professional society. At a minimum, the Visiting Committee questioned the continued presence under the NRC umbrella of a large annual meeting dedicated to transportation and the publication of its papers in the *Highway Research Record*. Carey understood that this recommendation undermined the purpose of the Board's Technical Activities Division as well as the Executive Committee's strategy for total transportation. In a nine-page personal letter, addressed from Bill to Saunders, Carey acknowledged that he had been asked only to correct factual errors, but took leave to plead the Board's case.[31]

Carey poured his heart out. The draft report did not give enough credit to the Board's significant efforts since the early 1960s to broaden its capabilities on economics, environmental problems, and land use. Because of its "highly interdisciplinary" activities and "multimodal" interests, the Board "could not survive as an adjunct to" any existing professional organization, such as the American Society of Civil Engineers or even AASHO. Unlike a professional society, Carey pointed out, 82 percent of the Board's revenue came from its federal and state government sponsors, a figure that did not include NCHRP. Being part of NRC, he added, "provides a very effective buffer towards the desirable end that permits us to be objective, sometimes in spite of sponsors' interest." He put forth the case that nothing the Board did was unusual to NRC, just on a much larger scale, asking rhetorically, "What is wrong with bigness per se as long as we are not bureaucratic?" Increasingly frantic, Carey closed by calling the regular technical activities "our backbone and raison d'être" and concluded, "Without them, we would be nothing and die."[32]

Carey's pleas were to no avail. The Visiting Committee judged that the Board was "well and effectively run" and then recommended separation. Whatever remained, including the Transportation Research Information Service, should be integrated into the planned Commission on Transportation. Arguing that "transportation is too important to our society to remain the exclusive domain of transportation experts," the Visiting Committee called for more involvement by high-level NRC staff and members of NAS and NAE. A streamlined board could then target "new style questions" such as highways and land use, urban growth, urban transportation, and "measuring and ameliorating environmental impacts." They also identified a need for additional studies on pedestrian and vehicle safety, and driver education.[33]

Although not issued as a minority report, one member of the Visiting Committee, Eugene P. Odum, submitted an "essay" with a different view on the National Academies, transportation, and the Board. A professor at the University of Georgia, Odum had helped define the field of modern ecology in the 1950s. He became an environmental activist in the 1960s and burst on the scene as a public intellectual in 1970 during the media attention catalyzed by the first Earth Day. Odum's essay presented recommendations that drew on his expertise in ecosystems. Highways had left their "exponential development" phase and entered the "mature maintenance phase," which "requires a reversal of many basic management strategies." Moreover, "the USA is especially in danger of continuing to rely too much on a one-crop economy based on the automobile." Mature systems needed diversity to create stability: not building more "superhighways," but integrating urban mass transportation, rail, and air transport should be priorities.[34]

For all these reason, Odum argued, the Board—and "American society as a whole"—needed NAS now more than ever. NAS members had the expertise in the environmental and social subjects required for a true interdisciplinary approach to transportation's transition. Moreover, Odum argued, the huge sums of investment that transportation required made it imperative that society set up firm "negative feedback control" to prevent "technological overdevelopment." Odum commended the Board's leaders for being "well aware of the need to shift priorities." It was NAS that appeared to be wavering, but Odum insisted, "NAS must now step in and help the HRB leadership accomplish agreed upon objectives."[35]

The NAS Council, however, remained skeptical. Their discussion at the August 1972 meeting acknowledged that the Board's leadership wanted to stay as part of the revamped NRC and noted that this desire offered leverage to achieve "constructive changes." In the end, however, too much of the Board—including its size—appeared to them to be only "tenuously connected" to NRC's mission. Moreover, the Council had a precedent and a model for its exit. The American Geophysical Union, launched by NRC in 1919, had just that year incorporated as a separate multidisciplinary scientific association. Citing an NAS policy to encourage groups "to assume independent status when they have reached organizational maturity and excellence," the NAS Council resolved that it was time for the Board to make plans to leave the nest.[36]

A Transportation Research Board

Odum's essay, however, did influence President Handler. His remarks at the Chairman's Luncheon during the 52nd Annual Meeting drew heavily from Odum's arguments. Handler also announced plans to create a new multidisciplinary commission within NRC on technology and society. Here would be the new home for the "somewhat altered" Highway Research Board. He glossed over the Board's possible departure and instead commended his audience's success in integrating additional modes. But Handler emphasized the need for more change: more attention must be paid to the urban modes, to land use, and to the environmental and societal costs of all transportation infrastructure. He closed solemnly: "I need not tell you nobody knows how to do that at this time. That is your job. You are going to have to learn how—and that is a great challenge."[37]

Three years into his own pursuit, Handler had firsthand knowledge that "nobody knows how to" organize NRC—let alone society—for total transportation. The committee he had convened to recommend reorganization for his Division of Transportation had floundered, after getting sidetracked by utopian solutions for society's transportation problems.[38] The Board's Visiting Committee became convinced by its intensive study that it "did not know enough to make such recommendations." Unable to even weigh in on whether the commission "should be organized by modes, by problems or by some other subdivision," Mac Lane tossed out the suggestion that the Board could become the "Road and Rail Research Board." During this same time, the American Transit Association and Institute for Rapid Transit, interested in a transit research program modeled after NCHRP, but wary of it in the same NRC board as highways, were considering a proposal for an "Urban Transportation Research and Development Board." And the Board, through its Executive Committee, had offered three successive proposals, culminating in a recommendation for three boards, one each for ground, air, and maritime transportation research.[39]

Although the Visiting Committee had no answers, it had outlined the major problem that was bedeviling Handler's ambitions: funding, or more specifically, the imbalance in potential funding. Shocked by the allocation of federal funding for highways versus mass transit, for infrastructure as well as research, the committee was concerned that a transportation research board's funding would be "erratic." Other

Dial-a-Ride van service in Ann Arbor, Michigan, was an attempt to boost transit ridership and ease travel in its congested downtown, 1973 (U.S. National Archives, 412-DA-7201).

modes—Mac Lane listed air travel and pedestrians as examples—did not even have a source equivalent to mass transit's meager-by-comparison-to-highways research funding. Nor was it obvious how to get funding for self-initiated studies that could target aspects of the transportation system as a whole. The Board's leaders, however, found the funding imbalance, in and of itself, to be less troubling. For them, funding was a matter of selling their services and reputation to new sponsors.[40]

The Board's greatest concern in January 1973 was the NAS Council's order for them to make plans to leave. Garrison, as incoming chair, easily won approval of a resolution protesting the decision and won a reprieve from President Handler. Preparing plans for separation could wait until after the NAE and NRC organizational dust had settled. In addition, NAS awarded Carey its Distinguished Service Award for NRC staff, citing his "significant contributions to transportation technology and his record of continuous leadership." Whether this award was meant to signal continued support and bolster Carey's morale or to thank him for a job well done is not clear.[41]

Whether through exquisite diplomacy or simple exhaustion, during fall 1973 the organizational pieces finally began to fall into place. The end result was a compromise. NAE would stay in the fold and manage its studies within NRC's Assembly on Engineering, according to NRC's procedural safeguards. Through its Assembly, NAE would also continue to manage the Committee on Transportation and studies advising government. The Board and the Maritime Transportation Research Board were slated for the new Commission on Sociotechnical Systems, but NAE's Marine Board went to the Assembly on Engineering. NRC organized the other three assemblies (behavioral and social sciences; life sciences; and mathematical and physical sciences) and three commissions (human resources, international relations, and natural resources) during the months it took for the final votes of NAS and NAE membership.[42]

Who first proposed that the Board revive its 1967 proposal to be a Transportation Research Board is lost to the National Academies' records, but it is not hard to imagine that Garrison seized the opportunity when he saw it. That Carey's feared "policy studies" had found another home in the new Assembly on Engineering also would have alleviated the executive director's concerns about the transformation. Or perhaps, the instigation came from a different party altogether: AASHO.

AASHO began in earnest to consider a broadened mandate in November 1972. Twenty-three states now had departments of transportation. Adding urgency, the Federal-Aid Highway Act of 1973, signed in August, significantly increased federal funding for mass transit infrastructure and required that some highway planning funds be reserved for metropolitan planning controlled by local governments. In addition, local officials could use certain federal funds for highways or mass transit projects. On November 13, 1973, AASHO adopted a new name, American Association of State Highway and Transportation Officials (AASHTO). Garrison and Carey, attending the November 1973 AASHTO meeting, aired their proposal for a Transportation Research Board during the luncheon for state and federal administrators. The Board's long-standing partners unanimously endorsed an NRC board and a research scope that matched their own.[43]

From this point, events moved so quickly that the Board dispensed with forming a subcommittee. Carey drafted a transition plan for Executive Committee approval at the January 1974 Annual Meeting. With formal support from AASHTO and federal administrators, the proposal's last stop was the NRC Governing Board. Mac Lane spoke in support of the proposal, but the most eloquent evidence of changed hearts and minds came from Harvey Brooks. Three years after publicly castigating the Highway Research Board, he wrote:

> Apparently the only serious argument against this change is that HRB is so committed to automobiles and highways that it cannot be relied upon to give balanced consideration to other modes.... That argument might have had some merit ten years ago, but I do not believe it does today. I am convinced that the present leadership of HRB—both staff and Board—is committed to the broad approach.

On March 9, 1974, the National Academies officially had a Transportation Research Board.[44]

President Handler's vision of one integrated unit for transportation, setting a model for how to put science and engineering into service on society's complex problems, had yet to come to fruition. However, NRC did have two transportation units with broad research scopes and a neat division of responsibility—policy advice and information—between them. That transportation came last, instead of first, in Handler's ambitious reorganization scheme reflected the true conceptual and management challenges that resided within the simple phrase, total transportation.

Just as importantly for the National Academies, the needed reforms were all in place before the 1975 publication of *The Brain Bank of America*, the book that Udall's broadside in December 1970 had inspired. Philip Boffey, its author, presented two main critiques: the lack of safeguards to ensure high-quality studies and the inability of the National Academies to get out in front, independently, on big-picture issues. Handler expressed confidence that NRC's new procedures added the necessary safeguards. He agreed with the second critique and put his faith in the reorganized NRC.[45]

However, TRB's leaders could not afford to be exhausted by the 10 years of controversy. Nor could they rest in satisfaction that the scientists and the engineers had finally admitted that they needed the highway experts after all. For the new TRB, its biggest challenges still lay ahead. It would be up to them to figure out whether the concept of the total transportation system would be the right solution for meeting society's total transportation needs.

CHAPTER 9

Building a *Transportation* Research Board, 1974–Present

THE COVER OF THE new Transportation Research Board's (TRB's) 1974 Annual Report celebrated its rebirth with the letters "HRB" fading into the growing bolder "TRB." Yet, inside, the report—typically full of photos—was surprisingly plain and even perfunctory. William N. Carey, Jr., TRB's executive director, explained why in the equally plain Annual Report for 1975. The high inflation and oil crises of the 1970s had eaten away at TRB's purchasing power in the same way they were distressing the transportation industry as a whole. Despite the economic headwinds, TRB's first steps found solid footing, only to be shaken as economic conditions weakened further and, as the 1980s dawned, federal policy appeared to abandon much of the intellectual underpinnings for TRB's expansion. Instead, TRB found a new—strategic—path to rejuvenation that accelerated growth throughout the 1990s and beyond. This chapter, and the four chapters that follow, portray this period for the institution as a whole and then how it unfolds for consensus studies, technical activities, strategic highway research, and cooperative research.

TRB's first Annual Report, 1974.

The First Steps

After spending nearly 10 years debating whether the Highway Research Board should become a Transportation Research Board, the speed of the final decision meant the Board had a new name, but no new sponsors. While TRB planned its expansion, the amount of sponsorship from the state departments of transportation, the Federal Highway Administration (FHWA), and the Urban Mass Transportation Administration (UMTA) stayed constant. Still, TRB formed planning committees for rail and air and started organizing technical committees.

TRB's first new federal funding came in the form of contracts to hold conferences, building on an established model. In the early 1970s, the Board had successfully used conferences to expand its presence in urban transportation, as called for in the revised scope approved in 1969. These were working conferences built around specific research or policy questions, and they often produced recommendations. Committees of the Regular Technical Activities Division typically lent assistance or even formally "sponsored" these conferences. For some, the Board convened a specialized committee. For example, the Board itself sponsored conferences on the use of Census data in urban transportation planning in 1970 and 1973, and it attracted support from the Engineering Foundation for a conference on public transportation in 1972. The Board joined the Massachusetts Institute of Technology (MIT) in co-sponsoring an annual conference on demand-responsive transportation systems (Dial-A-Ride) in 1972, to which the American Transit Association added its support in 1973. These annual conferences continued through the 1970s, under the sponsorship of TRB's new Committee on Urban Transport Service Innovations.

William J. Harris, Jr., led TRB's new Planning Committee for Rail Transport Activities. Then a vice president for the Association of American Railroads (AAR), Harris had a long history of affiliation with the National Research Council's (NRC's) National Materials Advisory Board. In 1975, AAR and the Federal Railroad Administration (FRA) sponsored a "total immersion" study, chaired by John Gratwick of Canadian National Railways. Held at the National Academies' facility in Woods Hole, Massachusetts, the study gathered 200 experts who over 5 weeks discussed research needs for all aspects of railroad transportation. In 1977, when TRB published the study's report, *Rail Transport Research Needs* (TRB Special Report 174), both AAR and FRA had become sponsors of TRB's regular technical activities, and Harris was elected to the National Academy of Engineering (NAE).[3]

For the new planning committee for air transport activities, TRB turned to Ronald Pulling, then a consultant and a 30-year veteran of the Federal Aviation Administration (FAA). That TRB would aggressively pursue aviation was not foretold by the planning done by NRC or the Board in 1972–1973 or in the Board's earlier attempt at total transportation in 1967–1969. The Airlie House Conference of 1968 had included representatives from FRA, but not FAA, and the Board's penultimate reorganization recommendation in 1973 had called for separate boards for surface, air, and maritime transportation. The new TRB embraced aviation. Pulling's committee was a large, diverse group representing all levels of government and facets of the aviation industry. Because aircraft design and air traffic control were well covered elsewhere, the committee recommended that TRB would have the most impact by addressing the economics of air travel and a comprehensive set of topics related to airports.[4]

William J. Harris, Jr., chaired the planning committee that began the process of integrating railroad research into the new TRB. Pictured here in 2004 upon his retirement from chair of the High-Speed Rail IDEA program (TRB).

Airports and aviation had been topics at annual meetings going back at least to the 19th meeting in December 1939. Runways, and the design and performance of their pavements, garnered most of the attention during the 1940s and 1950s. Indeed, the first report in the Board's Special Report series, launched in 1952, covered frost action in roads and airfields. Papers at annual meetings on airport planning and design dated to at least the 20th Annual Meeting, at which H. H. Houk, engineer in charge of building Washington National Airport, shared his experiences. As demand for air travel dramatically increased in the 1960s, ground access to airports became a frequent topic at annual meetings, including many papers exploring mass transit alternatives. Finally, not to be overlooked is the highway industry's early interest in aerial photography. The first research project advised by the Advisory Board on Highway Research in 1921, a highway travel survey in Connecticut, used "airplane photography" to collect data.[5]

In 1975, TRB's Advisory Committee on Airport Landside Capacity, chaired by Kenneth Heathington, University of Tennessee, organized a working conference on airport research needs. Sponsored by FAA, the conference brought together a wide range of experts, practitioners, and

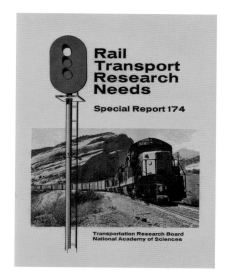

Rail Transport Research Needs, published in 1977, was the product of a 5-week immersion study sponsored by the Federal Railroad Administration and the Association of American Railroads.

customers to confront the quickly changing conditions at airports. After spiking upward in the 1960s, passenger travel had flattened in the 1970s, leaving great uncertainty over whether additional airport expansions were needed. In addition, during the expansion, greater attention and federal resources had been spent on the airside (getting planes to and from the gates) than on the landside (getting passengers to and from their flights). Over the course of 5 days, the committee produced a set of findings, including recommendations targeting government, and outlined 65 topics needing research. Showing the influence of TRB's work on highway capacity and level of service, chief among the conference's recommendations were developing techniques to measure and rate level of service and capacity at airports.[6]

Momentum seemed to be building. In addition to airports, TRB organized multiday conferences in 1975 on light rail transit and paratransit for UMTA and on transportation's air quality impacts for FHWA and the Environmental Protection Agency.[7] At the annual meeting in 1976, sessions on public transportation attracted the largest audiences, and the states responded well when the Executive Committee increased sponsorship fees for regular technical activities (the old Research Correlation Service) by 6 percent to offset inflation and pay for new subjects.[8] In the months ahead, TRB founded technical committees for rail (three), airports (two), and surface freight (two). TRB organized a conference in 1977 that informed the National Highway Traffic Safety Administration's (NHTSA's) response to a congressionally mandated study of the National Highway Safety Program. Also in 1977, FAA and NHTSA became sponsors, joining the Department of Transportation's (USDOT's) Secretary's Office, FHWA, UMTA, FRA, and AAR, as did the Maritime Administration even though it would not transfer from the Department of Commerce to USDOT until 1981.[9]

The always cautious Carey, therefore, had reason to be optimistic when he shared in the 1977 Annual Report that "The old Highway Research Board is really becoming a mature Transportation Research Board." Annual meeting sessions on rail and air numbered 34 that year, and the professional staff in the Regular Technical Activities Division were now visiting railroads and mass transit organizations along with their annual trips to state transportation departments. Conferences on new topics continued. FHWA's Julie Fee, chair of TRB's Committee on Pedestrians presented the keynote address at a conference on pedestrians. The CB radio craze, then rising to a peak with the 1977 hit film *Smokey and the Bandit,* inspired another conference on motorist communications. TRB also embarked on an international project, funded by the U.S. Agency for International Development.[10]

The new sponsors became ex officio members of the Executive Committee, which still numbered 20 appointed members despite added experts in railroads, aviation, and ports. Sponsors were generally on board with the model negotiated between the American Association of State Highway Officials (AASHO) and the Board in 1944, whereby they covered the cost of the professional and support staff who provided them a link to TRB's technical committees. However, the sponsors did push TRB to diversify its funding base by restructuring and raising fees for a new "associates" program that encouraged local governmental agencies, private companies, and educational institutions to help sustain TRB financially too.[11]

Transition to the 1980s

In spring 1979, Carey announced his intention to retire in 1980. As executive director, he had been a tireless advocate for TRB's traditional activities and had guided TRB through two significant expansions, first encompassing urban transportation and then total transportation. Between 1970 and 1979, the number of TRB's technical committees increased by nearly 50 percent, with the largest increase in Group 1, Transportation Systems Planning and Administration, which went from 9 to 40 committees. Attendance at annual meetings grew from 2,887 to 4,221. Sessions climbed even more, growing from 60 to nearly 200.[12]

Carey's replacement, however, would still have many challenges. Finances were stable, but precarious. Within the National Academies, President Philip Handler had negotiated an uneasy peace when he had maneuvered to keep the new TRB whole and within the fold in 1974. Handler's second, and final, 6-year term would expire in 1981.

TRANSPORTATION RESEARCH BOARD ANNUAL MEETING

1976

DATES January 19–23, 1976
LOCATION Sheraton-Park and Shoreham Americana Hotels
PRESIDING CHAIR Milton Pikarsky, Chicago Regional Transportation Authority

ATTENDANCE 3,900
NUMBER OF PAPERS 600
INTERNATIONAL ATTENDEES 5 percent
ORGANIZATION OF TECHNICAL ACTIVITIES Four groups hosting 140 committees and 16 task forces

WINNING PAPER TOPICS
- Needs of the elderly
- Passing zones
- Skid hazards
- Automatic warning devices at railroad crossings

BICENTENNIAL TIE-IN Chairman's Luncheon address "An American Travel Diary, 1776–1976" by Wilfred Owen
CHANGING TIMES Videotape shown at session on varved clays, but attendance limited by size of TV monitor

WHAT ELSE IS HAPPENING AT TRB IN 1976?
- NCHRP submits its 15th program of research projects, totaling $2.9 million
- TRB publishes eight Special Reports including on traffic flow theory, paratransit, air quality, fuel efficiency of vehicles and construction, and dual-mode transportation

In addition, TRB's embrace of total transportation took place during a time of tremendous change in the railroad, trucking, and airline industries. Since the 1950s, bipartisan support had been growing to end the decades-old federal regulatory system that dictated who carried what over which routes and at what prices. President Gerald Ford used the economic crisis and imminent railroad bankruptcies to push reform, with some small success at creating a railroad market. During the Carter administration, efforts continued, and Congress passed laws deregulating the airlines in 1978 and trucking and railroads in 1980. Newly competitive markets led to sharp cuts in the costs of shipping and travel. Mergers and acquisitions followed, and new types of companies emerged that managed freight across modes.[13]

President Ronald Reagan would accelerate the federal turn against regulation, including cutting funding for planning. Starting in 1954, federal housing legislation had supported grants for a growing portfolio of urban planning efforts conducted by cities, regions, and even states. Known as Section 701, the program was a source of support for the land use counterpart to the metropolitan transportation planning supported by federal-aid highway funding. The Reagan administration eliminated Section 701 grants entirely in 1981.[14]

Deregulation carried over into the federal–state–local relationship for transportation too. Ray A. Barnhart, federal highway administrator, told a TRB audience in late 1981 that "federal involvement will be curtailed or eliminated in areas in which the benefits of federal activity do not justify the intrusion of federal requirements or where the federal interest is questionable." National significance would be FHWA's criterion for action, and at the top of FHWA's list was reconstructing the older, deteriorating sections of the Interstate Highway System.[15]

Although Reagan's election was still months away, TRB's sponsors and the National Academies all sensed the importance of who next would lead this large, complex, and unique institution. TRB had a long tradition of promoting from within, and NRC had an equally strong tradition of its major units being led by people with significant experience in academia. The ideal person would need to be able to work with sponsors, administrators, and researchers from all of transportation. Paul Sitton, executive officer, led the process for NRC, while Thomas D. Larson, Pennsylvania Department of Transportation, led the Executive Committee's effort. Sitton knew Thomas B. Deen from when Sitton worked at UMTA. At

From left, FHWA Deputy Administrator Lester P. Lamm, former FHWA Administrator Frank Turner, Secretary of Transportation Elizabeth Dole, and FHWA Administrator Ray A. Barnhart at the dedication of the Francis C. Turner Building at the Turner-Fairbank Highway Research Center on May 5, 1983. Turner encouraged the Board's work in urban transportation, and Barnhart and Lamm supported TRB's initial study that eventually led to the Strategic Highway Research Program (FHWA).

first, Sitton reached out to Deen for candidate recommendations, but as the process bogged down in search of the elusive ideal, Sitton began twisting Deen's arm to consider the position himself.[16]

At the time, Deen was president of the consulting firm Alan M. Voorhees & Associates, but his background included a breadth of professional and geographic experience relevant to TRB. Deen had a civil engineering degree from the University of Kentucky and did advanced study at The University of Chicago and Yale University's Bureau of Highway Traffic. He then returned to the South, working in Nashville in the late 1950s and rising to direct the Nashville Area Transportation Study. In the early 1960s, he moved to Washington, D.C., for a position as a highway planner at the National Capital Transportation Agency (NCTA), a temporary federal agency organized to plan the region's heavy rail metro system and highway network. Deen rose to become NCTA's director of planning and oversaw studies making recommendations for both metrorail and highways, including canceling several planned Interstate routes. At Voorhees,

Bicycling Boomed in the 1970s, Including in TRB

ALTHOUGH THE BICYCLE inspired the Good Roads Movement in the late 19th century, bicycling received little more than an occasional aside during the Highway Research Board's first 50 years. Then came another bicycle boom. By 1973, the sale of bicycles for adults had more than tripled in a decade, spurred on by new light-weight, multispeed bicycles; the environmental movement; the oil crisis; and interest in exercise and recreation. The Transportation Research Board (TRB) was not going to let the latest bicycle boom pass it by.

Formal attention to bicycling as part of the Board's technical activities started as a subcommittee of the Committee on Pedestrians, which itself was created in 1970. The first major paper on bicycling, presented at the 1973 Annual Meeting, was bullish, proclaiming "the growing belief that bicycles are here to stay." The authors' survey of state highway departments found a majority doing research on bicycles. Nine states had already developed planning criteria and four had design criteria.[a]

The next year, bicycling research filled an entire session at the annual meeting, and in April 1974 the new TRB had a new Committee on Bicycles and Bicycle Facilities. Mark Akins, Washington Metropolitan Area Transit Authority, chaired the committee, and among its members

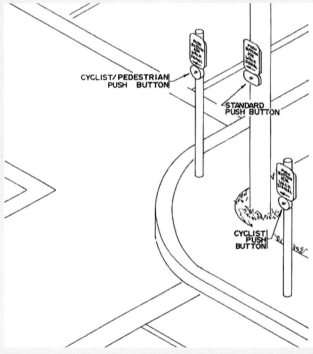

Figure from Peter Ju-Cheng Chao, Judson S. Mattias, and Mary R. Anderson, "Cyclist Behavior at Signalized Intersections," *Transportation Research Record* 683 (1978, 35).

were two women: Marie E. Birnbaum worked for the Department of Transportation and Nina Dougherty Rowe did transportation policy at the Environmental Protection Agency.[b]

Although the 1970s' boom cooled, research on bicycling within TRB continued. The Committee on Bicycle Transportation averaged three papers submitted per annual meeting in the early 1990s. Interest picked up in the early 2000s, rising to 15 submitted papers. Then bicycling research boomed. By early in the 2010s, the committee was reviewing roughly 80 papers per year.[c]

Research on bicycling found its way into other TRB research programs as well. The Transit Cooperative Research Program (TCRP) published *Integration of Bicycles and Transit* (TCRP Synthesis of Transit Practice 4) in 1994. As the National Cooperative Highway Research Program's (NCHRP's) work on highways became more multimodal, many studies included bicycle facilities or considered bicycles as part of research into geometric design. NCHRP published *Guidelines for Analysis of Investments in Bicycle Facilities* (NCHRP Report 552) in 2006 and 2014's NCHRP Report 797 (*Guidebook on Pedestrian and Bicycle Volume Data Collection*) looked anew at collecting data on bicycling.

Bicycle sharing services started making a splash in the *Transportation Research Record*

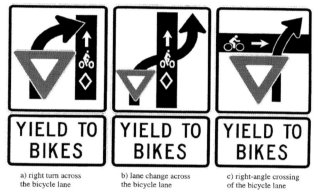

a) right turn across the bicycle lane   b) lane change across the bicycle lane   c) right-angle crossing of the bicycle lane

Figure from William W. Hunter, David L. Harkey, J. Richard Stewart, and Mia L. Birk, "Evaluation of Blue Bike-Lane Treatment in Portland, Oregon," *Transportation Research Record* 1705 (2000, 110).

around 2010. TRB has also long had a Committee on Motorcycles and Mopeds, which started as a task force in 1978. As the current decade comes to a close, the bicycle itself is changing, with e-bikes (electric assist) joining other types of "micromobility" on the streets. Questions rise anew on vehicle technologies, road design, and human behavior.

Deen had been vice president for transit planning and then senior vice president for international operations. Although not part of TRB's core leadership cadre, he had attended the annual meeting since his days at Yale and served on committees. Deen had also shown his research chops through numerous papers including co-authoring the 1975 winner of TRB's Pyke Johnson Award for best paper on transportation systems planning and administration. Finally, after months of effort, NRC and TRB's Executive Committee had found their man.[17]

Still, coming from the outside had its challenges for Deen, and it took 6 months of careful study to build confidence that he understood what made TRB tick. His outsider status also gave him fresh perspectives on TRB's difficult past. Deen had not been on the front lines during the total transportation disputes within NRC during the 1960s and 1970s, and he knew little about the AASHO Road Test until he took the job.[18] Unlike previous directors, Deen did not set himself up as the voice of TRB. He rarely used the annual reports or *TR News*, as *Transportation Research News* was renamed in 1983, to speak directly to TRB's constituencies. (In his reticence, Deen was most like Fred Burggraf, executive director from 1951 to 1964.) Instead, Deen elevated the voices of leaders from within the corps of volunteers.

Deen would also soon have a new boss. Frank Press assumed the NAS presidency in 1981. A geophysicist who specialized in seismology, Press advised numerous federal agencies under both Republican and Democratic administrations and had been director of the White House's Office of Science and Technology Policy during the Carter administration. Press had also served as president of the American Geophysical Union shortly after it had left NRC in 1972 to establish itself as an independent organization. Press, therefore, had an in-depth understanding of managing the government–science relationship and, for TRB, of what it would mean for both NRC and TRB if the National Academy of Sciences (NAS) Council's still unresolved 1972 decision that TRB should spin off parts of itself as an independent institution were realized.[19]

Merging Information and Policy

Press recognized that having two separate units dedicated to transportation was less than ideal. TRB was old, large, and had deep ties to federal and state highway researchers and growing relationships to urban transportation, aviation, and railroad research communities. The Committee on Transportation, founded by NAE just more than 10 years earlier, comprised around 15 top researchers in universities and private companies and former high-level federal officials. Even with their division of responsibility, information versus policy advice respectively, some sort of coordination was necessary.[20]

When the split between TRB and the Committee on Transportation worked well, coordination happened through overlapping leadership, and the two organizations succeeded in bringing new people to the table to share expertise. For example, anticipating the opening of the Bay Area Rapid Transit (BART) system, two Board committees on highway and passenger transportation economics joined forces in 1970 to hold a workshop conference to promote studying BART's socioeconomic and environmental impacts. Co-sponsored by the University of California, Berkeley, and held on the university's campus, officials from FHWA, UMTA, and the Department of Housing and Urban Development (HUD) were among the 65 participants who discussed research recommendations. The federal officials shared that they too were considering a major impact study.[21]

When USDOT and HUD did indeed join forces to launch the BART Impact Program in 1972, they turned to NAE's Committee on Transportation to organize an ongoing advisory committee. J. Douglas Carroll, a longtime TRB leader, participated in the effort, but the advisory committee also brought new people into NRC's transportation work. NAE and NRC selected as chair Milton Pikarsky, then with the Chicago Transit Authority and soon to be chair of northeastern Illinois' new Regional Transportation Authority. The advisory committee's Panel on Evaluation of Social, Political, and Economic Impacts included three African-American women: Dorothy S. Duke, a housing specialist and consultant to Secretary George Romney at HUD; Ann Gates, the first head of the Metro Regional Transit Authority Board in Akron, Ohio; and Aileen C. Hernandez, who had served in the Johnson administration and had been the second president of the National Organization for Women. Pikarsky was elected to NAE in 1973 and in the mid-1970s served on NAE's Committee on Public Engineering Policy, charged with making the connection to government policy making. Pikarsky had also joined the Board's Executive Committee in 1971 and took a turn as chair of TRB in 1975.[22]

Milton Pikarsky (left) talking to transit riders in Chicago, October 1974: Pikarsky served as chair in 1975 and would oversee TRB's policy studies in the 1980s (Chicago History Museum).

Although TRB was not directly involved in the BART Impact Program, the high profile of its research attracted attention at annual meetings, including a television crew from CBS in 1978.[23] However, if Carey needed a reminder, the BART research also revealed again the perils of association with controversial government programs. When *Transportation Research News* published an article titled "BART: Expensive Flop or Commuter's Delight?" Pikarsky demanded equal time for rebuttal. He made the case for rail transit and also argued that the federal government subsidized the automobile through dedicating the excise tax on gasoline to highways and federal programs supporting home mortgages and sewer and water infrastructure.[24]

Although the split between information and policy advice could work, in reality, as the 1970s came to a close, the line between NAE and TRB activities blurred. At first NAE's Committee on Transportation had the stronger representation across the modes, but TRB had successfully earned sponsorship from many of USDOT's constituent parts. While the Committee on Transportation supported controversial topics, such as co-sponsoring the first conference on women's travel behavior (see Chapter 14), the committee also held workshops on technical subjects such as forecasting freight demand and fostering innovation in transportation. TRB too moved into policy, conducting a study on promoting seat belt use for NHTSA as part of a congressional mandate.[25]

When the Reagan administration filled USDOT with a new crop of administrators, coordinating NRC outreach was paramount, but instead the Committee on Transportation and TRB became rivals.[26] TRB won early favor, leading to conferences in late 1981 and 1982, sponsored by FHWA and UMTA, on future directions for urban transportation planning and public transportation. These conferences produced findings, made recommendations, and in the case of public transportation, issued a consensus statement.[27]

Press and the NRC Governing Board conducted a thorough review of TRB's activities during the latter half of 1981, reexamining their fit within the larger institution. Until 1962, the Board had been *in* NRC, but as a federation of organizations with its own bylaws, not *of* NRC. Although the bylaw revision in 1962 brought the Board closer to the NRC norm, the compromise of 1974 had actually pushed the new TRB further away again. NAS, NAE, and NRC existed to advise government. Moreover, the late 1970s and early 1980s were such a tumultuous time in the federal government that almost any transportation topic raised questions of policy. (As the AASHO Road Test had shown, even pavement design could have controversial policy implications.) TRB was involved in policy whether it admitted it or not. Moreover, if the National Academies could bring the full resources of TRB to questions of policy, it would strengthen the entire institution.[28]

For TRB to reach its full potential, however, it was going to have to learn how to police itself. NAS had adopted procedural reforms to protect the credibility and integrity of the National Academies and its reports during the crisis of the early 1970s. These reforms developed rules for appointments to all committees and required peer review for reports. For what were called policy studies, which explicitly advised government, the procedural reforms also covered the shaping of the research question, the selection of committee members, and the process for reaching committee consensus on findings and recommendations. (Today, these studies are called consensus studies.) The modern TRB was so large and multidisciplinary that, as a practical matter, no other unit in NRC had the breadth of expertise or the capacity to provide rigorous oversight. Deen welcomed the challenge, although Carey, on hearing of the changes afoot, made a special visit to Deen's office to express his concerns.[29]

The elevation of TRB to a stand-alone unit within NRC finally resolved any lingering questions of its place in the National Academies. The executive director would report directly to the NAS president and the NRC Governing Board. Moreover, the organizational solutions put in place by Press over 1982 and 1983 tied TRB even more closely to NAS and NAE. TRB's promotion also clarified its role in managing research that touched on government activity. All studies that advised the federal government were required to be conducted according to NRC-supervised consensus study procedures. The NRC Governing Board would appoint members of NAS and NAE to TRB's Executive Committee. A separate

From left, Charles Potts (president, APAC, Inc.), Damian J. Kulash, Anthony Kane (FHWA executive director), Thomas B. Deen, and Thomas D. Larson in 1997 (Robert P. Turtil).

oversight committee, made up of NRC and TRB appointees, and with the support of specialized professional staff in TRB's executive office would ensure that TRB met NRC standards. (This Subcommittee on NRC Oversight is today called the Division Committee.) Pikarsky was first to chair this oversight committee, a position he held for 7 years, and a perch from which he was an enthusiastic proponent of TRB's ability to contribute to larger discussions about government policy.[30]

Deen, therefore, looked for policy experience when replacing the retiring Paul E. Irick, who had been in charge of TRB's special technical activities since completing his assignment as statistician for the AASHO Road Test. Damian J. Kulash joined the staff in late 1982. He had a Ph.D. in transportation systems analysis from MIT, and at the time of his hiring was deputy assistant director at the Congressional Budget Office and chair of TRB's Committee on Taxation, Finance, and Pricing.[31] Almost immediately, Deen, Kulash, and TRB were put to the test with federal requests for policy advice, and TRB would discover that the consensus study process was also a powerful tool to vet proposals of its own initiative. Consensus studies would prepare the ground for the Strategic Highway Research Programs (SHRPs) and new cooperative research programs (see Chapters 10, 12, and 13). In addition, the fears that policy studies, especially on controversial topics, might weaken support for TRB's traditional technical activities turned out to be misplaced. Instead, Deen found, sponsors' respect for TRB increased as they came to understand the significance and integrity of the consensus study process.[32]

Federal Policy, ISTEA, and TRB

The election of George H. W. Bush to the presidency in 1988 would bring momentous changes for transportation, including transportation research. TRB entered this new era with restored optimism. The 5 cent increase in the gas tax in the Surface Transportation Assistance Act of 1982 had helped rejuvenate TRB's technical activities. Federal funding for SHRP and increased state support for the National Cooperative Highway Research Program (NCHRP) in 1987 lifted TRB's spirits even more. The appointment of Samuel K. Skinner to secretary of USDOT, who served from 1989 through 1991, and Thomas D. Larson to federal highway administrator foretold an even more promising future. Skinner, long active in politics, had also chaired the Regional Transportation Authority for northeastern Illinois from 1984 to 1988, and Larson had been instrumental to the cultivation of a strategic approach to research within TRB. Among USDOT's achievements during the Bush administration were the release of a national transportation policy statement in 1990, followed by passage of the landmark Intermodal Surface Transportation Efficiency Act (ISTEA) in December 1991.

In July 1989, USDOT turned to TRB to host the kickoff event for the public outreach phase of its national policy statement. Secretary Skinner introduced speakers including the presidents of General Motors and USAir and the governor of Nebraska. NAE President Robert M. White, who had chaired the first World Climate Conference in 1979, spoke on the "environmental imperative" to address acid rain, oil spills, air pollution, and global warming as part of a national transportation policy.[33]

Six months later, Skinner previewed the new national transportation policy at TRB's annual Chairman's Luncheon. In response, Wayne Muri, chief engineer of Missouri Highway and Transportation Department and chair of TRB's Executive Committee in 1990 proclaimed: "Anyone involved in transportation research is entitled to lean toward the euphoric." Not only was "advancing transportation technology and expertise" one of the new policy's six "themes," but FHWA, FAA, and UMTA were all working to expand research and development programs.

Major industry groups also backed increased federal funding for research and development.[34]

Fulfilling USDOT's policy ambitions, ISTEA funded a huge increase in transportation research. In addition to congressional authorization for the Transit Cooperative Research Program (TCRP; see Chapter 13), the act increased State Planning and Research (SP&R) funds from 1.5 percent to 2 percent of federal highway aid and required that states spend one-quarter of SP&R funds on research and technology transfer. Between 1982 and 1993, annual federal and state spending on research and technology increased 250 percent to $276 million.[35]

TRB grew too, so much and so quickly that Deen and William W. Millar, chair of the Executive Committee in 1992, spoke in the Annual Report of "the problems of growth and success." Between 1991 and 1993, TRB's budget increased from $18 million to $30 million and staff from 95 to 115. Annual meeting attendance grew 20 percent between 1992 and 1993 alone, from 5,600 to 6,700 registrants. TRB began actively looking for ways to continue to meet its longtime standards of service, while accommodating growing demands for expansion, especially in the work of technical committees.[36]

In addition to funding research, ISTEA and 1990's Clean Air Act Amendments had also put in place new regulatory regimes. Just as significantly, ISTEA renegotiated the federal–state–local relationship, encouraging more locally driven planning and decision making. Requirements for metropolitan planning and management systems for congestion, pavement, bridges, and highway safety all brought new research issues—or new attention to old issues—to TRB's doorstep. For governments, how best to implement the regulations and coordinate among themselves, all while being inclusive of modes, was not just conceptually difficult, but also politically delicate. TRB's sponsors and constituencies looked to it to play host to numerous workshops and conferences in "neutral settings to achieve consistent and accepted procedures."[37]

One of the most significant efforts was a series of activities under the umbrella "Reinventing Planning" that fully embraced multimodalism. Despite "intermodal" being the "I" in ISTEA, "intermodalism" as an organizing concept for transportation was fading into the sunset. At its height in the late 1960s and early 1970s, intermodalism was the belief that systems analysis would help society rationally decide "between" the modes to create a unified system. In other words, intermodalism sought to identify "the most efficient way of moving from point to point in a system." The deregulation impulse, market orientation, and preference for decentralization of the 1980s, however, were more compatible with multimodalism. As the American Association of State Highway and Transportation Officials (AASHTO) recognized in its centennial history, ISTEA birthed "the era of transportation choice" that continues to today.[38]

To reinvent planning, TRB convened a series of conferences, culminating in a gathering in December 1992 that was TRB's first conference co-sponsored by all five of USDOT's modal administrations (FAA, FHWA, FRA, Federal Transit Administration, and the Maritime Administration). Notable to attendees, the December conference also invited representatives from the private sector to discuss their approaches to transportation planning and policy. The conferences led to NCHRP's sponsorship of a workshop in November 1993 "to support and improve multimodal transportation planning as practiced by publicly funded transportation agencies." AASHTO then used NCHRP for five linked studies covering data, freight and passengers, performance, land use, and partnerships for multimodal transportation (NCHRP Project 8-32).[39]

Maintaining Excellence and Continued Growth

After what would be only the first wave of an extended period of dramatic growth, Deen retired in 1994 and Robert E. Skinner, Jr., transitioned from director of special projects to executive director. Skinner had joined TRB's staff in 1983 from Alan M. Voorhees & Associates to assist in TRB's expansion into policy studies. Over 11 years, he had managed more than 30 studies that often took him far afield from his bachelor's and master's degrees in civil engineering from the University of Virginia and MIT, respectively. For TRB, the revolutions of past decades had finally settled. For the next 21 years, Skinner's challenges would be maintaining excellence and adapting proven models in an ever larger, and increasingly diverse, institution.[40]

During Skinner's tenure, TRB welcomed NRC's Marine Board as a special unit under the TRB umbrella in 1999. In the early 2000s, volunteers guided a reorganization of the standing technical committees that introduced modal groups (see Chapter 11). Mid-decade, TRB built the Airport Cooperative Research Program (see Chapter 13) and concurrently

launched the second SHRP. Unlike for the first SHRP, TRB managed
SHRP 2 itself, requiring a large, but temporary expansion of capacity
and staff (see Chapter 12). TRB's annual budget went from just less than
$30 million in 1994 to $130 million at the peak of SHRP 2 spending in
2011. Attendance at the annual meetings also continued to grow, reaching 12,000 in 2015, the first year it was held at the Walter E. Washington
Convention Center.

In 2008, TRB opened up the exhibit hall at the annual meeting to
commercial exhibitors, carving out an exception to the National Academies'
long-standing prohibition against any commercial advertising. Selling
exhibit space to businesses required special care and deliberation. From
the Board's 1925 decision to encourage experts from the private sector to
participate fully in the Board's activities, the strict prohibition on even
the appearance of the endorsement of a commercial product sent the
message that when people participated in TRB's activities, they did so as
individuals in service to the nation and the public interest. By the 2000s,
the National Academies' rigorous procedures governing committee
and panel appointments, conflicts of interest, transparency, and report
review made possible a select relaxation of the prohibition. The annual

meeting's exhibit hall soon hosted more than 200 exhibits and became another place for lively exchanges with public agencies, institutions and associations, and commercial enterprises.[41]

Just as importantly, commercial exhibits have been an independent source of funding for TRB's core technical activities, including the work of staff and volunteers on the more than 200 standing technical committees. TRB continues to develop sources of funding supplemental to government sponsorship for its traditional capacities. In addition to providing a hedge against the vicissitudes of government funding, independent funding helps ensure that TRB's traditional technical activities can provide a base—or a reserve corps—from which to respond to emergency or quickly evolving needs.

September 11, 2001

Both TRB and the National Academies as a whole mobilized within days of the September 11, 2001, terrorist attacks. TRB's Committee on Critical Transportation Infrastructure Protection quickly disseminated security research for aviation, waterways and ports, and surface transportation on a special website and launched, with AASHTO, a survey of the states.[42] In December, the National Academies appointed a 24-member committee to advise on "an integrated science and technology plan to combat terrorism." Mortimer L. Downey, former USDOT deputy secretary and a member of the full NRC committee, chaired the study's Panel on Transportation. In addition, NCHRP and TCRP directed $6 million to transportation security research. TCRP put its first (post-9/11) security-related project under contract in November 2001, and NCHRP quickly initiated the Report 525 series on surface transportation security.[43]

That TRB was prepared to act, however, had gotten a boost in the mid-1990s. In September 1996, Congress mandated that USDOT conduct a transportation system vulnerability assessment and requested that NAS form an advisory committee on surface transportation security. The work of this advisory committee, a large cross-NRC initiative, got under way in May 1998 and issued its final report, *Improving Surface Transportation Security: A Research and Development Strategy*, in 1999.[44] Even before this study got under way, however, the terrorist bombings of the World Trade Center in 1993 and the federal building in Oklahoma City in 1995 had prompted TRB's Executive Committee to ask "How vulnerable is the U.S. surface system to threats of terrorism and sabotage?" when it highlighted transportation security in its 1997 Critical Issues List (see Chapter 11). This set in motion the formation of a Task Force on Transportation Security in February 1999 that then became the Standing Committee on Critical Infrastructure Protection.[45]

Within 2 years of the September 11 attacks, TCRP and NCHRP completed 25 projects on transportation security. TCRP released the first volumes of its new research report series on public transportation security in 2002. NCHRP's Report 525 series eventually produced 16 concise volumes, starting with *Responding to Threats: A Field Personnel Manual* (2004).[46] Downey's panel also released its report in 2002. *Deterrence, Protection, and Preparation: The New Transportation Security Imperative*, published as part of the full NRC report and also as TRB Special Report 270, built on the 1999 consensus study's emphasis on "the need for a systems approach for transportation security." Special Report 270 is dedicated to Fred V. Morrone, a member of the 1998–1999 committee and director of public safety and superintendent of police for The Port Authority of New York & New Jersey, who died while responding to the attacks on the World Trade Center.[47]

TRB and the National Academies are now a mature, large, and multidisciplinary organization. Through the consensus study, the standing technical committee, and the cooperative research programs, they connect robust and dynamic expertise to government policy makers and the people on the front lines. Each of these tools is impressive in its own right. When coordinated, the whole becomes greater than the sum of its parts. They stand ready to take on the challenges of the future.

CHAPTER 10

Advising Government: Consensus Studies

COINCIDENTAL TO THE Transportation Research Board's (TRB's) 1982 promotion to a stand-alone unit within the National Research Council (NRC) and its acceptance of the responsibility to oversee consensus studies, Congress was working on an update to surface transportation legislation. Although major legislation is a typical vehicle for requests to the National Academy of Sciences (NAS), the timing meant that TRB was not going to be able to ease into its new responsibilities. Between September's Bus Regulatory Reform Act and December's Surface Transportation Assistance Act, five congressional requests were knocking on TRB's door when the Executive Committee met in January 1983. Congress had added some of the requests just days before passage, so even staff tracking the legislations' progress did not know they were coming. In addition, TRB had persuaded the Federal Highway Administration (FHWA) to sponsor a consensus study that would eventually lead to the first Strategic Highway Research Program (see Chapter 12).

With six studies waiting in the wings, members of the Executive Committee were filled with questions for the NAS representative in attendance. Could they refuse a request? Technically, yes, but only for "very serious considerations." However, the NRC Governing Board, which gave

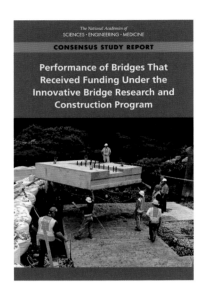

Commissioned by USDOT at the direction of Congress, *Performance of Bridges That Received Funding Under the Innovative Bridge Research and Construction Program* (TRB Special Report 330, 2019) is a recent example of a long line of studies assessing federal programs.

final approval to all studies, allowed revisions to the legislative language to make a study "more manageable, more sensible, and to make them doable." For the surprise requests, should they wait for the Department of Transportation (USDOT) to approach them? Here, the National Academies advised getting prepared before USDOT's overtures, although any eventual hiring of additional staff would have to wait until they were further along in the process. As with all the National Academies' committees, appointees to consensus study committees volunteered their time and experience. Funding covered travel, staff, and publication costs and offered modest recompense for commissioned research, which typically took the form of a resource paper summarizing information on a specific topic, but could include more in-depth research by agreement with the sponsor.[1]

Members of the Executive Committee also wanted to understand their responsibilities for whatever came out of a consensus study. Must they agree with a study's findings and recommendations? Ultimately, they learned, the National Academies needed to be able to endorse, with confidence, that the study committee "had the right people on it; that they brought in the right techniques; and that they did an honest job." TRB's Executive Committee provided oversight for the study process, including arranging for peer review of the report by third parties. Although the National Academies typically publicized the final reports, conclusions and recommendations belonged to the study committee, not the larger organization, a distinction that, the NAS representative admitted, "is very fine indeed."[2]

Between 1984, when TRB published *America's Highways: Accelerating the Search for Information* (TRB Special Report 202), and January 2019, TRB has been in the lead on more than 100 consensus studies that produced book-length reports. TRB has also supervised the production of numerous "letter reports," shorter documents advising federal agencies. These studies conformed to the strict set of practices and norms that the National Academies have developed over the years that govern study definition, committee selection, committee conduct during information gathering and deliberations, report drafting, and peer review. Study appointees must also comply with the National Academies' rules requiring the avoidance of conflicts of interest and forthrightness about biases (see Chapter 8). Many of these practices, including for public notice and transparency, were eventually codified in the Federal Advisory Committee Act Amendments of 1997.[3]

TRB's consensus studies program has enjoyed a continuity of leadership. Stephen R. Godwin, a member of the team that initiated consensus studies, succeeded Robert E. Skinner, Jr., as division director in 1994 and continued in the role until Thomas R. Menzies, Jr., who joined the unit in 1987, ably took over in 2017. This chapter examines the variety of types and uses of consensus studies through examples that illustrate differing sponsor relationships, study committees, and steps to study completion. It concludes with an in-depth examination of how TRB has been involved in, and initiated, consensus studies on sustainable transportation and climate change. More on consensus studies, including *America's Highways*, can be found in Chapters 12 and 13.[4]

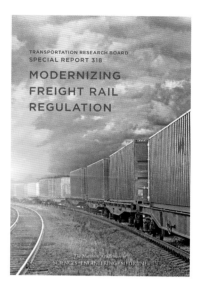

Congress funded a study sponsored by USDOT of freight railroads since the Staggers Rail Act of 1980 that resulted in *Modernizing Freight Rail Regulation* (TRB Special Report 318, 2015).

The Uses of Consensus Studies

The first five congressional requests covered the gamut: CB radios on intercity buses; twin trailer trucks on the Interstates; a feared retirement crisis among transportation professionals; design criteria for resurfacing, restoring, and rehabilitating ("RRR" [sic]) roads; and the 55-mile-per-hour national speed limit. For some, achieving consensus was straightforward. The committee on trucks concluded that twin trailer trucks were unlikely to affect safety, but would cause additional pavement wear, and the RRR committee determined criteria for federal aid for cost-effective RRR projects. However, presaging debates that would continue for decades, the CB radio committee, chaired by B. J. Campbell, a professor of psychology at the University of North Carolina at Chapel Hill, split over whether there was enough evidence to conclude that the benefits from in-vehicle communication outweighed the potential harm from distracted driving.[5]

Of the five, TRB knew that the speed limit study would be the most politically controversial, and over the course of the study, the committee exercised its independence, including the right to change its mind. At the height of the early 1970s oil crisis, Congress conditioned federal highway aid on states adopting a top speed limit of 55 miles per hour (mph). Effective March 1974, the law aimed to save fuel and ended up saving lives. However, the law had also broken with tradition that speed limits were a state prerogative. The study request, as it came from Congress, stacked the deck for continuing the 55-mph speed limit: it asked for a study of only the limit's benefits. NRC approved a revised scope to study the limit's benefits and *costs*. In the beginning, the committee, chaired by Alan A. Altshuler, New York University, a political scientist and former secretary of transportation for Massachusetts, expected that they would lay out the evidence without making policy recommendations, in recognition that ultimately this was a matter for politics. However, as evidence mounted that the lower speed limit was saving between 2,000 and 4,000 lives annually, the committee reconsidered. In the study's 1984 report, they came out unanimously, and strongly, for retaining a 55-mph limit on all urban highways and nearly all rural highways. Congress relaxed and eventually removed federal incentives for lower speed limits, and most states promptly raised them.[6]

In the first 10 years of consensus studies, TRB proved itself capable by conducting a wide variety of studies across the transportation modes. TRB won sponsorship from the Urban Mass Transportation Administration (UMTA) for the study that led to the Transit Cooperative Research Program (see Chapter 13). The Federal Aviation Administration commissioned a study, *Measuring Airport Landside Capacity* (TRB Special Report 215, 1987), chaired by Marjorie Brink, Peat Marwick Airport Consulting Services, and inspired in part by TRB's work on capacity and performance measurement in its long-running studies on highway capacity. After a deadly pipeline explosion, TRB worked with liaisons from the National Transportation Safety Board, USDOT's Office of Pipeline Safety, and private industry on damage prevention and emergency preparedness (TRB Special Report 219, 1988). Lawrence D. Dahms, head of the Bay Area's Metropolitan Transportation Commission, chaired a study on the potential for high-speed rail or maglev technology (TRB Special Report 233, 1991), and the Maritime Administration asked TRB to look at impediments and barriers to intermodal marine containers (TRB Special Report 236, 1992). Even the American Association of State Highway and Transportation Officials (AASHTO) requested a consensus study, after a particularly controversial proposal for heavy-weight trucks became too much for the National Cooperative Highway Research Program (NCHRP) (TRB Special Report 227, 1990).[7]

TRB also pursued self-initiated studies. For studies it proposes, TRB can follow one of three funding paths: external sponsorship alone, pooled

55: A Decade of Experience

Transportation Research Board
Special Report 204
National Research Council

In *55: A Decade of Experience* (TRB Special Report 204, 1984), the committee concluded that the lower speed limit saved 2,000–4,000 lives annually.

sponsorship with TRB funding, or solely TRB funded. *America's Highways* is the signature example of a self-initiated, but then fully sponsored, study. Most self-initiated studies, however, have required at least some TRB funding. In addition, TRB discovered that pooled sponsorship, if possible, was usually the most desirable route for a self-initiated study. Broader sponsorship, especially from those with authority to advance a study's recommendations, maximized its potential for impact. In 1989, TRB founded an Institute for Strategic Transportation Studies to attract unrestricted funds to support self-initiated studies. Donations from the Association of American Railroads, CONRAIL, the Norfolk Southern Corporation, and the UPS Foundation provided the needed funds for about a decade. Today, TRB funds self-initiated studies out of the interest earned on its reserve fund.[8]

Self-initiated studies are an important tool for TRB and the National Academies to express national leadership. As Thomas D. Larson, then secretary of Pennsylvania Department of Transportation and president of AASHTO, testified before Congress in 1986, "In the long run, the objectivity and independence of these organizations [TRB and NRC] will be enhanced if their expertise can be focused on the concerns of knowledgeable technical experts, regardless of whether government agencies are willing or able to finance [studies]." In his testimony, Larson shared how TRB had successfully courted corporate sponsorship for a "visionary" study of safety and mobility for older persons. The 3M Foundation, the Amerace Corporation, the Hartford Insurance Companies, and the Motor Vehicle Manufacturers Association all contributed funds to a study that was conducted with liaisons to NRC units on vision and human factors and to the American Association of Automotive Medicine. In 1987, Congress requested to join the study too. The committee of specialists in gerontology, traffic engineering, and automotive design, chaired by James L. Malfetti, director of the safety research and education project at Columbia University, completed "one of the most ambitious programs ever undertaken on behalf of elderly drivers, riders, and pedestrians." *Transportation in an Aging Society* (TRB Special Report 218, 1988) recommended a wide range of improvements to roadways, vehicle safety, driver licensing, and alternatives to driving.[9]

Consensus studies can also be used to promote research fundamentals such as the collection of data and the government institutions that

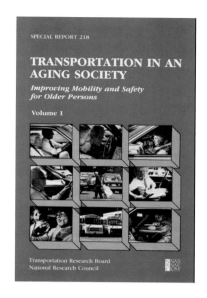

For *Transportation in an Aging Society* (TRB Special Report 218, 1988), TRB attracted sponsorship from numerous organizations, including Congress, for a "visionary" study on the elderly and driving, riding, and walking.

maintain such collections. As the first wave of enthusiasm for systems analysis crested in 1974, William N. Carey, Jr., TRB's executive director, warned that "an abysmal lack of data" stood in the way of using systems analysis for a comprehensive national transportation policy. The situation was not much better in 1989, when USDOT began work on such a national policy. The department turned to TRB for an evaluation of the data required for policy making and for advice on how to make such data permanently available. Chaired by Lillian C. Liburdi, then with The Port Authority of New York & New Jersey, the study recommended the creation of a permanent, independent data center that would track key trends through a national transportation performance monitoring system and provide a "framework" for more in-depth analyses of policies. In late 1991, even though *Data for Decisions: Requirements for National Transportation Policy Making* (TRB Special Report 234, 1992) had not yet officially gone to press, Congress was briefed on its contents and, in the Intermodal Surface Transportation Efficiency Act (ISTEA) of 1991, directed USDOT to create the Bureau of Transportation Statistics.[10]

At a Washington, D.C., press briefing for *Does the Built Environment Influence Physical Activity?* (TRB Special Report 282, 2005), committee chair Susan Hanson summarizes the findings (TRB).

The National Academies' consensus study framework also accommodates ongoing advisory relationships. As part of USDOT's 1990 policy encouraging research and technology advancement, FHWA and TRB entered into an advisory agreement in 1991 for continuing review and strategic advice on federal research programs. The resulting Research and Technology Coordinating Committee (RTCC) has produced, in addition to regular letter reports, three major studies in 1994, 2001, and 2008. Following recommendations in *The Federal Role in Highway Research and Technology* (TRB Special Report 261, 2001), conducted while C. Michael Walton, The University of Texas at Austin, chaired the RTCC, Congress in 2005 provided for a 10-fold increase in funding for higher risk, advanced research and for practices to improve research processes.[11]

The Federal Transit Administration (FTA) also supports a similar ongoing advisory process, the Transit Research Analysis Committee (TRAC). Since its first meeting in 2004, TRAC has issued around a dozen letter reports assessing and recommending changes to FTA's strategic approach to research. FHWA has also used ongoing TRB advising for long-term research projects on pavement performance (1997–2017) and bridge performance (2012–2016), and starting in 2017 for its infrastructure research and development program.[12]

The modal and subject breadth of TRB's consensus studies has continued into the present. To select only a few recent studies: In aviation, staffing levels for air traffic controllers received attention in two studies (TRB Special Report 301, 2010, and TRB Special Report 314, 2014). For freight rail, a committee recommended modernizing economic regulations (TRB Special Report 318, 2015). Studies revisited the collection and coordination of data for freight and passenger movement in 2003 (TRB Special Reports 276 and 277) and in 2011 (TRB Special Report 304). Studies on safety examined such topics as the relative risks of school travel (TRB Special Report 269, 2002); technologies to increase seat belt use (TRB Special Report 278, 2003); automotive electronics (TRB Special Report 308, 2012); and how to improve the study of guardrails (TRB Special Report 323, 2017). Studies also covered the safety of pipelines (TRB Special Report 281, 2004, and Special Report 311, 2013) and the movement of hazardous materials (TRB Special Report 325, 2018).[13]

As TRB closed in on its first century, it completed a major study of the Interstate Highway System. Congress allocated up to $5 million

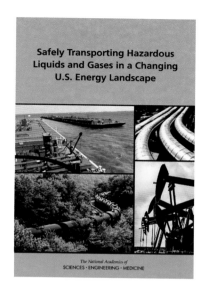

Safely Transporting Hazardous Liquids and Gases in a Changing U.S. Energy Landscape

TRB's Executive Committee self-initiated and sponsored a study of safety in the rail, pipeline, and barge industries that produced *Safely Transporting Hazardous Liquids and Gases in a Changing U.S. Energy Landscape* (TRB Special Report 325, 2018).

for the Future Interstate System Study in 2015's *Fixing America's Surface Transportation* (FAST) Act and instructed USDOT to work with TRB. The study, chaired by NAS and National Academy of Engineering (NAE) member Norman R. Augustine, retired chair and chief executive officer of Lockheed Martin Corporation, hosted numerous listening sessions and conducted scenario modeling, in addition to more typical information gathering. In *Renewing the National Commitment to the Interstate Highway System: A Foundation for the Future* (TRB Special Report 329, 2019), the committee advised that the "worn and overused" Interstate Highway System would require an increase from $25 billion to $45–$70 billion annually over the next 20 years. Furthermore, they warned that this estimate could be low, as it did not include improving the resilience of corridors vulnerable to the impacts of climate change.[14]

Finally, consensus studies require a set of skills and talents that often go unrecognized. The art of the study begins with the staff who set out to find people who have the subject expertise and the personality to work in the spirit of true collaboration. Once selected, chairs and staff need to be able to bring together high-achieving people from academic and practice backgrounds and to bridge the communications and cultural gaps that often stymie true cross-disciplinary efforts. Staff support the committee in their information gathering, deliberations, and response to peer review. Staff also often write draft reports. This specialized and unusual task requires the writer to work both under the direction of and in close collaboration with the committee, which is ultimately responsible for all of a report's content. The best consensus study reports transform the intention of a committee, sometimes even a divided committee, into a holistic document written in a unified, credible voice. In addition, much of what a committee of experts can just assume, staff must clearly articulate in a way that makes the persuasive case to an audience of non-experts.[15]

Sustainable Development and Climate Change

Starting in the 1990s, TRB exercised leadership on some of the most challenging environmental issues, including climate change. Over the span of more than 20 years, TRB used the consensus study as one tool to push action on sustainable transportation and mitigating climate change, even in studies prompted by Congress. The resulting series of studies allows an examination of the consensus study's strength as a

To inform the recommendations in *Renewing the National Commitment to the Interstate Highway System: A Foundation for the Future* (TRB Special Report 329, 2019), the study committee held numerous listening sessions and modeled scenarios.

collaborative tool. They also illustrate the challenge of emerging issues, especially when it is not clear whether science is adequate—or even appropriate—for the task society assigns it. TRB's interest in environmental topics, however, did not start with sustainable transportation.

In the early 1970s, as the Highway Research Board worked to court sponsors for public transportation, it also attempted to attract funding for environmental topics. The Task Force on Highways and the Environment, chaired by William B. Drake of the Kentucky Department of Highways, sponsored a special Summer Meeting in 1973 in Madison, Wisconsin, dedicated to environmental considerations in planning, design, and construction. Although top FHWA and Environmental Protection Agency (EPA) officials attended, the majority of speakers came from state governments. A spirit of optimism flowed through the meeting. Ray Lappegaard, Minnesota Department of Highways, encouraged attendees to improve the environmental quality on "spaceship Earth," and Lewis A. Posekany, Wisconsin Department of Natural Resources, shared that, thanks to cooperative efforts with the state's highway department dating to 1953, any trout stream crossed by a new Interstate Highway was "as high a caliber after construction as it was before."[16]

Whereas the revamped Highway Research Board in 1970 had two technical committees that addressed environmental issues, by 1979 TRB's Technical Activities Division had two entire sections (collections of committees below the group level) with "environmental" in their names. Environmental values had also started to transform construction and maintenance practices, so much so that some committee names evolved to reflect the new orientation. Thus, the Committee on Surface Drainage of Highways had become the Committee on Hydrology, Hydraulics, and Water Quality, and the Committee on Roadside Development had evolved into the Committee on Landscape and Environmental Design. During the 1970s and early 1980s, TRB also held conferences or workshops on noise control, conserving energy in construction, assessing transportation's impact on air quality, fuel efficiency, and the transportation of hazardous materials.[17]

Although environmental topics received less emphasis or sponsorship in the 1980s, concerns about transportation's role in urban vitality, suburbanization, and environmental quality came roaring back in the 1990s. The Bush administration's national transportation policy, released in February 1990, proclaimed one of its six defining policy directions

Using Economics to Manage Congestion: Is It Fair?

"**N**OT UNCONTROVERSIAL" IS how the Transportation Research Board's (TRB's) 1994 Annual Report described the consensus study *Curbing Gridlock: Peak-Period Fees to Relieve Traffic Congestion* (TRB Special Report 242). The Committee for Study on Urban Transportation Congestion Pricing had dared to suggest that the federal government should encourage tolls on the country's congested streets and highways.

Using pricing to manage travel during peak hours of traffic was not a new idea. As far back as the Fifth Annual Meeting in December 1925, Jacob Viner, The University of Chicago, examined the "economic control of traffic through the development of fees based on the use of road space at peak periods." In the mid-1970s, TRB hosted a major series of workshops on urban transportation economics, sponsored by the Department of Transportation (USDOT), the Environmental Protection Agency, and the Federal Energy Administration, that dedicated days to discussions of pricing alternatives.[a]

In the early 1990s, the time was ripe for revisiting congestion pricing. Federal transportation policy put a stronger emphasis on demand management. In addition, new technologies promised to make it easier to collect tolls and feasible to vary the price by time of

FHWA and FTA jointly sponsored *Curbing Gridlock*, TRB Special Report 242, in the early 1990s. The 1994 report recommended moving forward on congestion pricing and identified needed research on tolling's impact on lower-income groups.

day or traffic conditions. Because central to the analysis was how people respond to price changes, TRB partnered with the National Research Council's Commission on Behavioral and Social Sciences and Education.[b]

The Federal Highway Administration (FHWA) and the Federal Transit Administration (FTA) jointly sponsored the consensus study. The study also invited an unusually large number of liaisons. In addition to representatives from FHWA and FTA, liaison experts—who participate but do not vote on final recommendations—hailed from American Association of State Highway and Transportation Officials, American Automobile Association, Ford Motor Company, Highway Users Federation for Safety and Mobility, and American Trucking Associations. The committee, chaired by Martin Wachs, University of California, Los Angeles, commissioned 18 research papers on topics such as pricing and travel behavior, parking, urban form, and motor vehicle emissions, in addition to learning about electronic toll collection and the experience in other industries with peak-period pricing.

Although *Curbing Gridlock* recommended expanding experiments in congestion pricing and easing policy barriers to tolling, the committee also recognized that imposing new tolls would be politically difficult. Drawing heavily on a commissioned paper by Genevieve Giuliano on "Equity and Fairness Considerations of Congestion Pricing," the committee also recommended additional research and better policies addressing the needs of lower income groups.

In the years following *Curbing Gridlock*, federal transportation laws did indeed ease restrictions on adding toll lanes to Interstate highways and allowing solo drivers to pay a toll

In 2008, TRB self-funded the consensus study leading to *Equity of Evolving Transportation Finance Mechanisms* (TRB Special Report 303, 2011).

to use carpool lanes. Electronic toll collection has made variable pricing popular too.[c]

Political controversy continued, however, and the term "Lexus Lanes" entered the public debate. (In the early 1900s, "peacock lanes" was the term of choice to cast aspersions on highways designed and operated to speed wealthy car owners.) In the 2000s, TRB's Executive Committee began emphasizing "transportation equity" in periodic updates of its critical issues list.[d]

In 2008, TRB's Executive Committee decided to confront the fairness of how the country pays for transportation. TRB funded a consensus study on the *Equity of Evolving Transportation Finance Mechanisms* (TRB Special Report 303). Chaired by Joseph L. Schofer, Northwestern University, the committee worked to deepen political conversations about equity in all its "various dimensions" and encouraged policy makers to more fully "engage the public in decision making."[e]

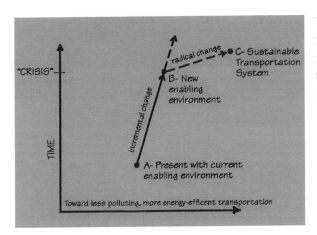

Labels within figure:
"CRISIS"
TIME
radical change
C- Sustainable Transportation System
B- New enabling environment
incremental change
A- Present with current enabling environment
Toward less polluting, more energy-efficent transportation

The Deen Paradigm, published in *TR News* in 1994, provides a way to conceptualize research needs when incremental change is predicted to fall short of societal goals.

to be "protect the environment and the quality of life."[18] Putting policy into action, FHWA requested that TRB convene a Conference on Transportation, Urban Form, and the Environment, which also attracted sponsorship from the Secretary's Office and UMTA, to identify research needs for "solutions and innovative institutional and technical approaches to provide for future urban mobility." Convened in December 1990, representatives from environmental advocacy organizations were among the attendees, and David Burwell, president of Rails-to-Trails Conservancy, served on the conference's steering committee and co-authored a resource paper on energy and environmental research needs.[19]

Burwell then joined TRB's Executive Committee in 1992, a symbol of TRB's recognition that expertise could be found outside of the traditional government–academia–consulting nexus. As a co-founder of the Surface Transportation Policy Project, a coalition of advocates for increased federal support for mass transit, walking, and bicycling, Burwell had helped shape USDOT's and then ISTEA's philosophy that used federal transportation policy to further multiple objectives, including environmental quality. Burwell also served on TRB's RTCC, which provided ongoing advice to FHWA.[20]

Since the early 1990s, TRB has conducted numerous consensus studies on transportation and environmental quality, many of which were self-initiated and self-funded. TRB, with NRC oversight, also continued to appoint researchers and experts to the study committees from environmental advocacy organizations and the transportation industries, including those with ties to automotive and energy companies. Although the discussion that follows focuses on consensus studies, environmental topics have also continued to find a home in annual meetings, the technical committees, the cooperative research programs, and the Strategic Highway Research Programs.

The Executive Committee's addition of "sustainable transportation" to its critical issues list in 1994 catalyzed much of TRB's subsequent environmental work. The Executive Committee argued, "The concept of sustainability ties together economic, environmental, social, and energy goals, all of which affect and are affected by transportation. Thus, transportation must be a part of sustainable development."[21] When the Executive Committee initiated the corresponding consensus study in 1995, it aimed high, planning "to lay out an achievable path toward sustainable transportation."[22]

TRB's sustainability work also continued the long tradition of defining terms and concepts to build a shared understanding around new transportation phenomena. One such concept, nicknamed the "Deen Paradigm," developed out of the work of the RTCC in 1994. Goal-oriented approaches to sustainable transportation revealed significant shortfalls between what researchers believed incremental change could achieve and the desired long-term goals. The gap between likely outcome and desired goal was especially large for reducing greenhouse gas emissions. Should researchers respond by trying to speed up incremental improvements, however inadequate, or by targeting radical change, however uncertain? The Deen Paradigm added the concept of an "enabling environment" or context that might allow radical change to happen. Essentially, it advocated assessing research needs along two tracks: incremental improvements in the near term and preparations to strike while the iron is hot, as it were, when shifts in the enabling environment make radical changes appear possible.[23]

Before TRB's sustainable transportation study could be completed, TRB published another self-initiated consensus study, *Expanding Metropolitan Highways: Implications for Air Quality and Energy Use* (TRB Special Report 245, 1995). Unlike the abstract concepts at play in sustainable transportation, this study was designed to weigh in on a hard reality: the Clean Air Act Amendments of 1990 had led, as TRB's *Annual Report* put it, to "litigation that threatens to stall metropolitan highway construction programs." The study, which attracted additional funding from AASHTO, EPA, and FHWA identified "courts with oversight responsibilities" as among its "primary audience" as it sought "to narrow the areas of disagreement about the impacts of highway capacity additions on traffic flow characteristics, travel demand, land use, vehicle emissions, air quality, and energy use." More specifically, could the best science really say whether a single highway project, typically adding lanes to an existing highway, made a significant difference to air quality and energy use?[24]

The 16-member committee chaired by Paul E. Peterson, professor of government, Harvard University, failed to come to consensus. The new environmental politics had created a rift over evaluating scientific uncertainty.

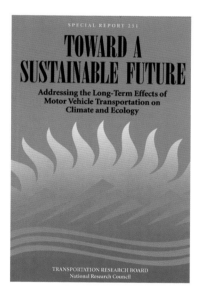

Toward A Sustainable Future (TRB Special Report 251, 1997), a product of a TRB-initiated study, highlights the importance of limiting greenhouse gas emissions and protecting biological diversity.

Fifteen members agreed that "the analytical methods in use are inadequate for addressing regulatory requirements." In other words, the best science just was not precise enough. However, Michael A. Replogle, a civil engineer with prior experience in local government and then co-director of the transportation project at the Environmental Defense Fund, issued a 26-page minority statement, which argued "the problem is not a lack of good science to support analysis, but institutional resistance to the use of good science in transportation analysis." In the end, the committee advised that direct approaches to reducing air pollution, through technology for cleaner cars or pricing incentives to reduce driving, were a better bang for the buck than tinkering with a highway system that was already largely in place.[25]

Toward a Sustainable Future: Addressing the Long-Term Effects of Motor Vehicle Transportation on Climate and Ecology (TRB Special Report 251) came out in 1997. Using its own funds as seed money, TRB had attracted sponsorship from the Energy Foundation, the Department of Energy (DOE), FHWA, FTA, AASHTO through NCHRP, and local transit agencies through the Transit Cooperative Research Program (TCRP). James D. Ebert, a biologist affiliated with both the Marine Biological Laboratory and Johns Hopkins University and a former vice president of NAS, chaired the 19-member, science-heavy committee. Most of the members came from universities or private research centers. Only two were affiliated with state highway departments, and Burwell, representing Rails-to-Trails Conservancy, also contributed his expertise.

From its ambitious beginnings, the limits of knowledge had soon set in. Instead of tackling all of sustainability to develop "an achievable path," the study targeted only motor vehicles in the United States. The committee picked two long-term risks that it determined needed more attention: greenhouse gas emissions and the loss of biological diversity because of air pollution and habitat disruption. It also limited its scope to raising awareness of the latest scientific findings and outlining research needs targeted at "reducing the uncertainties and risks." Burwell issued a concurring opinion. Although he diplomatically agreed that limiting the scope may have been necessary, Burwell pointed out that in doing so the committee had sacrificed the strength of the sustainability paradigm. Sustainability, Burwell argued, meant embracing a systems analysis that included the environment, the economy, and social equity. Sustainability should be about doing "more of good things and less of bad things," while the consensus report's "threat analysis" limited it to mitigating the bad. Even in its reduced scope, the study alarmed some in the transportation industry, who openly expressed their concerns that TRB had gone too far.[26]

Although a consensus study may not have been the place to pursue the sustainability paradigm as a whole, in 1999 TRB formed a Task Force on Transportation and Sustainability within its Technical Activities Division. Burwell chaired the Task Force from 2002 until it transitioned to a standing technical committee in 2005, at which time another veteran of the original consensus study committee, Daniel Sperling, became chair. A professor of civil engineering and environmental science and policy at the University of California, Davis, Sperling joined TRB's Executive Committee in 2010 and served as chair for 2015. Symbolic of TRB's embrace of sustainability and environmental issues, Sperling received TRB's Roy W. Crum Distinguished Service Award for 2018. The award cited his "distinguished achievements in transportation research in the areas of energy, air quality, climate change, and policy."[27]

Two very different types of congressionally requested studies on environmental issues arrived in the Transportation Equity Act for the 21st Century (TEA-21), enacted in 1998. Congress requested an evaluation of a federal air quality program that funded a long list of local projects to reduce automobile emissions, chiefly by encouraging less driving. Although the study was charged with determining the cost-effectiveness of various projects, *The Congestion Mitigation and Air Quality Improvement Program: Assessing 10 Years of Experience* (TRB Special Report 264, 2002), chaired by Martin Wachs, then at the University of California, Berkeley, reported that, unfortunately, neither the program's structure nor available data allowed such an analysis. The committee recommended that the federal program continue, but that it be more tightly focused on projects with a direct relationship to the biggest gains in public health.[28]

The second TEA-21-requested environmental study, *Surface Transportation Environmental Research: A Long-Term Strategy* (TRB Special Report 268, 2002), followed the pattern set by strategic transportation research studies explained more fully in Chapters 12 and 13. Chaired by Elizabeth Deakin, University of California, Berkeley, the 16-member committee outlined a multiyear national agenda for energy and environmental research around six recommended areas: human health, ecology and natural

NAS President Ralph J. Cicerone speaks at the 2006 Annual Meeting (Risdon Photography).

systems, environmental and social justice, emerging technologies, land use, and planning and performance measures. Congress funded the program in 2005 at more than $15 million annually and endorsed the report's recommended quality control measures. Although Congress gave USDOT the option of having TRB manage the program, the department instead decided to manage the program in house.[29]

Between 2008 and 2011, TRB published a suite of four consensus studies related to climate change, three of which were self-initiated. TRB's continued focus on climate change fit within the National Academies' strategic direction. Ralph J. Cicerone, known as an atmospheric scientist but trained as an electrical engineer, had become president of NAS in 2005. Cicerone had led a major National Academies study requested by President George W. Bush on climate change science in 2001 and had even presented to TRB's sustainable transportation study committee in the mid-1990s. In 2008, Congress commissioned another major set of studies on climate. The five studies—four technical reports and one overview of recommended strategies—appeared in 2010 and 2011 under the banner *America's Climate Choices*.[30]

Of the four TRB studies, the congressionally requested study came through the Energy Policy Act of 2005, and even here, TRB and NRC pushed the study further on climate change. Funded by DOE and conducted jointly with NRC's Board on Energy and Environmental Systems, the original request asked whether changes in land use patterns could reduce petroleum use and for a determination of the benefits of certain policy interventions. Because any conclusions on vehicle-miles traveled and oil consumption were only a short step away from greenhouse gas emissions, NRC negotiated adding emissions to the study's scope. In developing *Driving and the Built Environment* (TRB Special Report 298, 2009), the 12-member committee chaired by Jose A. Gomez-Ibanez, professor of urban planning and public policy, Harvard University, demurred on the requested evaluation of the listed policy interventions. The committee determined that, for some interventions, existing studies were insufficient to draw conclusions and, for others, the likelihood of successful implementation was a question of politics, not science. For the remaining question, the committee commissioned papers and modeled scenarios. Consistent with TRB's other studies looking at indirect means to reach environmental goals, the committee concluded that altering land use patterns would produce only very modest reductions in driving. Still, in the spirit of no harm done, the committee encouraged adopting policies that supported more compact land development patterns.[31]

TRB's Executive Committee geared the two self-initiated and solely self-funded studies in anticipation of a federal legislative context that then radically shifted. TRB published *A Transportation Research Program for Mitigating and Adapting to Climate Change and Conserving Energy* (TRB Special Report 299) and *Policy Options for Reducing Energy Use and Greenhouse Gas Emissions from U.S. Transportation* (TRB Special Report 307), in 2009 and 2011, respectively, and Robert E. Skinner, Jr., TRB's executive director, drew heavily from Special Report 299 when testifying before Congress in November 2009. When power in the House of Representatives shifted in 2011 from Democrats to Republicans, who took both climate change legislation and tax increases to fund surface transportation off the table, the reports lacked a ready audience.[32]

TRB played to its strengths, however, with *Potential Impacts of Climate Change on U.S. Transportation* (TRB Special Report 290, 2008), especially by making the connection between basic and applied research. The study attracted funding from AASHTO through NCHRP, transit agencies through TCRP, USDOT, EPA, and the U.S. Army Corps of Engineers and was a joint effort by TRB and the Climate Research Committee of NRC's Division on Earth and Life Studies. Henry G. Schwartz, Jr., NAE member and retired from Sverdrup/Jacobs Civil, Inc., chaired the 14-member committee. Eight members were experienced transportation officials or had other practice occupations.[33]

The study committee concurred with another, overlapping, NRC study that had concluded that although knowledge about climate change had accelerated, the tools needed to use this knowledge to make better decisions lagged behind. For example, for flooding—the greatest climate change risk to transportation, especially in coastal areas—better maps and models would be needed before even simple inventories of additional at-risk infrastructure could be assessed. Tools were needed to incorporate climate change into transportation planning, as well. Ultimately, the committee made 14 specific recommendations to support improved decision making for both infrastructure and operations.[34]

AASHTO, through NCHRP, then took up sustainable transportation and the impacts of climate change for its Foresight Series (NCHRP Research

Potential Impacts of Climate Change on U.S. Transportation (TRB Special Report 290, 2008) attracted funding from NCHRP, TCRP, USDOT, EPA, and the U.S. Army Corps of Engineers and made 14 specific recommendations about needed tools (Houston Metro buses in HOV lane in advance of Hurricane Harvey, 2017; Mark Mulligan/© Houston Chronicle, used with permission).

Report 750). Volume 2 in the series, published in 2014, provides step-by-step recommendations for assessing and responding to the impacts of climate change and extreme weather on infrastructure. Volume 4 provides tools for a transportation agency to use to advance a sustainable society.[35]

Looking at a series of consensus studies as they play out over time reveals that it is not necessarily obvious how they can best be deployed during political controversies, or how best to respond when the desire for hard-nosed, definitive analysis is in tension with what is achievable with available data and methods of analysis. However, the long view shows that it is possible to build a body of work out of both requested and self-initiated studies. Nor are TRB and the Marine Board alone in this work. The Board on Energy and Environmental Systems in the National Academies' Division on Engineering and Physical Sciences conducts consensus studies and continuing reviews of research programs on fuel efficiency, alternative fuels, and electric vehicles. TRB has a significant history of and continuing role to play in raising awareness, defining concepts, outlining needs, directing attention to effective solutions, and playing its part in bringing the multidisciplinary strength of the National Academies to bear on the most difficult questions of the day.

CHAPTER 11

The Work of the Committees

UNTIL THE ADOPTION of consensus studies in 1982, the Transportation Research Board (TRB), the Highway Research Board, and the Advisory Board on Highway Research had been the collective noun for the technical committees, or—as they came to be called in the 1980s—the "standing technical committees." The National Cooperative Highway Research Program's (NCHRP's) launch in 1962 did little to reorient the meaning of the Board as, tellingly, the program was not even included in the financial statements of annual reports until 1977. The technical committees were and are the lifeblood of TRB. Even today, many use "TRB" as a synonym for the annual meeting of these committees and the conference that has grown up around them. These committees' organizational home, TRB's Technical Activities Division, is also the direct descendent of the original Research Correlation Service (RCS) launched in 1945.

The elevation of TRB to a stand-alone unit within the National Research Council (NRC) in 1982 also precipitated additional changes in the work of TRB's top committees. Although the 1962 bylaw change that integrated the Board fully into NRC meant that the Executive Committee was no longer operational or administrative, but advisory to TRB's staff and NRC's Governing Board, what this meant in practice was still fluid until 1982. This chapter begins with the activities of TRB's top committees, including the development of critical issues lists, and concludes with the organizational evolution and myriad activities of the standing technical committees.

Strategic Advice and Oversight

Although the reorganization of 1967 created four divisions—Regular Technical Activities, Special Technical Activities, Administration, and NCHRP—the technical committees still constituted both technical activities divisions. In effect, the reorganization split the RCS into two administrative units. The Regular Technical Activities Division (or Division A) handled ongoing activities, including conferences and workshops, and the Special Technical Activities Division (or Division B) was dedicated to project-based work. The Special Technical Activities Division finally created an administrative home for the major research projects that the technical committees had always "sponsored" or conducted themselves and for funded, staff-led projects, which were also always advised by a committee. The Special Technical Activities Division also assumed responsibility for the TRB Special Report series of research reports and conference proceedings, founded in 1952, and the NCHRP Synthesis of Highway Practice series. Both divisions had top councils made up of technical committee members.

With the promotion to a stand-alone unit, TRB needed to augment the Executive Committee with two additional committees. One committee conducted oversight for NRC's rules governing committee (or panel) appointments and research products and was chaired by an elected member of the National Academies, who also served ex officio on NRC's Governing Board. (This is today's Division Committee, as "division" is the organizational label for the other National Academies' units that report directly to the NRC Governing Board.) The other committee advised TRB's Executive Committee on policy (consensus) studies. Originally called the Subcommittee on Policy Review (SPR), in 1988 it became the Subcommittee on Planning and Policy Review (SPPR), fulfilling an additional role formerly played by the long-range planning committees of the 1960s and 1970s. Because the SPPR also made necessary decisions between Executive Committee meetings, for the full committee's later concurrence, the SPPR grew into a de facto executive committee of the Executive Committee.[1]

Current and past Executive Committee chairs gather to commemorate 90 years of TRB: (Front row, left to right): William W. Millar (1992), Genevieve Giuliano (2003), former Executive Director Thomas B. Deen, Executive Director Robert E. Skinner, Jr., Debra L. Miller (2008), Martin Wachs (2000), Joseph M. Sussman (1994). (Back row, left to right): Neil J. Pedersen (2011), Herbert H. Richardson (1988), Michael R. Morris (2010), C. Michael Walton (1991), E. Dean Carlson (2002), and David N. Wormley (1997) (Risdon Photography).

SPR/SPPR also soon replaced the Special Technical Activities Council and in 1983 the division became the Special Projects Division. The division would now focus mostly on consensus studies. Moreover, the regular technical activities committees that in the past had taken actions making recommendations or advising government needed to be rechanneled to conform with NRC policies. This had implications for the work of TRB's standing technical committees, explored at more length below. Emblematic of the change, TRB's Special Report series became reserved for consensus studies and conference proceedings approved by NRC's Governing Board. In the mid-1990s, with the launch of a new TRB Conference Proceedings series, TRB's Special Report series was dedicated to consensus studies only. In the early 1990s, the division became the Studies and Information Services Division and in 2018, the Consensus and Advisory Studies Division.

Thomas B. Deen, TRB's executive director from 1980–1994, also introduced the policy session to the Executive Committee's agenda. Its members—leaders with expertise in all modes and from the public and private sectors and academia—wanted to make a bigger contribution than simply advising TRB on its projects and activities. Deen emulated the model that the National Academy of Sciences (NAS) President Frank

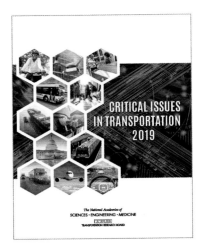

Critical Issues in Transportation 2019, TRB's 13th critical issues list, poses 63 challenging questions to frame future research, policy analysis, and debate.

Press used with the NRC Governing Board, which produced robust discussions about policy-related topics without crossing the line into making recommendations. For what came to be called "red meat" sessions, TRB's Executive Committee selected topics for both its January and June meetings, invited guests to give presentations, and designated a rapporteur to summarize the subsequent discussion. Over the decades, the sessions have covered the sweep of transportation topics, including in recent years: electric vehicles, freight transportation, the concept of livability, cybersecurity, and smart cities. In addition, the findings of a consensus study or presentations related to other TRB partners, such as the international research community, have made the agenda. The Executive Committee has also dedicated sessions to briefings on major changes in federal policy. The sessions can lead to the consideration of new projects, and even when no tangible outcome is immediate, they are credited with encouraging cross-fertilization among transportation leaders and decision makers.[2]

Identifying Critical Issues

One of the new Subcommittee on Policy Review's responsibilities would be to prepare and recommend lists of critical issues to the Executive Committee. The first "critical issues list," however, dates to TRB's transition from highways to total transportation. The Commission on Sociotechnical Systems, TRB's new institutional home within NRC in 1974, asked TRB what it would do if money or time were no object. NRC was attempting to nudge TRB's leaders to think bigger than applied research to solve problems. William N. Carey, Jr., the always practical executive director, resisted and, instead, invented a time frame (10 years) and budget ($100 million) and proposed a list of "specific problems that would respond to research."[3] Next time around, the Commission asked TRB's Executive Committee for a list of the 10 most critical issues in transportation, in the present and near future and irrespective of research potential. NRC's leadership wanted a list that represented transportation from the perspective of society, not just researchers, to use as a guide when evaluating TRB's activities.[4]

Although NRC's intent was an internal planning tool, TRB published "The Ten Most Critical Issues in Transportation" in *Transportation Research News* in late 1976. Still, the Executive Committee felt the whole exercise was fraught, as it prefaced the list with the caveat that "some of these issues should ***not*** be given substantial attention within TRB itself" [emphasis in original]. Indeed, all 10 issues had at least some government policy component and four—finance, intergovernmental responsibility, effects of regulations, and land use control—solely targeted government policies. By publishing the list, the committee hoped to "encourage support by administrators for research," but it also reassured TRB's sponsors and volunteers that "there will be no dilution of TRB efforts toward the solution of these long-standing problems in soils, materials, design, traffic, law, maintenance, and so on."[5]

Despite such trepidations, publication may have also felt necessary because TRB used its traditional, bottom-up process to create the first few lists. Nearly every member of TRB's technical committees participated in some way as the division's four groups produced their own top-10 lists for consideration by the Executive Committee. After the second critical issues list came out in 1978, *Transportation Research News* even published the groups' ranked lists and engaged in a little public soul-searching about the fate of safety as a critical issue. Even though each of the four groups had included it on their respective lists, safety had somehow not made the Executive Committee's list. TRB also used publication to invite feedback from the larger transportation community.[6]

To TRB's excitement, the second critical issues list received coverage in the transportation press. When the Executive Committee produced the third list in 1981, Deen planned for an accompanying publicity campaign with distribution to the transportation press, major newspapers, and congressional committees. Pleased with the attention the 1981 list had attracted, Deen planned the same for the 1984 list. Whether purposefully or organically, TRB had taken an internal bureaucratic requirement and turned it into a long-lived tool for outreach.[7]

With TRB's embrace of policy studies, the angst that had accompanied earlier lists subsided. The 1984 list, the first that the Subcommittee on Policy Review prepared for Executive Committee consideration, introduced a definition of a critical issue: "An unresolved aspect of transportation, national in scope, on which there are a wide variety of viewpoints, where the impacts of possible actions are not known, and where decisions will be made at the policy level." In addition, Deen and the Executive Committee took stronger steps to integrate the critical issues into TRB's own work. Sessions targeting the critical issues became a regular

Low-Volume Roads

A Path Around the World

T HEY MET IN June 1975 in Boise, Idaho, for a workshop organized by the Transportation Research Board's (TRB's) Special Task Force on Low-Volume Roads. Although the field trip took them over humble forest roads, workshop participants had global ambitions. Among the workshop's sponsors were the U.S. Agency for International Development (USAID) and the International Bank for Reconstruction and Development, which today is part of the World Bank.[a]

Governments across the world consulted with the workshop's chair, Eldon J. Yoder, Purdue University, an expert on pavement design. (Yoder would receive TRB's Roy W. Crum Distinguished Service Award in 1982.) Although this first workshop only attracted participants from the United States, Canada, and the United Kingdom, in 1977, USAID awarded TRB a 3-year grant to boost the international community of expertise on low-volume roads and improve rural transportation worldwide.

TRB, through a steering committee and a consultant, Lloyd Crowther, began to replicate its formula for shared expertise, but on a global scale. They sent letters of invitation to 200 potential correspondents in 65 developing countries. Correspondents accepted the job of making sure TRB publications got into the right hands. Review correspondents had the added responsibility of helping to plan the research topics and organizing an evaluation of how well publications met local needs. Crowther made tours of developing countries to see first-hand how TRB's information could be used. TRB also organized colloquiums at annual meetings for international students attending American universities.[b]

In 1979, the Second International Conference on Low-Volume Roads (the 1975 workshop having been rechristened the First International Conference) was held in Ames, Iowa. The USAID-funded project brought together project chair Kermit L. Bergstrahl and Philip Allsopp from Guyana, Pascual Cabellero from the Philippines, Ruslan Diwiryo from Indonesia, Guy Otobo from Nigeria, Luiz Soares from Brazil, and Said Beano from Jordan for a panel on low-volume roads in their countries.[c]

Although the USAID grant lasted only 3 years, the international seeds it planted continue today, as do being inclusive of road needs beyond highways. The 11th International Conference, held in Pittsburgh in 2015, was sponsored by The Pennsylvania State University, University of Belgrade, Pontificia Universidad Católica de Chile, and the University of Pretoria as well as by the Bureau of Indian Affairs and the Fish & Wildlife Service in the Department of the Interior, the Forest Service, the Department of Agriculture, and the Federal Highway

Students from Ecuador attend the 10th International Conference on Low-Volume Roads in Lake Buena Vista, Florida, 2011 (TRB).

Effective and Sustainable Road Slope Stabilization and Erosion Control, National Cooperative Highway Research Program (NCHRP) Synthesis of Highway Practice 430, published in 2012; and *Roadway Safety Tools for Local Agencies,* NCHRP Synthesis of Highway Practice 321, published in 2003. He also highlighted the committee's concern for environmental issues, formally added to its scope in 2009, and members' participation in a project sponsored by the Environmental Protection Agency and the Pennsylvania Department of Transportation that produced a guide on "Environmentally Sensitive Maintenance for Dirt and Gravel Roads" in 2006.[d]

Surdahl and the committee also celebrated the contributions of emeritus member Asif Faiz. After more than 30 years with the World Bank, working in more than 40 countries, Faiz had distilled a lifetime of experience into what became "The Promise of Rural Roads: Review of the Role of Low-Volume Roads in Rural Connectivity, Poverty Reduction, Crisis Management, and Livability," Transportation Research Circular E-C167, published in September 2012.[e]

In the Committee on Low-Volume Roads, TRB's origin in the movement for "good roads" for rural areas lives on well into the 21st century.

Administration (FHWA). International members of the Committee on Low-Volume Roads also hail from Canada, Chile, Italy, South Africa, and Tanzania and work with the World Bank and the Asian Development Bank.

When asked in 2014 to look back at its accomplishments, Roger Surdahl, FHWA, shared the committee's contributions to the American Association of State Highway and Transportation Officials (AASHTO) Guidelines for Geometric Design of Very Low-Volume Local Roads, also known as the "Little Green Book"; *Cost-*

Members of the Marine Board examine cyber-security while touring the Ports of Los Angeles and Long Beach, 2015 (Scott Brotemarkle).

feature at annual meetings. In 1989, the Executive Committee issued an accompanying action plan that called on the TRB community to help decision makers understand "the complex topics" and challenged researchers to connect their research to its "broader context." During 1990 and 1991, TRB formally integrated the critical issues list into its first strategic plan.[8]

A content analysis of the 12 critical issues lists produced through 2013 is made difficult by the different approaches taken over time. Some lists presented a few broad headings—1997's "Safety and Security" or 2006's "Congestion," for example—followed by short essays or lists of broad research questions. Other lists put forth bold declarative statements with only a paragraph or two of elaboration: 1981's list included "The viability of components of U.S. railroads" and "Survival of public transit systems" and 2002's list identified "An aging population poses special safety and mobility challenges" and "Consumer benefits from deregulation are threatened by industry consolidation." Taken as a whole, however, each iteration was usually broad enough to cover the bases of transportation: funding and finance, capacity, performance, safety, and interactions with the economy and the environment all found their way onto most lists.[9]

The critical issues lists typically stopped at raising awareness; they were not advocacy briefs with policy recommendations. Moreover, any priority rankings within the lists were not made public. Over time their use as an educational tool became more prominent. The lists grew from 3 pages to upward of 12 pages, with longer explanations and illustrative images and data in charts and graphs. Consistent with their nature, they have also tended to focus on what was thought wrong or worrisome about transportation. However, when the Executive Committee identified opportunities, they could be prescient. Already in 2002, the Executive Committee highlighted that "the merging of telecommunications and information technologies with transportation offers the greatest potential for innovation in transportation."[10]

For its most recent list, *Critical Issues in Transportation 2019*, TRB took additional steps to strengthen its content and distribution. Still a product of the Executive Committee, the 2019 list is now also a consensus study subject to independent report review. TRB published two versions, one for the general public and another, lengthier version, for transportation professionals that examines critical issues in a depth appropriate to inspire and guide research. Twelve broad categories signal the importance of transformational technologies, growing and shifting populations, equity, system performance, and the capacity of the transportation workforce in addition to more traditional transportation issues. For the transportation professional, the broad headings organize 63 topics for further discussion and research.[11]

TRB's critical issues lists have an important role to play, both internally and externally, in connecting the researcher and practitioner to big-picture issues important to society as a whole. Students and professionals alike can look to them for ideas for potential research projects or when making decisions about research programs. The regular identification of critical issues may have had the most significant impact on TRB itself.

Although throughout the 1970s and 1980s lists regularly included environmental protection and/or energy conservation, TRB's Executive Committee purposely reframed the issue in 1994 as "sustainable transportation." It drew inspiration from the intellectual forces that had gathered to produce the 1992 Earth Summit. In addition to the usual publicity efforts, TRB followed up by initiating a consensus study for sustainable transportation that attracted foundation and government sponsors and produced *Toward a Sustainable Future* (TRB Special Report 251) in 1997.[12]

Critical issues lists were a similar source of inspiration for the self-initiated and self-funded consensus study *Equity of Evolving Transportation Finance Mechanisms* (TRB Special Report 303), published in 2011. Starting in 2002, the list included a brief paragraph on the cost of owning and operating vehicles for low-income families. In 2006 the list introduced the term "equity," defining it as encompassing "burdens on the disadvantaged" and raising equity to the level of more traditional transportation issues such as congestion or finance. More information on both TRB Special Reports 251 and 303 can be found in Chapter 10.[13]

Organization of the Standing Technical Committees

TRB began the modern era in 1974 with 146 standing technical committees, rising to 174 in 1980. In response to the era's financial constraints, Charley V. Wootan, director of the Texas Transportation Institute at Texas A&M University, and chair of the Executive Committee in 1980, began

The importance of data for decision making is reflected in numerous committees and task forces for travel surveys, freight data, information systems, artificial intelligence, data privacy and security, and visualization (Sky Graph courtesy of the Center for Advanced Transportation Technology Laboratory [CATT Lab] at the University of Maryland).

the difficult process of shrinking the number of committees, which were reduced to 165 by 1983. Through the 1980s, TRB tried to enforce a policy of no net increase in their number. The Intermodal Surface Transportation Efficiency Act's (ISTEA's) emphasis on research, however, spurred their expansion, and TRB had just more than 200 by the early 2000s. In recent years, the number of committees has stabilized at around 210. (For more on committee membership, including the history of "friends of committees," see Chapter 14.)[14]

The Board's decision, implemented in 1970, to use the phases of transportation systems—and not mode—to organize the technical committees lasted until the early 2000s. Using system phases was intended to, if not transcend mode, at least foster communication and cross-fertilization among modal experts. When TRB officially embraced total transportation in 1974, committees organized by mode did become necessary. However, the four groups—Transportation Systems Planning and Administration; Design and Construction of Transportation Facilities; Operations and Maintenance of Transportation Facilities; and Legal Resources—each encompassed multiple modes. Even sections, a suborganization between committees and group for the larger groups, contained multiple modes. For example, within the Planning and Administration Group, the Transportation Forecasting Section had committees on forecasting passenger travel demand, aviation demand, and urban activity, and the Management and Finance Section included three committees on the state role in air transport, rail transport, and waterborne transport. The mode-neutral section model was not absolute, however, as already in 1979 there was a Public Transportation Section in the Planning and Administration Group and a Railway Section in the Design and Construction Group.[15]

In the early 1980s, modal organization began to assert its appeal. In a move to strengthen aviation activities—including their visibility—TRB consolidated all committees related to air travel in one Aviation Section, housed in the Planning and Administration Group. At the same time, it created a fifth group—Other Intergroup Resources—for broadly relevant topics that housed committees on the conduct of research; education and training; and microcomputers. Finding these former special committees a home in a group also made them eligible for session time at annual meetings. Finally, it added "Safety" to the name of the operations and maintenance group. Although safety had always been part of this group's scope, highlighting it in the group name again gave visibility to an activity of interest to sponsors.[16]

Although individual technical committees came and went and sections sometimes realigned, the five groups stayed stable until the early 2000s. Bringing an outsider's perspective at a time deemed right for change, in 2000 Mark Norman left the Institute of Transportation Engineers to take over from a retiring Robert E. Spicher who had directed TRB's Technical Activities Division since 1988. Although the committees and their activities had expanded, the Division A Council was still made up of a chair and the chairs of the five groups. It was just too small to accommodate the growing diversity within TRB.

Under the leadership of Harold "Skip" Paul, with the Louisiana Transportation Research Center of the state's Department of Transportation and Development and Division A Council chair from 1999 to 2001, the council initiated a Quality Improvement Program in 2001 and held a major summit in 2002. Two conclusions drove the subsequent reorganization: the need to reinvigorate leadership to restore a productive balance between bottom-up and top-down forces and the need for each mode or "functional component" (the new term for "system phase") to feel strong enough in their own community that they would be able to contribute more directly to TRB's larger transportation mission.[17]

Anne P. Canby chaired the Division Council from 2002 to 2005 during the reorganization. She had been secretary of the Delaware Department of Transportation from 1993 to 2001, earning a reputation for leadership on multimodalism and new technologies and became president of the Surface Transportation Policy Project during the reorganization effort. TRB leadership and staff used an iterative process that expanded the 5 groups to 11. The aim was not to create groups balanced in size: the organization of committees into sections and then into groups prioritized what was best for cross-fertilization and for service to sponsors. The largest group, Design and Construction, opted to stay together essentially

Anne P. Canby (right), Surface Transportation Policy Project, is joined by Lucy Garliauskas, FHWA; Janette Sadik-Khan, Parsons Brinckerhoff; and Debbie Niemeier, University of California, Davis, to discuss women in the transportation workforce and leadership at the 2006 Annual Meeting (Risdon Photography).

TECHNICAL ACTIVITIES DIVISION: GROUPS AND SECTIONS IN 2019

TECHNICAL ACTIVITIES COUNCIL
Committee on International Coordination
Young Members Council

POLICY AND ORGANIZATION GROUP
Management and Leadership (4)
Transportation Policy (9)
Research and Education (5)
Data and Information Systems (11)
Transportation Systems Resilience (3)

PLANNING AND ENVIRONMENT GROUP
Transportation System Policy, Planning, and Process (6)
Travel Analysis Methods (5)
Environment and Energy (8)
Social, Economic, and Cultural Issues (5)

DESIGN AND CONSTRUCTION GROUP
Design (8)
Pavements (8)
Structures (8)
Construction (9)
Asphalt Materials (5)
Concrete Materials (4)
Geological and Geoenvironmental Engineering (7)
Geotechnical Engineering (7)

OPERATIONS AND PRESERVATION GROUP (1)
Operations (13)
Maintenance and Preservation (14)

LEGAL RESOURCES GROUP (7)

SYSTEM USERS GROUP
Safety (10)
Users Performance (4)
Pedestrians and Cycles (3)

PUBLIC TRANSPORTATION GROUP (14)

RAIL GROUP (8)

FREIGHT SYSTEMS GROUP (11)

AVIATION GROUP (9)

MARINE GROUP (4)

Numbers in parentheses refer to the number of standing committees.

Source: TRB Online Directory, March 2019.

unchanged, dispensing with consideration of a 12th group. They even attempted a three-dimensional organizational model for crosscutting issues, but in the end decided this was too complex.[18]

Crucially, when they were done, all modes had a seat at the table on the renamed Technical Activities Council (TAC). By introducing groups for rail, aviation, marine, and public transportation, the new group structure, in many ways, also mirrored the organization of USDOT. For example, the "executive board" for the Rail Group includes the chairs of its eight committees and ex officio liaisons to the Federal Railroad Administration and the Association of American Railroads. "Highway" is not in the name of any group, although the Design and Construction Group and the Operations and Preservation Group are almost exclusively focused on roads. More broadly constructed are the Legal Resources Group, Safety and Systems Users Group (which includes a section for pedestrians, bicycles, and motorcycles), Policy and Organization Group, Planning and Environment Group, and the Freight Systems Group. Despite—or perhaps because of—the reorganization's alignment by mode, new standing committees have addressed safety, security, environmental issues, special user groups, and disaster mitigation and response, regardless of mode.[19]

TRB credits the expanded Technical Activities Division leadership structure with unleashing a new synergy and creativity among the groups, enhancing their capacity to tackle both new and long-standing crosscutting issues. The TAC has 14 members, representing the groups, young members, and state departments of transportation (DOTs). With "more players at our decision-making table," as Canby described it, the expanded leadership structure also made it easier to foster diverse perspectives. Cross-fertilization takes place formally in the "executive boards" at the section or group level. These boards are hierarchical in that chairs of committees make up a section board and chairs of the sections make up the group board, but they also include other key individuals. For example, the board of the Freight Systems Group includes a formal liaison from the Data and Information Systems Section within the Policy and Organization Group. Two or more committees can also form joint subcommittees, informal working bodies whose participants need not be appointed members of the parent committees.[20]

The Work of the Technical Committees

The work of TRB's standing technical committees is the result of a potent combination of sponsorship from governments and other institutions and a 5,000-strong volunteer corps. "Friends" of committees add thousands more. States, collectively, have been the largest sponsors of the work of the technical committees and TRB's associated information and professional development services. Although the technical committees operate without budgets, they have always been formed around a set of objectives, which now take the form of 3-year strategic plans. They are responsible for arranging their own meetings and agendas and maintaining their own communications, including websites. Unlike for consensus study committees or research program panels, for which the project budget covers travel costs, volunteers on technical committees pay their own way. Unless they are a committee chair, they also pay registration fees for the annual meeting.[21]

All technical committees include at least two TRB staff members. The senior program officers are the subject-matter experts, filling the positions formerly held by the RCS's staff engineers. Their task is to facilitate the work of committee volunteers, offering advice and support but also ensuring that the committees meet TRB's standards for integrity and quality. Senior program officers also manage TRB's relationships with its core program sponsors. Associate program officers support the senior officers and committee chairs. Both senior and associate officers are assigned to numerous committees. TRB's staff working in library and information services, publishing, and meetings and conferences also support the goals of sponsors and the work of technical committees.[22]

In addition, the senior program officers continue their roles as field agents in the former RCS's state visits program. As TRB's sponsors expanded in the 1970s, staff embarked on visits to transit agencies, ports,

Participants at a green trucking workshop examine the energy and emission impacts of different vehicle configurations at the 2011 Annual Meeting (Risdon Photography).

aviation, freight rail, and safety organizations, in addition to visiting state DOTs every year. Staff tailor visits to the needs of the sponsor, making each visit its own unique combination of large- and small-group meetings, personal conferences, and tours, with outreach to everyone from top management to young researchers first learning about TRB.[23]

TRB also depends heavily on a special class of volunteers employed by sponsors. The "contact men" of the early decades have evolved into sponsor representatives. These positions are particularly important for TRB's relations with state DOTs. Although the states recommend candidates, TRB state representatives are formal TRB appointments, and appointees are as much TRB's representatives in the states as they are the state DOTs' formal liaisons to TRB. TRB depends on them to help connect TRB and its services to new teams of executive administrators, as well as to make recommendations for new volunteers for TRB's committees and research panels. Symbolic of their importance, TRB acknowledges state representatives by name and state in annual reports.[24]

The annual meeting is the most visible work of TRB's technical committees, as they have always been responsible for curating a large majority of the program, in addition to planning the agendas for their own meetings. They take strategic direction from the Executive Committee and initiatives of the TAC and translate them into sessions. Through their own specialized calls for papers and posters or arrangements for panels of speakers, they can help foster new directions in their fields and disciplines. They also review all papers submitted for consideration, assigning those accepted to lectern sessions or poster sessions and recommending the selected few for publication in *Transportation Research Record*. (Hopeful participants still submit complete papers, not abstracts, for annual meeting consideration.)

Even in today's world of proliferating specialty conferences, TRB's annual meeting still plays the role of host

TRANSPORTATION RESEARCH BOARD ANNUAL MEETING

1996

DATES January 7–11, 1996

LOCATION Sheraton Washington, Washington Hilton, and Omni Shoreham Hotels

PRESIDING CHAIR Lillian C. Borrone, The Port Authority of New York & New Jersey

ATTENDANCE In a record-breaking snowstorm, 4,000 (out of an expected 7,000) attend, some arriving on skis

NUMBER OF PAPERS AND PRESENTATIONS 1,500 scheduled

ORGANIZATION OF TECHNICAL ACTIVITIES Five groups hosting 240 standing technical committees, subcommittees, and task forces

WINNING PAPER TOPICS
- Estimating truck vehicle-miles traveled
- Cost analysis for crack sealing
- Relationship of environmental and acquisition law
- Heavy-duty, hot-mix asphalt pavements

CELEBRATION Historian David McCullough delivers an inspirational address at the Chairman's Luncheon to celebrate TRB's 75th Annual Meeting

WHAT ELSE IS HAPPENING AT TRB IN 1996?
- TCRP publishes Report 10 on new technologies such as "smart cards" for fare payment
- TRB-SHRP Committee continues to advise AASHTO and FHWA on implementing SHRP's products

Welcome Sessions at annual meetings allow committee leaders to meet, brief, and recruit first-time attendees. Jeannie Beckett, chair, Ports and Channels Committee (right) talks with Karin Foster (left), Baltimore Metropolitan Council, and Megan Smirti, University of California, Berkeley, in 2006 (Risdon Photography).

to unique gatherings. John Bullough, Rensselaer Polytechnic Institute, points out that meeting activities associated with the Committee on Visibility, affecting all forms of transportation, is "the only large gathering of people who do research in my area and the people and organizations that actually implement this type of research." Outside of the annual meeting, TRB too offers its own specialty conferences. The technical committees participate in—and even take charge of—planning conferences, symposiums, and workshops, of which TRB typically sponsors dozens and co-sponsors an equal number in any given year.[25]

The identification of research needs is among the oldest of technical activities. Through the decades, the technical committees have stayed committed to the founding spirit that the identification of research needs is a collective, cooperative exercise. Technical committees provide the community to which individuals can bring their ideas. Whereas the individual or even a single agency acting alone would be likely to have only limited impact, within TRB's community and infrastructure are the means to traverse from problem or idea all the way to solutions disseminated to global audiences. For Michael Culmo, CME Associates, Inc., this capacity to go from idea all the way to implementation, making "a difference in the engineering world" and contributing "to the improvement of our practice on a national and international scale," was part of what was "most gratifying" about being part of the Committee on Steel Bridges and Committee on Concrete Bridges.[26]

TRB's technical committees can also advance research and practice through the cooperative research programs. Because the Transit Cooperative Research Program (TCRP) and the Airport Cooperative Research Program (ACRP) host open solicitations for research needs statements, it is relatively straightforward for TRB's committees to submit. NCHRP,

Eun Sug Park (left), Vichika Iragavarapu, Susan Chrysler, and Kay Fitzpatrick, TTI, celebrate receiving TRB's 2011 D. Grant Mickle Award for their paper on detection distances to crosswalk markings with an homage to the famous cover of the Beatles' *Abbey Road* album (Texas A&M Transportation Institute).

however, requires courting American Association of State Highway and Transportation Officials' (AASHTO's) committees. Over the decades, TRB's committees have learned how to craft research needs statements of likely interest to AASHTO and take pride when one of their needs statements appears on a final NCHRP program. For example, the Committees on Geometric Design and Operational Effect of Geometrics have systematically coordinated the development of their research needs statements with NCHRP's annual schedule and in consultation with AASHTO committees, earning TRB's "Blue Ribbon Committee" award in 2014 for advancing research. Between 2006 and 2018 their research needs statements had found their way into NCHRP projects totaling roughly $8 million. The technical activities committees–AASHTO–NCHRP relationship is truly symbiotic. When surveyed in 2014 about key research achievements in their respective fields over the past 20 years, numerous TRB technical committees identified specific NCHRP projects.[27]

This same dynamic can play out at the scale of an emerging field of study or even an area of transportation. Susan Shaheen, University of

California, Berkeley, came to TRB in the mid-1990s looking for a community interested in what came to be called "shared mobility." In the Committee on Automated Transit Systems, Shaheen "found colleagues, supporters, and friends from across the globe to share and advance ideas" and they "formed a large and growing community in shared and automated mobility." TRB awarded Shaheen its Roy W. Crum Distinguished Service Award for 2017.[28]

Launching projects with the goal of publishing the results has also been a long-standing technical committee activity. Updated editions of the *Highway Capacity Manual* and the *Landslide* books are legacies of the Board's practice of encouraging its technical committees to take on large projects, including seeking outside funding. One of the last projects under this model produced *Traffic Flow Theory* (TRB Special Report 165), a textbook for graduate students and other specialists published in 1975. When TRB Special Report 79, *An Introduction to Traffic Flow Theory* (1964) went out of print in 1968, the Committee on Traffic Flow Theory decided to pursue an update. With the green light from its department (group) Council, it persuaded the Federal Highway Administration (FHWA) to fund the project and facilitated a contract between FHWA and professors at the University of Minnesota, who worked under an advisory committee sponsored by the technical committee and supported by TRB's engineer of traffic and operations.[29]

With the adoption of policy studies in 1982 and then the launch of additional cooperative research programs, technical committees became less likely to facilitate large, funded projects themselves. However, TRB still provided them with means to continue to publish their products. The Highway Research Correlation Service Circular series, which dated to 1945, became dedicated to technical committee products starting in 1956. Rebooted as the Highway Research Circular in 1965, the Transportation Research Circular in 1974, and the Transportation Research E-Circulars in 1997, the series continues to publish their work. (The circulars come with the caveat that they are

Participants in the 30th Annual TRB Summer Port, Waterways, and International Trade Conference in Boston tour Massport's Conley Terminal in July 2005 (TRB).

not official National Academies reports subject to report review.) The E-Circular series alone, for electronic publication only, numbers almost 250 as the centennial draws near. The E-Circular series began with the proceedings of a workshop convened for USDOT by three TRB technical committees on geometric design, roadside safety features, and operational design of geometrics on "simultaneous vehicle and infrastructure design" (E-C001, 1997). E-C242, published in January 2019, provides a literature review of railroad trespassing and suicide prevention research, put together by a subcommittee of the Committee on Highway-Rail Grade Crossings.[30]

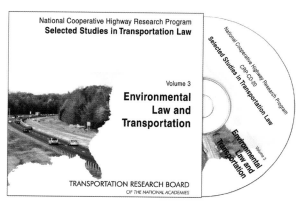

The Selected Studies in Transportation Law series grew out of a project of the Legal Resources Group in the 1970s.

The E-Circular series also contains records of significant collaborations with federal agencies. In 2001, the Federal Aviation Administration (FAA) and TRB's aviation committees partnered on three 1-day seminars on *Aviation Gridlock: Understanding Options and Seeking Solutions*. Designed as briefings for the press and governmental staff, all three seminars were opened by Jane Garvey, FAA administrator, and were also televised on C-SPAN. A task force of all eight aviation committee chairs, itself chaired by Agam N. Sinha, The MITRE Corporation, designed the curriculum on airport capacity and demand management, infrastructure, and weather and weather technology. Complete transcripts of the seminars, with presentation slides, were then published as E-Circulars (E-C029, E-C032, E-C034, all 2001).

TRB's Legal Resources Group maintains a unique presence among the technical activities committees, which dates to its early growth as a funded project that was a precedent for NCHRP (see Chapter 6). During the 1970s, the Group developed Selected Studies in Highway Law, under NCHRP sponsorship. The award for outstanding TRB publication or presentation on transportation law, sponsored by the Legal Resources Group, is named after John C. Vance, its first editor. Representative James J. Howard, member of Congress from New Jersey, called "the breadth, scope, and detail" of the volumes "splendid," when he wrote to Vance in 1979 that "there is no limit to the extent of my appreciation over having these precious volumes made available to me by the Transportation Research Board." The multivolume set was the first project of its kind to create what Lynn B. Obernyer called a "legal encyclopedia on the topics that most affect transportation officials." Obernyer, Colorado's chief highway counsel and chair of TRB's Legal Resources Group Council in the 1980s, believed that one of TRB's strengths was that its research was accessible to both the attorney and the client, the transportation professional.[31]

Selected Studies became Selected Studies in Transportation Law in the early 2000s with additional sponsorship from TCRP. NCHRP, TCRP, and ACRP also sponsor reports in their Legal Research Digest series on timely legal issues and case law. Funding from ACRP's governing board for the digest series began in 2006, after the Legal Resources Group championed the proposal. Today's Legal Resources Group, with seven technical committees, still takes on new legal questions. Emerging law around drones, automated vehicles, data privacy, and procurement through public–private partnerships are just some of the topics found in recent workshops and annual meetings.[32]

Taking Stock and Looking Forward

In addition to 3-year strategic plans, once per decade (or so) technical committees may choose to participate in a more formal process of taking stock and looking forward. One of the largest of these efforts took place in 1999 and produced the "Millennium Papers." Technical committees took on the task of distilling, in just a few pages, the current state of practice and likely future directions, for more than 150 topics ranging from aviation system planning to tort law, from cementitious stabilization to intercity passenger rail. The Technical Activities Division organized a similar undertaking as part of TRB's centennial celebration.[33]

Neil J. Pedersen admits that, at first, his committee balked at the Millennium Paper assignment. The future executive director was then chair of the Committee on Statewide Multimodal Transportation Planning and in the middle of a long tenure with the Maryland Department of Transportation's State Highway Administration. Pedersen's interest in planning had been piqued decades earlier when he combined the study

Neil J. Pedersen, TRB's executive director, presents Sandra Q. Larson with TRB's Roy W. Crum Distinguished Service Award in 2016. Larson would continue her service as chair of the TRB Centennial Task Force (Risdon Photography).

of civil engineering and urban studies during his undergraduate work at Bucknell College followed by earning a master's degree in civil engineering from Northwestern University. But in the middle of all of the other responsibilities of a TRB technical committee, taking the time to look forward just seemed like a burden.[34]

Instead, Pedersen concluded that the assignment turned out to be the best thing they had ever done. In scanning and contemplating the future of internal processes and external demands, they had created a much more robust agenda for research that guided their actions for years to come. Pedersen would take this lesson into new roles as group chair in 2003, TAC chair from 2006 to 2008, and chair of TRB's Executive Committee in 2011. He also volunteered in a leadership capacity for the Strategic Highway Research Program 2 (SHRP 2) before joining TRB's staff in 2012 as the program's deputy director for outreach to state DOTs. When appointed TRB's executive director in 2015, he continued to emphasize the need for research, and researchers, to look to the future.[35]

Looking to the future means exploiting new technologies and, with the explosive success of its webinars (live, interactive presentations via the Internet), TRB has extended its global reach. TRB first experimented with video conferencing in the early 1980s, but after disappointing

The Fifth National Seismic Conference on Bridges and Highways, which TRB co-sponsored, included a tour of bridges and bridge construction in the San Francisco Bay Area in 2006 (TRB).

results decided the technology was not up to delivering the desired experience. Although some webcasts occurred in the early 2000s, TRB formally launched a webinar series for professional development in 2007. Its popularity, especially in a time of spreading travel restrictions for state government staff, led TRB to expand it from one to two webinars per month in 2009. TRB's webinar program soon took off, the 2009 webinars attracting an average of 300 participants. TRB hosted nearly 600 webinars between 2007 and 2017 and currently produces webinars at a clip of about two new episodes per week.[36]

In many ways, webinars are the perfect augmentation of TRB's historical programs and traditions. They serve longtime sponsors and reach new, global audiences. They fulfill TRB's commitment to fostering interaction between research and practice. They expand opportunities for volunteer experts, of all ages and geographic locations, to contribute their knowledge and get their names out there as someone who wants to share what they have learned. Webinars typically last only 90–120 minutes and feature a new cooperative research program report or a topic chosen, presented, and sponsored by a standing technical committee. Volunteers submit proposals and compete for slots. All are recorded and archived and most come with the professional development/continuing education credits required to maintain professional licenses and certifications, as appropriate.

Webinars on roundabouts always draw crowds, sometimes more than 1,000 attendees. (A Task Force on Roundabouts started in 2006 and became a standing committee in 2012.) Webinars also allow TRB to match specialized experts with specific audiences, such as those interested in learning the details of airport bathroom design or hearing from maintenance experts eager to share the ecological and financial implications of roadside mowing techniques. In one sponsored by the Standing Committee on Seismic Design and Performance of Bridges in 2015, Elmer Marx, Alaska Department of Transportation & Public Facilities, wowed the audience with his physics equations and methods for checking computer-generated results by hand. He has since built a following for his webinars.[37]

Renewed International Activities: TRB and the World

Both TRB's Executive Committee and Technical Activities Division have formal structures to act internationally, following the precedents set by its home institution. The founders of NAS purposefully created an organization that would have an international presence. A foreign secretary was among the original officers, and members elected 10 "foreign associates" from France, Germany, Ireland, Italy, and Scotland at the First Annual Meeting in 1864. NRC, founded to be of service during World War I, set an even stronger precedent for international engagement. Today, all three academies elect a foreign secretary from among their members and continue to elect foreign associates. Through its Office of International Affairs, the National Academies addresses global challenges and coordinates with other countries' national academies and scientific organizations.[38]

TRB and its predecessors always had some international participants, especially from Canada and Mexico. By 1951, individual "associates"—those who paid an individual fee and received publications—also came from all over Africa, Australia, Europe, India, Japan, and Latin America. The American Association of State Highway Officials

(AASHO) Road Test attracted international attention, including a visit from a delegation from the Union of Soviet Socialist Republics. The Lacy–Zarubin Agreement for cultural and scientific exchanges, negotiated by the American and Soviet ambassadors in 1958, designated NAS as the U.S. institution responsible for reciprocal scientific tours. Seizing the opening of relations with the country of his birth, Gregory P. Tschebotarioff, professor of civil engineering at Princeton University, approached the Board's Executive Committee with a proposal for an exchange of experts on soil and foundation engineering. With funding from the National Science Foundation, the 21-day American and Soviet tours, held in spring and fall 1959, are documented in TRB Special Report 60 (1960).[39]

In the late 1970s, TRB began an organized outreach effort that resulted in the international project on low-volume roads. At the time, international attendees at annual meetings was about 5 percent of general attendance, although the percentage of international speakers and presenters was typically slightly higher. Still, TRB was more oriented toward domestic research and institutions than the National Academies as a whole. In 1983, TRB's Executive Committee adopted an action plan intended to boost its international profile, which led to the founding of the Standing Committee on International Cooperation in 1984 and a provision allowing technical committees four additional international members. Both SHRPs included international exchanges (see Chapter 12) and, at times, the cooperative research programs have funded "international scans" (see Chapter 13).[40]

TRB's 2002 strategic plan called for renewed attention to international activities, and a subsequent task force recommended that the Executive Committee appoint a member to be international secretary, formalizing the Executive Committee's leadership on international affairs. Memoranda of understanding (MOUs) with their international counterparts is the typical route for Executive Committee action. Many MOUs are already in their second iteration. The agreement with the World Road Association (PIARC), signed in 2017, builds on a relationship that dates back to 1926 and preparations for the Sixth World Road Congress, held in Washington, D.C., in 1930. The MOU's joint action plan, which is also coordinated with FHWA and AASHTO,

Former Secretary of Transportation Norman Y. Mineta (second from left) meets with a special delegation of transportation officials from Iraq at the 2008 Annual Meeting. Heading the delegation was Iraq's Construction and Housing Minister Bayan Dezei (right) (Risdon Photography).

lays out a series of activities that nurture cross-participation on the Committee on International Cooperation, technical committees, and conferences. The plan also provides for jointly produced webinars and even an avenue for PIARC to propose research need statements to AASHTO for NCHRP.[41]

In 2012, TRB embarked on a new joint project with USDOT and the European Commission. For a series of four planned (later expanded to six) annual symposia, the project created joint activities with equal representation of Americans and Europeans for everything from the planning committees to co-authorship of white papers and briefing documents. Held alternately in the United States and Europe, funding covered the travel cost for officials and experts who would have been otherwise unable to travel. The symposia produced "potential portfolios" for research on cutting-edge topics such as automated transport, freight logistics in cities, and adapting to climate change. Although invitation only, their papers and findings were published in TRB's Conference Proceedings series.[42]

As of 2019, nearly 15 percent of standing technical committee members reside outside the United States, and around 90 percent of technical committees have international members. Formal, funded international initiatives have their place, but even they depend on the larger symbiotic relationship between TRB's sponsors and volunteers and the culture that encourages individual initiative within the context of a supportive community. With modern communication technologies, operating on a global scale is more feasible than ever. Yet, just as important is the ability of the technical committees to also foster small-scale interactions that lead to action on the challenges, problems, and opportunities of the future.

CHAPTER 12

Strategic Highway Research Programs

EARLY IN THOMAS B. DEEN'S tenure as executive director, he studied the Transportation Research Board's (TRB's) traditional mission— providing an information clearinghouse, supporting professional development for researchers and practitioners, and stimulating research— and decided the third needed the most attention. The oil shocks of 1973 and 1979 and the high inflation of the 1970s had eroded the purchasing power of research funding. Deen also brought to TRB an understanding of how the private sector prioritized investing in research, including how the private sector sold its top management on research's value. He found an ally in Thomas D. Larson, who had become secretary of the Pennsylvania Department of Transportation after many years as a professor of civil engineering at The Pennsylvania State University. Larson had joined TRB's Executive Committee in 1980 and served as chair for 1981. Larson also shared Deen's concern that state departments of transportation (DOTs)—TRB's largest and oldest constituency—were losing faith in the utility of research.[1]

In addition to a founding mission to stimulate research, TRB had important tools at its disposal, ready to be combined in new ways. TRB's nearly two decades managing the National Cooperative Highway Research Program (NCHRP) had made it an expert at facilitating the elements of a client's research program: selecting projects, developing research plans and budgets, and managing contracted researchers. TRB also had a new tool: the National Academies' consensus study, recently reinvigorated to add credibility and gravitas when advising the federal government on policy issues. Deen and Larson would seek to use the consensus study to produce a plan for an entire research program. With little to lose, Deen and Larson also decided to go big in a way that had not been attempted since the American Association of State Highway Officials (AASHO) Road Test. The success of the first Strategic Highway Research Program (SHRP, pronounced "Sharp"), 1987–1993, led to a second program, 2006–2015. A set of unique circumstances for both SHRP and SHRP 2 allows a closer examination of how these programs went beyond listing research needs to making strategic choices about fostering innovation.

A Strategic Approach to Research

Deen and Larson highlighted the need for a new approach to transportation research at the 61st Annual Meeting in January 1982. In his address at the Chairman's Luncheon, Larson observed that NCHRP and state research programs, by adopting annual programs, do a "good job at the narrowly focused microscopic level." However, he continued, "there is also a need, largely unfulfilled, for a more macroscopic overview that looks at the status of research from a more strategic perspective." Larson announced that he would be leading a Strategic Transportation Research Task Force made up of "high-level policy oriented individuals" to tackle large-scale research strategies during 1982.[2]

Unlike with the activities leading up to the AASHO Road Test or NCHRP, Larson and Deen did not start with a specific research problem or develop a list of research needs. Instead, at a special kickoff session at the 1982 Annual Meeting, they organized discussions on the role of partnerships: building support within the state DOTs, understanding the federal perspective, reaching out to Congress, and other means to expand the constituency for transportation research. They asked, how do we generate enthusiasm for research to better manage, maintain, and reconstruct mature transportation systems? As L. Gary Byrd, consultant with Byrd, Tallamy, MacDonald and Lewis, put it: How do we build excitement for the reality that "the future highway will be physically old?"[3]

By March 1982, TRB had ready for circulation a proposal, endorsed by the Executive Committee, for its first Strategic Transportation

Research Study (STRS, pronounced "stars"). TRB also had moral support from the National Academy of Sciences (NAS) President Frank Press and the National Research Council (NRC), who were pleased that TRB was taking the initiative.[4]

From the outset, the proposal for the first STRS had three important features: a focus on highways, an outline of strategic criteria, and inclusion of research program management. The proposal described tasks for a 1-year study that would, in turn, produce a 5-year plan for strategic research for the highway industry, defined as the governments that provide, operate, and maintain roadways. The proposal also defined criteria for prioritizing and scaling elements of the research program: big "payoffs." Direct payoffs reduced highway industry expenditures. Indirect payoffs produced "benefits or savings to users and/or society at large." Additionally, the criteria called for aligning the eventual research program with the size of highway expenditure categories (e.g., for materials, construction, or administration). Finally, the proposal called for the Highway STRS to include a survey of best practices in initiating and managing large research programs.[5]

Although not stated in the initial proposal, Larson and Deen also decided early in the process to go big. At the time, states invested $4 million annually in NCHRP, and state and federal highway research spending totaled about $55 million per year. Larson and Deen reasoned that it would be the same work to sell a proposed 5-year program costing $100 million as one costing $10 million. They also predicted—correctly—that it would be much easier to develop enthusiasm for a program impressive in its size. A large program also fit Deen's diagnosis of the problem. Highway research had fallen from 0.25 percent of total highway expenditures in 1965 to 0.15 percent in 1982, at a time when similar industries invested at least 1–2 percent on research. Technology industries spent much more.[6]

Deen piqued the interest of Lester P. Lamm, the Federal Highway Administration's (FHWA's) deputy administrator and a longtime FHWA employee. Lamm then facilitated a meeting between Deen and Ray A. Barnhart, federal highway administrator. With the Reagan administration intent on downsizing government, Barnhart did not initially express much interest in a study that would make the case for a new federally funded research program. However, after several rounds of consultation among FHWA, AASHTO, and NRC's Governing Board, FHWA funding for the first STRS was in place by October 1982.[7]

The First Strategic Transportation Research Study

When the Highway STRS got under way, TRB was only in the early stages of adopting NRC's formal policy (consensus) study process. The study's 13-member "steering committee," chaired by Larson, was small but broadly representative of those with expertise in building, maintaining, and using highways. The three university professors specialized in planning and system operations, and two appointees managed research in private industries. County government and public transportation each had one expert, and the remaining six members came from state transportation departments or AASHTO. Federal liaisons included staff from FHWA and the Congressional Research Service. Unusual for the time, Deen and Larson purposely recruited committee members representing state governments from the top level of management. A research program responsive to the concerns of administrators, Deen and Larson reasoned, would enhance prospects for funding.[8]

Asphalt was then a special source of frustration for state DOTs. Many in the highway industry were convinced that asphalt "wasn't as sticky as it used to be," and some blamed changes in the petroleum industry during the 1970s. Whatever the cause, tried and true methods were suddenly producing road surfaces that prematurely failed, and administrators wanted solutions. Physical—or hard-side—research was a top concern. FHWA's Barnhart, too, was on public record prioritizing the reconstruction of the Interstate Highway System. Finally, although TRB staff began the Highway STRS without preconceived recommendations for a research program, the original proposal's emphasis on "payoffs"—essentially a commitment that the research would quickly pay for itself—framed the universe of choices.[9]

TRB published the Highway STRS report as *America's Highways: Accelerating the Search for Innovation* (TRB Special Report 202) in June 1984. It was at Larson's insistence that *America's Highways* did not include the word "research" anywhere in its title. Drawing on the business management theories of Peter Drucker and Tom Peters, Larson brought the conviction that "we either innovate constantly, and with a passion, or die" to his work with TRB and beyond.[10] Following Larson's lead, the steering committee had set out to foster innovation, because research itself, as they explained to the TRB Executive Committee, was only one part of an innovation process that also included development and application. The innovation process, moreover, was not linear, "but the linkages in both directions are important if research is to succeed."[11]

America's Highways recommended spending $150 million over roughly 5 years on a Strategic Highway Research Program encompassing what came to be called the "Big Six" promising research areas: asphalt, long-term pavement performance, maintenance cost-effectiveness, concrete bridge components, cement and concrete pavements and structures, and control of snow and ice. "Big" was not just a measure of their importance. The steering committee purposely chose research areas with the potential to "make dramatic advances" through large-scale, concentrated research. Moreover, physical research dominated. After 20 years of a transportation community agog with the promises of computers, systems thinking, regional planning, and new vehicle technologies, one of the oldest types of highway research won the day. Five of the Big Six research areas sought their "payoff" through extending the life or reducing the maintenance costs of highways, roads, and bridges. Even for snow and ice control, the research area with the clearest connection to safety, the economy, and water quality, the report emphasized the "payoff" from reducing the cost of maintenance.[12]

America's Highways: Accelerating the Search for Innovation (TRB Special Report 202, 1984), TRB's first consensus study, outlined what would become the first Strategic Highway Research Program and set a precedent for using the National Academies' consensus study process for strategic plans for significant research programs.

America's Highways marked another stark shift in the framing of research in its bold assertion that research should develop products. Previously, in major Board-led research efforts such as the Highway Capacity Manual or the AASHO Road Test, researchers framed their tasks as investigations to reveal facts or truths that could be used to inform standards, practices, and policy. They often invented concepts and tools in the course of research that helped them solve problems. For example, Fred Burggraf, the Board's fourth director, had developed the Burggraf Shear Machine for field tests of flexible pavements. Likewise, William N. Carey, Jr., and the engineers on the AASHO Road Test invented the CHLOE profilometer to measure pavements. The goal of research, however, was knowledge. The word "product" does not appear in the AASHO Road Test's summary report and appears only once in the Proceedings of the AASHO Road Test Conference, which was dedicated to getting the research into use. This discussion defined the "end product" as "efficient highway transportation."[13]

America's Highways uses the noun "product" more than 100 times, both in its analysis of innovation in the highway industry and in its recommendations for a research program. Indeed, the highway itself was a product, in the same way that an automobile was a product. The ultimate aim of the planned research program was to solve problems by improving existing products and producing new products.

TRB's Executive Committee went into the Highway STRS believing that funding for a large highway research program was "a long shot." However, the bet that once state administrators crafted a research program tailored to their concerns, they would then lead the charge for funding began to bear fruit even before the report's completion. The study's members from state transportation departments overlapped with AASHTO's leadership, and they developed a proposal that would direct 0.25 percent of federal-aid funding for highways and bridges to the program for 5 years. AASHTO even began publicizing funding for the program in advance of the report's official completion and release, much to the consternation of the NRC process watchers for consensus studies. Larson, however, was delighted that the Highway STRS seemed to be generating "new enthusiasm ... for practical, down-to-earth research" as a solution to "some big, costly, and embarrassing problems" in the highway industry.[14]

Because the Surface Transportation Assistance Act of 1982 put federal transportation on 5-year authorization cycles, Congress was not scheduled to address funding until 1987. In the interim, FHWA and AASHTO used NCHRP to fund the creation of detailed plans so that SHRP could hit the ground running when funded. TRB appointed Byrd as interim director, and more than 200 individuals contributed their expertise and feedback to devising the detailed plans.[15]

The Strategic Highway Research Program

FHWA, AASHTO, and NAS signed the three-party agreement to manage SHRP in May 1986. SHRP would be managed as a stand-alone program within the National Academies, outside the TRB umbrella, which was one of several management options that had been outlined in *America's Highways*. Although a short-term program, SHRP's annual budgets would be nearly twice TRB's. In addition, Deen and NRC were concerned that such a large program of physical research for highways would distract TRB from its mission to serve all of transportation.[16]

Funding arrived in April 1987 in the Surface Transportation and Uniform Relocation Assistance Act, which identified SHRP and NAS by name and did indeed set aside 0.25 percent of federal-aid funding for highways and bridges. Larson chaired the program's executive committee until tapped to be federal highway administrator, serving in the George H. W. Bush administration from 1989 to 1993. John R. Tabb, Mississippi Department of Transportation, then stepped in as chair. Damian J. Kulash left his staff position as head of TRB's Special Projects Division to be SHRP's executive director, and Deen also served on SHRP's executive committee.

During the life of the program, SHRP produced or evaluated more than 100 products that turned out to be promising enough to move into the adoption phase. The Big Six became consolidated into four major programs: asphalt, concrete and structures, maintenance and work-zone safety, and a long-term pavement performance study. Although the SHRP budget did not include implementation, Larson and AASHTO secured significant funding for technology transfer and implementation activities in the Intermodal Surface Transportation Efficiency Act of 1991. As the findings began to come out, state DOTs also used their own resources to test and adopt the new products and procedures. In the decade after completion, FHWA and state governments funded implementation in roughly equal amounts. Already in the mid-1990s, an FHWA study of the likely long-term benefits of SHRP products found that the cost savings easily paid for the initial research investment many times over.[17]

Superpave® and methods and procedures for snow and ice control are two of SHRP's most well-known and revolutionary products. Superpave targeted the asphalt problem and ended up advancing best practices across the entire industry. The most expensive project in the SHRP budget at $53 million, researchers spread across nine universities or research institutes developed a system that created recipes for the components of asphalt concrete according to expected weather and traffic conditions. The new system relied on innovative equipment for material testing and evaluation and on the development of models that could predict the performance of materials and mixes. NAS trademarked Superpave in order to protect the system from interlopers, with the intent of keeping the knowledge contained within the Superpave "brand" freely available. To hasten adoption, FHWA founded the National Asphalt Training Center in Lexington, Kentucky, and states partnered with universities to initiate regional Superpave training and research centers as well. By 1999, 45 percent of new asphalt surfaces put down that year in the United States used the Superpave system.[18]

Pretreatment was SHRP's innovative approach to snow and ice control. Applying salt and chemicals shortly before a storm hit maintained safer conditions longer and made cleanup easier, because the snow and ice would not bond to the pavement. Pretreatment, however, required getting better—and faster—information about weather conditions across often far-flung road networks. SHRP researchers devised information systems to monitor pavement and weather in real time. Getting the trucks out early saved personnel and chemical costs, but the overwhelming benefits come from reducing the economic disruptions and hazardous conditions caused by snowy and icy weather.[19]

Another of SHRP's lasting legacies is the first IDEA program for "innovations deserving exploratory analysis," which not only survives, but has multiplied as part of the cooperative research programs (see Chapter 13). Although TRB did not manage SHRP's research itself, with *America's Highways,* TRB had returned, forcefully and enthusiastically, to the arena of stimulating large-scale research programs. TRB had also set a precedent for using the National Academies' consensus study process to produce a strategic plan for a research program.

Strategic Highway Research Program 2

Congress set the stage for the second Strategic Highway Research Program in 1998. The Transportation Equity Act for the 21st Century (TEA-21) requested that TRB conduct what amounted to another strategic transportation research study for a "future strategic highway research program" (Future SHRP). C. Michael Walton chaired the committee for the consensus study. A member of the National Academy of Engineering and chair of TRB's Executive Committee in 1991, Walton held a dual appointment at The University of Texas at Austin in civil engineering and public affairs. Like the Highway STRS committee, the Future SHRP committee consisted of 13 members: 6 with ties to state DOTs, 2 academics, 2 engineering consultants, and 3 from advocacy organizations for safety, environmental issues, and trucking. Ann Brach joined TRB's staff to lead the study. A member of TRB's Conduct of Research Committee, Brach had been providing policy and budget leadership for FHWA's research and technology program and had managed the research program at the Maryland State Highway Administration.[20]

From the beginning, the committee committed to extensive outreach. Because the Future SHRP study had come out of Congress, rather than from a TRB proposal as had prepared the way for the Highway STRS, the

Signing the memorandum of understanding to establish SHRP 2, January 25, 2006 (at table, left to right): J. Richard Capka, FHWA; John C. Horsley, AASHTO; and Ralph J. Cicerone, National Academy of Sciences; (standing, left to right): Brian McLaughlin, Federal Motor Carrier Safety Administration; Stephen R. Godwin, TRB; Robert E. Skinner, Jr., TRB; Dennis Judycki, FHWA; Anne P. Canby, Surface Transportation Policy Partnership; Allen D. Biehler, Pennsylvania Department of Transportation; Nicholas Garber, University of Virginia; Ann Brach, TRB; C. Michael Walton, University of Texas; Neil J. Pedersen, Maryland State Highway Administration; Rebecca Brewster, American Transportation Research Institute; John R. Njord, Utah Department of Transportation; Neil F. Hawks, TRB; and Henry G. Schwartz, Jr., Washington University in St. Louis (TRB).

committee began its work with less of a preestablished framework. The Future SHRP committee engaged dozens of stakeholders and experts at every stage of plan development. Because of the commitment to openness, the committee also took the unusual step of including the evolution of the plan in the final report. *Strategic Highway Research: Saving Lives, Reducing Congestion, and Improving Quality of Life* (TRB Special Report 260, 2001), details the participation process and summarizes the plan's iterations in its appendixes.[21]

Strategic Highway Research, therefore, provides an unusual opportunity to follow the creation of a large strategic research plan as its committee brainstormed, sought feedback, created a long list of ideas, and then modified the short lists until it had a finalized plan. Whereas the Highway STRS committee had organized its report around a limited set of evaluation criteria, the Future SHRP committee followed a similar path, but organized its work around setting research objectives. The initial committee brainstorming session in June 1999 produced a list of seven

*Strategic Highway Research
Saving Lives, Reducing Congestion,
and Improving Quality of Life
(TRB Special Report 260)*

VISION

Providing Outstanding Customer Service
for the 21st Century: A highway system that
actively contributes to improved quality of life
for all Americans by providing safe, efficient
mobility in an economically, socially, and
environmentally responsible manner.

GOALS

RENEWAL: Accelerating the Renewal of America's Highways

To develop a consistent, systematic approach to performing highway renewal that is rapid, causes minimum disruption, and produces long-lived facilities.

SAFETY: Making a Significant Improvement in Highway Safety

To prevent or reduce the severity of highway crashes through more accurate knowledge of crash factors and of the cost-effectiveness of selected countermeasures in addressing these factors.

RELIABILITY: Providing a Highway System with Reliable Travel Times

To provide highway users with reliable travel times by preventing and reducing the impact of nonrecurring incidents.

CAPACITY: Providing Highway Capacity in Support of the Nation's Economic, Environmental, and Social Goals

To develop approaches and tools for systematically integrating environmental, economic, and community requirements into the analysis, planning, and design of new highway capacity.

Source: *Strategic Highway Research: Saving Lives, Reducing Congestion, Improving Quality of Life*, Special Report 260 (National Academy Press, 2001), 47, 49, 71, 98, 117.

"focus areas" that were then circulated widely for stakeholder comment. Two focus areas—"accelerating the renewal of America's highways" and "making a quantum leap in highway safety"—had so much support that they stayed virtually unchanged from day 1, but the other five underwent considerable revision and prioritization.

In March 2000, the committee introduced the concept of an "over-arching theme" to guide the selection of focus areas and research topics: "providing outstanding customer service for the 21st century." The over-arching theme would play a similar guiding role as the Highway STRS's "big payoffs" criteria. To add definition to the focus areas, the committee then generated lists of research questions. Questions likely to produce significant progress toward the research objective and likely to thrive only under a large, concentrated research program rose to the top of the list. At one point, the committee produced a draft program that contained only one additional focus area—"delivering a sustainable highway system"—but stakeholder feedback led the committee to reintroduce a fourth focus area—"increasing mobility by optimizing system performance"—into the final program recommendations. Finally, one weakness of planning efforts with significant stakeholder engagement is that the goals tend to become less precise and more open to interpretation over time. Notably, the Future SHRP committee did the opposite. As the process reached its conclusion in 2001, the objectives defining the four research focus areas actually became more targeted and specific.

AASHTO passed a resolution on December 2, 2001, in support of Future SHRP's recommended $450 million research program, which followed the first SHRP's precedent of a funding amount equal to 0.25 percent of federal-aid funding for highways and bridges. As with SHRP, AASHTO and FHWA used NCHRP to conduct more detailed planning while waiting for Congress to take up the next transportation authorization. The interim planning process, structured as a large oversight panel and four technical panels corresponding to each program goal, identified more than 100 individual projects in enough detail to produce project budget estimates totaling $450 million.[22]

Congress authorized SHRP 2 in the Safe, Accountable, Flexible, Efficient Transportation Equity Act: A Legacy for Users (SAFETEA-LU) in 2005. The law references Special Report 260 by name and summarizes the four recommended focus areas. Unlike for SHRP, SHRP 2 was managed within TRB. Neil F. Hawks, who had worked on SHRP, became director. Ann Brach assumed the role of deputy director and rose to director in 2012. Allen D. Biehler, secretary of transportation, Pennsylvania Department of Transportation, chaired the oversight committee until 2008, when Kirk T. Steudle, director, Michigan Department of Transportation, took over.[23]

In operation from 2006 to 2015, SHRP 2 invested $217 million in 132 research contracts that yielded 130 promising products. TRB managed the research projects with a structure similar to that used for interim planning. Expert task groups played a role similar to panels in the cooperative research programs. They helped draft requests for proposals, reviewed proposals from consultants, and provided other technical

SHRP 2's Naturalistic Driving Study and the Power of Fundamental Research

FROM ITS FIRST meeting in June 1999, the Committee for a Future Strategic Highway Research Program (Future SHRP) knew that it wanted something big in the field of highway safety research. Relatively simple interventions—seatbelts, air bags, campaigns against driving while intoxicated, etc.—had succeeded in reducing the rate of fatalities and injuries, but increases in driving had kept total fatalities stubbornly high. The equivalent of a jumbo jet full of people still died every day on America's highways and streets.[a]

For what would become SHRP 2, the Future SHRP committee recommended that highway safety needed fundamental research into the causes of crashes. The SHRP model, with its large, multiyear research program, was particularly well suited to big leaps in both applied and fundamental research. In addition, new technology made it feasible to take another run at safety research's ultimate data set: tracking the road, vehicle, and driver together in real-life situations.

Rapid technological advances also made new solutions feasible. The National Cooperative Highway Research Program's (NCHRP's) Safety Technical Panel, chaired by John L. Craig, Nebraska Department of Roads, and charged with advance planning for a Future SHRP, observed in 2003 that improvements in

Julie McClafferty (pointing) and Julie Hodge work on NDS data reduction at the secure data enclave (Virginia Tech Transportation Institute).

vehicle technologies, such as automated collision avoidance, could soon be widely available. But they also warned—4 years before the release of the iPhone—that new technologies could just as easily increase driver distraction.[b]

With congressional funding in 2005's Safe, Accountable, Flexible, Efficient Transportation Equity Act: A Legacy for Users, SHRP 2 launched the largest naturalistic driving study (NDS) to date. Researchers recruited more than 3,500 drivers—men and women of all ages—from six states representing different driving environments throughout the country. They outfitted each driver's personal vehicle—cars, pickup trucks, SUVs, and minivans—with video cameras to track their face and feet and the view from the vehicle's front and rear. Sensors and in-vehicle diagnostics also tracked acceleration, speed, turn signals, illumination of the road, and other variables. They created a separate geographic information system–based database of road conditions, including weather and traffic, for 12,500 centerline miles.[c]

Then the participants drove and drove and drove, racking up 32.5 million miles over 3 years. The drivers also got into roughly 2,000 crashes and—just as important for research—7,000 close calls. For each incident, researchers could diagnose exactly what was happening with the road, the vehicle, and the driver.

To make the data as widely available as possible, the Transportation Research Board (TRB) contracted with the Virginia Tech Transportation Institute to host the driving data, and with Iowa State University to host the road information database. To manage privacy protections and costs, but still encourage research, several levels of access are available, including free downloads of some data sets. TRB is currently working to ensure that the data will be available to researchers for many years to come.

Since 2015, researchers from all over the world have tapped the data for hundreds of topics. At the 2018 Annual Meeting alone, papers used the NDS to examine driving behavior at rural intersections, at right turns, on horizontal curves, in the fog, in the rain, and also while drowsy, distracted, following another car, overtaking bicyclists, or interacting with pedestrian infrastructure, to state a few examples.

Researchers hail from dozens of universities, including from Asia, Canada, and Europe, in addition to American universities. Federal agencies are using the data to study energy and public health. Insurance companies have also expressed interest.

The prescience of the Future SHRP committee really shows, however, in the numerous companies from the automobile and technology industries using the NDS data. The same technology that made the NDS possible is now being deployed for everything from advanced driver assistance systems to autonomous vehicle trials.

Although it is still too early to be certain about the future of driving, the industry can get together to mull over its progress at the Automated Vehicles Symposium, sponsored annually by the Association for Unmanned Vehicle Systems International and TRB since 2014.[d]

We can pray, however, that a dramatic reduction in crashes will be part of the future of driving. In 2016, motor vehicle crashes killed more than 100 people per day in the United States. Globally, the annual toll is approximately 1.25 million.[e]

guidance. More than 150 volunteers served on SHRP 2 committees and task groups in just its first year, and over the life of the program, 158 committees and task groups mustered 853 volunteers and liaisons into service.[24]

SHRP 2 also continued TRB's history of international collaborations on major research programs. During the AASHO Road Test, consulting resident-observers from Canada and Germany participated on-site in Illinois. For the first SHRP, a cooperative relationship with Canada began during the NCHRP-funded planning stages and a Canadian, Boris Hryhorczuk, Manitoba Department of Transportation, was an ex officio member of SHRP's executive committee. The Canadian provinces even formed their own parallel "C-SHRP" to coordinate Canadian test sites and materials. C-SHRP also facilitated loaned staff from Canadian governments. For Superpave, a major mid-course meeting included researchers from 11 foreign countries.[25]

SHRP 2's top oversight committee and three of the four technical coordinating committees included a liaison to Canada. In addition, loaned staff from Canada, the French Institute of Science and Technology for Transport, Development and Networks, and the Ministry of Infrastructure and the Environment of the Netherlands maintained their presence for years and truly became part of the SHRP 2 staff team. They contributed their expertise to coordinating and managing SHRP 2's research projects, as well as conducting international outreach.[26]

Attendees at annual meetings could track progress on future SHRP 2 products: Michael Townley (left), Michigan Department of Transportation, and Steven Ziegler, ICF International, use a tablet to try out the Web-based decision support tool that would become PlanWorks (Risdon Photography).

SHRP 2 Solutions

The same law that funded SHRP 2 also requested a report from TRB on implementing the program's results. Over the decades of managing research programs, FHWA, AASHTO, and TRB had grown more sophisticated in their attention to research implementation and technology and knowledge transfer. Indeed, the Future SHRP report recommended integrating potential users into every step of the research process. This included designating those responsible for implementation during the earliest stages of the program. In addition, Future SHRP noted that identifying likely products, conducting demonstrations, testing in real-world

Charles
Robert Fay

circumstances, and providing user training may also be appropriate to incorporate into the research program itself.[27]

TRB published the consensus study *Implementing the Results of the Second Strategic Highway Research Program* (TRB Special Report 296) in 2009, only a couple of years into the research phase. Using the experience gained from SHRP and NCHRP projects, the committee, chaired by Steudle, recommended investing $400 million over 6 years for SHRP 2 implementation. Although research results were only preliminary, nascent, or even embryonic, the committee also identified promising products, potential users, barriers to assimilation, and incentives for adoption for all four focus areas. For example, for the reliability focus area, the report pointed out that SHRP 2's projects that were assessing best practices in incident management—for everything from a stalled car to multiple-vehicle crashes to spilled freight—would require training programs for transportation professionals, and also emergency responders, law enforcement, and private tow truck drivers. In addition, the report advised, training could not be limited to just those on the front lines, but would also require targeting management at higher levels of organizations.[28]

FHWA, in partnership with AASHTO, took the lead in implementation. The states collectively agreed to redirect to FHWA 4 percent of their federal-aid funding for planning and research, contributing more than $60 million for the $172 million, 7-year implementation program. AASHTO also created an Implementation Task Force, which over the course of three workshops assessed which products were suitable for prioritized funding.[29]

For each of the 64 chosen "SHRP 2 Solutions," researchers worked with state officials to develop a customized implementation plan to be

Both SHRP and SHRP 2 benefited from international participation and attracted international interest: Jinquan Zhang, deputy director general of China's Research Institute of Highways; Neil F. Hawks, first director of SHRP 2; and Charles Fay, SHRP 2 senior program officer, at the China–U.S. Seminar on Highway Technology in June 2011 (RIOH).

SHRP 2 conducted research on accelerated bridge construction: A worker guides a bridge section into place (Minnesota Department of Transportation).

funded by an Implementation Assistance Program that developed proof-of-concept pilots, supported early adopters, and offered user incentives. The implementation program also supported peer exchanges and technical assistance and even helped early adopters become "champions" for products. States, and for some products, metropolitan planning organizations and regional agencies, competed to participate, and all 50 states, the District of Columbia, and Puerto Rico advanced the implementation of at least one product. Most states organized trials on 5 or more products; 12 states implemented 10 or more during the program.[30]

With 63 SHRP 2 Solutions, some only a couple of years old, there is only room here to present a few examples that are making the biggest impact right out of the gate. For traffic incident management, SHRP 2 worked to perfect an integrated training program that would be appropriate for all emergency responders. By the end of 2017, 300,000 responders had participated. The training encouraged coordination and took participants from start to finish including initial assessment, dispatch, arrival, medical care for the injured, protocols to prevent secondary crashes, and site clearance. A second curriculum trained the trainers too. Post-training evaluation revealed 81 percent felt safer on-site and 87 percent said they had increased their efforts to prevent secondary crashes.[31]

SHRP 2's customer orientation came through strongly in Renewal's accelerated bridge construction project. Building bridges out of

SHRP2 by the Numbers

From Research into Practice: SHRP2's Implementation Progress

SHRP 2 Solutions' *2018 Implementation Highlights* summarizes activities to date (FHWA-HOP-19-001, December 2018).

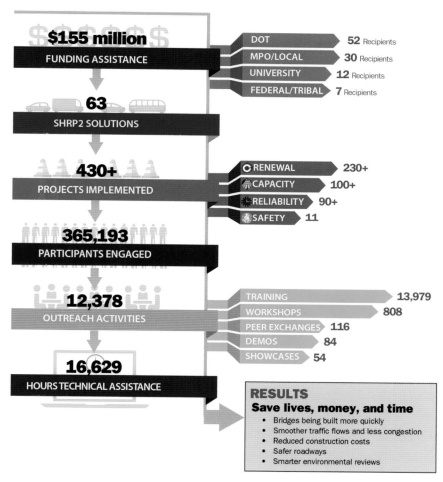

$155 million
FUNDING ASSISTANCE

DOT	**52** Recipients
MPO/LOCAL	**30** Recipients
UNIVERSITY	**12** Recipients
FEDERAL/TRIBAL	**7** Recipients

63
SHRP2 SOLUTIONS

430+
PROJECTS IMPLEMENTED

RENEWAL	230+
CAPACITY	100+
RELIABILITY	90+
SAFETY	11

365,193
PARTICIPANTS ENGAGED

12,378
OUTREACH ACTIVITIES

TRAINING	13,979
WORKSHOPS	808
PEER EXCHANGES	116
DEMOS	84
SHOWCASES	54

16,629
HOURS TECHNICAL ASSISTANCE

RESULTS
Save lives, money, and time
- Bridges being built more quickly
- Smoother traffic flows and less congestion
- Reduced construction costs
- Safer roadways
- Smarter environmental reviews

prefabricated, modular systems can drastically reduce traveler disruptions. However, prior to SHRP 2, only exceptional, unique bridges were usually deemed worthy of the customized engineering required. The SHRP 2 project targeted typical bridges, and the researchers developed standardized approaches that could be adopted by local contractors using conventional equipment. They developed a toolkit that was piloted on bridge replacement projects in Iowa, New York, and Vermont. Early adopters included the Gila River Indian Community in Arizona, where the toolkit reduced a bridge closure from 6 months to 11 days, and Rhode Island Department of Transportation, which reduced construction disruption of a busy highway ramp from 330 to 21 days.[32]

Under the Capacity focus area, SHRP 2 developed guidance on how to fulfill the promise of "Eco-Logical: An Ecosystem Approach to Developing Infrastructure Projects," an interagency agreement that had been signed in April 2006 by eight federal agencies responsible for infrastructure or environmental conservation. Instead of infrastructure projects getting bogged down by controversial environmental reviews that in the end might only lead to piecemeal mitigation, the agreement proposed that the parties come together early in the process and be open to creative approaches to the win-win: timely project completion and enhanced natural environments. SHRP 2's job was to take this nice-sounding theory and turn it into a replicable step-by-step process, which is today part of a dedicated website called PlanWorks. Maine Department of Transportation used SHRP 2's guidance to protect habitat for the Atlantic salmon when it replaced culverts, speeding interagency consultation by 7 months. When planning to replace 20 miles of I-75 along Lake Erie, Michigan Department of Transportation used it to collaborate with stakeholders to improve the entire watershed and ended up reducing permitting time and land acquisition costs.[33]

SHRP 2 took on the exceptional and made it standard; the innovative and made accessible to even the most routine projects. It married objective-driven research to the soft side—the human side—of transportation. Building on a nearly century-long partnership, FHWA, AASHTO, and TRB integrated decades of growing sophistication on implementing research results, including that the users should be in the lead.

At a time when research funding was flagging and state and federal highway administrators seemed unwilling to direct new funds to research, TRB used its new tool—consensus studies—to fulfill its mission to stimulate research. The Highway STRS and the first SHRP bolstered faith in Congress and among administrators in the value of research, cultivating favorable conditions for SHRP 2. In addition, the Highway STRS would lead to additional strategic transportation studies that set the stage for the next generation of cooperative research programs.

CHAPTER 13

Cooperative Research Programs

AS WORD SPREAD of the $150 million being proposed for a
Strategic Highway Research Program (SHRP) in *America's Highways*
(TRB Special Report 202, 1984), advocates for other modes and topics
began to clamor for Strategic Transportation Research Studies (STRS)
of their own. In response, Thomas B. Deen, the Transportation Research
Board's (TRB's) executive director, cautioned that TRB might consider
such studies for other modes, but only if there "is a large perceived need
for research." In fact, TRB had already embarked on the next proposal
for a STRS. The contract that funded the STRS that produced *America's
Highways* included in its scope of work preparing a proposal for another
STRS for a second mode.[1]

The congressional authorizations for the Transit Cooperative Research
Program (TCRP) in 1991 and the Airport Cooperative Research Program
(ACRP) in 2003 followed the path that had led to SHRP: a proposal for
a strategic research plan, which led to a consensus study that produced a
program plan, followed by congressional authorization of the research
program. The consensus studies for the transit and airport research
programs, however, did not recommend the short-term, concentrated
research program used by SHRP. Instead, the studies advised emulating
the National Cooperative Highway Research Program (NCHRP).

In the mid-1980s, NCHRP was in its second decade and a recognized success in the transportation research community. Indeed, when Congress reduced the funding authorized for highway planning and research (the old 1½ percent funds) in the Surface Transportation and Uniform Relocation Assistance Act of 1987, the states rallied to maintain NCHRP's purchasing power. Through the American Association of State Highway and Transportation Officials (AASHTO), they voted to increase the allocation from 4.5 to 5.5 percent of highway planning and research funding. In support of the increase, AASHTO's Standing Committee on Highways praised NCHRP for providing benefits "many times in excess of its investment," specifically citing the *Highway Capacity Manual*, and also AASHTO's guides, manuals, policies, and standards for pavement structures, subsurface investigations, geometric design, and highway bridges that had built on NCHRP research.[2]

Three directors shepherded TRB's cooperative research programs (CRPs) through the modern era. Coming to the position in the mid-1980s, Robert J. Reilly led the expansion into transit and airports. Christopher W. Jenks, after building a sound footing for TCRP, assumed the director role in 2007 and Christopher J. Hedges became director in 2016. This chapter examines the modern era of NCHRP and how it inspired additional CRPs, including TCRP and ACRP. The transit and airport industries then adapted that NCHRP model to their particular needs and circumstances to produce their own impressive record of research. NCHRP and TCRP also began hosting Innovations Deserving Exploratory Analysis (IDEA) programs, a legacy of the first SHRP. The chapter concludes with look inside the expert panel process that underpins the success of TRB's research programs.

NCHRP's Flexible Deployment

NCHRP's huge volume of research—and its impacts—have been celebrated in publications honoring the program's 25th and 50th anniversaries. Research reports produced by NCHRP will total more than 1,000 by TRB's centennial. In addition, NCHRP has published more than 500 Synthesis of Highway Practice reports and numerous other documents in the Research Results Digest and Legal Research Digest series. Funding has remained strong. The states, through AASHTO, have continued to peg NCHRP funding to federal funding for planning and research. NCHRP funding from the Intermodal Surface Transportation Efficiency Act (ISTEA) reached

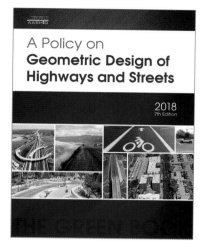

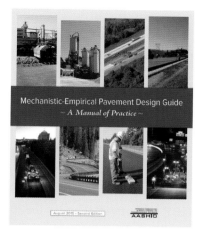

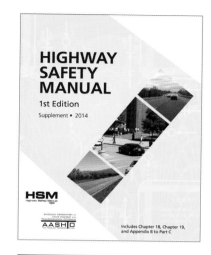

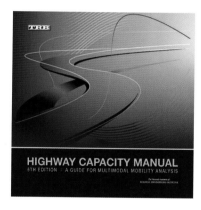

$17 million annually, and the next authorization, 1998's Transportation Equity Act for the 21st Century (TEA-21), bestowed a 50 percent increase. Increases followed in subsequent surface transportation legislation so that, as of 2018, the NCHRP program totaled around $42 million annually.[3]

By the very nature of its applied, cooperative structure, all NCHRP research is important to some corner of the highway transportation world. However, part of NCHRP's strength, and longevity, is due to the many different ways it can be deployed. Indeed, NCHRP's founders recognized the need for flexibility and the benefits of creativity by setting up at the outset a funding subcategory especially designated for Special Projects (Project Area 20). NCHRP's sponsors have also used other tactics, such as linked or coordinated projects, to great effect.

NCHRP research continues to contribute to national guidance and standards, including for AASHTO's *A Policy on Geometric Design of Highways and Streets*, *Mechanistic-Empirical Pavement Design Guide*, *Highway Safety Manual*, and *LRFD Bridge Design Specifications*; TRB's *Highway Capacity Manual*; and FHWA's *Manual on Uniform Traffic Control Devices* (AASHTO, TRB, and FHWA).

The basic sequence to developing an NCHRP product, or any CRP product, starts with a *research problem statement*, which is transformed into a *project statement* that becomes *contracted research* that produces a *research report*. As applied research, the execution of this simple sequence for straightforward problems often shows through in the titles of the reports: *Detection and Repair of Fatigue Damage in Welded Highway Bridges* (NCHRP Report 206, 1979); *Partial Lighting of Interchanges* (NCHRP Report 256, 1983); *Roadway Widths for Low-Traffic-Volume Roads* (NCHRP Report 362, 1994); and *Long-Term Performance and Lifecycle Costs of Stormwater Best Management Practices* (NCHRP Report 792, 2014).

NCHRP also provides a way for states to collectively co-sponsor and coordinate research with other agencies. NCHRP's first special project, co-sponsored with the Bureau of Public Roads, computerized the Highway Research Information Service in 1964. NCHRP has also been a vehicle to co-sponsor the National Academies' consensus studies. When TRB's Executive Committee initiated the study that led to *Expanding Metropolitan Highways: Implications for Air Quality and Energy Use* (TRB Special Report 245, 1995), AASHTO used NCHRP to join the Federal Highway Administration (FHWA), the Environmental Protection Agency (EPA), and TRB in co-sponsoring the study. More recently, NCHRP sponsored the consensus study *In-Service Performance Evaluation of Guardrail End Treatments* (TRB Special Report 323, 2018).

NCHRP's annual program also gives it the flexibility to meet emerging needs, even on short notice. For both SHRPs, NCHRP funded planning studies during the interval between consensus study and congressional authorization that accelerated their launch. When TEA-21 reduced FHWA's research funds putting two of the first SHRP's legacy research programs, Superpave® and the Long-Term Pavement Performance Project, in jeopardy, the state departments of transportation (DOTs) and AASHTO mobilized to "Save SHRP." They directed some NCHRP funding to FHWA to continue the planned research, while also continuing NCHRP's own planned work refining and implementing Superpave. For many years, NCHRP also supported "quick response" research contracts for AASHTO's standing committees on highways, planning, the environment, and public transportation.[4]

AASHTO has also used NCHRP's special project designation to expand into workforce and professional development. NCHRP Project 20-24 specifically serves the needs of chief executive officers and senior managers in state DOTs. Since its launch in 1987, NCHRP has executed more than 100 projects on topics such as leadership, performance management, communications, and workforce development including diversity. In the 1990s, the project developed an educational outreach program for high schools to raise awareness of careers in transportation and civil engineering, especially among underrepresented groups (Project 20-24(3)A). The National Academy of Sciences (NAS) President Bruce Alberts (1993–2005) commended the result, AASHTO's transportation and civil engineering (TRAC) program, in the pages of *TR News* for advancing the priorities he too had set for the National Academies to help students and workers adapt to the "increasingly technological society." AASHTO's member states can still today bring TRAC to high school classrooms, and NCHRP has also continued to assist the cultivation of transportation professionals, such as 2011's *Strategies to Attract and Retain a Capable Transportation Workforce* (NCHRP Report 685).[5]

NCHRP's ability to foster coordination with other agencies combined with the flexibility of a continuing fund for annual research programs has also encouraged the development of coordinated and linked research projects that extend over years, even decades. The process that supports regular updates of manuals and guides, such as TRB's *Highway Capacity Manual* and AASHTO's Green Book on geometric design, regularly draw on NCHRP. Influence works in both directions: the update of a manual can trigger additional NCHRP research in response to newly identified needs, and NCHRP research that points in new directions can trigger an update to guidance documents.

NCHRP's ability to support the long-term evolution of coordinated research played out significantly in the development of a body of work around safety. After AASHTO adopted a Strategic Highway Safety Plan in 1998, NCHRP managed 19 different research projects furthering plan implementation. One of the 19 projects produced the NCHRP Report 500 series, individual guides that covered each of the plan's 22 "key emphasis areas," such as seatbelt use, drowsy and distracted drivers, work-zone safety, and vehicle collisions involving pedestrians, bicyclists, or young drivers.[6]

NCHRP again came to the rescue to develop an "authoritative document" on highway safety. In 1999, participants in a conference session at TRB's annual meeting discussed the desirability of such a document. Without an authoritative manual to estimate the reduction in the frequency and severity of crashes from changes to facility design and

Celebrating the 100th Synthesis of Highway Practice, Setting a Model for Transit and Airports

T HE TRANSPORTATION Research Board (TRB) paused in 1983 to honor reaching the 100th National Cooperative Highway Research Program (NCHRP) Synthesis of Highway Practice in less than 15 years. To celebrate, TRB shared an insider view in *TR News* of how synthesis reports came to be and reviewed the impacts of numbers 1 through 100.[a]

NCHRP funded the Synthesis of Highway Practice series as a continuing special project starting in 1967, and TRB produced the first report, *Traffic Control for Freeway Maintenance,* in 1969. In its early years, the Highway Research Board and then TRB kept the project in-house. The project closely aligned with the heart of TRB's mission. They also wanted to keep close tabs on the process and evaluate how well the reports helped users translate research into practice.[b]

By design, synthesis reports covered relatively narrow topics that also suffered from fragmented and scattered information. The early project committees also worried that existing information was underevaluated. They set their goals high: synthesis reports were to contain "the best knowledge available."

Every year, the project committees agonized over which 10–11 topics rose above the 75 suggestions. In 1983, Bryant Mather, a top specialist in concrete research who had been a civilian employee of the U.S. Army Corps of Engineers since 1941, worked the chalkboard, and Herbert A. Pennock, on TRB's staff, tracked everything on his specially designed computer program. Prioritization could be painful.[c]

NCHRP's Synthesis of Highway Practice series, first funded in 1967, inspired TCRP and ACRP to develop their own series of reports promising "the best knowledge available."

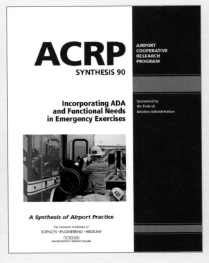

Topics chosen, the project committee then refined each project's scope and recommended a panel to manage the synthesis report. To make the tie to practice, all panels strove to include at least one active practitioner. For the first 100 reports, panelists came from 47 states and two Canadian provinces.

TRB proudly pointed to its synthesis reports being used in undergraduate, graduate, and continuing education courses. Two of the first 100 had informed special conferences on pavement rehabilitation and corridor management. Synthesis reports on highway finance and studded tires had reached state legislatures. *Bridge Approach Design and Construction Practices* (NCHRP Synthesis of Highway Practice 2) had been translated into Portuguese and *Bituminous Emulsions for Highway Pavements* (Synthesis 30) into Japanese.[d]

TRB's work on NCHRP's synthesis reports set the model for the Transit Cooperative Research Program (TCRP) and the Airport Cooperative Research Program (ACRP). TCRP published *Safe Operating Procedures for Alternative Fuel Buses* (TCRP Synthesis of Transit Practice 1) in 1993 and reached *Elevator and Escalator Maintenance and Safety Practices* (TCRP Synthesis 100) in 2012. In 2007, ACRP produced its first synthesis, *Innovative Finance and Alternative Sources of Revenue for Airports* (ACRP Synthesis of Airport Practice 1), and reached Synthesis 90, *Incorporating ADA and Functional Needs in Emergency Exercises*, in 2018.

NCHRP's synthesis series is still kicking too. *Control of Concrete Cracking in Bridges* (Synthesis 500) came out in 2017.

What was the topic of NCHRP's celebrated 100th synthesis? Managing state highway finance.

operations, AASHTO's website explains, "safety considerations often carried little weight in the project development process." A joint TRB task force got the ball rolling on what would become AASHTO's first *Highway Safety Manual* (2010), building off of NCHRP research and with additional support from FHWA and the Institute of Transportation Engineers (ITE). TRB's Committee on Highway Safety Performance coordinates additional research, and in 2015 NCHRP launched a project to produce the *Highway Safety Manual*'s second edition. In addition, NCHRP has supported research that dives deeper into human factors. *Human Factors Guidelines for Road Systems* (NCHRP Report 600) already in its second edition in 2012, translated research into how people perceive and react in specific environments into guidance on road design.[7]

NCHRP also played a critical role in finally overcoming one of the Advisory Board on Highway Research's original research problems: understanding pavement, especially concrete slabs. The Committee on Structural Design of Roads had set out in 1919 "to establish reliable scientific engineering theory" for how pavements behaved under actual traffic and varying temperatures and subgrades. Fifty years later, the Highway Research Board lamented that so little had been accomplished toward this goal. The American Association of State Highway Officials (AASHO) Road Test, as Francis Hveem critiqued, had produced equations based on statistical correlations without advancing understanding of pavement mechanics. In other words, the equations appeared to work, but they contained insufficient theory as to why. The equations had also been based on the deterioration of new pavement, giving little guidance on the performance of rehabilitated pavement.[8]

In 1996, AASHTO felt the time was right to take on pavement mechanics again. NCHRP launched Project 1-37A, which ran from 1998 to 2004, and invested nearly $7 million into creating the *Mechanistic and Empirical Pavement Design Guide*. The research produced a sea change in the understanding of pavements and, just as importantly, in a way that could be translated into practice. The project spawned numerous additional NCHRP studies, including a crucial cooperative study with FHWA that in 2007 conducted an international scan of Canadian and European approaches to long-life pavements.[9]

Finally, AASHTO has used NCHRP's flexibility to peer into the unknown. The Foresight Series, initiated in 2008 and published in 2014 as *Strategic Issues Facing Transportation*, NCHRP Report 750, includes six volumes whose topics were chosen to help state DOTs manage an uncertain future. As John Halikowski, director of the Arizona Department of Transportation and chair of AASHTO's Standing Committee on Research, described the series, "the topics in this series represent big-picture, strategic thinking: we will have to deal with and manage these issues no matter what else the future holds." Many of the volumes used scenario planning or established other indicators of the future to help states get a handle on the future of freight; preparing for extreme weather; evaluating new technologies; organizing transportation to support a sustainable society; energy and fuels; and demographics.[10]

Transit Cooperative Research Program

Mass transit turned out to be the lucky mode for the second strategic transportation research study. To develop the proposal for a Transit STRS, TRB began holding preliminary conversations with the American Public Transit Association (APTA) and others in the transit industry in late 1983. During the proposal development phase, industry feedback already indicated that the "big payoff" approach that framed the Highway STRS (see Chapter 12) may not be the most appropriate way to approach a Transit STRS or to screen research priorities for the mass transit industry.[11]

With sponsorship from the Urban Mass Transportation Administration (UMTA), TRB began the year-long consensus study for the Transit STRS in 1986 and published its final report, *Research for Public Transit: New Directions* (TRB Special Report 213) in 1987. The 22-member committee was chaired by William W. Millar, then with the Port Authority of Allegheny County. Committee members came from small and large transit agencies and included academics and consultants with expertise in mechanical engineering, system planning, and business administration. Millar would go on to be chair of TRB's Executive Committee for 1992 and APTA's president from 1996 to 2011.[12]

At the time of the Transit STRS, TRB already managed a small CRP for mass transit modeled after NCHRP. Launched in 1980 and funded at the discretion of UMTA, the National Cooperative Transit Research and Development Program (NCTRP) had struggled to gain momentum. Its organizers' hopes went unfulfilled that UMTA's initial $1 million in annual funding would attract additional funding from transit agencies, as originally conceived. Eventually, even UMTA's funding became erratic. The Transit STRS committee saw much in NCTRP that worked well, however. They agreed that its near-term "problem-solving" orientation was what was most needed in transit research. They also identified a need to continue to support the priorities of those running local transit agencies, which NCTRP did by proposing research projects to UMTA via a Technical Steering Committee managed by APTA. Federally funded transit research in the 1970s (on new technologies) and in the 1980s (on efficient federal oversight) had been tailored mostly to federal priorities. The Transit STRS committee believed that research that focused only on federal priorities, however worthy, meant missed opportunities for bottom-up innovations and local input on effective implementation.[13]

Instead of a short-term, big-payoff research program, *Research for Public Transit* advised that the elements of NCTRP—problem-solving orientation, local direction, and funding for annual programs—be put on stronger footing. They also outlined several management options in addition to continuing within TRB. To keep the proposed program focused on local problem solving, the report also recommended seven priority problem areas: human resources management, service configuration and marketing, service delivery models, internal efficiencies, maintenance, equipment, and innovative financing. APTA welcomed the research program proposal and began advocating for federal funding.[14]

Congress authorized the revitalized TCRP in ISTEA in 1991, the law that also transformed UMTA into the Federal Transit Administration (FTA). ISTEA required an independent governing board to recommend projects and identified NAS as the preferred research manager. By cooperative agreement signed on May 13, 1992, FTA sponsors TCRP, and APTA's Transit Development Corporation created the TCRP Oversight and Project Selection (TOPS) Committee, which acts as the required governing board. TRB manages the research program. For funding, although *Research for Public Transit* recommended emulating NCHRP by setting aside a small percentage of total federal transit funding for research, the actual TCRP funding amount has been set in each authorization. After reaching a high of $10 million in 2009, funding has declined in recent years. However, the Fixing America's Surface Transportation (FAST) Act

TCRP has produced numerous research reports on modern light rail transit since TCRP Report 2 (1995) on the applicability of low-floor vehicles in North America (Metro Transit Minneapolis/St. Paul).

of 2015 put TCRP funding on sounder footing by moving it to the Mass Transit Account of the Highway Trust Fund.[15]

Over TCRP's first 25 years, TRB staff have managed around 200 research reports and published an additional 130 Synthesis of Transit Practice reports. The program released its first Synthesis of Transit Practice report on *Safe Operating Procedures for Alternative Fuel Buses* in 1993 and its first research report on *Artificial Intelligence for Transit Railcar Diagnostics* in 1994. The typical size of a research project is around $250,000 per year of work. A Research Results Digest series publishes shorter documents designed to speed results into practice. TCRP also includes a Legal Digest series, which briefs transit agencies on topical legal issues, and runs its own IDEA program. In addition, TCRP funds a continuing contract with APTA for research dissemination and implementation.

TCRP operates much like NCHRP. The TOPS Committee solicits and selects research problem statements, which are presented annually to the National Academies for acceptance. This committee numbers around 30 members, representing a range of transit agencies from across the country plus a few members from consulting firms and unions. Unlike NCHRP, TCRP welcomes research problem statements from anyone and maintains an open Web portal for submissions. Nearly 3,000 research

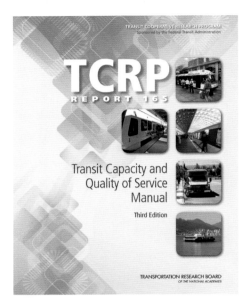

TCRP's *Transit Capacity and Quality of Service Manual* reached its third edition in 2013 and has become the standard reference manual for the industry.

problem statements have vied for consideration over the years. Most research problems have come from transit agencies or APTA committees, but FTA, TRB committees, universities, consultants, and even state DOTs have submitted a healthy share. For each research problem selected, TRB staff create an oversight panel, which crafts the request for proposals, selects the consultants, monitors progress, and reviews results.

TCRP's most popular reports show the breadth of topics in need of problem-solving. Transit passes for college students, the legal implications of video surveillance, financing infrastructure through land value capture, staffing levels for fleet maintenance, track design for light rail, and new shared mobility services all make appearances on the list of most downloaded reports over recent years. As app-based transportation network companies (TNCs) and "shared-use" business models for vehicles have burst on the scene, TCRP has been able to meet a hunger for information. *Broadening Understanding of the Interplay Among Public Transit, Shared Mobility, and Personal Automobiles* (TCRP Research Report 195, 2018), which analyzed data on TNC trips in five metropolitan regions, received nearly 5,000 downloads in just a few months.[16]

TCRP, not surprisingly given the huge role of labor in delivering quality transit services, has put substantial resources into workforce development. In 2004, TCRP contracted with the National Institute for Automotive Service Excellence to develop certification tests for eight mechanical systems in transit buses (TCRP Project E-06). By July 2017, nearly 3,500 technicians had passed more than 11,500 tests; more than 800 had earned Automotive Service Excellence Transit Bus Master Technician status. For rail transit, a similar project designed a certification program that transit agencies have implemented through an apprenticeship framework approved by the Department of Labor (TCRP Report 170, 2014).[17]

Any list of TCRP's most important contributions is incomplete without the *Transit Capacity and Quality of Service Manual*. First released as a Web-only document in 1999, TCRP's TOPS Committee had been inspired by TRB's *Highway Capacity Manual*, then in its third edition. No single comprehensive and authoritative source for transit practitioners existed to help them design elements of the transit service to achieve desired speed, reliability, and capacity. Nor did the transit industry have robust ways to measure the quality of transit service from the rider's perspective. Although the first edition could only synthesize existing research, the second (TCRP Report 100 in 2003) and third (TCRP Report 165 in 2013) editions incorporated newly developed research and best practices to close gaps identified in previous manuals. In addition to its use as a standard reference work, the manual has been adopted in university courses and transit agency training programs across the English-speaking world.[18]

Airport Cooperative Research Program

The congressional request for a consensus study outlining an airport research program came in April 2000 in the Federal Aviation Administration's (FAA's) reauthorization bill, and the legislation specifically directed the study to evaluate the applicability of NCHRP and TCRP. Congress' action followed decades of interest within the aviation industry. Studies in the 1980s and 1990s, conducted outside of TRB, stressed that airport operators had little influence over federal aviation and aeronautics research programs and no mechanism to cooperate as an industry on research. In 1992, the National Association of State Aviation Officials even pointed specifically to NCHRP and TCRP as models.[19]

At the time of Congress' request for the consensus study, FAA, the National Aeronautics and Space Administration (NASA), the Department of Defense, and the Transportation Security Administration all conducted research, but no federal agency's research was organized around the needs of the 5,000 airports open to the public, including the 525 designated commercial-service airports. FAA's research program aligned with federal priorities for policy, legislation, and rulemaking, and NASA researched technologies on medium- and long-term horizons. Airports, the majority of which were owned by local governments or regional authorities, had no research program specifically designed to meet their needs, even as environmental and security concerns, shifting patterns of demand, and rapidly evolving technologies had made their operations and planning more complex.[20]

The Committee for a Study of an Airport Cooperative Research Program, chaired by James C. DeLong, manager of aviation for the

From left, Bhoomin Chauhan, Abdullah Bouran, Donna Wilt, and Erin Egoroff, advised by Debra Carstens, Florida Institute of Technology, celebrate their win at the 2018 ACRP Design Competition Awards Ceremony (Sherry DiBari/Virginia Space Grant Consortium).

Louisville International Airport, published its report, *Airport Research Needs: Cooperative Solutions* (TRB Special Report 272) in 2003. The study made recommendations for financing, governing, and managing a CRP for airports and emphasized that airport operators should be directly involved in every phase of such a research program. Two members of the study committee would later become chair of TRB's Executive Committee. Adib K. Kanafani, University of California, Berkeley, who had been elected to the National Academy of Engineering in 2002 in part for his "significant contributions to national and international air transportation," served as chair in 2009, and James M. Crites, Dallas/Fort Worth International Airport, served in 2016.[21]

Congress authorized ACRP in December 2003 in the Vision 100: Century of Aviation Reauthorization Act and appropriated the first $10 million a year later. Following the NCHRP and TCRP model, ACRP finds solutions to practical problems. Like the transit industry, the airport industry is highly dispersed, making it unfeasible to emulate NCHRP's funding mechanism by pooling annual contributions from individual airport operators. FAA directly sponsors ACRP. The ACRP Oversight Committee, whose members are appointed by the secretary of USDOT, hail mostly from agencies that run airports. Five industry organizations and EPA assign ex officio members. The oversight committee selects and

crafts the annual research programs that TRB then manages using the
established CRP procedures and suite of publication series.[22]

From the program's launch in October 2005 through 2017, ACRP has
invested $126.5 million in 555 projects across 11 research topic areas. Like
TCRP, ACRP accepts research problem statements from any interested
party through an open solicitation. In 2017, ACRP took the open solicitation approach a step further with IdeaHub, an online platform designed
to turn proposing and shaping research problem statements into a
collaborative experience and to lower barriers to participation. IdeaHub
encourages industry practitioners to offer ideas, comment on proposed
ideas, and receive support from subject matter experts. Committed to
transparency, participants will be able to follow ideas through to the
development of final annual research programs.[23]

Environmental concerns—storm water, air quality, noise, alternative
fuels, energy efficiency, public health, etc.—make up the largest category of
ACRP funding (27 percent), a proportion that does not include numerous
studies on wildlife and habitat management that have been funded in the
safety and operations categories.[24] Environmental sustainability is also
the topic of one of ACRP's most popular products. The Sustainable Aviation
Guidance Alliance (SAGA), a volunteer organization of industry leaders,
had created an award-winning database of solutions that
airports of all sizes can incorporate into their sustainability
plans. ACRP responded when both the database's user interface and its stable of sustainable solutions needed updating.
Two ACRP panels worked together to guide the creation of
an interactive website populated with innovative and tested
sustainability activities. The website, a nontraditional product
for TRB's CRPs, led to the question of hosting and branding.
User needs ordained the answer: chosen via solicitation,
Dallas/Fort Worth International Airport hosts the website
under the SAGA brand, airportsustainability.org.[25]

ACRP's most popular (traditional) report to date comes
out of the design research area. *Airport Passenger Terminal
Planning and Design* (ACRP Report 25), published in 2010,
offers a modern, comprehensive guidebook. An 11-member
panel chaired by Robin R. Sobotta, Embry-Riddle Aeronautical

ACRP also covers the needs
of general aviation aircraft
and airports in its reports,
syntheses, and legal
digests (Harvey Douthit,
Alaska Department of
Transportation & Public
Facilities).

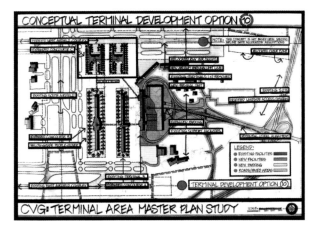

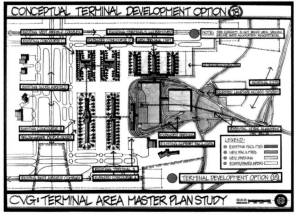

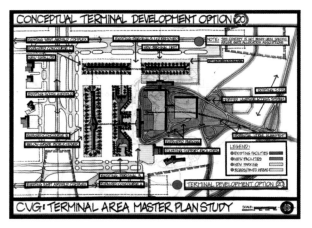

Illustration from Airport Passenger Terminal Planning and Design (ACRP Report 25, 2010): Since its release, the report has been downloaded 18,000 times (courtesy of Landrum & Brown, Incorporated & Cincinnati/ Northern Kentucky International Airport).

University, oversaw the integration of techniques to address new security concerns, quickly evolving technologies, and business practices such as low-cost airlines, in addition to traditional passenger terminal considerations. Spreadsheet models that accompany the report allow airport operators to plug-and-play the guidance with their own data. Since release, the report has received 18,000 downloads, more than half of which have come from outside the United States.[26]

In 2015, ACRP began an Impacts on Practice publication series that curates stories of its research in action. *Wayfinding and Signing Guidelines for Airport Terminals* (ACRP Report 52, 2011) made it easier to travel through Philadelphia International Airport, Fort Lauderdale-Hollywood International Airport, and Changi Airport in Singapore. Austin–Bergstrom International Airport used the *Guidebook for Airport Terminal Restroom*

Planning and Design (ACRP Report 130, 2015) to redesign its bathrooms. ACRP Synthesis of Airport Practice reports helped Orlando International Airport reduce bird strikes from cattle egrets (ACRP Synthesis of Airport Practice 23, 2011, and 39, 2013), and Sterling Municipal Airport in Colorado used ACRP research to manage swallows (ACRP Report 32, 2010). For light fixtures, when should incandescent be replaced with LEDs? Manchester-Boston Regional Airport in Manchester, New Hampshire, and King County International Airport in Seattle, Washington, used *Issues With Use of Airfield LED Light Fixtures* (ACRP Synthesis 35, 2012) to guide this decision for airfield taxiway lighting.[27]

ACRP too has tackled workforce development on topics such as *Helping New Maintenance Hires Adapt to the Airport Operating Environment* (ACRP Synthesis 48, 2013), training programs for firefighters and rescue workers (ACRP Report 103, 2014), and management leadership (ACRP Report 75, 2013). Building off of ACRP Report 75's recommendations, Florida Department of Transportation, the Florida Aviation Council, and the University of South Florida collaborated to design a 3.5-day airport leadership development program. In its first 4 years, 40 Florida airports sent 150 professionals through the program. ACRP reports and syntheses are also regularly used in classrooms, and the Airport Management program at Kansas State University Polytechnic Campus went a step further and developed its core curriculum around ACRP products.[28]

Innovations Deserving Exploratory Analysis

Today, both NCHRP and TCRP include IDEA programs, but the IDEA concept is a legacy of the first SHRP. To balance SHRP's highly prescribed research program that left little to chance, 2 percent of its funding went to small-scale investments in research projects solicited through an open competition. Although limited to proposals that targeted the four SHRP research areas, SHRP-IDEA encouraged imagination and risk taking and even funded projects that were still in the concept development stage. In 4 years, SHRP-IDEA reviewed 400 proposals and funded 40. SHRP's sponsors discovered that the program attracted a broad set of researchers and disciplines to transportation research. Could the secret to stronger pavements be in dental adhesives? Could arctic fish teach us better snow and ice control? SHRP-IDEA had opened an avenue that encouraged inventive and unusual approaches to transportation problems.[29]

In 1993, as SHRP wound down, FHWA and AASHTO arranged to integrate IDEA into NCHRP, and TCRP adopted a similar IDEA program. Over the years, the IDEA model has also lent itself to short-term research programs, including for intelligent transportation systems, SHRP 2's reliability objective, and high-speed rail. IDEA programs help innovators develop concepts and prototypes, and they can act as match-makers between inventors and transportation agencies willing to field test their products. Although IDEA programs favor high-risk, big-leap types of ideas, an NCHRP-IDEA assessment in 2015 found that over the program's lifetime, 40 percent of its projects had either been adopted or had a high potential for implementation.[30]

A bridge beam that weighs one-tenth of a typical precast concrete beam, steel that does not corrode, ultraviolet light that kills germs in the air conditioners on buses, automatic warning systems for rail work zones—IDEA seed money helped all find success. Project ideas come from universities, state DOTs, and transit agencies, and also small engineering firms and individuals such as Gary Rayner. IDEA funded his DriveCAM incident video recording system in 1999, long before cameras were a ubiquitous part of everyday life. Rayner's product, which came packaged with software to manage fleets and encourage safe driving, went on to be adopted by more than 1,000 enterprises in the business of everything from garbage pickup to public buses to long-distance trucking. IDEA programs also continue to attract innovators from outside of transportation, such as researchers at medical schools who have devised better ways to make wheelchair users safe and comfortable on transit vehicles.[31]

In addition, IDEA has offered another way for TRB to first attract volunteers. "The NCHRP IDEA program was my first exposure to the NCHRP program and to TRB," wrote

The Transit IDEA program supported Peter Bartek's rail warning system to increase track worker safety (2004 Annual Meeting, Risdon Photography).

Susan Martinovich, who served a year as AASHTO president while director of Nevada Department of Transportation from 2007 to 2011. When so much of research reacts to existing problems, she grew to strongly support NCHRP's IDEA program because "research should also be proactive and look for views and opinions outside of the normal way of doing business." Through the IDEA programs managed by TRB, participants on AASHTO's research committees and on the other IDEA committees can maintain continuous contact with the world of cutting-edge innovation.[32]

Targeted Cooperative Research Programs

Since 2000, Congress has also authorized several cooperative research programs that targeted specific topics. Although the programs operated on a shorter time frame, they used the cooperative model—for which an advisory committee of representatives from across the industry select a slate of projects. Congress authorized the National Cooperative Freight Research Program in the 2005 Safe, Accountable, Flexible, Efficient Transportation Equity Act: A Legacy for Users (SAFETEA-LU) and charged it with achieving a specified research agenda for freight movement, including by truck and rail, according to a multiyear strategic plan. Sponsored by USDOT's Research and Innovative Technology Administration, the program published 38 reports between 2009 and 2017 that addressed the needs of specific modes or took a multimodal approach to freight movement.[33]

SAFETEA-LU also included a pilot CRP for hazardous materials transportation sponsored by USDOT's Pipeline and Hazardous Materials Safety Administration. The Hazardous Materials Cooperative Research Program published 14 reports between 2009 and 2014 that targeted safer day-to-day operations and emergency preparedness. The Commercial Truck and Bus Safety Synthesis Program, authorized by Congress in 2001 and sponsored by the Federal Motor Carrier Safety Administration, modeled itself after NCHRP's Synthesis series. The program produced 24 Synthesis of Safety Practice reports between 2003 and 2011 of immediate use to practitioners.[34]

Research Management

Like SHRPs, the modal CRPs have been extraordinarily successful, as measured by both their productivity and

The Transit IDEA program supervised the testing of an audio-enhanced ticket machine for transit riders with impaired vision in 2004 (TRB).

U.S. Representative Elijah E. Cummings, Maryland, discusses the provisions he drafted for a Hazardous Materials Cooperative Research Program at the 2006 Annual Meeting (Risdon Photography).

longevity. What most distinguishes the two research program models—strategic versus cooperative—is not their content, size, or even their duration, but their approaches to planning and prioritizing research projects. The strategic highway (transportation) research program model is built around a single, objective-driven strategic plan that lays out research over a multiyear time frame. The CRP model is built around the annual creation of a slate of research projects selected by those heavily involved in applying the results. The former is ideally suited to large projects or a concentrated set of coordinated projects, while the latter contributes a series of research advances that accumulate over years, even decades, and excels in producing results relatively quickly.

Whether under a strategic or cooperative program, all TRB-managed research benefits from the protocols and procedures mandated by the National Academies that are designed to maintain the credibility and integrity of the research process and, by extension, its results. Although the contracted consultants are ultimately responsible for the content of their research and reports, equally important to research quality are the panels of volunteer experts and the National Academies' report review (peer-review) process. In addition, the National Academies limit contracted research to presenting information on findings or best practices. Only consensus studies may recommend specific policies to government.

TRB's senior program officers each manage their assigned research projects from forming the expert panel to publishing the final report. The chair plays a crucial role in the success of a panel. As one senior program officer put it: the program officer manages the process, the chair manages the people. Group facilitation skills are a must. A good chair can draw the best ideas out of everyone and bring each individual panelists' strengths to the table so that the proverbial whole is greater than the sum of its parts.[35]

Everything builds on gathering the right mix of 8 to 10 volunteers for the panel. The call for panel nominees goes out when the annual list of projects is released. The program officer determines the desired range of subject-matter expertise and diversity of backgrounds. For most of the panel slots, the program officer will often have a choice of three to four nominees with the right expertise and background. For one or two slots, however, the program officer may need to seek out and invite potential panelists. The CRPs have discovered that mid-level transportation professionals are excellent candidates for panels. They often have untapped expertise, enthusiasm for the novel opportunity, and bring new diversity to the larger TRB community.

Getting the right balance can be tricky. Panelists need to be able to work collaboratively, but there is no point to convening a panel if everyone is in lock-step agreement. Conflicts of interest, of course, are prohibited. Biases, however, while important to acknowledge, are not necessarily avoided. Instead, biases in one panelist should be balanced by other panelists. Upon completing the roster, the program officer sends a proposed panel to the National Academies' oversight process for review. After any appropriate tweaking, the National Academies then officially appoints volunteers to their panel.

A panel's first task is to take the assigned problem statement and turn it into a research project description for the request for proposals. The panelists meet in person for 1.5 days, and TRB staff and panelists alike describe what happens during this stage as "magical." This first meeting is often the most dynamic and exciting part of the process. Almost invariably, there is a moment, usually toward the end of the first day, when everyone thinks it will never come together, and then by the end of the second day, something better than anyone had imagined is the result.

In 90 days, the panel meets in person again to evaluate the submitted proposals. Requests for proposals, in addition to describing the project, include a budget. Prospective consultants compete on quality, approach, and the amount of research they can provide for the given budget. The program officers depend on the strength of the relationships and enthusiasm created during the first two meetings to keep panelists engaged during the research phase, when a year or more may pass before their third meeting. At the third meeting—a mid-project review—the panelists meet with the researchers to review work to date and to plan the final stretch of the research phase. The trick is to schedule this third meeting during the "sweet spot" when enough research has been done to make review meaningful, but there is still enough time and budget remaining for any needed course corrections.

Panelists individually review the draft final report, giving comments in writing. If everything goes right, at this point the panel's task is done. Researchers must indicate how they have addressed the panelists' comments, but the final report is reviewed by the National Academies' oversight process, not the panel. TRB's report review officer and division committee chair review the final product to ensure that it meets National Academies' standards. To speed getting the research results out to practitioners, CRPs may release prepublication, unedited versions of a research report, which is then replaced with the final published report when available. In addition to senior program officers, the staff who support convening the panelists and producing the final products are critical to the success of CRPs.

As TRB reaches its centennial, staff stand ready to adapt the CRP model to new problems and constituencies. In October 2017, the National Highway Traffic Safety Administration, the Governors Highway Safety Association, and the National Academies acting through TRB signed a three-party agreement for a new Behavioral Traffic Safety Cooperative Research Program. Its first products delivering solutions to unsafe behaviors on streets, roads, and highways are expected in 2019.[36]

CHAPTER 14

To Be Part of Something Bigger

IN HIS *TR NEWS* article celebrating the Transportation Research Board's (TRB's) 90th Anniversary, Thomas B. Deen, executive director from 1980–1994, offered a provocative subtitle, "Everyone Loves It, But No One Can Explain Why." In many ways, this history project started with Deen's challenge. Although understanding motivation is difficult, the historian can look at words and deeds. For the people who engage TRB's communication and knowledge-generating infrastructure, there is something akin to love going on: the love of friendship, the love of place, the love of service. Their actions reflect the values of the men of the founding highway generation. But the word "everyone" in Deen's subtitle, and indeed in the subtitle of this book, is just as important. Who is everyone? TRB's expansion generation began the work of redefining everyone, and the effort was about more than multiple modes. It meant encompassing new ways of thinking, confronting new critical issues, and reaching across the barriers that divide us as people.

Because of TRB's dependence on volunteers, every type and amount of participation—beyond inert!—are important to TRB's mission. Although this book has emphasized the chairs of committees by including their names and institutions, a chair without a committee is just a person sitting alone in a room. Moreover, research without a responsive audience questions its value. Yet, TRB has always attracted a significant subset of participants who volunteer on a (geometric) plane beyond simple professional responsibility. To understand TRB requires acknowledging this group. When asked why, they will often reply that to participate in TRB is to be part of something bigger.[1]

As a supplement to the research, TRB put out a call for stories in spring 2018 that asked its volunteers, "How has TRB influenced you as a transportation professional?" Although only a few of the responses are directly referenced, all of them influenced the analysis.

A Commitment to Diversity

Integral to the National Academies' founding principle that government should be advised by a committee was the recognition of the importance of diversity. Consensus was never to be confused with group think. In the early 1980s, the National Academies operationalized this principle through seeking balance in committee appointments by fields of expertise, geography (defined by regions of the United States), ethnic and racial groups, age, institutional affiliation, and potential sources of bias. Although "sex" was not an official variable to be balanced, TRB reported the number of women when proposing committees for approval.[2]

The new TRB emerged at a time of tremendous change in education, especially for women, and in immigration, as the United States welcomed immigrants from Africa, Asia, and Latin America. In the early 1970s, women earned less than 2 percent of the bachelor's degrees awarded in civil engineering in the United States. By the early 1980s, 12 percent went to women. During the same time period women earning bachelor's degrees in geosciences rose from 12 to 25 percent and in physics from 7 to 12 percent.[3] Although women awarded bachelor's degrees in engineering had reached 20 percent by 2004, the proportion since then has struggled to remain this high. Women also began to lose ground in the computer sciences and the earth, atmospheric, and ocean sciences, although they now earn more than half of the master's degrees in planning. In the professions related to transportation research, statistics from 2017 show that in the United States women make up less than 10 percent of construction or engineering managers and around 14 percent of civil engineers, 36 percent of environmental scientists and geoscientists, and 38 percent of chemists and materials scientists.[4]

Aviation Group Chair James M. Crites, Dallas/ Fort Worth International Airport, assists first-time attendee Silpa Yanduru, Purdue University, at the 2007 Annual Meeting (Risdon Photography).

Overall, however, women now earn more than 60 percent of all bachelor's degrees, and a generational shift in race and ethnicity is under way in the United States. Encouraging gender and racial diversity in TRB's disciplines is not just an issue of fairness, but of competing for talent. TRB data on female participation were not readily available until 2010, when the Annual Report revealed that 22 percent of volunteers on committees and panels were women. By 2018, the percentage had ticked up to 26 percent overall and 28 percent for chairs. For underrepresented minorities, chiefly African Americans and Hispanic Americans, their status as under-represented is as true for TRB as for the professions as a whole.[5]

To support diversity, the National Academies require the regular rotation of standing committee members. The Highway Research Board first confronted the tension between respect for longtime committee members and the necessity of diversity in 1970. The Board's reorganization and the National Academies' reforms, including term limits on committee membership, meant some dedicated participants in technical committees were suddenly left without a home. In response, the Board invented "membership" in a Technical Activities Group "so that the expertise of these former committee members will not be lost to the Board." Although without voting rights, these "members" were encouraged to attend open meetings, suggest "areas of concern," offer papers, and participate in other activities "at the pleasure of the committee chairman."[6]

This same impulse motivated the evolution of "friends of committees," a status or cultural practice already prominent enough to be recognized in 1997's Annual Report. With committee membership limited to 25, the practice evolved for the chair of a committee to keep a "friends list"—literally a list of names on a piece of paper—of people to call on for information on an emerging topic or advice on planning a conference. Some chairs enlisted "friends" to review papers submitted for the annual meeting. Eventually, friends lists migrated to electronic listservs that allowed easy one-to-many communication, and in the mid-2000s TRB's leadership began urging all committees to nurture such lists. Today, TRB encourages everyone interested to self-identify as a "friend" through its committee information system.[7]

TRB currently rotates one-third of the membership of its technical committee every 3 years. This ensures that opportunities cyclically rise for those interested, but also puts pressure on volunteers to maintain a pipeline for individuals with characteristics that may be in short supply. The "friend of the committee" status, as evolved, is a powerful tool to address both the problems of oversupply and undersupply of volunteers with certain characteristics. TRB also incentivizes diversity by raising the cap on 25 appointed members with "bonus slots" for age (young members and emeritus honorees), international members, and personnel from state departments of transportation (DOTs). For other volunteer characteristics, however, more informal methods are used.

Maintaining the pipeline requires fostering the next generation. Even in the first decades of the Board, its leaders worked to attract young transportation professionals into the fold. Opening the annual meeting to everyone interested was a key tool, and at the 30th Annual Meeting, the Board proudly reported that, for two decades, half of the names on annual meeting programs had been first-time presenters. The Board still achieved this benchmark 15 years later when D. Grant Mickle, the Board's director, announced a new award named in memory of his predecessor, Fred Burggraf, for the best paper by young researchers. The award, they hoped, would further one of the Board's "most important functions" because "many a youthful researcher has, over the years, received his first national recognition and encouragement through participation in the Board's annual meetings."[8]

Using the annual meeting to encourage young researchers received a boost from the Dwight David Eisenhower Transportation Fellowship Program, administered by the Federal Highway Administration (FHWA). For its more than 4,000 student awardees since 1983, TRB's annual meeting has become a major gathering and milestone for their research.[9] During the rejuvenation of the Technical Activities Council (TAC) in the early 2000s, TRB again started experimenting with and perfecting additional techniques to encourage those new to TRB, especially the young. Welcoming sessions for first-time annual meeting attendees, webinars, and networking job fairs expanded organization-wide outreach, while the committees themselves continued their own recruitment efforts. The TAC founded a Young Member Council in 2011, whose chair is also a member of the TAC. The young members sponsored new types of engagement, such as their "Six-Minute Pitch" competition inspired by technology start-up culture.[10]

For researchers from some ethnic and immigrant groups, TRB's traditional engagement methods of encouraging young researchers and then building a long-term relationship has worked well.

When *Highway Research News* profiled T. C. Paul Teng in 1974, he was a research and development engineer for the Mississippi State Highway Department and his enthusiasm for applied research still practically leaps from the page. Born in China and educated in Taiwan, he had earned a master's degree in civil engineering from the University of Mississippi in 1966 and, by 1974, had already served on three Board committees and a National Cooperative Highway Research Program (NCHRP) panel. In 1981, Teng joined FHWA, specializing in pavement design and rehabilitation. In 1992, as the Strategic Highway Research Program (SHRP) prepared to hand off the Long-Term Pavement Performance Project to FHWA, Teng led the transition. Teng completed his career as director of FHWA's Office of Infrastructure Research and Development (1999–2005).[11]

Alejandro Miramontes (center) and Victor Manuel Garcia (right), undergraduates at The University of Texas at El Paso, were among the 15 Minority Student Fellows attending the 2015 Annual Meeting. Their paper, "Understanding Sources of Variability of Overlay Test Procedure," was published in *Transportation Research Record* 2507 (2015, 10–18) (Risdon Photography).

SHRP staff gather at the Einstein statue at the NAS main building in 1992, before the Long-Term Pavement Performance Project section moved to FHWA. T. C. Paul Teng is bottom row, second from right (Ankers, Anderson & Cutts).

From 1995 to 2010, Kumares C. Sinha led the Joint Transportation Research Program of Purdue University and the Indiana Department of Transportation, a position that traces its lineage through Kenneth B. Woods, lead Board volunteer on the American Association of State Highway Officials (AASHO) Road Test, to William K. Hatt, the Board's first director. In 1972, Sinha won the Fred Burggraf award for co-authoring a paper that used computer simulations to show why it is more difficult to merge onto a freeway from the left than from the right. He then continued to be active on numerous technical committees and NCHRP panels, chairing the Intergroup Resources group, 1998–2000, and also the International Activities Committee. He was elected to the National Academy of Engineering (NAE) in 2008, and TRB recognized his contributions to both transportation research and as a volunteer with the 2009 Roy W. Crum Distinguished Service Award.[12]

For the National Academies, the start of directly confronting the legacies of centuries of racial discrimination and segregation in the United States also began in the early 1970s. Robert C. Seamans, NAE president in 1974, called on NAE to "take care to see to our own house" by working to increase the participation of racial minorities in engineering.[13] TRB's move into mass transit in 1971 brought it face to face with American racial realities. As the private sector pulled out of the collapsing mass transit industry and urban governments, supported by the Department of

Housing and Urban Development (HUD) and the Urban Mass Transportation Administration (UMTA), took over, the industry became a place where African-American transportation professionals could flourish. TRB's commitment to connecting research to practice and decision making brought it into contact with African-American leaders in the transit industry. It is not a coincidence, therefore, that the first African Americans appointed to and then rising to leadership of the Executive Committee, Carmen Turner (1988–1990), Sharon D. Banks (chair, 1998), and Michael S. Townes (chair, 2004), all came out of the mass transit industry.[14]

In addition, the Conference of Minority Transportation Officials (COMTO), founded in 1971, connects to TRB through the Transit Cooperative Research Program (TCRP). Since 1998, working through a program facilitated by the American Public Transportation Association, COMTO members can apply to become TCRP ambassadors. Ambassadors improve the relationship between research and practice in both directions. They help raise awareness of TCRP products and also help transit agencies and professionals participate in TCRP's research processes. As liaisons, they also assist TCRP to better understand the uses and successes of its products in the field. TRB signed a formal memorandum of understanding with COMTO in 2018.[15]

TRB began attempting to increase the number of women and minorities on its technical committees in the mid-1980s. In 1986, the Planning and Administration Group recommended, and the Division A (Technical Activities) Council concurred, that the Executive Committee should form two task forces, one on women and TRB and one on minorities and TRB, aimed at increasing their participation in committee life. Deen, TRB's director, was also targeting the recruitment of women and minorities, and in 1987 the Executive Committee recruited Lillian C. Liburdi and Edward L. Davis to be task force chairs. (The task forces may have been informal because they do not appear in the National

Sharon D. Banks, Executive Committee chair, speaking during the 1999 Annual Meeting (Cable Risdon).

Michael R. Morris, Executive Committee chair, and Beverly Scott, Executive Committee member, talk with students from TransTech Academy at the 2011 Annual Meeting (Risdon Photography).

Research Council [NRC] records.) These recruiting efforts continued into the early 1990s and consisted chiefly of canvassing transportation organizations to develop lists of candidates for committees. Lacking a bit of introspection, the 1991 Annual Report noted that "the response had been excellent" and they had found "many potential candidates for service."[16]

The attention paid to recruiting women and minorities may have been prompted in part by a conference sponsored by FHWA and UMTA in October 1984 on education and training. The wide-ranging agenda covered transportation engineers at all levels of government, personnel for transit agencies, and the needs of carriers and shippers. Liburdi authored the resource paper on the education and training needs of women in transportation. Another commissioned resource paper examined transportation careers for minorities. This paper emphasized the importance of making connections to historically black colleges and universities (HBCUs), which the conference findings also reinforced. TRB experimented with summer internships, sponsored by UMTA, for minority college students in 1983, although the program was short lived.[17]

In 1991, however, TRB did form a long-lived partnership with the Cardozo Education Campus in Washington, D.C. Shirley Clair McCall helped found the high school's TransTech (now TransSTEM) Academy that connects a classroom curriculum in aerospace engineering, civil engineering, electronics, and computers to real-world experiences with transportation professionals and workplaces. More than 750 students have graduated from the program and 85 percent have continued their education. TRB is one of many industry partners, and students present research to staff and attend the annual meeting, including the Chair's Luncheon. In 2004, TRB awarded McCall the Sharon D. Banks Award for Innovative (now Humanitarian) Leadership in Transportation, an award that honors the chief executive officer of AC Transit, Oakland, California, from 1991 to 1999.[18]

The TRB Minority Student Fellows Program, now a decade old, reinforces TRB's relationships with universities, faculty members, and students. Participating HBCUs and Hispanic-serving institutions select student researchers and designate faculty mentors. The students then present their research at poster or lectern sessions at annual meetings. Started in 2009 to prepare students for the 2010 Annual Meeting, only a handful participated during the program's first years. For 2017–2018, 14 schools sent 21 undergraduate and master's degree students and 15 faculty mentors from programs in civil engineering, environmental engineering, transportation planning, and transportation systems. FHWA and TRB co-sponsor the program, which is also open to sponsorship from institutions and companies and donations from individuals.[19]

In the 1990s, Native American communities utilized TRB's strength as a meeting ground for those engaged in complex intergovernmental relationships. The 556 federally recognized Native American tribes in the United States are sovereign governments, with decision-making authority over land and roads in rural and urban areas. A TRB-organized conference on Native American transportation and economic development in 1993 catalyzed attendees to found the Inter-tribal Transportation Association. Around the same time, TRB's Standing Committee on Historic Preservation formed a Subcommittee on Native American Issues in Transportation, which began planning a major conference in 1999. By the time the conference convened nearly 140 attendees in Albuquerque, New Mexico, in October 2001, TRB had approved a standing technical committee by that name. This committee covers a full range of transportation topics and in 2014 sponsored a special issue of *TR News* (September–October) to bring transportation issues in Indian Country to larger audiences. In addition, both NCHRP and TCRP have produced reports tackling issues related to tribal interests, including transit, cooperation and coordination, and archeological investigations.[20]

Pete Red Tomahawk speaks at the 2013 National Tribal Transportation Conference (John Velat, Michigan Technological University).

Maintaining a commitment to diversity requires constant care. In 2016, TRB again formed a Diversity and Inclusion Task Force charged with creating a new strategic plan. The plan outlines measures intended to address diversity and inclusion in TRB's committees and also with contractors and staff. Malcolm Dougherty, chair of the Executive Committee in 2017, spearheaded the effort to ensure that people from all backgrounds feel welcome at TRB.

Women and a Path to Leadership

The Board and the early decades of TRB were overwhelmingly male environments and cultures. Until around 1970, members of committees were literally referred to as "committee men" and liaisons in state agencies and universities designated "contact men." And yet, as Dava Sobel writes, the history of science is full of "unsung female presences of the past." However, Sobel also warns that their circumstances may have been unique and not, instead, a path that today's women have followed. TRB's history has both unsung women and women and men who paved the way for generations of women to come.[21]

Even in the earliest days of the Advisory Board on Highway Research, women were present. Hatt, the Board's first director, thanked Miss Agnes W. Ayres and Miss Elise Hatt, his daughter, for their work as assistants to the director in the preparation of the Board's first report, a bibliography of 479 unpublished research projects from around the country. What exactly they did while the senior Hatt was traveling to promote the Board and advise on studies is not known, but soon thereafter the younger Hatt began a long stint as a researcher and a university instructor affiliated with an institute dedicated to the study of child development.[22]

Mary J. Cairns came to the Board's employ as a data expert for the safety studies of the late 1930s (see Chapter 3). When the Board finally landed funding for permanent professional staff for the Research Correlation Service in 1944, it prioritized hiring engineers and a librarian, Dorothy Bright, to a position filled by women for decades to come. During the 1950s, Mary O. Eastwood and Helen J. Schwartz were among the five attorneys who worked on the Highway Laws Project from 1956 to 1960.[23]

From the early days of the Board, women, including, as time went on, African-American women, filled the clerical ranks and, crucially, they also managed the committee appointments records, meetings, and conferences, and edited and managed publications. By the 1980s, women dominated or were at parity on TRB's information services, meetings and conferences, program assistant, and editorial and communication staffs. Many stayed for decades. At the Board's 50th Anniversary it celebrated the hiring of Ellen Arendes (1927) and Marilou Damon (1946, retired 1987) and at its 75th Anniversary the hiring of Jewelene G. Richardson (1969, retired in 2011). Reflective of the times, the wives of senior staff and volunteer leaders also had regular roles to play at events. For decades at annual meetings, Joan Carey, Bettie Deen, and then Dianne Skinner hosted a "Ladies Hospitality Center" that morphed into morning receptions offering "coffee and conversation." Their events were advertised in promotional materials and programs and included in annual meeting recaps.[24]

Not until the late 1980s and early 1990s, however, did women make inroads into the transportation technical staff. In 1986, Elaine King was hired as a rail transport specialist, Nancy Humphrey joined policy studies, and Suzanne Schneider became special assistant to the executive overseeing report review. All three stayed for decades. In the cooperative research programs, the advent of TCRP opened doors: Stephanie Robinson came on board in 1992; Gwen Chisholm-Smith in 1993; and Dianne Schwager in 1994. As of 2019, both Chisholm-Smith and Schwager were still with TCRP, Chisholm-Smith as program manager.[25]

For women in the transportation research industry, it was not until 1970 that the Board began to acknowledge the small number in its midst. Three who had long been there—Alice Bourquin, Katharine Mather, and Willa Mylroie—were the product of unique circumstances. Bourquin, the daughter of the president of Continental Motors Company, joined Michigan's highway department in 1935 after training in landscape architecture. For the next 39 years, she participated in designing more than 100 roadside parks. For Mather and Mylroie, World War II and the U.S. Army Corps of Engineers had opened the door to careers in transportation research. Mylroie did pioneering work on traffic gravity models, first presenting at the annual meeting in 1954. By 1970, she had already served on three Board technical committees and would soon be appointed head of research for the Washington State Department of Transportation. When *Highway Research News* profiled Mather in 1972, she chaired the Board's Committee on

Poster Sessions

An International Bazaar for Ideas

POSTER SESSIONS at the Transportation Research Board (TRB) annual meeting are something to behold. They mix the enthusiasm of a youthful science fair with the entrepreneurial spirit of an international bazaar. People from all over the world come to pitch new knowledge and haggle over ideas.

Hundreds of 4- by 8-foot posters pack each time slot, lined up in rows that fill a cavernous convention hall. Activity is constant, as people milling about sample the content or linger to go in-depth with the authors. The generations mingle freely; a first-year graduate student may be presenting next to a veteran of decades of annual meetings. Old friends catch up in the aisles, and the exchange of business cards cements new relationships. Smartphone cameras snap to capture a poster for future reference or to celebrate the achievement.

The annual meeting began experimenting with posters in the early 2000s because too

Crowds at a poster session during the 2019 Annual Meeting (Risdon Photography).

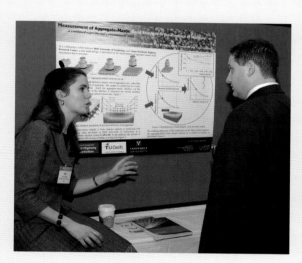

Niki Kringos, Delft University of Technology, the Netherlands, discusses a study measuring aggregate–mastic bond strength in the presence of moisture with Dan Micco at the 2007 Annual Meeting (Risdon Photography).

Ranjani Prabhakar shares her findings on predicting bikeshare trips between stations with Alex Erath at the 2017 Annual Meeting (Risdon Photography).

many quality research papers were being left behind because of a lack of time in lectern sessions. At first the unfamiliar form struggled, and annual meeting planners realized that they needed to either give up or go big. Successful poster sessions require a critical mass of posters and attendees to create the right invigorating energy. By 2006, 43 percent of annual meeting papers were presented during poster sessions.[a]

The secret to the quality of TRB poster sessions is that, for many participants, poster sessions are not an alternative way to partici-pate in the annual meeting. The poster session is an alternative way to present a paper at the annual meeting. Standing behind these posters are fully reviewed research papers, eligible for consideration for publication in the *Transportation Research Record*.

Indeed, during its early years, TRB promoted poster sessions as "meet the author" events. As the poster form flourished, committees began experimenting with "calls for posters" to highlight research that is best explained in graphical form. Still, authors are instructed that the poster itself is simply a visual aid. TRB advises that they also have a brief talk at the ready for small audiences. And to wear comfortable shoes.[b]

Basic Research on Portland Cement and Concrete, was chief of X-Ray and Petrography in the Concrete Division of the Army's Waterways Experiment Station, and along with Bryant Mather, one-half of TRB's own concrete power couple.[26]

The generation of women who arrived in the 1970s did blaze trails for others to follow. They were young, energetic, and eager to dive head first into new problems and research questions. In these traits, they had much in common with the men of the Board's founding generation. As TRB expanded into new modes and issues, the edifice opened to a wider group of participants and range of expertise. Many women followed Patricia F. Waller into safety and human factors research. Waller chaired TRB's Operation and Maintenance Group starting in 1980, a year that achieved, not coincidentally, new sponsorship from the National Highway Traffic Safety Administration for technical committees on highway safety statistics. True to her cross-disciplinary spirit, she would go on to chair the Intergroup Resources group in 1992.[27]

Others followed the path of Kathleen E. Stein into the planning committees. She came in through NCHRP, working on a research project that eventually became the American Association of State Highway and Transportation Officials' "Guidelines on Citizen Participation in Transportation Planning" (1978) while she chaired TRB's technical activities committee of the same name (1976–1982). She then chaired three additional committees before becoming chair of the Division A (Technical Activities) Council in 1995.[28]

FHWA's investment in women also began to pay off. Julie Fee, first employed in the Bureau of Public Roads' (BPR's) Office of Research in 1964, joined TRB's Committee on Operational Effects of Geometrics in 1968 while earning a master's degree in transportation. She became chair in 1973, served on NCHRP panels, and then moved on to chair TRB's Committee on Pedestrians, keynoting a conference it organized in New York City in 1977. For all but one of the conference's five sessions and two workshops, the rosters of speakers featured only men.[29]

One woman, however, made an impact that in its significance is almost beyond measure. TRB hired Sandra Rosenbloom as a consultant to organize and then produce the final report for what was recognized at the time as a groundbreaking conference on paratransit, held in 1975 and sponsored by UMTA. Rosenbloom had just finished her Ph.D. in political science from the University of California, Los Angeles, and despite her youth, then presided over a packed session on paratransit at TRB's 1976 Annual Meeting. When *Transportation Research News* profiled Rosenbloom in 1981, she was an associate professor at The University of Texas at Austin and had already completed numerous studies for NCHRP, UMTA, and NRC and had been part of organizing another TRB conference on paratransit, plus a conference on transportation system management. Yet, the profile failed to mention that she had actually been responsible for another groundbreaking conference, even though it had been held in the National Academy of Sciences' (NAS's) grand building on Constitution Avenue in Washington, D.C.[30]

In 1978, USDOT and NAE's Committee on Transportation co-sponsored a conference on women's travel behavior. At the time, NAE's Committee on Transportation and TRB split their responsibilities between policy and information respectively, and TRB assiduously avoided anything politically controversial (see Chapter 9). This conference would have met TRB's definition. The organizers received hate mail, USDOT was nominated for a Golden Fleece Award for government waste, and a prominent conservative columnist subjected it to ridicule. Courtland Perkins, president of NAE and an aeronautical engineer, welcomed the 100 attendees to what he described as the first known conference dedicated to the study of women's travel, but no TRB representative spoke or registered in attendance.[31]

Rosenbloom chaired the conference's steering committee and, as speaker after speaker attested, had done the lion's share of the work to pull it all together. Katherine O'Leary, on the steering committee from HUD, made sure the attendees also knew that the conference had been Rosenbloom's idea. In addition, Rosenbloom edited the proceedings, writing an extensive preface about the significance and nuance of research on women and transportation that still reveals insights 40 years later.[32]

For TRB, what is even more striking about the importance of the 1978 conference are the participants. Examining just the conference's list of speakers and research presenters reveals many who would become TRB's future. Adriana Gianturco, director of the California Department of Transportation (1976–1983) would be the first woman appointed to TRB's Executive Committee in 1980, when she was not yet 40.[33] Carmen Turner, Washington Metropolitan Area Transit Authority (WMATA), would serve as WMATA's general manager from 1983 to 1990 and would be appointed to TRB's Executive Committee starting in 1988.[34] Lillian C. Liburdi, then an associate administrator for UMTA, would be appointed to TRB's Executive Committee in 1992. In 1995, she—then Lillian C. Borrone and director, Port Department, The Port Authority of New York & New Jersey—would be the first woman to chair TRB's Executive Committee. Martin Wachs, University of California, Los Angeles, would be TRB's chair in 2000. Catherine Ross, who would join TRB's Executive Committee in 2001 when she was executive director of the Georgia Regional Transportation Agency, offered her research, as did Lalita Sen and Susan Hanson. Sen, today on the faculty at Texas Southern University, would go on to be recognized for her work by TRB's Committees on Accessible Transportation and Mobility and on Paratransit.[35] Hanson, a geographer at Clark University, would be appointed to her first TRB committee in 1982 and was elected to NAS in 2000. She served on more than 40 National Academies or TRB committees, including TRB's top oversight committee (today's Division Committee), contributing, by one measure, 110 years of terms of service. In 2018, TRB named her the recipient of the W. N. Carey, Jr., Distinguished Service Award.[36]

FHWA would not sponsor another national conference on women's travel until 1996. Rosenbloom again chaired the steering committee, which also included Hanson, Ross, Sen, and Wachs. In their continuity, they were able to christen it the second national conference, in honor of the gathering in 1978.[37] One year later, TRB founded a task force on women's transportation, which had grown out of a subcommittee formed in 1994 by the Committee on Safety Data, Analysis, and Evaluation. After much advocacy, TRB finally had a Standing Committee on Women's Issues in Transportation in 2001. Ten years later and "intensely focused on promoting the awareness of gender dimensions in all aspects of transportation research," its friends list ran 200 names. TRB and the committee organized the third conference in 2004; it became international with the fourth conference in 2009, and the fifth conference met in Paris in 2014. The sixth conference was in 2019.[38]

Lillian C. Borrone, Executive Committee chair in 1995, examines freight systems and global trade in her Thomas B. Deen Distinguished Lecture at the 2005 Annual Meeting (Risdon Photography).

In pursuit of diversity, an examination of women on TRB's Executive Committee shows success, but also gives a lesson in the fragility of small numbers. Of the six women appointed to the Executive Committee from the 1980s through the mid-1990s, two left transportation shortly thereafter. The first academic on the committee, Della Martin Roy, a materials scientist at The Pennsylvania State University, had been elected to NAE in 1987 for her work in cement and concrete. Roy represented NAE on the committee, serving from 1991 to 1993. Carmen Turner (1988–1990) died in 1992 at the age of 61. Sharon D. Banks died in 1999, less than 1 year after serving as chair. She was not yet 55. This left only Borrone as the experienced TRB member, to play model and mentor to those who would come after. Since 2010, of the 25 appointed members on TRB's Executive Committee, 5 to 7 annually have been women. Women have also continued to contribute as chair: Genevieve Giuliano (2003), Linda S. Watson (2007), Debra L. Miller (2008), Sandra Rosenbloom (2012), Deborah H. Butler (2013), Katherine F. Turnbull (2018), and Victoria Arroyo (2019).[39]

C. Michael Walton (left) and Deborah H. Butler (center) lead applause for outgoing Executive Committee chair Sandra Rosenbloom (right) at the 2013 Annual Meeting (Risdon Photography).

Small numbers also held back TRB's Division A Council, whose six members led the standing technical committees. Women started serving as group chairs and thus on the council in the 1980s and made regular appearances on the council in the 1990s. In 1998, in what could have been a watershed year, three of the six members were women. Instead, in 2001 men again occupied all six seats. The expanded TAC in the early 2000s was a crucial reform for diversity (see Chapter 11).

When Rosenbloom, as incoming chair of the Executive Committee, spoke in January 2012 to young professionals about TRB, she urged: "We need your talents, we need your energy, we need your skills, and we need you to feel that this is a warm and welcoming community." Rosenbloom would have known well the consequences of having, and not having, a welcoming community to support the work of connecting research and practice. She was saying to the next generation that they should seek out a warm and welcoming community, as well as contribute to its nurture.[40]

The continuing challenge of a commitment to diversity is that the mere presence of a person who meets the identified criteria is not evidence on its own that the organization has created a path for others to follow. A trail, once blazed, can still be obstructed. A path, once paved, still needs maintenance and perhaps eventually reconstruction.

The Bonds That Build

There is a joke that attendees to the annual meeting often tell: I'm going to Washington, D.C., in January to hang out with 13,000 of my closest friends. (The quip was once 7,000 and then 10,000.) For many decades, the quintessential annual meeting experience was to take an hour to cross the crowded Sheraton-Park Hotel lobby, or to make your way down the hallway after a session, because you kept running into so many old friends. People interested in the work of a technical committee do not get on an e-mail list, but a list of friends. The choices of words, jokes, and stories transmits TRB's culture to people across the generations. The men of the founding highway generation purposely created much of what still shapes TRB's culture. Other aspects grew out of their values and circumstances. TRB's expansion generation then began the work to bring the best of these practices to the larger world of transportation.[41]

The purposeful cultivation of friendship is a cultural tradition that runs deep. In 1958, Edwin B. Eckel, U.S. Geological Survey, paused in the introduction to the first landslides report to speak not as chair or editor, "but as a person" and closed his statement of gratitude: "From all our discussions, formal and informal, has come a comradeship and a mutual understanding of the problems of engineers and geologists that is all too rare. We have worked together—and we have had fun doing it." The technical reports are full of these heartfelt testaments to friendship, as are the memorials published in the *Proceedings*. Collaborative projects were just one way to form intense bonds. In addition to the annual meetings, many committees met, and still meet, at summer or mid-term meetings designed to be more intimate. A committee or a small group of committees often meets at locations chosen as a retreat from daily obligations or for an experience, such as a tour, to foster collective education.[42]

Friendship was not the objective, obviously. The objective, and reward, lay in the contribution to transportation by helping solve a problem or advance an innovation, but also by holding each other accountable to high standards and, sometimes, painful realities. Friendship sustained the necessary culture of trust. TRB was designed to—and still must—bring people from across disciplines, institutions, and regions to engage in discussions for which the stakes are measured in millions and billions of dollars, the health of the economy and environment, and the lives and welfare of travelers. In their conversations, participants needed to feel encouraged to be honest about what they do not know and forthright about their disagreements. They needed to be willing to share their failures, while being generous with their successes.

As Roy W. Crum explained at the 30th Annual Meeting, his last, the Board wanted a forum where the highway researcher can "talk shop to his heart's content with co-workers from all over the country without distractions. He can discuss the papers and reports presented at these meetings as controversially as he desires, to the benefit of all concerned."[43] Howard E. Hill, administrator, Michigan Department of State Highways, in 1966 commended the Board's high standards for being a "valuable discipline," and a "tremendous experience" for staff. For himself, he admitted to attending his first meeting with "misgivings," but "the after-hour 'bull sessions' provided the kind of communication and camaraderie that made every minute of the time valuable." Hill also emphasized the importance of participating in "discussions defending or attacking new ideas or departures from conventional processes."[44] Mehmet C. Anday, senior research scientist, Virginia Department of Highways and Transportation, expressed gratitude in 1983 that the people he met through TRB "constitute a network for consultations on problems of mutual interest throughout the rest of the year" and that TRB "is allowing us to avoid mistakes made by others—mistakes seldom reported in the

TRANSPORTATION RESEARCH BOARD ANNUAL MEETING

2016

DATES January 10–14, 2016
LOCATION Walter E. Washington Convention Center and Marriott Marquis Hotel
PRESIDING CHAIR Daniel Sperling, University of California, Davis

ATTENDANCE 12,500
NUMBER OF SESSIONS AND WORKSHOPS 865
INTERNATIONAL ATTENDEES 17 percent
ORGANIZATION OF TECHNICAL ACTIVITIES
11 groups hosting 200+ standing technical committees

SPOTLIGHT THEME AND "HOT TOPICS"
• Theme: Research convergence for a multimodal future
• Transformational technologies
• Resilience
• Transportation and public health

HIGHLIGHT Chairman's Luncheon speech on Google's self-driving cars
DEEN LECTURESHIP Hani S. Mahmassani, Northwestern University, speaks on "Micromodels and Megadata"

WHAT ELSE IS HAPPENING AT TRB IN 2016?
• Consensus study report published on new mobility technologies
• ACRP releases 16 reports, including four volumes of a report on NextGen

literature." TRB perpetuates this combination of progress through frank conversation buffered by what Veronica Murphy, New Jersey Department of Transportation, called in 2018 an "amazing spirit of sharing and helping each other."[45]

In addition to the work of the committees and panels, contribution also happens through additional forums. For the more scholarly, there is the *Transportation Research Record*. Transportation agencies with research success stories can submit them to the "Research Pays Off" column in *TR News*, a constant presence since 1983. Agency researchers can now propose a webinar too (see Chapter 11). The Pooled Fund Study (see Chapter 4) still provides a way for researchers in transportation agencies, such as Bernhard Izevbekhai, Minnesota Department of Transportation, to run with their own ambitious initiatives. In search of a quiet concrete surface, their study produced "the largest data base of rolling resistance testing of various surface types" through a partnership with Texas Department of Transportation, FHWA, and others including researchers in Poland and Sweden.

Trust and contribution is not just the work of the collective, but also from person to person, especially in helping each other prepare for leadership. Borrone acknowledged the dedicated support she received from Louis J. Gambaccini, who was general manager, Southeastern Pennsylvania Transportation Authority (SEPTA), Philadelphia, when he chaired TRB's Executive Committee in 1989. For Hyun-A Park, chair of the TAC in 2017, the mentor was Stein.[46]

The point of traveling hundreds or thousands of miles to meet in person is to build relationships, sometimes through serendipitous interaction. For Arlyn Purcell, Port of Seattle, lady luck was a seating at a dinner in Washington, D.C. She struck up a conversation with Richard Altman from the Commercial Aviation Alternative Fuels Initiative and one thing led to another and then another and ended with facilitating a 26-week transatlantic demonstration on alternative jet fuel.[47]

Receiving his final "pink slip" from a TRB committee in 1980, John L. Beaton, California Division of Highways, succinctly summed all three: friendship, contribution, and progress through frank conversation. After 30 years of participation, he reflected, "Thinking of this, I am reminded of all the good times, good friends, and good feelings I have experienced through your organization.... We could not only expose your work to the industry [in California] but also achieve the peer criticism that is so essential to good research."[48]

The chance to be in a room with the brightest minds and industry leaders has also been a lure for the young. Leslie W. Teller, Sr., structural engineer for research at BPR, remembered in 1966 what it was like at to see Hatt in action in Washington, D.C., in 1922. Hatt, TRB's first director on leave from Purdue University, "dignified the occasion and impressed me no end by appearing in striped trousers and a cutaway coat." TRB, thankfully, no longer relies on the sartorial choices of professors to impress. Professors are still, though, an important entryway for the next generation of researchers, practitioners, and administrators.[49]

Purdue University students fill a chartered bus on the way to the 2016 Annual Meeting (Dr. Darcy M. Bullock, Purdue University).

Professors have long built reputations for strongly encouraging, even insisting, that students at all levels and transportation career paths attend and participate in TRB's annual meeting. Through such encouragement, professors send the message that TRB is a forum for everyone. For Donald S. Berry, professor of civil engineering at Northwestern University, Executive Committee chair in 1965, and elected to NAE in 1966, his dedication to encouraging students to make the trip is even noted in his official NAE memoir. For generations of students, the all-American road trip—albeit in January—by bus, van, or recreational vehicle from New England, Texas, or the Midwest was part of their formative TRB experience. The fellowship and travel funding programs have formalized, and upgraded, an old tradition.[50]

TRB's more senior leaders have also left huge impressions on the next generation through exchanges of interest and invitation. Especially powerful are interactions that send signals that TRB is a place where the value of a contribution will be measured by its usefulness, not by status hierarchies.

For C. Michael Walton, Executive Committee chair in 1991 and Division Committee chair 2004–2013, the moment came after he delivered his first paper. A researcher he knew only by esteemed reputation approached him to talk. Decades later, Walton still remembered how the conversation meant so much to him that he floated all the way back to Austin. For Alvaro Rodriguez-Valencia, Universidad de los Andes, it was 30 minutes spent talking to Patricia Mokhtarian in the Hilton Hotel lobby in 2011. TRB had accepted the paper he had submitted as an instructor in Columbia. Fellow researchers from Latin America not only recommended talking with Mokhtarian, one set up the meeting. He completed his Ph.D. from the program Mokhtarian directed at the University of California, Davis, in 2015.[51]

For Stephanie Dock, research manager at the District of Columbia Department of Transportation, it was feeling encouraged to speak up in committee meetings, even when she was the youngest person in the room. For Mena Souliman, assistant professor at The University of Texas at Tyler, it was a chance to work with the "top-notch" engineers on the Committee on Design and Rehabilitation of Asphalt Pavements.[52]

Three out of multitudes of interactions at the 2018 Annual Meeting capture how TRB's culture is today still transmitted in ways small and profound.

It is Nancy Aguirre, a Ph.D. candidate at The University of Texas at El Paso, telling the story of standing in front of her poster, ready to give her presentation when Georgene Geary walked up. Retired after 30 years at Georgia Department of Transportation and chair of the Committee on Design and Rehabilitation of Concrete Pavements, Geary engaged Aguirre in a discussion of her research and invited her to the committee meeting. Aguirre attended, which led to productive exchanges and an appointment to the committee in 2017. Aguirre is speaking before TRB's Minority Student Fellows Program, teaching them—peer to peer—the culture of TRB.[53]

It is W. M. Kim Roddis, The George Washington University, presiding over a lectern session on steel bridges. She briefly halts an intense back-and-forth discussion between researchers and state engineers to address the young people growing restless in the back of the room. She speaks not to quiet them, but to invite them to come closer, so that they can witness the best of TRB.[54]

It is William W. Millar at the Chairman's Luncheon receiving the Sharon D. Banks Award for Humanitarian Leadership in Transportation. Knowing people's memory of Banks is fading, he speaks of what she

TRB Minority Students Fellow Chelse Hoover (left), Texas Southern University, discusses her research on calculating delay time using global positioning system data at the 2013 Annual Meeting (Risdon Photography).

meant to him and to transportation, of their time together endeavoring to get TCRP off the ground. In his words, Millar reenacts Carey and Burggraf speaking of friendship and inspiration decades after the passing of their beloved director, Crum.

TRB is many things to many people. For some, it is a professional conference: a great event for networking and keeping up to date in their fields and a healthy environment to invite others to engage with their research. For others, TRB is their technical committee: a community for support and contribution to the advancement of the field through crafting a research needs statement, issuing a call for papers, or organizing a conference. For people on the front lines, TRB is the unseen force behind guidelines, reports, and webinars that seem to just be there, waiting for them, when they have a new task to learn or a problem to solve.

For those in search of advice, TRB is one of many loci of expertise within the National Academies that can be deployed via consensus study. For government, TRB is a trusted institution in which to place funding for research programs. For researchers, TRB is the manager of contracts for compelling work. For officials and administrators, TRB is where they can find the best minds and assuage any fears that a stone may have been left unturned as they make decisions affecting the travel of millions.

For transportation, as TRB begins its second century, echoes of the 50th Anniversary resonate. The polity is divided, unsure of who and what to trust. We live with daily reminders that transportation problems, and questions, are fundamental to the strength of the economy, the health of the environment, the bonds of community, and the well-being of people and, indeed, the human race. We also have much in common with TRB's founding generation: we can see the world around us changing, but are filled with uncertainty about when, where, and how the future will unfold. As it has in the past, transportation will continue to present problems and inspire innovations for decades to come. There is still much work to be done.

Learning from the History of the Transportation Research Board's First 100 Years

Neil J. Pedersen, TRB Executive Director (2015–Present)

THE STORY OF THE TRANSPORTATION RESEARCH BOARD'S (TRB's) first 100 years helps us to gain a deeper appreciation of how TRB came to be the influential and valued organization that it is today. At the same time, it serves as a basis for lessons for the next 100 years. In her thoroughly researched and insightful history of TRB, Sarah Jo Peterson reveals the many intentional and circumstantial factors that were instrumental to TRB's success, and at times to its near demise. The responsibility of TRB's leaders is to learn from this history and to position TRB to be even stronger and more relevant over the next 100 years.

This is an important time for TRB to think about its future. Dramatic changes in transportation are on the horizon. Advances in technology have the potential to revolutionize how both people and goods move. Demographic trends, such as dramatic increases in the elderly population and shifts of population into megaregions, will affect where and how travel occurs. Driven by concerns about climate change and its impacts, the resilience of the transportation system and the sources and forms of energy used in transportation will be a focus of public attention for decades to come. The gap between public spending and the investment levels needed to renew and modernize an increasingly congested and aging transportation infrastructure continues to grow, demanding new and innovative funding solutions as well as improved performance and asset management and materials that are more durable. Despite improvements in transportation's safety performance, countering the tragedy of death and injury will remain a central challenge for the transportation community and society. Shifts in demand and evolving consumer expectations, as well as advances in technology, are resulting in new approaches to how goods are moved. All of these changes create major challenges for governance, and for the capacity of institutions and the transportation workforce to adapt.

These many developments, as well as many more that will undoubtedly emerge, will present complex and vexing challenges that TRB can, and must, play a prominent role in addressing. The interdisciplinary nature of these issues will require the expertise of professionals from many different fields and researchers and practitioners who will be aided in coordinating their efforts by relying on open and trusted institutions to facilitate collaboration and convening activities. The rapid evolution of transportation technology will require changes in the transportation workforce and will impose new requirements regarding the skills and knowledge that transportation professionals must possess. Federal, state, and local decision makers will need independent and fact-based advice to inform the many policy choices that lie ahead. Transportation's critical role in society and the economy will need to be conveyed not only to transportation professionals, but also to decision makers and the public through effective communication. The need for TRB and the role that it plays has never been greater.

The story of TRB's first 100 years is a story about adaptation to change. For a century, TRB has remained attuned to evolving issues in transportation, and to issues external to transportation that affect transportation. It has responded to the changing needs of its sponsors and stakeholders while also being responsive to demographic shifts in the transportation professional community. TRB has both tracked and helped guide a growing field: the disciplines that fall within it, the research methods that lead to new knowledge, and the technology and innovation that drive the field forward. It has also invested heavily in communication and in the question of how to most effectively access and transfer knowledge within the transportation field. Some of these changes occurred as a result of forethought and planning on the part of TRB's leaders. Others occurred based on unforeseen circumstances. However, all of these changes, and many more, required TRB to adapt, and that will be as true in its second century as it was in its first 100 years.

TRB takes seriously its responsibility to focus on future transportation issues, so it pursues research, information exchange, policy analysis, and communication all while looking ahead. I am particularly pleased that TRB's standing technical committees have prepared "centennial papers" that document the history of how issues in specific subject areas have been dealt with by TRB, but also seek to identify the future issues that TRB should be addressing within the scope of the committees. The Executive Committee's latest version of *Critical Issues in Transportation* addresses what it believes are the strategic issues of the next 10–20 years in an effort to focus its attention on them in as timely a manner as possible. TRB's Technical Activities Council is doing a strategic realignment to ensure that its committees and programs are structured to address the most important issues of the future. Particularly in light of how rapidly change is occurring in transportation, it will be essential that forward-looking planning of this type continue to occur throughout the next 100 years.

TRB will also need to adapt to changes in technology and the way that policy makers and transportation professionals obtain information. We have entered an age when "digital first" is how TRB must think both about its products and services and how it communicates with its stakeholders. TRB will continue to offer opportunities for face-to-face information exchange, but more and more collaboration and professional development activities will occur digitally or virtually. TRB offers some of the best professional development opportunities available to transportation professionals, but it must adapt as the professional development field evolves.

The story of TRB is one of bringing together researchers and practitioners. TRB gathers transportation professionals from all levels of government, academic researchers, and private-sector representatives so they can all learn from each other's work, benefit from each other's perspectives and knowledge, and use this shared information to help advance transportation policy and practice in the United States and worldwide. TRB's "heart and soul" have always been its volunteers, members of its committees and research panels, and participants in its annual meeting and other convening activities. Volunteers will continue to be the lifeblood of TRB for decades to come.

Over the course of its first 100 years, TRB has become a far more diverse organization, both among its volunteers and staff, which is a major source of its strength today. Evolving from an organization that was dominated by white male highway engineers from the United States, TRB today has expanded to include all modes of transportation, scores of different professional disciplines, ever-increasing percentages of women and other under-represented groups, and ever-increasing numbers of participants from outside the United States. In its next 100 years, TRB will grow even stronger if its volunteers and staff reflect not just the diversity of the transportation professional community, but also the diversity of the public that the profession serves. Transportation professionals from the United States can learn so much from their counterparts in other parts of the world. One of the keys to TRB's future success will be ever-increasing involvement of professionals from nations outside the United States. The diversity of professions involved in TRB also provides an opportunity for TRB to address issues that benefit from the input of persons from multiple disciplines. The fact that TRB is housed within the National Academies of Sciences, Engineering, and Medicine will enable it to continue to benefit from some of the greatest experts in science, engineering, and medicine, as well as the credibility that comes from the National Academies' standards for objectivity, independence, non-partisanship, and an evidence base for conclusions that TRB is expected to uphold.

The story of TRB is also one of new programs being introduced to meet the needs of sponsors and the TRB stakeholder community. It is difficult to predict what new programs will be introduced in the next 100 years, but one of the key ways TRB's success will be measured is by the degree to which it meets sponsor needs. TRB's principal sponsors have been the state departments of transportation and the U.S. Department of Transportation. It will be critical that the needs of these primary sponsors continue to be met, even as TRB seeks additional sponsors and financial support from other organizations to ensure its future growth.

TRB has met a need in the transportation community through the applied research that is conducted in its cooperative research programs. Ensuring that these programs produce research results and products that make an impact on practice in the field will continue to be a key to the success of these programs. As strategic needs are identified for large applied research programs, the success of the first two Strategic Highway Research Programs will hopefully serve as a basis for TRB being asked to manage large strategic research programs in the future.

From its early days, TRB has been a place for students and young professionals to gain exposure to top professionals in the field and to learn about the latest developments in transportation. Many top professionals in the transportation field talk about their introduction to TRB when they were in school or when they first entered their profession. TRB needs to continue to focus on reaching and serving these future leaders of the transportation field and adapting how it involves and serves them, because they will be the future leaders of TRB.

I have had the good fortune to be continuously involved in TRB since 1975 when I attended my first TRB Annual Meeting as a graduate student. TRB has been instrumental in my professional development. It was where I interacted with and learned from experts and colleagues who I could turn to for advice and support. I have used hundreds of TRB reports and journal articles over the course of my career. I have benefited from participating in, and in many cases helped in the planning of, dozens of TRB conferences and annual meetings. Over the course of my career, I had the opportunity to serve in a number of TRB volunteer leadership roles. Both as a volunteer, but especially since becoming Executive Director in 2015, I have come to appreciate the key role that both TRB's volunteer leaders and the hard-working TRB staff play in ensuring the success of TRB. Both will be key elements to the future direction and success of TRB during its second 100 years. I hope that future transportation professionals have similar opportunities to benefit from TRB's programs, products, and activities.

In its latest strategic plan the TRB Executive Committee adopted a vision that "TRB is where the nation's leaders and the global transportation community turn for research, innovations, information exchange, and advice on current, emerging, and critical transportation issues to foster a high-performing multimodal transportation system that enhances society." In order for TRB to achieve this vision, participants in TRB need to learn from and build on the past, but also need to continually adapt, as the world around us changes, and as transportation evolves in the future. If TRB adapts successfully, it will help ensure that it plays a key role in helping to achieve this vision.

APPENDIX

Leadership

Executive Committee Chairs

2019	Victoria Arroyo, Georgetown Climate Center
2018	Katherine F. Turnbull, Texas A&M Transportation Institute
2017	Malcolm Dougherty, California Department of Transportation
2016	James M. Crites, Dallas/Fort Worth International Airport
2015	Daniel Sperling, University of California, Davis
2014	Kirk T. Steudle, Michigan Department of Transportation
2013	Deborah H. Butler, Norfolk Southern Corporation
2012	Sandra Rosenbloom, Urban Institute
2011	Neil J. Pedersen, Maryland State Highway Administration
2010	Michael R. Morris, North Central Texas Council of Governments
2009	Adib K. Kanafani, University of California, Berkeley
2008	Debra L. Miller, Kansas Department of Transportation
2007	Linda S. Watson, Central Florida Regional Transportation Authority
2006	Michael D. Meyer, Georgia Institute of Technology
2005	Joseph H. Boardman, New York State Department of Transportation
2005	John R. Njord, Utah Department of Transportation
2004	Michael S. Townes, Hampton Roads Transit
2003	Genevieve Giuliano, University of Southern California
2002	E. Dean Carlson, Kansas Department of Transportation
2001	John M. Samuels, Jr., Norfolk Southern Corporation
2000	Martin Wachs, University of California, Berkeley
1999	Wayne Shackelford, Georgia Department of Transportation
1998	Sharon D. Banks, AC Transit
1997	David N. Wormley, The Pennsylvania State University
1996	James W. van Loben Sels, California Department of Transportation
1995	Lillian C. Borrone, The Port Authority of New York & New Jersey
1994	Joseph M. Sussman, Massachusetts Institute of Technology
1993	Adrian Ray Chamberlain, Colorado Department of Transportation
1992	William W. Millar, Port Authority of Allegheny County, Pennsylvania
1991	C. Michael Walton, The University of Texas at Austin
1990	Wayne Muri, Missouri Department of Transportation
1989	Louis J. Gambaccini, Southeastern Pennsylvania Transportation Authority
1988	Herbert H. Richardson, Texas A&M University
1987	Lowell B. Jackson, Greenhorne & O'Mara, Inc.

1986	Lester A. Hoel, University of Virginia
1985	John A. Clements, New Hampshire Department of Public Works and Highways
1984	Joseph M. Clapp, Roadway Express, Inc.
1983	Lawrence D. Dahms, Metropolitan Transportation Commission, California
1982	Darrell V. Manning, Idaho Department of Transportation
1981	Thomas D. Larson, Pennsylvania Department of Transportation
1980	Charley V. Wootan, Texas A&M University
1979	Peter G. Koltnow, Highway Users Federation for Safety and Mobility
1978	Albert S. Lang, Massachusetts Institute of Technology
1977	Robert N. Hunter, Missouri State Highway Department
1976	Harold L. Michael, Purdue University
1975	Milton Pikarsky, Regional Transit Authority, Chicago
1974	Jay W. Brown, Florida Department of Transportation
1973	William L. Garrison, University of Pittsburgh School of Engineering
1972	Alan M. Voorhees, Alan M. Voorhees & Associates
1971	Charles E. Shumate, Colorado Department of Highways
1970	D. Grant Mickle, Highway Users Federation for Safety and Mobility
1969	Oscar T. Marzke, U.S. Steel Corporation
1968	David H. Stevens, Maine State Highway Commission
1967	Edward G. Wetzel, Port of New York Authority
1966	J. Burch McMorran, New York State Department of Public Works
1965	Donald S. Berry, Northwestern University
1964	Wilbur S. Smith, Wilbur Smith Associates
1963	Charles D. Curtiss, Bureau of Public Roads
1962	Ralph R. Bartelsmeyer, Illinois Division of Highways
1961	William A. Bugge, Washington State Highways Commission
1960	Pyke Johnson, Automotive Safety Foundation
1959	Harmer E. Davis, University of California
1958	Charles H. Scholer, Kansas State College
1957	Rex M. Whitton, Missouri State Highway Department
1956	Kenneth B. Woods, Purdue University
1954–1955	G. Donald Kennedy, Portland Cement Association
1954	Walter H. Root, Iowa State Highway Commission
1952–1953	Robert H. Baldock, Oregon State Highway Commission
1950–1951	Ralph A. Moyer, Iowa State College
1948–1949	Fred V. Reagel, Missouri State Highway Department
1946–1947	Roger L. Morrison, University of Michigan
1944–1945	Stanton Walker, National Sand and Gravel Association
1942–1943	Fred C. Lang, Minnesota Department of Highways and University of Minnesota
1940–1941	Warren W. Mack, Delaware State Highway Department
1938–1939	Burton W. Marsh, AAA Foundation for Traffic Safety

1936–1937	Hobart C. Dickinson, Bureau of Standards
1934–1935	Albert T. Goldbeck, National Crushed Stone Association
1932–1933	George E. Hamlin, Connecticut State Highway Department
1930–1931	Horatio S. Mattimore, Pennsylvania Department of Highways
1928–1929	Frank H. Eno, The Ohio State University
1927	Thomas R. Agg, Iowa State College
1923–1926	Arthur N. Johnson, University of Maryland
1920–1922	Anson Marston, Iowa State College

Division Committee Chairs

The Transportation Research Board (TRB) Division Committee provides liaison between the Governing Board of the National Research Council (NRC) and TRB. The committee ensures that TRB meets NRC's standards for objectivity, monitors for conflicts of interest of potential committee and panel members, and ensures that its activities are appropriate for NRC. In addition, the committee monitors TRB's specially funded project committee and panel appointments, report review, and programs that are approved by the NRC Governing Board. The committee chair assists the Executive Committee with special project approvals requested of the Governing Board. The chair must be a member of the National Academy of Sciences, the National Academy of Engineering, or the National Academy of Medicine.

2019–Present	Chris Hendrickson, Carnegie Mellon University
2013–2019	Susan Hanson, Clark University
2004–2013	C. Michael Walton, The University of Texas at Austin
2007–2016	Henry Gerald Schwartz, Jr., Jacobs Civil, Inc.*
1995–2004	Lester A. Hoel, University of Virginia
1989–1995	L. Gary Byrd, Consulting Engineer
1982–1989	Milton Pikarsky, City University of New York

*Vice-Chair responsible for the second Strategic Highway Research Program.

Technical Activities Council Chairs

2017–2020	Hyun-A Park, Spy Pond Partners, LLC
2014–2017	Daniel S. Turner, The University of Alabama
2011–2014	Katherine F. Turnbull, Texas A&M Transportation Institute
2008–2011	Robert Johns, Volpe National Transportation Systems Center
2005–2008	Neil J. Pedersen, Maryland State Highway Administration
2002–2005	Anne P. Canby, Delaware Department of Transportation
1999–2002	Harold (Skip) R. Paul, Louisiana Transportation Research Center
1995–1999	Kathleen E. Stein, Howard Stein Hudson
1993–1995	Wayne Muri, Missouri Department of Transportation
1989–1993	William M. Spreitzer, General Motors

1986–1989	Charley V. Wootan, Texas A&M University
1982–1986	Lester A. Hoel, University of Virginia
1980–1982	Lawrence D. Dahms, Metropolitan Transportation Commission, California
1979–1980	Charley V. Wootan, Texas A&M University
1976–1979	Kurt W. Bauer, Southeastern Wisconsin Regional Planning Commission
1973–1976	Harold L. Michael, Purdue University
1972–1973	William L. Garrison, University of Pittsburgh School of Engineering
1971–1972	Alan M. Voorhees, Alan M. Voorhees & Associates
1970–1971	Charles E. Shumate, Colorado Department of Highways

Executive Directors

2015–Present	Neil J. Pedersen
1994–2015	Robert E. Skinner, Jr.
1980–1994	Thomas B. Deen
1966–1980	William N. Carey, Jr.
1964–1966	D. Grant Mickle
1951–1964	Fred Burggraf
1928–1951	Roy W. Crum
1924–1928	Charles M. Upham
1921–1923	William K. Hatt

Endnotes

Introduction

1 National Research Council, *Colleges of Agriculture at the Land Grant Universities: A Profile* (National Academy Press, 1995), 9.

Chapter 1

1 This account of the National Academy of Sciences' founding and early years is largely drawn from Rexmond C. Cochrane, *National Academy of Sciences: The First Hundred Years, 1863–1963* (National Academy Press, 1978) and Frederick. W. True, ed., *A History of the First Half-Century of the National Academy of Sciences, 1863–1913* (Lord Baltimore Press, 1913).

2 Office of Coast Survey, "The Nation's First Scientific Agency," accessed March 14, 2018, https://nautical charts.noaa.gov/about/history-of-coast-survey.html.

3 True, *History NAS*, 204–205.

4 True, *History NAS*, 213–217.

5 Cochrane, *National Academy of Sciences*, 84–87; True, *History NAS*, 219–222.

6 Cochrane, *National Academy of Sciences*, 88; True, *History NAS*, 226–227.

7 True, *History NAS*, 230–232.

8 Cochrane, *National Academy of Sciences*, 97; True, *History NAS*, 247–253.

9 True, *History NAS*, 267–268.

10 Cochrane, *National Academy of Sciences*, 156.

11 David A. Pfeiffer, "Working Magic with Cornstalks and Beanpoles: Records Relating to the U.S. Military Railroads During the Civil War," *Prologue Magazine* 43, no. 2, Summer 2011, accessed March 18, 2018, https://www.archives.gov/publications/prologue/2011/summer/usmrr.html.

12 Association of American Railroads, accessed May 19, 2019, https://en.wikipedia.org/wiki/Association_of_American_Railroads; AREMA, "Predecessor Organizations," accessed May 19, 2019, http://www.arema.org/AREMA_MBRR/Predecessor_Organizations.aspx.

13 Cochrane, *National Academy of Sciences*, 127–129; True, *History NAS*, 269–271.

14 Cochrane, *National Academy of Sciences*, 130–133; True, *History NAS*, 271–279.

15 Cochrane, *National Academy of Sciences*, 143–145.

16 Cochrane, *National Academy of Sciences*, 148–150, 166–168.

17 Cochrane, *National Academy of Sciences*, 136, 207.

18 Cochrane, *National Academy of Sciences*, 177–179, 194–197; Walter S. Adams, *Biographical Memoir of George Ellery Hale, 1868–1938*, National Academy of Sciences, 1939, 195, accessed April 25, 2018, http://www.nasonline.org/publications/biographical-memoirs/memoir-pdfs/hale-george-ellery.pdf.

19 Cochrane, *National Academy of Sciences*, 208–213.

20 Cochrane, *National Academy of Sciences*, 212–215; United Engineering Foundation, "Historical Timeline," accessed April 27, 2018, https://www.uefoundation.org/the-uef-story/historical-timeline.

21 Cochrane, accessed April 27, 2018, 223–233; *Third Annual Report of the National Research Council* (Government Printing Office, 1919), 48.

22 Millikan quoted from Robert. A. Millikan, "Contributions of Physical Science," 35–37, and James. R. Angell, "The National Research Council," 417–438, in Robert. M. Yerkes, ed. *The New World of Science: Its Development During the War* (Books for Library Press, 1920, Reprint, 1969); Cochrane, *National Academy of Sciences*, 241; *Third Annual Report of the National Research Council*, 7.

23 Cochrane, *National Academy of Sciences*, 227, 234.

24 Cochrane, *National Academy of Sciences*, 235–236; Wilson's Executive Order is also reprinted in full in *Ideas & Actions: A History of the Highway Research Board* (HRB, 1971), 178–179.

25 Cochrane, *National Academy of Sciences*, 237; National Academy of Sciences, *The National Academy of Sciences Building: A Home for Science in America* (The National Academies Press, 2013), 26–33.

26 Cochrane, *National Academy of Sciences*, 248–249, 252, 256, 258.

a "Preliminary Report Upon the Possibility of Controlling the Land Slides Adjacent to the Panama Canal," *Proceedings of the National Academy of Sciences* 2, no. 4 (1916), 193–207.

b J. David Rogers, "Landslides of the Panama Canal," Pacific Section Meeting of the American Association for the Advancement of Science, June 13, 2011, https://web.mst.edu/~rogersda/Panama-Canal-2012/Rogers-Landslides-Panama-Canal-minimum.pdf.

c *Landslides and Engineering Practice*, Highway Research Board Special Report 29 (HRB, 1958).

d *Landslides: Analysis and Control*, Transportation Research Board Special Report 176 (TRB, 1978); Landslides: Investigation and Mitigation, Transportation Research Board Special Report 247 (TRB, 1996).

e "Ta Liang," eCommons, Cornell University, accessed July 21, 2018, http://hdl.handle.net/1813/19169.

f A. K. Turner and G. P. Jayaprakash, "Rockfall: Characterization and Control," *TR News*, January–February 2013, 39–41.

Chapter 2

1 Bruce E. Seely, *Building the American Highway System: Engineers as Policy Makers* (Temple University Press, 1987), 11–12; *Historical Statistics of the United States, Colonial Times to 1970*, accessed May 20, 2019, https://www.census.gov/library/publications/1975/compendia/hist_stats_colonial-1970.html.

2 Seely, *Building the American Highway System*, 14–16.

3 Seely, *Building the American Highway System*, 13–14.

4 "Rural Free Delivery," *Encyclopedia Britannica*, https://www.britannica.com/topic/Rural-Free-Delivery, accessed March 20, 2018; Richard F. Weingroff, "Creation of a Landmark: The Federal Aid Road Act of 1916," *Highway History*, accessed March 21, 2018, https://www.fhwa.dot.gov/highwayhistory/landmark.pdf.

5 Seely, *Building the American Highway System*, 18, 21.

6 Seely, *Building the American Highway System*, 21–22.

7 Seely, *Building the American Highway System*, 24–30.

8 Seely, *Building the American Highway System*, 33–34.

9 *Historical Statistics of the United States, Colonial Times to 1970*; Seely, *Building the American Highway System*, 36–40.

10 Weingroff, "Creation of a Landmark," 51–52.

11 Weingroff, "Creation of a Landmark," 52–54.

12 Weingroff, "Creation of a Landmark," 57, 60; Chris Becker, *AASHTO 1914–2014: A Century of Achievement for a Better Tomorrow* (AASHTO, 2014), 6–7.

13 Weingroff, "Creation of a Landmark," 61; Seely, *Building the American Highway System*, 41–42.

14 Seely, *Building the American Highway System*, 42–43; Weingroff, "Creation of a Landmark," 66–76.

15 Seely, *Building the American Highway System*, 47; Weingroff, "Creation of a Landmark," 78–86.

16 Quoted text from Seely, *Building the American Highway System*, 50–52.

17 Seely, *Building the American Highway System*, 52.

18 MacDonald quoted in Richard F. Weingroff, "Firing Thomas H. MacDonald-Twice," accessed April 28, 2018, https://www.fhwa.dot.gov/infrastructure/firing.cfm.

19 *Ideas & Actions: A History of the Highway Research Board* (HRB, 1971), 178–179; Vannevar Bush, "Comfort Avery Adams," NAS Memoirs, accessed May 9, 2018, http://www.nasonline.org/publications/biographical-memoirs/memoir-pdfs/adams_comfort.pdf; "Anson Marston," History of Iowa State: People of Distinction, accessed March 21, 2019, http://historicexhibits.lib.iastate.edu/150/template/marston.html; "Arthur N. Talbot, Noted Engineer," *The New York Times*, April 4, 1942.

20 *Ideas & Actions*, 17.

21 Frederick W. Cron, "Highway Design and Motor Vehicles: A Historical Review," *Public Roads*, December 1974, 87; T. R. Agg, "Comprehensive Investigations of Highway Engineering Needed," *Public Roads*, August–September 1919, 35–36.

22 *Ideas & Actions*, 19, 181–182.

23 Anston [sic] Marston, "A National Program for Highway Research," *Public Roads*, January–February, 1920, 37.

24 Report of the Director, Advisory Board on Highway Research, Minutes, January 16, 1922, TRB Library.

25 "About SAE International," accessed May 14, 2018, https://www.sae.org/about/history.

26 *Education for Highway Engineering and Highway Transport*, Bulletin 1920, no. 42 (Bureau of Education, Department of the Interior, 1921), 46–48.

27 *Education for Highway Engineering and Highway Transport*, 78–102, 106–118.

28 *Education for Highway Engineering and Highway Transport*, 78–102, 106–118.

29 *Ideas & Actions*, 18–22.

30 *IIdeas & Actions*, 20–22.

31 Highway Research Conference, November 11, 1920, TRB Executive Committee Meeting Minutes Record Group (TRB ECMMRG), NAS-NRC Archives.

32 Highway Research Conference, November 11, 1920, TRB ECMMRG, NAS-NRC Archives.

33 Highway Research Conference, November 11, 1920, TRB ECMMRG, NAS-NRC Archives.

34 Highway Research Conference, November 11, 1920, TRB ECMMRG, NAS-NRC Archives.

35 Highway Research Conference, November 11, 1920, TRB ECMMRG, NAS-NRC Archives.

36 *Ideas & Actions*, 25–26.

37 Seely, *Building the American Highway System*, 60–64.

a Unless otherwise indicated, this sidebar draws from Leo Landis, *Building Better Roads: Iowa's Contribution to Highway Engineering 1904-1974* (Center for Transportation Research and Education, Iowa State University, 1997).

b   Iowa State Data Center, "Total Population for Iowa's Incorporated Places: 1850–1920," accessed May 9, 2018, http://www.iowadatacenter.org/archive/2011/02/citypop.pdf.

c   "Nation's Truck Routes Start in Iowa," *The Road-maker*, December 1918, 40–41.

d   Anston [sic] Marston, "A National Program for Highway Research," *Public Roads*, January–February 1920, 34–37.

e   "Thomas Radford Agg," Special Collections and University Archives, Iowa State University, accessed May 29, 2018, http://findingaids.lib.iastate.edu/spcl/arch/rgrp/11-1-12.html; T. R. Agg, "Comprehensive Investigations of Highway Engineering Needed," *Public Roads*, August–September 1919, 35–36.

f   "Walter Root," *Highway Research Board Proceedings* 34(1954), 625–626.

Chapter 3

1   Minutes, January 16, 1922, TRB Executive Committee Meeting Minutes Record Group (TRB ECMMRG), NAS-NRC Archives.

2   Mary A. Sego, "William K. Hatt papers," 1922–1929, Purdue University Libraries, Archives and Special Collections, accessed May 6, 2019, https://archives.lib.purdue.edu/repositories/2/resources/397#.

3   *Education for Highway Engineering and Highway Transport*, Bulletin 1920, no. 42 (Bureau of Education, Department of the Interior, 1921), 78.

4   Advisory Board on Highway Research, Proceedings of the Second Annual Meeting, published in *Bulletin of the National Research Council*, no. 32 (May 1923), 6–7.

5   Minutes, January 16, 1922, TRB ECMMRG, NAS-NRC Archives.

6   W. K. Hatt, "Paper for Conference on Highway Economics," University of Maryland, July 27, 1921, TRB ECMMRG, NAS-NRC Archives; "Automotive Industries" article reprinted in *Ideas & Actions: A History of the Highway Research Board* (HRB, 1971), 185–186; W. K. Hatt, "Outline of Highway Research Program," *Engineering News-Record*, September 15, 1921, 450–451.

7   W. K. Hatt, "The Coordination of Highway Research," December 8, 1921, TRB ECMMRG, NAS-NRC Archives.

8   See, for example, W. K. Hatt, "Discussion of Paper on Aspects of Research," Association of Land Grant Colleges, Washington, D.C., November 21, 1922, in TRB ECMMRG, NAS-NRC Archives; Rexmond C. Cochrane, *National Academy of Sciences: The First Hundred Years, 1863–1963* (National Academy Press, 1978), 238–239.

9   Advisory Board on Highway Research, Proceedings of the Second Annual Meeting, published in *Bulletin of the National Research Council*, no. 32 (May 1923).

10   Minutes, January 16, 1922, TRB ECMMRG, NAS-NRC Archives; "Connecticut Makes Detailed Study of Highway Traffic," *Engineering News-Record*, January 12, 1922, 48–52; J. Gordon McKay, "Analysis of Connecticut's Traffic Census Data Yields Facts on Truck Overloading," *Engineering News-Record*, May 18, 1922, 826–830.

11   W. K. Hatt, "Highway Research Projects in the United States," *Bulletin of the National Research Council* 4 (Part 3), no. 21 (October 1922).

12   The project appears in every director's report and annual meeting proceedings in 1921, 1922, and 1923. The most complete summary is in "Proceedings of Third Annual Meeting of the Advisory Board on Highway Research," November 8–9, 1923, *Bulletin of the National Research Council* 8, no. 43 (March 1924), 30–34.

13   "Proceedings of Third Annual Meeting of the Advisory Board on Highway Research," 25; *Ideas & Actions*, 31; Minutes, November 21, 1922, TRB ECMMRG, NAS-NRC Archives.

14   "North Carolina Road Commission Has Able Chairman and Engineer," *The Highway Magazine*, November 1921, 7–8; "Charles M. Upham Appointed Director of Advisory Board on Highway Research," *Public Roads*, July 1924, 18; "T. Coleman DuPont, Ex-Senator, is Dead," *The New York Times*, November 12, 1930.

15   Minutes, July 8, 1924, TRB ECMMRG, NAS-NRC Archives.

16   Cochrane, *National Academy of Sciences*, 290.

17   "Reorganization of the Engineering College, University of Maryland," *Good Roads*, September 15, 1920, 140; "Dr. A. N. Johnson Rites Tomorrow," *Baltimore Sun*, July 12, 1940.

18   Minutes, July 8, 1924, TRB ECMMRG, NAS-NRC Archives.

19   *Ideas & Actions*, 35.

20   Minutes, December 2, 1925, TRB ECMMRG, NAS-NRC Archives.

21   Minutes, July 8, 1924, and September 11, 1924, TRB ECMMRG, NAS-NRC Archives.

22   Minutes, September 11, 1924, TRB ECMMRG, NAS-NRC Archives.

23   The funding difficulties for both the low-cost roads and culvert investigations are documented in the Minutes, July 10, 1925; December 2, 1925; February 6, 1926; October 28, 1926; February 2, 1927; June 28, 1927; and December 9, 1927, TRB ECMMRG, NAS-NRC Archives; Highway Research Board News Letter, May 1, 1928, TRB Library; *Report of the National Academy of Sciences, Fiscal Year 1928–1929* (Government Printing Office, 1930), 68.

24 Minutes, January 20, 1928, TRB ECMMRG, NAS-NRC Archives.

25 Highway Research Board News Letter, July 1928, TRB Library.

26 "Roy W. Crum Award Given to William N. Carey, Jr.," *Transportation Research News*, March–April 1980, 11–12; *Ideas & Actions*, 40.

27 Highway Research Board News Letter, October 1928, TRB Library.

28 Business Meeting, December 14, 1928, TRB ECMMRG, NAS-NRC Archives; *Report of the National Academy of Sciences, Fiscal Year 1939–1940* (Government Printing Office, 1941), 29; *Ideas & Actions*, 44.

29 Minutes, October 15, 1928, and ByLaws of the Highway Research Board Effective July 1, 1939, TRB ECMMRG, NAS-NRC Archives.

30 *Highway Research Board Proceedings* 10 (1931), 7–8; "Biographies of Distinguished NBS Researchers," accessed June 8, 2018, https://www.nist.gov/el/energy-and-environment-division-73200/biographies-distinguished-nbs-researchers.

31 Highway Research News Letter, February 1929, July 1929, January 1930, August 1930, TRB Library; *Highway Research Board Proceedings* 10 (1931), 226–231, 238–247; "Burton W. Marsh," accessed March 22, 2019, https://www.ite.org/about-ite/history/honorary-members/burton-w-marsh; *Ideas & Actions*, 48.

32 "Committee Organization," Minutes, April 5, 1935, TRB ECMMRG, NAS-NRC Archives.

33 *Ideas & Actions*, 44–45, 122, 201.

34 *Ideas & Actions*, 43–44, 47; Highway Research Board News Letter, January 1931, March 1933, TRB Library. Hatt proposed a research information service in his final director's report, "Proceedings of Third Annual Meeting of the Advisory Board on Highway Research," *Bulletin of the National Research Council* 8, no. 43 (March 1924), 21–22.

35 Cochrane, *National Academy of Sciences*, 338–341.

36 *Report of the National Academy of Sciences for the Year July 1, 1930–1931* (Government Printing Office, 1932), 73.

37 "Proceedings of the Second Annual Meeting of the Highway Research Board," *Bulletin of the National Research Council* 6, no. 32 (May 1923), 73–78.

38 Peter D. Norton, *Fighting Traffic: The Dawn of the Motor Age in the American City* (MIT Press, 2011), 179–181, 184.

39 *First National Conference on Street and Highway Safety*, 1924, U.S. DOT Special Collections, accessed June 3, 2018, https://dotlibrary.specialcollection.net.

40 *First National Conference on Street and Highway Safety.*

41 *Second National Conference of Street and Highway Safety*, 1926, 11, accessed June 3, 2018, https://dotlibrary.specialcollection.net.

42 "Report of the Committee on the Causes of Accidents," Second National Conference on Street and Highway Safety, U.S. DOT Special Collections, accessed June 4, 2018, https://dotlibrary.specialcollection.net; Minutes, February 26, 1926, TRB ECMMRG, NAS-NRC Archives; Highway Research Board News Letter, July 1928, October, 1928, August 1930, TRB Library; *Report of the National Academy of Sciences for the Year July 1, 1930–1931*, 75–76; *Report of the National Academy of Sciences, Fiscal Year 1931–1932* (Government Printing Office, 1933), 78–80.

43 *Highway Research Board Proceedings* 10 (1931), 247–253; *Report of the National Academy of Sciences, Fiscal Year 1932–1933* (Government Printing Office, 1934), 61–63; *Report of the National Academy of Sciences, Fiscal Year 1933–1934* (Government Printing Office, 1935), 86–90; Minutes, December 6, 1935, TRB ECMMRG, NAS-NRC Archives.

44 The MUTCD Turns 80!, accessed June 6, 2018, https://mutcd.fhwa.dot.gov/mutcd_80_bday.htm.

45 Fourth National Conference on Street and Highway Safety, Summary of Proceedings (1934), 9, 39, U.S. DOT Special Collections, accessed June 4, 2018, https://dotlibrary.specialcollection.net; Bureau of Public Roads, *Guides to Traffic Safety* (Government Printing Office, Revised 1937).

46 Public Law 768, 74th Congress, June 23, 1936; House resolutions 6200, 8855, 10591, 74th Congress in Committee on Roads, U.S. House of Representatives Files, 1926–1942, Cartwright Collection, Carl Albert Center, University of Oklahoma, https://arc.ou.edu/repositories/3/archival_objects/136122; Minutes, November 20, 1936, TRB ECMMRG, NAS-NRC Archives; Williams quoted in *Highway Research Board Proceedings* 16 (1937), 234–235.

47 Raymond G. Paustian, *Speed Regulation and Control on Rural Highways* (Highway Research Board, 1940).

48 *Motor-Vehicle Traffic Conditions in the United States*, House Document no. 462, Parts 1–4, 75th Congress, 1938.

49 *Motor-Vehicle Traffic Conditions in the United States*, House Document no. 462, Part 5, 75th Congress, 1938.

50 *Motor-Vehicle Traffic Conditions in the United States*, House Document no. 462, Part 6, 75th Congress, 1938; Wilse B. Webb, "Harry M. Johnson: War Without Peace," *Psychological Reports* 64, no. 3 (June 1989), 907–913.

51 "Can Road Design Make Highways Completely Safe?" December 8, 1936, U.S. DOT Special Collections, https://dotlibrary.specialcollection.net.

52 "Highway Safety and the Bureau of Public Roads,"
September 27, 1938, U.S. DOT Special Collections,
https://dotlibrary.specialcollection.net; Bureau of Public
Roads, *Highway Accidents: Their Causes and Recommendations for Their Prevention* (Government Printing
Office, 1938), 1.

a AASHO Resolution included in *Ideas & Actions: A
History of the Highway Research Board* (HRB, 1971),
120.

b AASHTO, "About R&I and RAC," accessed June 22,
2018, https://research.transportation.org/about-r-and-
i-and-rac.

Chapter 4

1 Tom Lewis, *Divided Highways: Building the Interstate
Highways, Transforming American Life* (Viking Press,
1997), 58–67.

2 Tom Lewis, *Divided Highways*, 58–59.

3 *Toll Roads and Free Roads*, 76th Congress, House
Document no. 272 (Government Printing Office, 1939).

4 *Highway Research Board Proceedings* 20 (1941), 3–5, 27.

5 Sarah Jo Peterson, *Planning the Home Front: Building
Bombers and Communities at Willow Run* (University
of Chicago Press, 2013), 57–64, 148.

6 Rexmond C. Cochrane, *National Academy of Sciences:
The First Hundred Years, 1863–1963* (National Academy Press, 1978), 342–346.

7 Cochrane, *National Academy of Sciences*, 408, 416.

8 *Ideas & Actions: A History of the Highway Research
Board* (HRB, 1971), 136–137.

9 *Highway Research Board Proceedings* 24 (1945), 540;
Highway Research Board Proceedings 25 (1946),
479–480.

10 "Memoriam to Fred C. Lang," *Highway Research
Board Proceedings* 25 (1946), 483.

11 *Ideas & Actions*, 45, 49, 52–53.

12 Section 11 of the Act quoted in Richard Weingroff,
"'Clearly Vicious as a Matter of Policy': The Fight
Against Federal-Aid, Part Three: To Control the Levers,"
accessed June 25, 2018, https://www.fhwa.dot.gov/
infrastructure/hwyhist06a.cfm; Public Law No. 686,
74th Congress, June 16, 1936.

13 Bruce D. Greenshields, "The Photographic Method of
Studying Traffic Behavior," *Highway Research Board
Proceedings* 13 (1934), 382–386; *Celebrating 50 Years
of Traffic Flow Theory: A Symposium*, Transportation
Research Circular E-C197 (TRB, September 2015), i;
Highway Research Board Proceedings 12 (1933), 383–388;
"History of the Missouri Highway Department," 1943,
accessed June 16, 2018, https://www.scribd.com/
document/190505510/History-of-the-Missouri-
State-Highway-Department.

14 *Interregional Highways*, 78th Congress, House Doc.
No. 379 (Government Printing Office, 1944), ix–x.

15 *Interregional Highways*, 78th Congress, House Doc.
No. 379 (Government Printing Office, 1944).

16 Minutes, February 26, 1944, TRB Executive Committee
Meeting Minutes Record Group (TRB ECMMRG),
NAS-NRC Archives.

17 *Ideas & Actions*, 52–57; Federal-Aid Highway Act of 1944,
Public Law No. 521, 78th Congress, December 20, 1944;
Mark H. Rose and Raymond A. Mohl, *Interstate: Highway
Politics and Policy Since 1939*, 3rd ed. (University of
Tennessee Press, 2012), 19–28.

18 HRB, Annual Report, December 18, 1946, TRB Library;
Ideas & Actions, 126.

19 *Ideas & Actions*, 61, 103; Highway Research Board
News Letter, February 1929, TRB Library; *Report of the
National Academy of Sciences, Fiscal Year 1931–1932*
(Government Printing Office, 1933), 18–19.

20 HRB, Annual Report, December 18, 1946; HRB,
Annual Report, June 1949, TRB Library.

21 HRB, Annual Report, December 18, 1946, TRB
Library; HRB, Annual Report, June 1949, TRB Library;
Cochrane, *National Academy of Sciences*, 236.

22 HRB, Annual Report, June 1949, TRB Library.

23 Reagel quoted in HRB, Annual Report, June 1949,
TRB Library; "Memoriam to Fred C. Lang," *Highway
Research Board Proceedings* 25 (1946), 483.

24 Cochrane, *National Academy of Sciences*, 407–408;
Ruth Schwartz Cowan and Matthew H. Hersch, *A
Social History of American Technology* (Oxford University Press, 2018), 232–235.

25 HRB, Annual Report, June 1949, TRB Library.

26 HRB, Annual Report, June 1951, TRB Library.

27 HRB, Annual Report, June 1951, TRB Library.

28 HRB, Annual Report, June 1951, TRB Library.

29 "Ralph A. Moyer: Civil Engineering, Berkeley," *University of California: In Memoriam 1989*, Calisphere.

30 *Ideas & Actions*, 69; Richard Weingroff, "Firing
Thomas H. MacDonald—Twice," accessed on July 2,
2018, https://www.fhwa.dot.gov/infrastructure/firing.
cfm; Federal Highway Administration Administrators, accessed July 2, 2018, https://www.fhwa.dot.gov/
administrators.

31 *In Commemoration of the 40th Annual Meeting*,
Highway Research Board Special Report 63 (HRB,
1961), 27.

32 "Roy W. Crum Award Given to William N. Carey, Jr.,"
Transportation Research News, March–April 1980,
11–12.

a *Highway Research Board Proceedings* 29 (1950),
617–619.

b   Wayne K. Kittelson, "Historical Overview of the Committee on Highway Capacity and Quality of Service," in *Fourth International Symposium on Highway Capacity*, Transportation Research Circular E-C018 (TRB, 2000), 5–16.

c   Minutes, June 4, 1949, TRB ECMMRG, NAS-NRC Archives; *Highway Capacity Manual: Practical Applications of Research* (Bureau of Public Roads, 1950).

d   *Highway Capacity Manual 1965*, Highway Research Board Special Report 87 (HRB, 1966), iv–vi.

e   *Highway Capacity Manual 1965*, 7–8.

f   *Highway Capacity Manual 1965*, vii.

g   Hugh M. Gillespie, "AASHTO's National Cooperative Highway Research Program," *TR News*, September 1986, 6; *Highway Capacity Manual*, Transportation Research Board Special Report 209 (TRB, 1985).

h   *Highway Capacity Manual 2010* [HCM 2010], 5th ed., Vol. 1 (TRB, 2010).

i   Roger P. Roess, et al., "Level of Service: 2010 and Beyond," *Transportation Research Record* 2173 (2010), 20–27.

j   *Highway Capacity Manual: A Guide for Multimodal Mobility Analysis*, 6th ed., Vol. 1 (TRB, 2016), introduction.

Chapter 5

1   *Ideas & Actions: A History of the Highway Research Board* (HRB, 1971), 145; William K. Hatt, "Recent Developments in the Work of the Advisory Board on Highway Research," April 17, 1922, TRB Executive Committee Meeting Minutes Record Group (TRB ECMMRG), NAS-NRC Archives.

2   *Ideas & Actions*, 63; *The AASHO Road Test: History and Description of the Project*, Highway Research Board Special Report 61a (HRB, 1961), 2–3.

3   *The AASHO Road Test: History and Description of the Project*, 3, 11.

4   *Road Test One—MD*, Highway Research Board Special Report 4 (HRB, 1952), 3; *Ideas & Actions*, 146.

5   *Ideas & Actions*, 147. The WASHO Road Test was published in Special Reports 18 and 22.

6   *The AASHO Road Test: History and Description of the Project*, 4, 48–50.

7   *The AASHO Road Test: History and Description of the Project*, 5–6.

8   Mark H. Rose and Raymond A. Mohl, *Interstate: Highway Politics and Policy Since 1939*, 3rd ed. (University of Tennessee Press, 2012), 85–94; Federal-Aid Highway Act of 1956, Public Law 627, 84th Congress, June 29, 1956.

9   *The AASHO Road Test: History and Description of the Project*, 10–11.

10   *The AASHO Road Test: Proceedings of a Conference Held May 16–19, 1962*, Highway Research Board Special Report 73 (HRB, 1962), 3.

11   "Kenneth Brady Woods," *Highway Research Board Proceedings* 29 (1950), 616–618; K. B. Woods, H. S. Sweet, and T. E. Shelburne, "Pavement Blowups Correlated with Source of Coarse Aggregate," *Highway Research Board Proceedings* 25 (1946), 147–168.

12   *The AASHO Road Test: Summary Report*, Highway Research Board Special Report 61g (HRB 1962), 7.

13   *The AASHO Road Test: History and Description of the Project*, 6–7, 50–54.

14   *The AASHO Road Test: History and Description of the Project*, 6–7, 50–54.

15   *Pavement Lessons Learned from the AASHO Road Test and Performance of the Interstate Highway System*, Transportation Research Circular E-C118 (TRB, 2007), 11–12.

16   *The AASHO Road Test: History and Description of the Project*, 6, 8, 19–30.

17   *The AASHO Road Test: History and Description of the Project*, 12, 52; "Final Report of the Highway Cost Allocation Study" (Government Printing Office, 1961); "Who Pays for Highways: Is a New Study of Highway Cost Allocation Needed?" (Congressional Budget Office, 1978).

18   Minutes, March 31, 1961, TRB ECMMRG, NAS-NRC Archives.

19   *The AASHO Road Test: Proceedings of a Conference Held May 16–19, 1962*, 1–3.

20   "From a Road to Nowhere," *St. Louis Post-Dispatch*, May 17, 1962.

21   *The AASHO Road Test: Proceedings of a Conference Held May 16–19, 1962*, 256–289.

22   *The AASHO Road Test: Proceedings of a Conference Held May 16–19, 1962*, 270; *Pavement Lessons Learned from the AASHO Road Test and Performance of the Interstate Highway System*, 24–26.

23   Hveem's extensive critique: *The AASHO Road Test: Proceedings of a Conference Held May 16–19, 1962*, 284–286.

24   *The AASHO Road Test: Proceedings of a Conference Held May 16–19, 1962*, 275; *Pavement Lessons Learned from the AASHO Road Test and Performance of the Interstate Highway System*, 21.

25   S. J. Fenves, J. W. Fisher, and I. M. Viest, "Bridges of the AASHO Road Test: A Unique and Historic Research Endeavor," *TR News*, November–December 2005, 16–23; *The AASHO Road Test: Proceedings of a Conference Held May 16–19, 1962*, 97–101.

26 *The AASHO Road Test: Proceedings of a Conference Held May 16–19, 1962*, 290–438.

27 *Pavement Lessons Learned from the AASHO Road Test and Performance of the Interstate Highway System*, 1–5.

28 *The AASHO Road Test: Proceedings of a Conference Held May 16–19, 1962*, 1, 270.

29 *Ideas & Actions*, 105.

30 Minutes, January 15, 1960, and January 12, 1962; Highway Research Board, Bylaws, Approved October 1962, TRB ECMMRG, NAS-NRC Archives.

31 *The AASHO Road Test: Proceedings of a Conference Held May 16–19, 1962*, 270.

a   National Academy of Sciences, Annual Reports for 1952–1963; National Academy of Sciences, Organization and Members, volumes covering 1953–1983.

b   Brian J. Cudahy, "The Containership Revolution: Malcom McLean's 1956 Innovation Goes Global," *TR News*, September–October 2006, 5–9; Maritime Cargo Transportation Conference, *The NEAC Study: Comparison of Conventional Versus Unitized Cargo Systems* (NAS and NRC, 1956); *Comparative Economic Analysis of Break-Bulk and Unit Load Systems for Maritime General Cargo from Shipper to Consignee* (NAS and NRC, 1963); Maritime Cargo Transportation Conference, *San Francisco Port Study, Volume I: Description and Analysis of Maritime Cargo Operations in a U.S. Port* (NAS and NRC, 1964).

c   National Academy of Sciences, Organization and Members, volumes covering 1953–1983.

d   Geraldine Knatz, "Local Seaport Initiatives Driving International Policy: Eliminating the Effects of Air Pollution and Drawing up 'Green Prints' for Responsible Growth," *Transportation Research Record* 2100 (2009), 5–11.

Chapter 6

1   "Whitton Urges More Research on Construction of Highways," *St. Louis Post-Dispatch*, May 17, 1962.

2   *The Sagamore Conference on Highways and Urban Development: Guidelines for Action* (Syracuse University, [1959?]), 9–10.

3   Richard F. Weingroff, "Celebrating a Century of Cooperation," *Public Roads*, September/October 2014, https://www.fhwa.dot.gov/publications/publicroads/14sepoct/03.cfm; *The Sagamore Conference*, 4.

4   Survey of *Highway Research Board Proceedings* and *Highway Research Board Bulletin* in TRID, accessed August 24, 2018, https://trid.trb.org.

5   Frank Brink, Jr., *Detlev Wulf Bronk, 1897–1975* (National Academy of Sciences, 1978), 48; Rexmond C. Cochrane, *National Academy of Sciences: The First Hundred Years, 1863–1963* (National Academy Press, 1978), 518–519.

6   Detlev Bronk, Academy-Council Greetings to the Highway Research Board, January 12, 1954, Engineering and Industrial Research 1954: Highway Research Board, NAS-NRC Archives.

7   Minutes, January 15, 1954, TRB Executive Committee Meeting Minutes Record Group (TRB ECMMRG), NAS-NRC Archives.

8   *Highway Research Board Proceedings* 35 (1956), 831.

9   Minutes, June 10, 1954, TRB ECMMRG, NAS-NRC Archives.

10 Minutes, June 10, 1954, TRB ECMMRG, NAS-NRC Archives.

11 "D. Grant Mickle, President of HUFFSAM, Receives HRB's 1973 Roy W. Crum Award," *Highway Research News*, Spring 1974, 5.

12 Minutes, June 12, 1951, TRB ECMMRG, NAS-NRC Archives; *Parking as a Factor in Business*, Highway Research Board Special Report 11A-11D (HRB, 1953–1956).

13 Minutes, June 12, 1951, TRB ECMMRG, NAS-NRC Archives; *Parking as a Factor in Business*.

14 Coleman Woodbury, *A Framework for Urban Studies: An Analysis of Urban-Metropolitan Development and Research Needs*, Highway Research Board Special Report 52 (HRB, 1959), ii–iii.

15 Minutes, June 10, 1954, TRB ECMMRG, NAS-NRC Archives; see also Joseph F. C. DiMento and Cliff Ellis, *Changing Lanes: Visions and Histories of Urban Freeways* (MIT Press, 2013), 100–115.

16 National Committee on Urban Transportation, *Better Transportation for Your City: A Guide to the Factual Development of Urban Transportation Plans* (Public Administration Service, 1958).

17 I*The Sagamore Conference*, 2–3.

18 Woodbury, *A Framework for Urban Studies*, 12–18.

19 Woodbury, *A Framework for Urban Studies*, 22–27.

20 *Ideas & Actions: A History of the Highway Research Board* (HRB, 1971), 75; Minutes, January 5, 1959, January 15, 1960, and June 29–30, 1960, TRB ECMMRG, NAS-NRC Archives.

21 "Foreword," in Woodbury, *A Framework for Urban Studies*, v.

22 Minutes, June 29–30, 1960, June 30, 1961, June 21, 1962, and June 1963, TRB ECMMRG, NAS-NRC Archives.

23 Thomas D. Larson, "Rex Whitton—the Man from Missouri," November 16, 1990, https://www.fhwa.dot.gov/infrastructure/whitton.cfm.

24 "Better Laws for Better Highways," *Highway Research Board Bulletin* 88 (1954); "ASF's Lou Morony Continues to Pioneer in Highway and Traffic Law Research," *Highway Research News*, Winter 1967, 20.

25 *Highway Research Board Proceedings* 35 (1956), 831; *Ideas & Actions*, 73.

26 *Ideas & Actions*, 80, 129; Highway Research Board, Executive Committee Meeting Minutes, June 1963, TRB Library.

27 "ASF's Lou Morony Continues to Pioneer in Highway and Traffic Law Research," *Highway Research News*, Winter 1967, 22; "Victor J. Perini, Jr.," *TR News*, January–February 1985, 39–40.

28 *Ideas & Actions*, 151.

29 *Ideas & Actions*, 100–101; Highway Research Board, Bylaws, Approved October 1962, TRB Library.

30 *Ideas & Actions*, 201; D. Grant Mickle, "Commentary," *Highway Research News*, June 1965, 1; W. N. Carey, Jr., "The Transfer of Information," *Highway Research News*, Summer 1967, 1–2.

31 Minutes, June 28, 1958, TRB ECMMRG, NAS-NRC Archives.

32 Minutes, June 28, 1958, TRB ECMMRG, NAS-NRC Archives.

33 "Harmer E. Davis, Civil Engineering, Berkeley," University of California: In Memoriam 199, Calisphere, accessed on September 1, 2018, https://calisphere.org.

34 Minutes, January 9, and June 13, 1959, TRB ECMMRG, NAS-NRC Archives.

35 Minutes, June 13, 1959, TRB ECMMRG, NAS-NRC Archives.

36 Minutes, June 13, 1959, TRB ECMMRG, NAS-NRC Archives.

37 *Ideas & Actions*, 151; *In Commemoration of the 40th Annual Meeting*, Highway Research Board Special Report 63 (HRB, 1961), 18–21; Minutes, July 27, 1961, and January 12, 1962, TRB ECMMRG, NAS-NRC Archives.

38 *Ideas & Actions*, 150–154.

39 W. N. Carey, Jr., and M. Earl Campbell, "The National Cooperative Highway Research Program: An Overview After Three Years," *Highway Research News*, March 1965, 16–23.

40 *Ideas & Actions*, 152.

41 Carey and Campbell, "The National Cooperative Highway Research Program," 16–23; NCHRP, 2014 Summary of Progress, 2014, 22.

42 Carey and Campbell, "The National Cooperative Highway Research Program," 16–23; Google Books Ngram Viewer, accessed September 8, 2018, https://books.google.com/ngrams.

43 W. N. Carey, Jr., "The Transfer of Information," *Highway Research News*, Summer 1967, 1–2.

44 John L. Beaton, "Is Your Highway Research Being Implemented?" *Highway Research News*, Winter 1970, 21–24.

45 *Getting Research Findings into Practice*, NCHRP Synthesis of Highway Practice 23 (HRB, 1974), 18–19.

a T. Larson, P. Cady, M. Franzen, and J. Reed, *A Critical Review of Literature Treating Methods of Identifying Aggregates Subject to Destructive Volume Change When Frozen in Concrete and a Proposed Program of Research*, Highway Research Board Special Report 80 (HRB, 1964).

b "VTRC History," accessed on March 22, 2018, http://vtrc.virginiadot.org/DynamicPage.aspx?PageId=34; "NCHRP Pioneer Looks at Research and Innovation." *TR News*, September–October 1986, 2–3.

c "Thomas Duane Larson, 1928–2006," in National Academy of Engineering, *Memorial Tributes*, Vol. 12 (The National Academies Press, 2008).

d "Thomas D. Larson, 1989–1993, Federal Highway Administrator," Federal Highway Administration, U.S. DOT, accessed March 25, 2018, https://www.fhwa.dot.gov/administrators/tlarson.cfm.

e Tom Larson, "The Roberts Management and Leadership Model," *TR News*, November–December 2004, 15–17.

Chapter 7

1 Minutes, January 15, 1960, TRB Executive Committee Meeting Minutes Record Group (TRB ECMMRG), NAS-NRC Archives.

2 National Research Council, *Conference on Transportation Research: Report of a Study Group Convened by the National Academy of Sciences* (National Academy of Sciences, 1960).

3 *Conference on Transportation Research: Report of a Study Group Convened by the National Academy of Sciences*, 6–7.

4 FAA administrator and Johnson quoted in "Creation of Department of Transportation—Summary," accessed November 13, 2017, https://www.transportation.gov/50/creation-department-transportation-summary.

5 Johnson quoted in "Creation of Department of Transportation—Summary," accessed November 13, 2017, https://www.transportation.gov/50/creation-department-transportation-summary; "The Origin of Elements of the Department of Transportation," accessed November 13, 2017, https://www.transportation.gov/sites/dot.gov/files/docs/origins%20of%20DOT.pdf.

6 Rexmond C. Cochrane, *National Academy of Sciences: The First Hundred Years, 1863–1963* (National Academy Press, 1978), 567, 573–578; NAS, Organization and Members, 1975–1976, NAS-NRC Archives.

7 *The National Academy of Engineering: The First Ten Years* (National Academy of Engineering, 1976), 1, 4, 18.

8   *The National Academy of Engineering: The First Ten Years*, 6; Cochrane, 571; NAS, Organization and Members, 1965–1966, NAS-NRC Archives.

9   Seitz quoted in Cochrane, 571–573; NAS, Organization and Members, 1964–1965, NAS-NRC Archives.

10 NAS, Organization and Members, 1964–1965, NAS-NRC Archives.

11 *The National Academy of Engineering: The First Ten Years*, 11, 15, 121.

12 NAS, Organization and Members, 1975–1976, NAS-NRC Archives; *The National Academy of Engineering: The First Ten Years*, 51–52.

13 NAS-NAE-NRC, Annual Report, Fiscal Year 1964–1965 (Government Printing Office, 1967), 99; Minutes, January 15, 1965, and July 1, 1965, TRB ECMMRG, NAS-NRC Archives.

14 Minutes, January 21, 1966, TRB ECMMRG, NAS-NRC Archives.

15 For a short description of the Research Correlation Service in the mid-1960s, see HRB, Annual Report, 1966.

16 "Report of the Special Committee on Long Range Planning," Minutes, July 7, 1966, TRB ECMMRG, NAS-NRC Archives.

17 Minutes, July 7, 1966, TRB ECMMRG, NAS-NRC Archives; Chris Becker, *AASHTO 1914–2014: A Century of Achievement for a Better Tomorrow* (American Association of State Highway and Transportation Officials, 2014), 114; "The Man Who Saved the Interstate System," accessed November 14, 2017, https://www.fhwa.dot.gov/infrastructure/50man.cfm.

18 Minutes, July 7, 1966, TRB ECMMRG, NAS-NRC Archives.

19 *Pavement Lessons Learned from the AASHO Road Test and Performance of the Interstate Highway System*, Transportation Research Circular E-C118 (TRB, 2007), 19; "HRB Chief W. N. Carey, Jr., Named Recipient of Academy's Distinguished Service Award," *Highway Research News*, Summer 1973, 3.

20 W. N. Carey, Jr., "New Directions for the HRB," *Highway Research News*, Winter 1967, 1.

21 W. N. Carey, Jr., "New Directions for the HRB," *Highway Research News*, Winter 1967, 2.

22 "Report of the Special Committee on Long Range Planning," Minutes, June 22, 1967, TRB ECMMRG, NAS-NRC Archives.

23 "Report of the Special Committee on Long Range Planning," Minutes, June 22, 1967, TRB ECMMRG, NAS-NRC Archives.

24 HRB, Annual Report, 1966 and 1967.

25 Minutes, June 22, 1967, TRB ECMMRG, NAS-NRC Archives.

26 Special Committee on Long-Range Planning, Appendix B, Minutes, January 17, 1968, TRB ECMMRG, NAS-NRC Archives.

27 W. N. Carey, Jr., "Meeting the Challenge," *Highway Research News*, Winter 1968, 1–3; "Executive Committee Recommends Change in Board's Organizational Structure," *Highway Research News*, Winter 1968, 4–5.

28 "The Airlie House Conference," *Highway Research News*, Summer 1968, 7; "Report to the Executive Committee on Reorientation and Reorganization," Minutes, June 19, 1968, TRB ECMMRG, NAS-NRC Archives; HRB, Annual Report, 1968.

29 "The Airlie House Conference." *Highway Research News*, Summer 1968, 7; "Report to the Executive Committee on Reorientation and Reorganization," Minutes, June 19, 1968, TRB ECMMRG, NAS-NRC Archives; HRB, Annual Report, 1968.

30 George C. Sponsler to W. N. Carey, July 16, 1968, Highway Research Board Reorganization, Engineering 1968, NAS-NRC Archives.

31 "Report to the Executive Committee on Reorientation and Reorganization, June 19, 1968," and Minutes, June 19, 1968, TRB ECMMRG, NAS-NRC Archives.

32 Frances Hightower to J. H. Mulligan, Jr., July 8, 1970, Transportation 1970 Proposed, Subject: Transportation Proposals, National Academy of Engineering, NAS-NRC Archives; Oral history transcript, Frank W. Lehan, interview 2 (II), January 31, 1969, by David G. McComb, LBJ Library Oral Histories, LBJ Presidential Library, https://www.discoverlbj.org/item/oh-lehanf-19690131-2-05-10; Zachary M. Schrag, *The Great Society Subway: A History of the Washington Metro* (Johns Hopkins University Press, 2006), 126.

33 Schrag, *The Great Society Subway*, 119–122.

34 Tom Lewis, Divided Highways: Building the Interstate Highways, Transforming American Life (Penguin Books, 1997), 179–210.

35 Minutes, January 15, 1969, TRB ECMMRG, NAS-NRC Archives; *Ideas & Actions: A History of the Highway Research Board* (HRB, 1971), 89. *Ideas & Actions* includes the purpose and scope adopted in 1969 in its list of events for 1967. *Ideas & Actions* does not include the broader scope that the Executive Committee actually adopted in 1967 or the controversy within NRC that ensued.

36 HRB, Annual Report, 1970.

37 Oral history transcript, Frank W. Lehan, interview 2 (II), January 31, 1969, by David G. McComb, LBJ Library Oral Histories, LBJ Presidential Library, https://www.discoverlbj.org/item/oh-lehanf-19690131-2-05-10.

38 HRB, Annual Report, 1968; Minutes, June 25, 1969, TRB ECMMRG, NAS-NRC Archives.

39   Highway Research Board, *Research: The Common Denominator*, 1970, accessed September 12, 2018, https://www.floridamemory.com/items/show/253417.

40   *Joint Development and Multiple Use of Transportation Rights-of-Way*, Highway Research Board Special Report 104 (HRB, 1969); *Transportation and Community Values*, Highway Research Board Special Report 105 (HRB, 1969).

41   Joseph Dimento, et al., "The Century Freeway: Design by Court Degree," *Access*, Fall 1996, https://www.accessmagazine.org/fall-1996/the-century-freeway-design-by-court-decree.

a   Paul E. Irick and W. N. Carey, "The New Highway Research Information Service," Highway Research News, March 1965, 5–15.

b   "Highway Research Board Pushes Start-Button on Automated Highway Information System," Highway Research News, Summer 1967, 3–5.

c   Paul E. Irick, "'TRIS'—a New Step Forward," Highway Research News, Spring 1969, 1–2.

d   Paul E. Irick and Arthur M. Mobley. "HRIS Introduces Online Retrieval," Public Roads, December 1973, 256–260.

e   "Information Service News Briefs," Transportation Research News, Autumn 1974, 39–41.

f   TRB, Annual Reports, 1985, 1995, 1996, and 2000.

Chapter 8

1   Minutes, January 14, 1970, TRB Executive Committee Meeting Minutes Record Group (TRB ECMMRG), NAS-NRC Archives; "William L. Garrison Passed Away," Department of Civil and Environmental Engineering, University of California, Berkeley, February 24, 2015, https://www.ce.berkeley.edu/news/964.

2   NAS-NAE-NRC, Annual Report, Fiscal Year 1967–1968 (Government Printing Office, 1970), 144; *The National Academy of Engineering: The First Ten Years* (National Academy of Engineering, 1976), 121.

3   "The Highway Research Board and Urban Mass Transportation: Questions and Answers," Minutes, January 14, 1970, TRB ECMMRG, NAS-NRC Archives.

4   "Proposal for a Modified Highway Research Board," Minutes, January 14, 1970, TRB ECMMRG, NAS-NRC Archives.

5   Minutes, January 20, 1971, TRB ECMMRG, NAS-NRC Archives; Richard F. Weingroff, "Busting the Trust," *Public Roads*, July/August 2013, https://www.fhwa.dot.gov/publications/publicroads/13julaug/03.cfm.

6   HRB, Annual Report, 1971 and 1972; Carlos C. Villarreal, "Urban Mass Transportation Administrator Urges True Partnership of Transit Modes," *Highway Research News*, Winter 1972, 1–3; *Public Transportation Research Needs*, Highway Research Board Special Report 137 (HRB, 1973).

7   Minutes, June 23, 1971, and January 19, 1972, TRB ECMMRG, NAS-NRC Archives.

8   Emil L. Smith and Robert L. Hill, "Philip Handler: 1917–1981," Biographic Memoir, National Academy of Sciences, 1985, accessed December 31, 2017, http://www.nasonline.org/member-directory/deceased-members/20001161.html; "TRB's Distinguished Service Award for 1981: Philip Handler," *Transportation Research News*, January–February 1982, 18; W. N. Carey to Paul Sitton re Distinguished Service Award, December 1, 1981, COMMIS: Sociotechnical Systems 1981, Transportation Research Board, NAS-NRC Archives.

9   Philip M. Boffey, *The Brain Bank of America: An Inquiry into the Politics of Science* (McGraw-Hill, 1975), 115–129.

10   NAS-NAE-NRC, Annual Report, Fiscal Year 1969–1970 (Government Printing Office, 1973), 127–128, 142–143.

11   Philip Handler, "Remarks at Chairman's Luncheon," *Highway Research News*, Winter 1970, 1–4.

12   Handler, "Remarks at Chairman's Luncheon," 1970, 1–4.

13   Philip Handler to Ernst Weber, Chairman-Elect, Division of Engineering, June 10, 1970, Transportation 1970 Proposed, NAS-NRC Archives.

14   NAS-NAE-NRC, Annual Report, Fiscal Year 1970–1971 (Government Printing Office, 1974), 119.

15   Minutes, July 1, 1970, and June 23, 1971, TRB ECMMRG, NAS-NRC Archives; Carey to Ernst Weber, Subject: NRC Division of Transportation, May 7, 1971, Transportation 1971 Proposed, NAS-NRC Archives.

16   John Noble Wilford, "Ex-Interior Chief Calls for Moral Leadership," *The New York Times*, December 31, 1970; "Excerpts from Udall's Address at Scientists' Meeting," *The New York Times*, December 31, 1970.

17   Christopher Jensen, "50 Years Ago, 'Unsafe at Any Speed' Shook the Auto World," *The New York Times*, November 26, 2015; "History of the Center for Study of Responsive Law," accessed February 21, 2018, http://csrl.org/about.

18   NAS-NAE-NRC Annual Report, Fiscal Year 1970–1971 (Government Printing Office, 1974), 140; "Excerpts from Udall's Address at Scientists' Meeting," *The New York Times*, December 31, 1970.

19   Brooks interview in *National Journal* quoted in Boffey, *The Brain Bank of America*, 54; Lewis M. Branscomb, "Harvey Brooks, 1915–2004," Biographical Memoir, NAS, accessed February 13, 2018, http://www.nasonline.org/publications/biographical-memoirs/memoir-pdfs/brooks-harvey.pdf.

20   Philip Handler, "Remarks at the 50th Annual Meeting of the Highway Research Board," *Highway Research News*, Winter, 1971, 1.

21   Jeff Davis, "What's the Purpose of Mass Transit?—Part 4—What's the Underlying Goal of Transportation?,"

Eno Transportation Weekly, July 18, 2018, https://www.enotrans.org/article/whats-the-purpose-of-mass-transit-part-4-whats-the-underlying-goal-of-transportation.

22   NAS-NAE-IOM-NRC, Annual Report, Fiscal Year 1971–1972 (Government Printing Office, 1974), 131; Boffey, *The Brain Bank of America*, 228–244; Aileen Fyfe, "Peer Review: Not as Old as You Might Think," *Times Higher Education*, June 25, 2015; Melinda Baldwin, "In Referees We Trust?" *Physics Today*, February 2017, 44–49.

23   NAS-NAE-IOM-NRC, Annual Report, Fiscal Year 1971–1972, 131; "Reorganization of NRC," Letter to Members, Volume 2, no. 7, April 1972, 10, NASEM Archive; Philip Handler, "Scientific Volunteers in the National Service," in *The Work of the National Research Council: Organization and Structure, Committee Operations, and Measures of Effectiveness*. Three essays by Philip Handler reprinted from *The National Research Council in 1976/77/78* (National Academy of Sciences, 1979), 13–18; Minutes, July 1, 1970, and June 27, 1973, TRB ECMMRG, NAS-NRC Archives.

24   NAS-NAE-NRC, Annual Report, Fiscal Year 1970–1971, 135.

25   NAS-NAE-IOM-NRC, Annual Report, Fiscal Year 1971–1972, 28–29.

26   NAS-NAE-IOM-NRC, Annual Report for Fiscal Years 1973 and 1974 (Government Printing Office, 1975), 336–337.

27   *Highways and Air Quality*, Highway Research Board Special Report 141 (HRB, 1973); HRB, Annual Report, 1969; Boffey, *The Brain Bank of America*, 79–81.

28   *The National Academy of Engineering*, 16–17; NAS-NAE-IOM-NRC, Annual Report, Fiscal Year 1971–1972, 153–155.

29   Philip Handler to Members of the NAS Council, September 1, 1971, and Philip Handler to Visiting Committee, September 28, 1971, Engineering 1971, Highway Research Board, NAS-NRC Archives.

30   Minutes, June 21, 1972, TRB ECMMRG, NAS-NRC Archives.

31   W. N. Carey, Jr., to Saunders Mac Lane, July 14, 1972, Engineering 1972, Highway Research Board, NAS Visiting Committee Report to Council of the Academy, NAS-NRC Archives.

32   Carey to Mac Lane, July 14, 1972.

33   "The Highway Research Board in 1971: A Report of the Visiting Committee to HRB," July 20, 1972, Engineering 1972, Highway Research Board, NAS Visiting Committee Report to Council of the Academy, NAS-NRC Archives.

34   Betty J. Craige, "Eugene Odum (1913–2002)," New Georgia Encyclopedia, December 13, 2013, https://www.georgiaencyclopedia.org/articles/geography-environment/eugene-odum-1913-2002; Eugene P. Odum, "Overview with Special Reference to Environmental and Social Aspects," Engineering 1972, Highway Research Board: NAS Visiting Committee Report to Council of the Academy, NAS-NRC Archives.

35   Odum, "Overview with Special Reference to Environmental and Social Aspects."

36   "Excerpts from NAS Council Meeting, August 14–17, 1972," Engineering 1972, Highway Research Board: NAS Visiting Committee Report to Council of the Academy, NAS-NRC Archives; Innovation Research Interchange, "About," accessed September 27, 2018, http://www.iriweb.org/about.

37   Philip Handler, "Remarks at the Chairman's Luncheon During the 52nd Annual Meeting of the Highway Research Board," *Highway Research News*, Winter 1973, 1–2.

38   Ernst Weber to John S. Coleman, Dr. J. H. Mulligan, Jr., Mr. Paul L. Sitton, November 4, 1970, transmitting "Attempt to Outline the Objectives of the Division of Transportation," Transportation 1970 Proposed; Paul L. Sitton to Ernst Weber, Subject: Comments for May 19 Discussion of Division of Transportation, May 18, 1971, Transportation 1971 Proposed, NAS-NRC Archives.

39   Saunders Mac Lane, "The New Commission of Transportation of the NRC," Engineering 1972, Highway Research Board: NAS Visiting Committee Report to Council of the Academy, NAS-NRC Archives; "Suggested Structure for a Transportation Division with the New Commission on Sociotechnical Systems of the National Research Council, February 9, 1973," Minutes, January 24, 1973, TRB ECMMRG, NAS-NRC Archives.

40   Mac Lane, "The New Commission of Transportation of the NRC."

41   Minutes, January 24, 1973; June 6, 1973; and June 27, 1973, TRB ECMMRG, NAS-NRC Archives; "HRB Chief W. N. Carey, Jr., Named Recipient of Academy's Distinguished Service Award," *Highway Research News*, Summer 1973, 3.

42   NAS-NAE-IOM-NRC, Fiscal Years 1973 and 1974 (Government Printing Office, 1975), 186–187, 196–197, 241; *The National Academy of Engineering*, 16–17; NAS, Organization and Members, 1975–1976, NAS-NRC Archives.

43   "Remarks Introducing the Subject of Name Change and Broadening of Scope of the Highway Research Board, W. N. Carey, Jr., January 11, 1974" in Minutes, January 23, 1974, TRB ECMMRG, NAS-NRC Archives; Richard F. Weingroff, "100th Anniversary-An Evolving Partnership," *Public Roads*, November/December 2014, https://www.fhwa.dot.gov/publications/

publicroads/14novdec/03.cfm; Richard F. Weingroff, "Busting the Trust," *Public Roads*, July/August 2013, https://www.fhwa.dot.gov/publications/publicroads/13julaug/03.cfm.

44 Minutes of the Governing Board Meetings, March 9, 1974–April 20, 1974, NAS-NRC Archives.

45 NAS-NAE-IOM-NRC, Annual Report Fiscal Year 1974–1975, 1–2.

a "Harold L. Michael," in National Academy of Engineering, *Memorial Tributes*, Vol. 18 (The National Academies Press, 2014), 211–213; HRB, Annual Report, 1967 and 1968.

b "Probing the Human Factor in Transportation," *Transportation Research News*, Summer 1975, 5–8.

c "Highway Safety Is Challenging and Fascinating Says P. F. Waller, North Carolina University," *Transportation Research News*, Winter 1974, 34–35.

d "Probing the Human Factor in Transportation," 5–8.

e Pamphlet, Ninth Annual Workshop on Human Factors in Transportation, January 18, 1976, TRB Library; "Annual Meeting Photos," *Transportation Research News*, January–February 1981; "Annual Meeting Photos," *Transportation Research News*, January–February 1982.

f C. Rinehart and D. A. Sleet, "Patricia Fossum Waller, PhD (1932–2003)," *Injury Prevention* 9, no. 4 (2003), http://dx.doi.org/10.1136/ip.9.4.295.

Chapter 9

1 TRB, Annual Report, 1975.

2 *Issues in Public Transportation*, Special Report 144 (TRB, 1974); *Census Data and Urban Transportation Planning*, Transportation Research Board Special Report 145 (TRB, 1974); *Special Report 147: Demand-Responsive Transportation*, Transportation Research Board Special Report 147 (TRB, 1974). Note: The Board's and TRB's financial statements in the Annual Reports do not include funding for special studies, sponsored conferences, or NCHRP until 1977.

3 "Five-Week 'Total Immersion' Study Probes Research Needs of Railroads," *Transportation Research News*, Autumn 1975, 10–12; *Review of Rail Transport Research Needs*, Transportation Research Board Special Report 188 (TRB, 1980), 1.

4 TRB, Executive Committee Meeting Minutes, June 1975; HRB, Executive Committee Meeting Minutes, June 1968.

5 H. M. Westergaard, et al., "Stresses in Concrete Runways of Airports," *Proceedings of the Nineteenth Annual Meeting of the Highway Research Board Proceedings* 19 (1940), 197–205; H. H. Houk, "Cardinal

Principles in Location and Design of Commercial Airports and Their Application to the Washington Airport," *Highway Research Board Proceedings* 20 (1941), 455–480; A. W. Johnson, *Frost Action in Roads and Airfields*, Highway Research Board Special Report 1 (HRB,1952); Kenneth E. Cook, "Mass Transit to Airports—An Overview," *Highway Research Record* 330 (1970), 1–4; "Connecticut Makes Detailed Study of Highway Traffic," *Engineering News-Record*, January 12, 1922, 48–52.

6 *Airport Landside Capacity: Proceedings of a Conference Held in Tampa, Florida, April 28–May 2, 1975*, Transportation Research Board Special Report 159 (TRB, 1975).

7 *Light Rail Transit: Proceedings of a National Conference, June 23–25, 1975*, Transportation Research Board Special Report 161 (TRB, 1975); *Paratransit: Proceedings of a Conference Held November 9–12, 1975*, Transportation Research Board Special Report 164 (TRB, 1976); *Assessing Transportation-Related Air Quality Impacts: Proceedings of the Conference on the State of the Art of Assessing Transportation-Related Air Quality Impacts Held October 22–24, 1975*, Transportation Research Board Special Report 167 (TRB, 1976); *Future of the National Highway Safety Program*, Transportation Research Board Special Report 178 (TRB, 1977), 3; TRB, Annual Report, 1977.

8 TRB, Annual Report, 1976.

9 TRB, Annual Report, 1977.

10 TRB, Annual Report, 1977; "'Ten Four, Good Buddy' May Signal Help for Stranded Motorist," *Transportation Research News*, May–June 1977, 10–11; Pamphlet, "Conference on Pedestrians," Transportation Research Board, TRB Library.

11 TRB, Annual Report, 1978.

12 W. N. Carey, Jr., "A Personal Message to Friends of TRB from Executive Director W. N. Carey, Jr.," *Transportation Research News*, March–April 1979, 10.

13 Mark H. Rose, Bruce E. Seely, and Paul F. Barrett, *The Best Transportation System in the World: Railroads, Trucks, Airlines, and American Public Policy in the Twentieth Century* (University of Pennsylvania Press, 2006), 166–213; John W. Fischer, "Transportation Economic Regulation in Practice," *TR News*, May–June 2018, 3–8.

14 Carl Feiss, "The Foundations of Federal Planning Assistance: A Personal Account of the 701 Program," *Journal of the American Planning Association* 51, no. 2 (1985), 175–184.

15 *Urban Transportation Planning in the 1980s*, Transportation Research Board Special Report 196 (TRB, 1982), 7–8.

16 Thomas B. Deen, Interview with author, October 27, 2017.

17 "New Executive Director of TRB," *Transportation Research News*, May–June 1980, 16; Thomas B. Deen, Correspondence with author, December 2018.

18 Thomas B. Deen, Interview with author, October 27, 2017.

19 NAS, "Frank Press," accessed September 25, 2018, http://www.nasonline.org/about-nas/history/highlights/frank-press.html; American Institute of Physics, "Frank Press," accessed September 25, 2018, https://history.aip.org/phn/11601017.html.

20 Thomas B. Deen, Interview with author, October 27, 2017.

21 *Impact of the Bay Area Rapid Transit System on the San Francisco Metropolitan Region*, Highway Research Board Special Report 111 (HRB, 1970), 53.

22 Edward Weiner, *Urban Transportation Planning in the United States: An Historical Overview*, 5th ed. (U.S. Department of Transportation, 1997), 134–136; Anton Tedesko, "Milton Pikarsky," *Memorial Tributes: National Academy of Engineering*, Vol. 4, 1991, accessed September 26, 2018, https://www.nae.edu/MembersSection/MemorialTributes/51349/189128.aspx; "Aileen Hernandez, 90, Ex-NOW President and Feminist Trailblazer, Dies," *The New York Times*, February 28, 2017; "Akron loses an icon: Ann Lane Gates dies at 92," *Akron Beacon Journal/Ohio.com*, February 6, 2017, https://www.ohio.com/akron/news/top-stories-news/akron-loses-an-icon-ann-lane-gates-dies-at-92; "The President's National Commission on Fire Prevention and Control," Extensions of Remarks, February 15, 1972, https://www.gpo.gov/fdsys/pkg/GPO-CRECB-1972-pt4/pdf/GPO-CRECB-1972-pt4-1-2.pdf; NAS, *Organization and Members, 1975–1976*, NAS-NRC Archives.

23 "Annual Meeting Photos," *Transportation Research News*, March–April 1978.

24 "BART: Expensive Flop or Commuter's Delight?" *Transportation Research News*, January–February 1977, 2–3; "Is There a Case for Rail Transit?" *Transportation Research News*, May–June 1977, 2–5.

25 *Forecasts of Freight System Demands and Related Research Needs* (National Academy of Sciences, 1979); *Innovation in Transportation: Proceedings of a Workshop, September 24–26, 1979* (National Academy of Sciences, 1979); *Study of Methods for Increasing Safety Belt Use*, Transportation Research Board Unpublished Report 17 (TRB, 1980).

26 Minutes, June 25, 1981, TRB Executive Committee Meeting Minutes Record Group (TRB ECMMRG), NAS-NRC Archives.

27 *Urban Transportation Planning in the 1980s*, Transportation Research Board Special Report 196 (TRB, 1982); *Future Directions of Urban Public Transportation*, Transportation Research Board Special Report 199 (TRB, 1983).

28 Thomas B. Deen, Interview with author, October 27, 2017; "Minutes of the Meeting of the Governing Board, August 8, 1981," COMMIS: Sociotechnical Systems 1981: Transportation Research Board, NAS-NRC Archives.

29 Thomas B. Deen, Interview with author, October 27, 2017.

30 Thomas B. Deen to Philip M. Smith re Agreements reached by the Ebert Subcommittee on TRB Governance—March 13, 1982, March 15, 1982, Governing Board, 1982 Transportation Research Board, General, NAS-NRC Archives; "Organizational Change and Initiation of Policy Studies Highlight TRB Activities," *TR News*, March–April 1983, 11–13; Anton Tedesko, "Milton Pikarsky," "Minutes of Governing Board, October 31, 1983," Governing Board: 1983, Transportation Research Board, Program Plan, NAS-NRC Archives.

31 "CBO's Damian J. Kulash Predicts More Passive Federal Role," *TR News*, July–August 1982, 15.

32 Thomas B. Deen, Correspondence with author, December 2018.

33 U.S. DOT, *Moving America: A Look Ahead to the 21st Century: Proceedings of the Conference, Washington, DC, July 24, 1989* (U.S. DOT, 1989); E. Langer, "Robert M. White, Top Weatherman Under Five U.S. Presidents, Dies at 92," *The Washington Post*, October 15, 2015.

34 Elaine Chao, Thomas D. Larson, Anthony R. Kane, Wallace Burnett, "Development of a National Transportation Policy: The Process and the Product," *TR News*, July–August 1990, 9–12; TRB, Annual Report, 1990.

35 *Highway Research: Current Programs and Future Directions*, Transportation Research Board Special Report 244 (TRB, 1994), 6–9.

36 TRB, Annual Report, 1992; TRB, Annual Report, 1993.

37 TRB, Annual Report, 1993.

38 *ISTEA and Intermodal Planning: Concept, Practice, Vision*, Transportation Research Board Special Report 240 (TRB, 1993), 6; Chris Becker, *AASHTO 1914–2014: A Century of Achievement for a Better Tomorrow* (American Association of State Highway and Transportation Officials, 2014), 22.

39 *ISTEA and Intermodal Planning*, 4–6; TRB, Annual Report, 1995; C. S. Casgar and J. A. Scott, "ISTEA and Intermodal Planning: TRB Releases Fourth Report on ISTEA Planning Issues," *TR News*, January–February 1994, 19–21; B. D. McDowell, "Reinventing Planning Under ISTEA: MPOs and State DOTs: ISTEA's Impact," *TR News*, November 1994, 6–9, 29.

Endnotes **317**

40 TRB, Annual Report, 2014.

41 TRB, Annual Report, 2007; TRB, Annual Report, 2008.

42 TRB, Annual Report, 2002.

43 *Deterrence, Protection, and Preparation: The New Transportation Security Imperative*, Transportation Research Board Special Report 270 (TRB, 2002), v–x; TCRP, Annual Report of Progress, 2017; TRB, Annual Report, 2003; *Public Transportation Security: Communication of Threats: A Guide*, TCRP Report 86, Vol. 1 (TRB, 2002); "NCHRP at 50 Years," Transportation Research Board, 2012.

44 H. Rept. 104-863, September 28, 1996, 1187; *Improving Surface Transportation Security: A Research and Development Strategy* (National Academy Press, 1999), vii–ix.

45 "Critical Issues in Transportation," *TR News*, November–December 1997, 9–19.

46 TCRP, Annual Report of Progress, 2017; TRB, Annual Report, 2003; *Public Transportation Security*; "NCHRP at 50 Years," Transportation Research Board, 2012.

47 *Deterrence, Protection, and Preparation: The New Transportation Security Imperative*, Transportation Research Board Special Report 270 (TRB, 2002), x.

a A. Trent Germano, Paul H. Wright, R. Gary Hicks, and Paul H. Sanders, "The Emerging Needs of Bicycle Transportation," *Highway Research Record* 436 (1973), 8–18.

b TRB, Annual Report, 1974.

c ANF20—Bicycle Transportation, Key Research Achievements in Transportation, [2014?], accessed May 24, 2019, http://www.trb.org/AboutTRB/KeyResearchAchievements.aspx?srcaud=AboutTRB.

Chapter 10

1 Minutes, January 19, 1983, TRB Executive Committee Meeting Minutes Record Group (TRB ECMMRG), NAS-NRC Archives.

2 Minutes, January 19, 1983, TRB ECMMRG, NAS-NRC Archives.

3 National Academies, "Our Study Process," and "Federal Advisory Committee Act 1997," accessed October 10, 2018, http://www.nationalacademies.org/nasem/na_064188.html.

4 TRB, Annual Reports, 1983, 1987, 1994, and 2017.

5 TRB, Annual Report, 1982; *Designing Safer Roads*, Transportation Research Board Special Report 214 (TRB, 1987); *Twin Trailer Trucks*, Transportation Research Board Special Report 211 (TRB, 1986); *Should Intercity Bus Drivers Be Allowed to Use CB Radios?*, Transportation Research Board Special Report 205 (TRB, 1984).

6 *55: A Decade of Experience*, Transportation Research Board Special Report 204 (TRB, 1984); "Minutes of Governing Board, October 31, 1983," Governing Board,

1983, Transportation Research Board, Program Plan, NAS-NRC Archives.

7 *Measuring Airport Landside Capacity*, Transportation Research Board Special Report 215 (TRB, 1987); *Pipelines and Public Safety: Damage Prevention, Land Use, and Emergency Preparedness*, Transportation Research Board Special Report 291 (TRB, 1988); *In Pursuit of Speed: New Options for Intercity Passenger Transport*, Transportation Research Board Special Report 233 (TRB, 1991); *Intermodal Marine Container Transportation: Impediments and Opportunities*, Transportation Research Board Special Report 236 (TRB, 1992); TRB, Annual Report, 1987.

8 Minutes, June 28, 1982, TRB ECMMRG, NAS-NRC Archives; "Institute for Strategic Transportation Studies," *TR News*, September 1989, 21–22; TRB, Annual Report, 1994; Thomas B. Deen, Correspondence with author, December 2018.

9 "Thomas Larson, PennDOT Secretary, Focuses on TRB During Congressional Hearings on the Role of the National Academies in Science Policy," *TR News*, July 1986, 2–8; *Transportation in an Aging Society: Improving Mobility and Safety for Older Persons*, Transportation Research Board Special Report 218 (TRB, 1988).

10 W. N. Carey, Jr., "Commentary," *Transportation Research News*, Winter 1974, 3–4; Nan Humphrey, "Data for Decisions: Requirements for National Transportation Policy Making," *TR News*, May–June 1992, 24–27, 35.

11 *Highway Research: Current Programs and Future Directions*, Transportation Research Board Special Report 244 (TRB, 1994); TRB, Annual Report, 2005; *The Federal Investment in Highway Research, 2006–2009: Strengths and Weakness*, Transportation Research Board Special Report 295 (TRB, 2008).

12 TRAC, "Letter Report—June 2, 2005," Transportation Research Board, accessed October 11, 2018, http://onlinepubs.trb.org/onlinepubs/reports/trac_june_2005.pdf; "TRB Policy Study Letter Reports and Other Brief Reports," accessed October 11, 2018, http://www.trb.org/Publications/PubsPolicyStudiesLetterReports.aspx.

13 *Air Traffic Controller Staffing in the En Route Domain: A Review of the Federal Aviation Administration's Task Load Model*, Transportation Research Board Special Report 301 (TRB, 2010); *The Federal Aviation Administration's Approach for Determining Future Air Traffic Controller Staffing Needs*, Transportation Research Board Special Report 314 (TRB, 2014); *Modernizing Freight Rail Regulation*, Transportation Research Board Special Report 318 (TRB, 2015); *A Concept for a National Freight Data Program*, Transportation Research Board Special Report 276 (TRB, 2003); *Measuring Personal Travel and Goods Movement: A Review of The Bureau of Transportation Statistics'*

Surveys, Transportation Research Board Special Report 277 (TRB, 2003); *How We Travel: A Sustainable National Program for Travel Data*, Transportation Research Board Special Report 304 (TRB, 2011); *The Relative Risks of School Travel: A National Perspective and Guidance for Local Community Risk Assessment*, Transportation Research Board Special Report 269 (TRB, 2002); *Buckling Up: Technologies to Increase Seat Belt Use*, Transportation Research Board Special Report 278 (TRB, 2003); *The Safety Promise and Challenge of Automotive Electronics: Insights from Unintended Acceleration*, Transportation Research Board Special Report 308 (TRB, 2012); *In-Service Performance Evaluation of Guardrail End Treatments*, Transportation Research Board Special Report 323 (The National Academies Press, 2018); *Transmission Pipelines and Land Use: A Risk-Informed Approach*, Transportation Research Board Special Report 281 (TRB, 2004); *Effects of Diluted Bitumen on Crude Oil Transmission Pipelines*, Transportation Research Board Special Report 311 (TRB, 2013); *Safely Transporting Hazardous Liquids and Gases in a Changing U.S. Energy Landscape*, Transportation Research Board Special Report 325 (The National Academies Press, 2018).

14 "U.S. Interstate Highways Need Overhaul; System Requires Significant Commitment for Federal and State Coordination and Funding, Says New Report," National Academies Press Release, December 6, 2018, http://www8.nationalacademies.org/onpinews/newsitem.aspx?RecordID=25334; FAST Act, Public Law 114-94, December 4, 2015.

15 Tom Menzies, interview with author, January 23, 2018.

16 Minutes, January 19, 1972, TRB ECMMRG, NAS-NRC Archives; *Environmental Considerations in Planning, Design, and Construction*, Highway Research Board Special Report 138 (HRB, 1973), 23, 87–88.

17 HRB, Annual Report, 1970; TRB, Annual Report, 1979; *Motor Vehicle Noise Control*, Transportation Research Board Special Report 152 (TRB, 1975); *Optimizing the Use of Materials and Energy in Transportation Construction*, Transportation Research Board Special Report 166 (TRB, 1976); *Assessing Transportation-Related Air Quality Impacts*, Transportation Research Board Special Report 167 (TRB, 1976); *Strategies for Reducing Gasoline Consumption Through Improved Motor Vehicle Efficiency*, Transportation Research Board Special Report 169 (TRB, 1976), *Transportation of Hazardous Material: Toward a National Strategy*, Transportation Research Board Special Report 197 (TRB, 1983).

18 U.S. DOT, *Moving America: New Directions, New Opportunities*, Volume 2: A Statement of National Transportation Policy (U.S. DOT, 1990).

19 *Transportation, Urban Form, and the Environment*, Transportation Research Board Special Report 231 (TRB, 1991), vi.

20 *Toward a Sustainable Future: Addressing the Long-Term Effects of Motor Vehicle Transportation on Climate and Ecology*, Transportation Research Board Special Report 251 (TRB, 1997), 257–258; TRB, Annual Report, 1992; Mark H. Rose and Raymond A. Mohl, *Interstate: Highway Politics and Policy Since 1939*, 3rd ed. (University of Tennessee Press, 2012), 168–171.

21 "Critical Issues in Transportation," *TR News*, September 1994, 4.

22 TRB, Annual Report, 1995.

23 Thomas B. Deen and Robert E. Skinner, "A Paradigm for Addressing Change in the Transportation Environment," *TR News*, September–October 1994, 11–13.

24 TRB, Annual Report, 1995; *Expanding Metropolitan Highways: Implications for Air Quality and Energy Use*, Transportation Research Board Special Report 245 (TRB, 1995), 16.

25 *Expanding Metropolitan Highways*, 1–9, 354–380.

26 *Toward a Sustainable Future*, 253–255; Thomas B. Deen, Correspondence with author, December 2018.

27 "David G. Burwell: 1947–2017," *TR News*, March–April 2017, 44; "Daniel Sperling Awarded TRB's 2018 Roy W. Crum Distinguished Service Award," TRB News Release, January 10, 2019, http://onlinepubs.trb.org/onlinepubs/news/98AM/19Crum.pdf.

28 TRB, *Informing Transportation Policy Choices* (TRB, 2003), 52.

29 *Surface Transportation Environmental Research: A Long-Term Strategy*, Transportation Research Board Special Report 268 (TRB, 2002); TRB, Annual Report, 2005.

30 "Dr. Cicerone Goes to Washington," *The National Academies In Focus*, Fall 2005, 16–17; *Toward a Sustainable Future*, x; National Research Council, *America's Climate Choices* (The National Academies Press, 2011), 8.

31 *Driving and the Built Environment: Effects of Compact Development on Motorized Travel, Energy Use, and CO_2 Emissions*, Transportation Research Board Special Report 298 (TRB, 2009).

32 Testimony of Robert E. Skinner, Jr., Executive Director, Transportation Research Board, The National Academies, before the Technology and Innovation Subcommittee, Committee on Science and Technology, U.S. House of Representatives, November 19, 2009, http://www.nationalacademies.org/ocga/111session1/testimonies/OCGA_149809.

33 *Potential Impacts of Climate Change on U.S. Transportation*, Transportation Research Board Special Report 290 (TRB, 2008).

34 *Potential Impacts of Climate Change on U.S. Transportation*.

35 Michael D. Meyer, "Climate Change, Extreme Weather Events, and the Highway System," *TR News*, November–December 2015, 21–24.

a   J. Viner, "Report of Investigations of Urban Aspects of the Highway Finance Problem," *Highway Research Board Proceedings 5*, Part 1 (1926), 208–238; *Urban Transportation Economics*, Transportation Research Board Special Report 181 (TRB, 1978).

b   *Curbing Gridlock: Peak-Period Fees to Relieve Traffic Congestion*, Transportation Research Board Special Report 242 (TRB, 1994).

c   FHWA, "Guidance General Tolling Programs," September 24, 2012, https://www.fhwa.dot.gov/map21/guidance/guidetoll.cfm.

d   "The National Old Trails Road," Highway History, accessed September 30, 2018, https://www.fhwa.dot.gov/infrastructure/trailse.cfm; for a discussion of critical issues lists, see Chapter 11.

e   *Equity of Evolving Transportation Finance Mechanisms*, Transportation Research Board Special Report 303 (TRB, 2011), 1–3.

Chapter 11

1   TRB, Annual Report, 1988; Purposes and Duties of the TRB Executive Committee, accessed February 12, 2019, http://onlinepubs.trb.org/onlinepubs/ExComm/Duties.pdf.

2   Thomas B. Deen, Correspondence with author, December 2018; Minutes, June 2008–January 2019, TRB Executive Committee Meeting Minutes Record Group (TRB ECMMRG), NAS-NRC Archives.

3   W. N. Carey, Jr., "Commentary," *Transportation Research News*, Winter 1974, 3–4.

4   TRB, Annual Report, 1977.

5   Executive Committee, Transportation Research Board, "The Ten Most Critical Issues in Transportation," *Transportation Research News*, November–December 1976, 2–4.

6   Executive Committee, Transportation Research Board, "The Ten Most Critical Issues in Transportation: A 1978 Update," *Transportation Research News*, November–December 1978, 2–5; "How Transportation Specialists Rank Critical Issues," *Transportation Research News*, March–April 1979, 4–5.

7   "Response to 'Ten Most Critical Issues,'" *Transportation Research News*, May–June 1979, 13; Edward Epreman to Thomas Deen re Critical Issues in Transportation, July 24, 1981, COMMIS: Sociotechnical Systems 1981: Transportation Research Board, NAS-NRC Archives; Minutes, January 18, 1984, TRB ECMMRG, NAS-NRC Archives.

8   Minutes, January 18, 1984, TRB ECMMRG, NAS-NRC Archives; TRB, Annual Report, 1989, 1990, 1991.

9   "Critical Issues in Transportation," *TR News*, November–December 1997, 9–19; "Ten Most Critical Issues in Transportation: 1981 Update," *Transportation Research News*, July–August 1981, 2–5; "Critical Issues in Transportation 2002," *TR News*, November–December 2001, 3–11; *Critical Issues in Transportation*, Washington, D.C.: Transportation Research Board, 2006. See also Alan E. Pisarski, "Framing National Agendas for Transportation Research: Trends and Lessons from TRB's Critical Issues Statements, 1976–2013," *TR News*, March–April–May 2015, 26–34.

10 "Critical Issues in Transportation 2002," *TR News*, November–December 2001, 8.

11 *Critical Issues in Transportation 2019* (The National Academies Press, 2018).

12 TRB, Annual Report, 1994.

13 TRB, Annual Report, 2009; Critical Issues List 2002, 8; Critical Issues List 2006, 5–6; Critical Issues List 2009, 6–7.

14 TRB, Annual Report, 1983 and 2002.

15 TRB, Annual Report, 1979.

16 "TRB Announces Establishment of Fifth Group in Division A," *TR News*, November–December 1983, 38–39; "Reorganization of Division A–Regular Technical Activities," *TR News*, March–April 1984, 20; TRB, Annual Report, 1985.

17 "Louisiana Transportation Research Center Director Harold R. Paul W. N. Carey, Jr., Distinguished Service Award Recipient," TRB News Release, January 6, 2014, http://onlinepubs.trb.org/onlinepubs/news/93AM/14Carey.pdf; Mark Norman, Interview with author, February 27, 2018.

18 "STPP President Anne Canby Wins TRB'S 2006 W. N. Carey, Jr., Distinguished Service Award," TRB News Release, January 19, 2007, http://onlinepubs.trb.org/onlinepubs/news/86AM/carey.pdf; Mark Norman, Interview with author, February 27, 2018.

19 TRB Standing Committee database, 1970–2018.

20 "Technical Activities Division Restructures," *TR News*, January–February 2004, 43; Mark Norman, Interview with author, February 27, 2018.

21 TRB, Annual Report, 2018.

22 Neil Pedersen, "Perspectives from the TRB Executive Committee Chair," *TRB Annual Meeting Daily*, January 24, 2012.

23 Technical Activities staff, Interview with author, January 24, 2018.

24 "TRB State Representative Roles and Resources," 2014, accessed February 26, 2019, http://onlinepubs.trb.org/onlinepubs/dva/state/StateRepsRolesAndResources.pdf.

25 TRB Call for Stories, 2018.

26 TRB Call for Stories, 2018.

27 "Blue Ribbon Committee Advancing Research Success Stories: Standing Committees on Geometric Design and Operational Effect of Geometrics," accessed September 3, 2018, http://onlinepubs.trb.org/onlinepubs/dva/crc/resources/AFB10_AHB65_SUCCESS_STORY_PPT.pdf; "Key Research Achievements in Transportation," accessed September 3, 2018, http://www.trb.org/AboutTRB/KeyResearchAchievements.aspx?srcaud=AboutTRB.

28 TRB Call for Stories, 2018.

29 *Special Report 165: Traffic Flow Theory: A Monograph*, Transportation Research Board Special Report 165 (TRB, 1976), iii, 2–3.

30 *Index to Highway Research Correlation Service Circulars (Nos. 1–491)* (HRB, 1963).

31 "John C. Vance Is Selected First Winner of Award Named for Him," *Transportation Research News*, January–February 1979, 13–14; "Lynn B. Obernyer," *TR News*, January–February 1988, 23–24; "Letters," *Transportation Research News*, January–February 1979, 28–29.

32 TRB, Annual Report, 2006.

33 "Millennium Papers Home," accessed November 16, 2018, http://www.trb.org/publications/PubsMillenniumPapers.aspx.

34 Neil J. Pedersen, Interview with author, January 26, 2018; "Neil Pedersen Named TRB Executive Director – Effective February 1, 2015," accessed November 17, 2018, http://www.trb.org/Main/Blurbs/171671.aspx.

35 Neil J. Pedersen, Interview with author, January 26, 2018; Neil J. Pedersen, "Multimodal Transportation Planning at the State Level: State of the Practice and Future Issues," accessed November 17, 2018, http://onlinepubs.trb.org/onlinepubs/millennium/00076.pdf.

36 Neil J. Pedersen, Interview with author, January 26, 2018; TRB, Annual Report, 1982, 1996, 2006, 2007, 2009.

37 Lisa Marflak, Steven Andreadis, and Elaine Ferrell, Correspondence with author, July 19–20, 2018.

38 Rexmond C. Cochrane, *National Academy of Sciences: The First Hundred Years, 1863–1963* (National Academy Press, 1978), 76, 91; National Academies, "International Activities," accessed February 25, 2019, http://sites.nationalacademies.org/International/index.htm.

39 *Soil and Foundation Engineering in the Union of Soviet Socialist Republics*, Highway Research Board Special Report 60 (HRB, 1960); "Text of Lacy–Zarubin Agreement, January 27, 1958," *Passing Through the Iron Curtain*, accessed February 25, 2019, https://librariesandcoldwarculturalexchange.wordpress.com.

40 Kenneth B. Johns, "Looking Abroad: TRB's 'Action Plan' Aims to Expand International Activities Program," *TR News*, September–October 1983, 6–9.

41 *Ideas & Actions: A History of the Highway Research Board* (HRB, 1971), 37; PIARC-TRB MOU Item 3: Action Plan 2016–2108: CY 2018.

42 TRB, Annual Report, 2012; Transportation Research Board Conference Proceedings 50–53, 54, 56 (TRB, 2013–2019).

a *Low-Volume Roads: Proceedings of a Workshop Held June 16–19, 1975, in Boise, Idaho*, Transportation Research Board Special Report 160 (TRB, 1975).

b "Developing Countries Visited in Transportation Technology Support Project," *Transportation Research News*, September–October 1978, 10–11; TRB, Annual Report, 1979.

c "Correspondents from Developing Countries Discuss Low-Volume Road Concerns and Needs," *Transportation Research News*, November–December 1979, 9–11.

d AFB—30 Low Volume Roads, Key Research Achievements Database, [2014?], accessed March 29, 2018, http://www.trb.org/AboutTRB/KeyResearchAchievements.aspx?srcaud=AboutTRB.

e Doug Scott, "Faiz Elected ASCE Fellow," *ASCE News*, January 12, 2015, http://news.asce.org/faiz-elected-asce-fellow.

Chapter 12

1 Thomas B. Deen, Interview with author, October 27, 2017; Damian Kulash, Interview with author, December 12, 2017.

2 Thomas B. Deen, Interview with author, October 27, 2017; Thomas D. Larson, "Need for Continued Research Stressed by Thomas D. Larson, Retiring TRB Chairman," *Transportation Research News*, March–April 1982, 9; A detailed timeline for the Highway STRS and SHRP planning can be found in Appendix 12, Minutes, June 11, 1986, TRB Executive Committee Meeting Minutes Record Group (TRB ECMMRG), NAS-NRC Archives.

3 "Developing Support for Transportation Research," *Transportation Research News*, July–August 1982, 11–13.

4 Deen to Frank Press via Edward Epremiam, March 4, 1982, and Edward Epremiam to Frank Press, March 4, 1982, CSS: Transportation Research Board, 1982, General, NAS-NRC Archives.

5 Deen to Frank Press via Edward Epremiam, March 4, 1982, CSS: Transportation Research Board, 1982, General, NAS-NRC Archives.

6 Thomas B. Deen, Interview with author, October 27, 2017; Analysis of highway research expenditures occur in the initial proposal and various reports, including the final report, *America's Highways: Accelerating the Search for Information*, Special Report 202 (TRB, 1984), 1.

7 Thomas B. Deen, Interview with author, October 27, 2017; Thomas B. Deen, Correspondence with author, December 2018.

8 *America's Highways*, 165–169; Thomas B. Deen, Correspondence with author, December 2018.

9 Rebecca S. McDaniel, et al., *The Superpave Mix Design System: Anatomy of a Research Program*, NCHRP Web Document 186 (TRB, 2011), 6–7; *Urban Transportation Planning in the 1980s*, Transportation Research Board Special Report 196 (TRB, 1982), 7–8; Thomas B. Deen, Interview with author, October 27, 2017; Damian Kulash, Interview with author, December 12, 2017.

10 "NCHRP Pioneer Looks at Research and Innovation," *TR News*, September–October 1986, 2–3.

11 Minutes, January 19, 1983, TRB ECMMRG, NAS-NRC Archives.

12 *America's Highways*, v–vi, 3–4.

13 *Ideas & Actions: A History of the Highway Research Board* (HRB, 1971), 70; *Pavement Lessons Learned from the AASHO Road Test and Performance of the Interstate Highway System*, In Transportation Research Circular E-C118 (TRB, 2007), 19; *The AASHO Road Test: Summary Report*, Highway Research Board Special Report 61g (HRB, 1962); *The AASHO Road Test: Proceedings of a Conference Held May 16–19, 1962*, Highway Research Board Special Report 73 (HRB, 1962), 270–271.

14 Minutes, January 19, 1983, TRB ECMMRG, NAS-NRC Archives; Thomas B. Deen, Interview with author, October 27, 2017; Appendix 8, Minutes, January 6, 1984, TRB ECMMRG, NAS-NRC Archives; Thomas B. Deen, Correspondence with author, December 2018.

15 *Strategic Highway Research: Saving Lives, Reducing Congestion, Improving Quality of Life*, Transportation Research Board Special Report 260 (TRB, 2001), 34.

16 Thomas B. Deen, Interview with author, October 27, 2017; Damian Kulash, Interview with author, December 12, 2017.

17 Michael Halladay, "The Strategic Highway Research Program: An Investment That Has Paid Off," *Public Roads*, March/April 1998, https://www.fhwa.dot.gov/publications/publicroads/98marapr/shrp.cfm; *Strategic Highway Research*, 37–38.

18 McDaniel, *The Superpave Mix Design System*, 1, 24; Halladay, "The Strategic Highway Research Program"; *Strategic Highway Research*, 38.

19 Halladay, "The Strategic Highway Research Program."

20 *Strategic Highway Research*, 200–204; Ann Brach, Interview with author, February 6, 2018.

21 Thomas B. Deen, Interview with author, October 27, 2017; Damian Kulash, Interview with author, December 12, 2017; and Ann Brach, Interview with author, February 6, 2018; *Strategic Highway Research*, 42.

22 *Interim Planning for a Future Strategic Highway Research Program*, NCHRP Report 510 (TRB, 2003).

23 Safe, Accountable, Flexible, Efficient Transportation Equity Act: A Legacy for Users, Public Law 59, 109th Congress, August 10, 2005.

24 Ann Brach, Interview with author, February 6, 2019; SHRP 2, Annual Report, 2006.

25 McDaniel, *The Superpave Mix Design System*, 89–91, Appendix A.

26 Ann Brach, Correspondence with author, January 28, 2019.

27 *Strategic Highway Research*, 10, 145.

28 *Implementing the Results of the Second Strategic Highway Research Program*, Transportation Research Board Special Report 296 (TRB, 2009), 66–67, 142–147.

29 Pam Hutton, AASHTO, Correspondence with author, March 7 and July 31, 2018; "FHWA/AASHTO Implementation Assistance Program State Participation in Rounds 1–7," accessed August, 15, 2018, http://shrp2.transportation.org/Documents/SHRP2updatedIAPdocMay%202018.pdf.

30 Pam Hutton, AASHTO, Correspondence with author, March 7 and July 31, 2018; "FHWA/AASHTO Implementation Assistance Program State Participation in Rounds 1–7," accessed August 15, 2018, http://shrp2.transportation.org/Documents/SHRP2updatedIAPdocMay%202018.pdf.

31 *Training of Traffic Incident Responders*, SHRP 2 Report S2-L12-RW-1 (TRB, 2012); SHRP 2 Solutions, "Advancing the State of the Practice: 2017 Implementation Highlights," FHWA-OTS-18-001, December 2017.

32 "SHRP2 Moving Us Forward: Implementation Highlights 2015," FHWA-OTS-16-0001, December 2015; "A Toolkit for Accelerated Bridge Construction," SHRP 2 Project Brief (TRB, June 2013).

33 "Eco-Logical: An Ecosystem Approach to Developing Infrastructure Projects," April 2006, https://www.environment.fhwa.dot.gov/env_initiatives/eco-logical/report/ecological.pdf; *Practitioner's Guide to the Integrated Ecological Framework*, SHRP 2 Report S2-C06-RW-3 (TRB, 2014); "SHRP2 Moving Us Forward: Implementation Highlights 2015," FHWA-OTS-16-0001, December 2015; SHRP 2 Solutions, "Advancing the State of the Practice: 2017 Implementation Highlights," FHWA-OTS-18-001, December 2017; FHWA, "PlanWorks," accessed May 29, 2019, https://fhwaapps.fhwa.dot.gov/planworks.

a   *Strategic Highway Research: Saving Lives, Reducing Congestion, Improving Quality of Life*, Transportation Research Board Special Report 260 (National Academy Press, 2001).

b   *Interim Planning for a Future Strategic Highway Research Program*, NCHRP Report 510 (TRB, 2003).

c   TRB Staff Briefing Materials, "SHRP 2 Naturalistic Driving Study Data Unique Customer List," January 31, 2018; "SHRP 2 Safety Data Phase 2 Frequently-Asked Questions," October 9, 2017; "SHRP 2 Safety Data Update," February 2018.

d   Automated Vehicles Symposium, "Proceedings," accessed May 25, 2019, https://www.automatedvehiclessymposium.org/proceedings-printables.

e   Centers for Disease Control and Prevention, "Global Road Safety," accessed August 21, 2018, https://www.cdc.gov/motorvehiclesafety/global/index.html.

Chapter 13

1   Deen quoted in TRB, Annual Report, 1985; Appendix 14, Minutes, January 18, 1984, TRB Executive Committee Meeting Minutes Record Group (TRB ECMMRG), NAS-NRC Archives.

2   TRB, Annual Report, 1988.

3   Hugh M. Gillespie, "AASHTO's National Cooperative Highway Research Program: Solving Problems in Highway Transportation for a Quarter of a Century," *TR News*, September 1986, 3–8; NCHRP, 2014 Summary of Progress, 2014; NCHRP, Annual Report, 2018.

4   TRB, Annual Report, 2000.

5   A. W. Shute, "Teaching Transportation with TRAC," *TR News*, January–February 1999, 7–10; Bruce Alberts, "Preparing Tomorrow's Transportation Workforce," *TR News*, January–February 1999, 2; "Bruce Alberts: The Education President," *National Academies In Focus*, Summer 2005, 16–17; AASHTO, "TRAC and RIDES," accessed February 2, 2019, https://tracrides.transportation.org.

6   "NCHRP at 50 Years," Brochure, Transportation Research Board, 2012.

7   "Background: Highway Safety Manual," AASHTO, accessed February 1, 2019, http://www.highwaysafetymanual.org/Pages/hsm_background.aspx; *Proposed AASHTO Highway Safety Manual*, 2nd Edition, NCHRP Project 17-71, accessed February 1, 2019, http://apps.trb.org/cmsfeed/trbnetprojectdisplay.asp?projectid=3874; *Human Factors Guidelines for Road Systems*, NCHRP Report 600, 2nd Edition (TRB, 2012).

8   *Ideas & Actions: A History of the Highway Research Board* (HRB, 1971), 143, 182.

9   *Pavement Lessons Learned from the AASHO Road Test and Performance of the Interstate Highway System*, Transportation Research Circular E-C118 (TRB, 2007), 8–9; International Scanning Study Team, *Long-Life Concrete Pavements in Europe and Canada*, FHWA-PL-07-027 (Federal Highway Administration, 2007).

10   "Foresight Series Brochure," TRB, 2014, accessed January 31, 2019, http://www.trb.org/NCHRP750/ForesightReport750Series.aspx.

11   Appendix 14, Minutes, January 18, 1984, TRB ECMMRG, NAS-NRC Archives.

12   *Research for Public Transit: New Directions*, Transportation Research Board Special Report 213 (TRB, 1987); "TRB Selects William W. Millar as the Recipient of the 2018 Sharon D. Banks Award," January 4, 2018, http://onlinepubs.trb.org/onlinepubs/news/97AM/18Banks.pdf.

13   "NCTRP Publishes First Report, Accesses Results," *Transportation Research News*, July–August 1982, 8–10; *Research for Public Transit*, 68–69, 73–77.

14   W. W. Millar, "Transit STRS," *TR News*, July 1989, 6–7.

15   TCRP, Annual Report of Progress, 2017; TRB, Annual Report, 2016.

16   TCRP, "12 Most Popular Publications," June 6, 2018, TCRP Day Toolkit, https://www.apta.com/resources/tcrp/Pages/TCRP-Day-Toolkit.aspx; *Broadening Understanding of the Interplay Among Public Transit, Shared Mobility, and Personal Automobiles*, TCRP Research Report 195 (TRB, 2018).

17   Gwen Chisholm-Smith, Correspondence with author, July 13, 2018.

18   "Overview of TCQSM," Transit Capacity and Quality of Service Manual, Third Edition, accessed August 8, 2018, http://www.trb.org/Main/Blurbs/169437.aspx.

19   *Airport Research Needs: Cooperative Solutions*, Transportation Research Board Special Report 272 (TRB, 2003), 7–32.

20   *Airport Research Needs*, 7–32.

21   *Airport Research Needs*, ix–x, 7.

22   Tom Menzies, "Airport Research Needs: Cooperative Solutions," *TR News*, March–April 2004, 32–35; ACRP, Annual Report of Progress, 2017.

23   ACRP IdeaHub, accessed August 18, 2018, https://crp.trb.org/ideahub.

24   ACRP, Annual Report of Progress, 2017.

25   Joe Navarrete, Correspondence with author, August 9, 2018; "AIAA/AAAE/ACC Jay Hollingsworth Speas Airport Award Recipients," accessed August 18, 2018,

https://www.aiaa.org/HonorsAndAwardsRecipient
Details.aspx?recipientId=d1ac4131-980c-4d27-8faa-08
d2b8b49c47; SAGA, "About," accessed August 18, 2018,
http://www.airportsustainability.org/about.

26   *Airport Passenger Terminal Planning and Design*,
ACRP Report 25 (TRB, 2010); ACRP, Annual Report
of Progress, 2017; Theresia H. Schatz, Interview with
author, January 23, 2018.

27   *ACRP Impacts on Practice*, July 2018, November 2016,
September 2016, September 2015, and June 2015.

28   "Preparing the Next Generation of Airport
Leaders," *ACRP Impacts on Practice*, August 2016;
"ACRP and Higher Education: Building the Next
Generation of Airport Professionals," *ACRP
Impacts on Practice*, February 2017; "Implementing
Aircraft Rescue and Firefighting Training at Fresno
Yosemite International Airport," *ACRP Impacts on
Practice*, April 2018.

29   Damian Kulash, Interview with author, December 12,
2017; "Innovative Research: The SHRP-IDEA Program,"
TR News, November 1991, 17–19; K. Thirumalai,
"SHRP-IDEA Program: Successful Activity to Have
Wider Focus at TRB," *TR News*, May 1993, 6–9.

30   Thirumalai, "SHRP-IDEA Program," 6–9; Harvey
Berlin, et al., "TRB's IDEA Programs Turn 20,"
TR News, November–December 2012, 20–26; *NCHRP
IDEA Program: Products with an Impact or Potential
Impact on Current Highway Practice* (TRB, 2015).

31   Berlin, "TRB's IDEA Programs Turn 20," 20–26; TCRP,
Annual Report of Progress, 2017.

32   *NCHRP IDEA Program*, ii.

33   TRB, Annual Report, 2006, 45; NCFRP Publications,
accessed January 9, 2019, http://www.trb.org/NCFRP/
Blurbs.aspx?fields=PublicationType|NCFRP.

34   TRB Annual Report, 2006, 46; HMCRP Publications,
accessed January 9, 2019, http://www.trb.org/HMCRP/
Blurbs.aspx?fields=PublicationType|HMCRP; TRB,
Annual Report, 2002, 36; CTBSSP Publications,
accessed January 9, 2019, http://www.trb.org/
Publications/PubsCTBSSPSynthesisReports.aspx.

35   Cooperative Research Program staff, Interview with
author, January 23, 2018.

36   Behavioral Traffic Safety Cooperative Research
Program, accessed August 19, 2018, https://
onlinepubs.trb.org/onlinepubs/btscrp/
BTSCRPBrochureFinal.pdf.

a   "NCHRP Milestone from 1 to 100," *TR News*,
July–August 1983, 2–3.

b   Thomas L. Copas, "Synthesizing Existing Information,"
Highway Research News, Winter 1969, 1–2.

c   "Bryant Mather," *Standardization News,* May 2000,
https://www.astm.org/SNEWS/MAY_2000/
Mather_May.html.

d   Copas, "Synthesizing Existing Information," 1–2; *Con-
tinuing Project to Synthesize Information on Highway
Problems: 2018*, NCHRP Research Results Digest 402
(TRB, 2018).

Chapter 14

1   Russell Houston, associate executive director of TRB,
first suggested this chapter's title. Similar sentiments
also appear, almost verbatim, in the responses to the
call for stories.

2   Minutes, January 19, 1983, TRB Executive Committee
Meeting Minutes Record Group (TRB ECMMRG),
NAS-NRC Archives; Thomas B. Deen to Chairman, NRC,
via Robert W. Johnston, Request for Approval to Steering
Committee to Develop the Conference on Traveler
Behavior and Values, April 5, 1982, CSS: Transportation
Research Board, 1982, General, NAS-NRC Archives.

3   *Women: Their Underrepresentation and Career Differ-
entials in Science and Engineering: Proceedings of a
Conference* (National Academy Press, 1987), 58–60.

4   National Science Foundation and National Center for
Science and Engineering Statistics, *Women, Minorities,
and Persons with Disabilities in Science and Engineering:
2017*, Special Report NSF 17-310 (National Science
Foundation, 2017), http://www.nsf.gov/statistics/
wmpd; Planning Accreditation Board, "Student and
Faculty Composition in PAB-Accredited Programs: 2017
Annual Report," accessed November 13, 2018, http://
www.planningaccreditationboard.org/index.php?id=112;
Bureau of Labor Statistics, "Labor Force Statistics from
the Current Population Survey," 2017, accessed November
13, 2018, https://www.bls.gov/cps/cpsaat11.htm.

5   Report of the TRB Division Committee, June–
December 2018.

6   Minutes, July 1, 1970, TRB ECMMRG, NAS-NRC
Archives; W. N. Carey, Jr., "New 'Talent Pool' Is Formed
to Utilize Most Valuable Asset of HRB–Its People,"
Highway Research News, Summer 1971, 1–2.

7   TRB, Annual Report, 1997; Neil J. Pedersen, Interview
with author, January 26, 2018.

8   HRB, Annual Report, 1951, 9; D. Grant Mickle, "On
Recognizing Young Talent...," Highway Research News,
Summer 1966, 1.

9   Ewa Flom, Andy Lehrer, and Jenna Overton, "Inspiring
Successive Generations," *Public Roads*, Summer 2008,
https://www.fhwa.dot.gov/publications/publicroads/
18summer/05.cfm.

10   TRB, Annual Report, 2002; Young Members Council, "Key Research Achievements in Transportation,"
accessed November 21, 2018, http://www.trb.org/
AboutTRB/KeyResearchAchievements.aspx?
srcaud=AboutTRB.

11 "T. C. Paul Teng," *Highway Research News*, Spring 1974, 19–21; "Paul Teng: Honorary Member Since 2001," International Society for Concrete Pavements, accessed November 21, 2018, https://www.concrete pavements.org/team/paul-teng.

12 "Purdue University Professor Kumares C. Sinha Wins TRB's 2009 Roy W. Crum Distinguished Service Award," TRB News Release, January 7, 2010; Kumares C. Sinha, "What Have I Learned Over Half a Century of Studying Transportation Engineering?" accessed November 21, 2018, https://engineering.purdue.edu/ Engr/AboutUs/Administration/AcademicAffairs/ Events/Colloquia/Sinha.

13 *The National Academy of Engineering: The First Ten Years* (National Academy of Engineering, 1976), vi.

14 "Transit Leader Michael S. Townes Receives 2010 Sharon D. Banks Award," TRB News Release, January 7, 2010, http://onlinepubs.trb.org/ onlinepubs/news/89AM/10Banks.pdf.

15 COMTO, "TCRP Ambassadors Program," accessed November 23, 2018, https://www.comto.org/page/ TCRP; TRB, Annual Report, 2018.

16 TRB, Annual Report, 1986, 1987, and 1991.

17 *Transportation Education and Training: Meeting the Challenge*, Transportation Research Board Special Report 210 (TRB, 1985); Stephen E. Blake, "Venturing into Uncharted Waters: Summer Minority Undergraduate Intern Program in Transportation at TRB," *TR News*, September–October 1983, 24–26.

18 *Internship and Mentoring Programs*, Transportation Research Board Conference Proceedings 17 (TRB, 1998), 79; "Chairman's Luncheon," *TR News*, March–April 2004, 26; "TransSTEM Academy," Francis L. Cardozo Education Campus, accessed November 22, 2018, https://cardozohs.com/apps/pages/index.jsp? uREC_ID=187568&type=d&termREC_ID=&pREC_ ID=379397.

19 "TRB Minority Student Fellows Program," *97th Annual Meeting Final Program*, 2018; "Sharon D. Banks: 1945–1999," *TR News*, May–June 2000, 37.

20 Raquelle Myers and Cindy Ptak, "Safe Journeys: Improving the Role of Tribal Communities in the Development of Transportation Facilities in Indian Country," *TR News*, September–October 2014, 3–4; *Conference on Transportation Improvements: Experiences Among Tribal, Local, State, and Federal Governments, October 18–21, 2001, Albuquerque, New Mexico*, Transportation Research E-Circular E-C039 (TRB, September 2002).

21 Dava Sobel, "Science's Invisible Women," *The New York Times*, March 19, 2018.

22 William K. Hatt, "Highway Research Projects in the United States," *Bulletin of the National Research Council* 4 Part 3, no. 21 (October 1922); "Finding Aid for Elise Hatt Campbell Papers," Archives of Labor and Urban Affairs, Walter P. Reuther Library, Wayne State University, accessed November 15, 2018, http:// reuther.wayne.edu/node/7443.

23 *Highway Research Board Proceedings* 35 (1956), 831.

24 *Ideas & Actions: A History of the Highway Research Board* (HRB, 1971), 37, 61; "Annual meeting photographs insert," *Highway Research News*, Winter 1969; "Tentative Program," *Transportation Research News*, November–December 1976; TRB, Annual Report, 1987 and 2011; Bettie Deen and Dianne Skinner, Interview with author, October 27, 2017.

25 Analysis of staff lists in TRB Annual Reports, 1983–1999.

26 "Interstate Link Closes Book on Historic Wartime Expressway," *Transportation Research News*, March–April 1976, 4–6; "Alice and Jessie Bourquin papers: 1905–1991," Bentley Historical Library, University of Michigan; Willa Mylroie, "Evaluation of Intercity-Travel Desire," *Highway Research Board Bulletin*, no. 119 (1956), 69–94; "Willa W. Mylroie," *Highway Research News*, Spring 1970, 14, 16; C. Elton Troth, "Research Is the Backbone for Transportation Projects," *Transportation Research News*, January–February 1979, 7–9; "Katharine Mather," *Highway Research News*, Spring 1972, 32, 34.

27 TRB, Annual Report, 1980 and 1992.

28 "Kathleen Stein Hudson," *Transportation Research News*, November–December 1978; "Letters," *Transportation Research News*, January–February 1979, 28–29; "Transportation Trailblazer: Kathleen E. Stein," WTS International," accessed November 19, 2018, http://www.wtsinternational.org/assets/47/14/ stein.pdf.

29 "Julie Fee," *Transportation Research News*, January–February 1977; "Conference on Pedestrians," Conference Program, Transportation Research Board, 1977, TRB Library.

30 "University of Texas' Sandra Rosenbloom Is Champion of Transportation for Disadvantaged," *Transportation Research News*, July–August 1981, 29–30.

31 *Women's Travel Issues: Research Needs and Priorities* (Research and Special Programs Administration, U.S. DOT, 1978), Sandra Rosenbloom, "Understanding Women's and Men's Travel Patterns: The Research Challenge," *Research on Women's Issues in Transportation: Report of a Conference*, Transportation Research Board Conference Proceedings 35, Vol. 1 (TRB, 2006), 21.

32 *Women's Travel Issues*, 732.

33 Adriana Gianturco, Oral History Interview, conducted in 1994 by George F. Petershagen, California State University, Sacramento, for the California State Archives, State Government Oral History Program.

34 "A Pioneer for Public Transit: Carmen E. Turner (1930–1992)," accessed November 14, 2018, https://www.transportation.gov/connections/pioneer-public-transit.

35 "Resources," TRB Committee on Accessible Transportation and Mobility, accessed November 18, 2018, http://www.trbaccessmobility.org/resources.html.

36 "Susan Hanson, 2018 W. N. Carey, Jr., Distinguished Service Award Recipient," accessed November 22, 2018, http://onlinepubs.trb.org/Onlinepubs/news/98AM/19Carey.pdf.

37 *Women's Travel Issues: Proceedings from the Second National Conference* (Federal Highway Administration, 2000).

38 "About," TRB Committee on Women's Issues in Transportation, accessed November 13, 2018, https://sites.google.com/site/trbwomensissues/about; Women's Issues in Transportation, "Key Research Achievements in Transportation," accessed November 13, 2018, http://www.trb.org/AboutTRB/KeyResearchAchievements.aspx?srcaud=AboutTRB.

39 "A Pioneer for Public Transit: Carmen E. Turner (1930–1992)," accessed November 14, 2018, https://www.transportation.gov/connections/pioneer-public-transit.

40 "Young Professionals Reception," TRB Annual Meeting AM Daily, January 2012, http://www.trb.org/AMDaily/AMD1225A100.aspx.

41 Howard Newlon, Jr., "Lost: A Historic Transportation Resource–the Sheraton-Park Lobby," *Transportation Research News*, March–April 1980, 7–8; TRB, Call for Stories, 2018.

42 *Landslides and Engineering Practice*, Highway Research Board Special Report 29 (HRB, 1958) Washington, 5.

43 HRB, Annual Report, 1951.

44 Howard E. Hill, "A Highway Administrator Looks at the HRB," *Highway Research News*, Autumn 1966, 2–4.

45 M. C. Anday and C. F. Potts, "Transportation Professionals Make TRB Annual Meeting Work for Them," *TR News*, November–December 1983, 23–24; TRB Call for Stories, 2018.

46 Lillian Borrone, Interview with author, December 12, 2017; "Hyun-A Park," *TR News*, November–December 2015, 38.

47 TRB, Call for Stories, 2018.

48 "Letters," *Transportation Research News*, March–April 1980, 30.

49 *Ideas & Actions*, 30.

50 Raymond J. Krizek, "Donald S. Berry: 1911–2002," *Memorial Tributes*, Vol. 11, 2007, accessed November 18, 2018, https://www.nap.edu/read/11912/chapter/5; Thomas B. Deen, "The Transportation Research Board at 90," *TR News*, November–December 2010, 7–8; "Annual Meeting Photo Spread," *Transportation Research News*, March–April 1979.

51 C. Michael Walton, Interview with author, December 13, 2017; TRB, Call for Stories, 2018.

52 TRB, Call for Stories, 2018.

53 Nancy Aguirre, Minority Fellows Reception, TRB Annual Meeting, January 7, 2018.

54 Author's observation, January 10, 2018.

a   Mark Norman, Interview with author, February 27, 2018; TRB, Annual Report, 2006.

b   TRB Annual Meeting Poster Session Guidelines, accessed May 25, 2019, http://onlinepubs.trb.org/onlinepubs/am/2019/PosterSession.pdf.

Index

(including definitions of acronyms)

New Mexico, 281

New York, 20, 32, 34, 40, 45, 58, 64, 69, 101, 108, 136, 154, 249, 286, 301, 302

New York State Department of Public Works, 136, 302

New York State Department of Transportation, 301

New York State Thruway, 101

New York University, 192

NHTSA (*see* National Highway Traffic Safety Administration)

Nicaragua, 13

Niemeier, Debbie, 217

Nigeria, 212

Nixon, Richard, 142, 158–159

Njord, John, 241, 301

Norfolk Southern Corporation, 193, 301

Northern Kentucky International Airport, 266

Norman, Mark, 217

Normann, Olav K., 73, 78, 79

North Carolina, 30, 31, 49

North Carolina State Highway Commission, 49

North Central Texas Council of Governments, 301

North Dakota, 114, 115

Northern Kentucky International Airport, 266

Northwestern University, 199, 293, 302

NRC (*see* National Research Council)

O

O'Leary, Katherine, 287

O'Neal, Emmot, 61

Obernyer, Lynn B., 226

Odum, Eugene P., 164, 165

Office of Civil and Defense Mobilization, 126

Office of Public Road Inquiry, 27

Office of Public Roads (OPR), xxiv, 27–29, 30–31, 33, 50

Office of Road Inquiry (ORI), 25, 26

Office of Science and Technology Policy, 178

Office of Scientific Research and Development, 69

Ohio, 83, 145, 179

Ohio State University, The, 39, 56, 126, 303

Oil crisis of 1970s, 176, 191, 233

Oklahoma, 64, 69, 134, 151, 187

Oklahoma Department of Transportation, 134

Older, Clifford, 34

OPR (*see* Office of Public Roads)

Oregon, 156, 177, 302

Oregon State Highway Commission, 302

Organisation for Economic Co-operation and Development, 133

Organization of American States, 99

ORI (*see* Office of Road Inquiry)

Otobo, Guy, 212

P

Page, Frank, 39

Page, Logan, xxiv, 27–28, 30–31, 33

Panama Canal, 14–15, 41

Paratransit/Dial-a-Ride, 145, 166, 170, 172, 173, 286–287, 288

Park, Eun Sug, 223

Park, Hyun-A, 292, 303

Parking studies, 68, 105, 107–108, 116, 145, 199

Passenger transportation

    air, 171–172, 265–266

    data collection and coordination, 195

    economics, 39, 47–48, 92, 179

    forecasting demand, 216

    human factors workshop, 152

    intercity, 226

    motor vehicles, 39, 92, 104

    multimodal, 172, 185

    rail, 154, 226

    traffic surveys, 47–48

    urbanization and, 104

Paul, Harold (Skip), 217, 303

Pavements (*see also* Asphalt materials and pavements; Concrete materials and pavements)

    airport runways, 171

    design standards/regulations, 97, 101, 184, 258

    profilometers, 97, 237

    Project 1-37A, 258

    pumping phenomenon, 96–97

    serviceability index, 97, 100

    snow and ice control, 69–70, 120, 123, 237, 239–240, 267

    Superpave®, 239, 246, 254

Peat Marwick Airport Consulting Services, 192

Pedersen, Neil J., xxv, 209, 226–227, 241, 301, 303, 304

Pedestrians/walking, 6, 59, 79–80, 105, 109–110, 145, 152, 153, 163, 166, 172–173, 176, 177, 193, 200, 218, 219, 245, 255, 286

Peirce, Benjamin, 10

Pennock, Herbert A., 256

Pennsylvania, 67, 68, 174, 193, 213, 233, 241, 243, 302, 303

Pennsylvania Department of Highways, 303

Pennsylvania Department of Transportation, 174, 193, 213, 233, 241, 243, 302

Pennsylvania State University, The, 112, 212, 233, 289, 301

Pennsylvania Transportation Institute, 113

Pennsylvania Turnpike, 67, 68

Pennsylvania Turnpike Commission, 67

Perini, Victor J., Jr., 115

Perkins, Courtland, 287

Peters, Tom, 236

Peterson, Paul E., 201

Philadelphia International Airport, 266–267

Philippines, 212

PIARC (*see* World Road Association)

Pikarsky, Milton, 173, 179, 180, 182, 302, 303

Pipeline and Hazardous Materials Safety Administration, 269

Pipelines, 126, 133, 192, 195

Pittsburg Road Test, 85

Planning (*see* Transportation planning)

PlanWorks, 246, 250

Poland, 292

Policy studies (*see* Consensus studies)

Pontificia Universidad Católica de Chile, 212

Port Authority of Allegheny County, 259, 301

Port Authority of New York & New Jersey, The, 131, 188, 194, 288, 301

Port of Los Angeles, 99

Port of New York Authority, 131, 302

Port of Seattle, 292

Portland Cement Association, 50, 77, 89, 94, 96, 115, 302

Ports, 32, 98, 99, 160, 173, 187, 214, 220, 222, 224

Posekany, Lewis A., 197

Post Office Department Appropriation Bill of 1912, 29

Potts, Charles, 182

Prabhakar, Ranjani, 285

President's Science Advisory Committee, 150

Press, Frank, 178–179, 180–181, 209–210, 235

Princeton University, 230

Public Works Administration, 67

Puerto Rico, 74, 91, 111, 248

Pulling, Ronald, 171

Purcell, Arlyn, 292

Purdue University, 44, 49, 91, 92, 95, 152, 212, 275, 278, 293, 302, 304

Pyke Johnson Award, 178

R

Rail transportation (*see also* Light rail transit)
    Civil War and, 14
    construction, 149
    freight movement, 32, 87, 191, 195, 220–221, 269
    high-speed rail or maglev, 171, 192, 268
    interface between other modes, 27–28, 136
    regulation/deregulation, 174
    research needs, 170, 214
    roadbuilding promotion, 27–28
    safety, 173, 225
    security, 225
    and survey expeditions, 14, 16–17
    TRB and, xxv, 170, 171, 172, 173, 174, 178–179, 191, 193, 214, 218–219
    World War I and, 32–34

Railroad Research Information Service (RRIS), 132

Rails-to-Trails Conservancy, 200, 202

Rayner, Gary, 268

RCS (*see* Research Correlation Service)

Reagan, Ronald, 174, 180, 235

Reagel, Fred V., 70, 77–78, 83, 118, 302

Reconstruction Finance Corporation, 67

Red Tomahawk, Pete, 281

Reed, Joseph, 112

Regional Transit Authority, Chicago, 302

Reilly, Robert J., 252

Rensselaer Polytechnic Institute, 222

Replogle, Michael A., 202

Research and Innovative Technology Administration, 269

Research and Technology Coordinating Committee (RTCC), 195, 200, 201

Research Correlation Service (RCS), xxiv, xxv, 6, 52, 70–78, 115, 117, 121, 123, 134, 138, 207, 208, 220, 224, 282

Research information service, HRB, xxiv, 46, 48, 58, 71, 76, 132, 134

Research Information Service, NRC, 21, 76

Research Institute of Highways, 247

Research Results Digest series, 252, 261

RFD (*see* Rural Free Delivery)

Surdahl, Roger, 213
Surface Transportation and Uniform Relocation
    Assistance Act, 238, 252
Surface Transportation Assistance Act of 1982, 183, 189,
    238
Surface Transportation Policy Partnership, 241
Surface Transportation Policy Project, 200, 217
Sussman, Joseph M., 152, 209, 301
Sustainable Aviation Guidance Alliance (SAGA), 265
Sustainable development/transportation, 191, 196,
    197, 200–201, 204–206, 212–213, 215, 243,
    259, 265
Sverdrup/Jacobs Civil, Inc., 204, 303
Sweden, 80, 292
Sweet, Harold S., 91–92
Synthesis of Airport Practice series, 257, 267
Synthesis of Highway Practice series, 124, 213, 252, 256,
    257
Synthesis of Transit Practice reports, 177, 257, 262
Syracuse University, 110
Systems approach to research, 126–127, 158, 164, 194

T

Tabb, John R., 239
TAC (*see* Technical Activities Council)
Taiwan, 277
Talbot, Arthur N., 34, 35
Tanzania, 213
TCRP (*see* Transit Cooperative Research Program)
TCRP Oversight and Project Selection (TOPS)
    Committee, 260, 261, 262
TEA-21 (*see* Transportation Equity Act for the 21st
    Century)
Technical Activities Council (TAC), xviii, 209, 218,
    219, 221, 227, 277, 279, 286, 289, 292, 298,
    303–304
Technical committees of HRB and TRB
    cooperative research programs, 222–224, 228
    correlation of research, 76–77, 149
    friends of committees, 219, 276
    international participation, 229–232
    meetings and conferences, 3–4, 56, 115, 207, 221–222,
        290, 291
    membership, xviii, 45, 220–221, 230, 231–232,
        275–276, 279
    Millennium Papers, 226–229

number of, xvii, 55, 115, 143, 149, 172, 173, 197,
    215–216, 291
organization/reorganization, xviii, xxiv, xxv, 1, 24,
    38, 40, 44, 56, 135, 138, 139–140, 143–144, 170, 185,
    207–208, 215–219
oversight, 208–210
professional staff, xxiv, xxv, 6, 52, 71, 75, 134, 173
project concept, 57–58, 82
publications, 47, 70, 76–77, 82–83, 109–110, 224–226,
    298
research needs/critical issues list, 6, 56, 121, 188, 199,
    210–211, 214–215, 222
rotation of members and term limits, 275, 276
sponsor funding for, 173, 187, 208, 226
strategic advice, 208–210
structure, 3, 82
webinars, 227–229, 231, 277, 292, 299
women and minorities on, 279–281, 283, 286, 289
work of, 219–226
Teller, Leslie W., Sr., 293
Teng, T. C. Paul, 277, 278
Texas, 20, 65, 83, 101, 119, 130, 139, 292, 293
Texas A&M Transportation Institute, 83, 119, 215, 301,
    303
Texas A&M University, 301, 302, 304
Texas Department of Transportation, 130, 139, 292
Texas Highway Department, 101, 119, 139
Texas Southern University, 288, 295
Texas Transportation Institute, 119
Thomas B. Deen Distinguished Lectureship, 99, 288,
    291
Thornburgh, Richard, 113
3M Foundation, 193
Tilden, Charles J., 47, 56, 63–64
TOPS (*see* TCRP Oversight and Project Selection
    Committee)
Townes, Michael S., 279, 301
Townley, Michael, 246
TRAC (*see* Transit Research Analysis Committee)
TRAC program, AASHTO, 255
Traffic
    behavior studies, 71–72, 153, 193, 272–273
    congestion/gridlock, 69, 149, 154, 184, 198–199, 214,
        215, 241, 242
    economic studies, 39, 47–48, 198
    forecasting/flow theory, 120, 121, 149, 152, 224

gravity models, 283

incident management, 247, 248

and level of service (capacity), 78, 201

origin–destination studies, 73

and pavement behavior, 92, 95, 97, 258

regulation/control, 60, 62, 64, 79, 105, 107, 115, 118, 123, 152, 153, 198, 253, 256

rural, 66

safety, 44, 47–48, 61, 62, 63, 64, 66, 153, 272–273

speed limits, 68, 69, 191–192

surveys, 47–48, 57, 71–72, 73

truck, 86–87

urban, 105, 121, 154

volume estimates, 57, 73

and weather conditions, 239, 245

Transit Capacity and Quality of Service Manual, 80, 262

Transit Cooperative Research Program (TCRP), xxv, 7, 80, 177, 184, 187–188, 192, 202, 205, 206, 221, 222–223, 226, 251, 252, 256, 257, 259–263, 264, 265, 267, 268, 279, 283, 294–295

Transit Research Analysis Committee (TRAC), 195

Transportation Equity Act for the 21st Century (TEA-21), 203, 240, 253, 254

Transportation planning

    airports and aviation, 171, 226, 263, 265–267

    bicycles and bicycling, 176–177

    citizen participation in, 146, 286

    education programs, 281

    environmental considerations, 197, 205, 218, 219, 250

    funding for, 252

    highways, xxiv, 167, 250, 252

    intermodalism, 184–185

    land use, 174

    multimodal, 185, 226

    systems approach, 173, 178, 216

    3 Cs planning process, 114

    traffic flow, 120, 121, 149, 152, 184, 224

    urban, 109, 111, 121, 131, 134, 139, 144, 146, 160, 167, 170, 174, 180

Transportation Research Board (TRB)

    AASHO/AASHTO and, 167–168, 173, 185, 187, 192, 193, 201, 202, 205–206, 213, 221, 222–223, 230–231, 235, 236, 238, 239, 241, 243, 246, 247, 250, 252, 253, 254, 255

challenges for the future, 297–300

committee structure, xxv, 2–3 (*see also* Technical committees of HRB and TRB)

conferences, 170–172

cultural tradition of friendship, 290–296

diversity commitment, 274–282

division structure, 208–209, 239

excellence during growth, 185–187

executive directors, 304 (*see also specific individuals*)

FHWA and, 170, 172–173, 174, 180, 185, 189, 195, 198, 200, 201, 202, 221, 224, 230–231, 235, 236, 238, 239, 241, 243, 247, 250, 254, 258, 268, 277, 281, 286, 288, 292

formation, xxv, 169–173

funding, 165–166, 173, 187

growth and expansion, 184

how it works, 2–4

information and policy merger, 178–183

international participation, 173, 210, 212–213, 229–232, 278–279, 284–285

Internet home page, xxv

ISTEA and, 183–185

key developments in history of, xxiv–xxv, 4–7

leadership, 301–304

learning from history of, 297–300

meetings, 3–4, 7, 284–285

mission, 1

mobilization after 9/11 terror attacks, 187–188

NRC and, xvii, 140–141, 178, 180

oversight, 182, 208, 288, 293–294, 303

policy studies, xvii, 180, 181–183, 185, 211, 224 (*see also* Consensus studies)

Regular Technical Activities Division, 138, 140, 142, 143, 149–150, 162, 163, 170, 172, 203, 207, 208, 209

self-initiated studies, 166, 192–193, 195, 200, 201, 204, 205, 206, 215

sponsors/sponsorship, xviii–xix, xxv, 1, 170, 171, 172, 173, 174, 179, 180, 183, 184, 185, 187, 189, 190, 191, 192–193, 197, 198, 200, 202, 211, 212, 213, 215, 217, 219, 220–221, 224, 225, 226, 232, 253, 254, 259, 260, 267, 269, 280, 281, 286–287, 288, 298, 299

as stand-alone unit, xxv, 5, 207, 208

standards for integrity and quality, 181–182, 220

standing technical committees (*see* Technical committees of HRB and TRB)

About the Author

SARAH JO PETERSON has more than 25 years of experience specializing in transportation and land use, including working with state and local governments, academia, and the real estate community. She has a master's degree in urban and regional planning from the University of Wisconsin–Madison and a Ph.D. in history from Yale University. Her first book, *Planning the Home Front: Building Bombers and Communities at Willow Run* (University of Chicago Press, 2013) won an Honorable Mention for the Lewis Mumford Prize for best book in American planning history from the Society for American City and Regional Planning History.